Wars within a War

Civil War America

Gary W. Gallagher, EDITOR

WARS WITHIN A WAR

Controversy and Conflict over the
❧ AMERICAN CIVIL WAR ❧

EDITED BY
Joan Waugh & Gary W. Gallagher

THE UNIVERSITY OF NORTH CAROLINA PRESS
Chapel Hill

© 2009 The University of North Carolina Press
All rights reserved
Manufactured in the United States of America

Designed by Rebecca Evans
Set in MT Walbaum and MT Latin
by Tseng Information Systems, Inc.

The paper in this book meets the guidelines for permanence
and durability of the Committee on Production Guidelines
for Book Longevity of the Council on Library Resources.

The University of North Carolina Press has been a
member of the Green Press Initiative since 2003.

Library of Congress Cataloging-in-Publication Data
Wars within a war : controversy and conflict over the American Civil War /
edited by Joan Waugh and Gary W. Gallagher.
p. cm. — (Civil War America)
Includes bibliographical references and index.
ISBN 978-0-8078-3275-2 (cloth : alk. paper)
1. United States—History—Civil War, 1861–1865—Social aspects. 2. United States—
History—Civil War, 1861–1865—Influence. 3. Social conflict—United States—History—
19th century. 4. Social conflict—Southern States—History—19th century. 5. United
States—Social conditions—To 1865. 6. United States—Social conditions—1865–
1918. 7. Confederate States of America—Social conditions. 8. Southern States—
Social conditions—19th century. 9. War and society—United States—History—19th
century. 10. War and society—Southern States—History—19th century.
I. Waugh, Joan. II. Gallagher, Gary W.
E468.9.W29 2009
973.7'1—dc22
2008050487

cloth   13 12 11 10 09   5 4 3 2 1

To the memory of

MARY L. ARBOIT

(1918–2007)

and

PHILIP JAMES CALLAHAN

(1949–2007)

⊰ CONTENTS ⊱

The Civil War saw the United States and the Confederacy create huge armies that waged some of the bloodiest and most famous battles in American history. The governments headed by Abraham Lincoln and Jefferson Davis sought to make the most of their respective human and material resources and strove to achieve national unity. Yet on February 28, 1863, *Harper's Weekly* offered its readers a vivid portrayal of northern political dissent. The cartoon depicts a beleaguered yet defiant Columbia, her shield emblazoned with "UNION," determined to slay three copperhead snakes threatening the U.S. war effort. Three months later, a cartoon in *Frank Leslie's Illustrated Newspaper* showed southern women concerned with shortages of bread and other food rioting in Richmond's streets. Armed with clubs and pistols, the women strike belligerent poses in front of a store's smashed windows. Such acknowledgments of political and social conflict would not have surprised anyone at the time because both the United States and the Confederacy experienced internal dissent throughout most of the war. Union victory ensured reunion and emancipation, but heated disagreements over the war's meaning and memory remained bitter in the immediate aftermath of the war and have continued in various forms to the present day.

Civil War dissent sometimes has been obscured amid popular conceptions of the conflict as a tragic but ultimately triumphant testing of the nation. Celebratory views accurately capture the degrees to which the people of both sides sacrificed in the course of a struggle that exacted a terrible human and material toll. Bruce Catton's "Centennial History of the Civil War" and Shelby Foote's *The Civil War: A Narrative*, two beautifully written and widely read trilogies published between 1958 and 1974, exemplify this tradition, as does Ken Burn's immensely influential PBS documentary, titled *The Civil War* and first aired in 1990. Yet any account of the war that diminishes the extent and severity of dissatisfaction, North and South, leads to a flawed understanding — a fact long recognized by historians. Works such as A. B. Moore's *Conscription and Conflict in the Confederacy* (1924), Frank L. Owsley's *State Rights in the Confederacy*, (1925), James G. Randall's *Constitutional Problems Under Lincoln* (1926), Ella Lonn's *Desertion During the Civil War* (1928), and, more recently, Mark E. Neely Jr.'s *The Union Divided: Party Conflict in the Civil War North* (2002), Armstead L. Robinson's *Bitter Fruits of Bondage: The Demise of Slavery and the Collapse of the Confederacy, 1861–1865* (2005), David Williams's *A People's History of the Civil War: Struggles for the Meaning of Freedom* (2005), and Amy Murrell Taylor's *The Divided Family in Civil War America* (2006) document the widespread disaffection and political disagreement that confronted both nations.[1]

The contributors to *Wars within a War* explore internal stresses that posed serious challenges to each country's viability, as well as some of the ways in which wartime disputes and fissures carried over into the postwar years and well beyond. Their twelve essays are not meant to offer a comprehensive treatment. Rather, they are designed to suggest some of the many forms of conflict that arose among civilians, soldiers, politicians, and military leaders during the war. The essays extend the discussion of controversies far past the death of the Confederacy in the spring of 1865, analyzing, among other things, Walt Whitman's poetry, handling of the Union and Confederate dead, treatment of disabled and destitute northern veterans, Ulysses S. Grant's imposing tomb, and Hollywood's long relationship with the Lost Cause narratives. Reflecting disparate methodologies, the essays, as a group, provide a starting point for anyone interested in how Americans have argued about the prosecution, meaning, and memory of the war. They also underscore the variety of approaches adopted by current historians and convey, in several cases, arguments and evidence from recently published or forthcoming books.[2]

The essays can be placed in five broad categories. The first, comprising pieces by Stephanie McCurry and William Blair, deals with the respective home fronts. McCurry investigates the response of Confederate women, especially poor soldiers' wives, to the hardships brought on by a war that witnessed enormous expansion of the Confederate state. Focusing on a series of sometimes violent demonstrations triggered by shortages of food, she finds examples of interstate political communication and organization among non-elite white women that suggests a major shift in the relationship between citizens and their government. Blair takes up the thorny issues of how the North (the United States) would define and punish treason and handle the confiscation of Rebel property in a war that quickly assumed a scale and level of carnage no one anticipated in the spring of 1861. He offers a fresh interpretation of the Second Confiscation Act of July 1862, describing it as a moderate measure rather than a radical attempt to strike at Confederate slaveholders.

The second category, devoted to military affairs, offers three essays. James M. McPherson looks at the relationship between Abraham Lincoln and Maj. Gen. George B. McClellan, evoking the profound gulf that separated the two in terms of their approach to prosecuting the war. Despite his best efforts, Lincoln could do little to prevent McClellan from treating Republican politicians as a greater threat than the Rebel army — or from molding the Army of the Potomac in his own cautious image. Robert E. Lee, McClellan's great opponent on the battlefield, is the subject of Joseph T. Glatthaar's essay. Like McClellan, Lee put his stamp on an army, contending with a range of critics who lacked his vision and ability to improve discipline, morale, and military prowess in the Army of Northern Virginia. Three regiments of black soldiers serving in Florida take center stage in J. Matthew Gallman's essay. The battle of Olustee, fought on February 20, 1864, provides a point of departure for Gallman to highlight the varied experiences, positive and negative, of men in different U.S. Colored Troops (USCT) units. The essay provides a useful reminder that the heroes of the film *Glory* cannot stand in for all black men who donned blue uniforms.

Three essays on the war in literature and the visual arts comprise the third category. Harold Holzer offers a perceptive reading of political caricatures of Lincoln and Jefferson Davis, teasing out meanings that would escape many viewers. Slavery, emancipation, and race figure prominently in many of the cartoons, and the overall tenor of the images reminds modern Americans that politics has always been an arena in which national leaders come under brutal attack. Stephen Cushman uses Walt Whitman's *Memoranda During the War*, with its allusion to "the seething hell and the black infernal background of countless minor scenes and interiors" of the war, to underscore the tension between those who understand the conflict as a contest between generals and armies and those who prefer to highlight the common folk who shouldered the burden of killing and suffering. In Cushman's skillful analysis, Whitman emerges as a pioneer of the type of "bottom-up" history that would sweep the scholarly world more than a century later. However prescient Whitman might have been, he reached an infinitesimal audience compared to Hollywood's filmmakers. Gary W. Gallagher's essay traces the cinematic history of the heroic Lost Cause narrative created by ex-Confederates in the postwar years. After a long ascendancy established by *The Birth of a Nation* (1915) and *Gone with the Wind* (1939), argues Gallagher, the Lost Cause fell out of favor beginning in the mid-1960s — only to reappear in *Gods and Generals*, which was released shortly before *Cold Mountain* in 2003. Those two films revealed that competing memories of the Confederacy remained viable in a Hollywood that, just a few years earlier, seemingly had banished the Lost Cause.

A fourth category, consisting of a pair of essays, demonstrates that burying the war's dead and caring for its veterans prompted acrimonious disputes. Drew Gilpin Faust explains how efforts by the U.S. government to provide proper burials for the Union dead — a commitment that changed the definition of the nation's obligation to its citizen-soldiers — prompted former Confederates to complain that their slain men were being dishonored. As the federal government set up the national cemetery system, groups of southern women took up the challenge of establishing cemeteries for dead Confederates. Memorialization on both sides bristled with political meaning, stoking the fires of sectional enmity for many years. During those same years, as James Marten illustrates, the question of pensions for disabled veterans sparked sharp debate in the North. The debate revealed a chasm between former soldiers and those who had not served and, as with the discussion about national cemeteries, raised the issue of the role of national government in caring for men who had defended the republic. The creation of soldiers' homes brought other questions to the fore, including whether their residents gave up some measure of manhood in accepting governmental support.

Carol Reardon and Joan Waugh close the volume with essays on the memories of the Union's two greatest military heroes. It is a commonplace that William Tecumseh Sherman's "March to the Sea" provoked the enmity of generations of white Georgians — a view dramatically bolstered by *The Birth of a Nation* and *Gone with the Wind*. Reardon's essay suggests a more complex memory of Sherman among white Georgians, one that juxtaposed a bitter Lost Cause interpretation with a more conciliatory one influenced by the New South mentality and the rise of Jim Crow. Waugh explores the building of Ulysses S. Grant's famous tomb on Riverside Drive in New York City. A towering figure whose heroic and well-publicized struggle against cancer added further luster to his reputation, Grant stood as the most famous American of the postwar decades. Waugh reveals that Grant's death precipitated wrangling about where the tomb should be built (many veterans touted Washington, D.C., as the most appropriate site), what design should be adopted, and how best to raise the necessary funds. Her essay provides an important reminder that public monuments, whether commemorating individuals such as Grant or national traumas such as the Vietnam War and the attacks on the World Trade Center, often ignite heated public debate.

Readers should keep in mind that the contributors to this volume could have selected different topics for their essays. Sources relating to virtually every aspect and episode of the Civil War can be mined for evidence of controversy. The key to understanding the conflict, as it played out between 1861 and 1865 and as it has been portrayed and remembered since Appomattox, lies in determining how disaffection and dissent fit within the overarching story of the North's success in saving the republic and the white South's costly effort to establish a new slaveholding nation.

THIS BOOK GREW out of a conference at the Henry E. Huntington Library in October 2006. We thank Roy Ritchie, W. M. Keck Foundation Director of Research at the Huntington, for his generous support in making the conference possible. Our thanks go as well to Carolyn Powell and Susi Krasnoo, whose combined expertise ensured the smooth planning and running of the event. We are most indebted to our ten colleagues, who took time from hectic schedules to prepare excellent lectures and then cheerfully turn them into the essays that appear in *Wars within a War*. This book is dedicated to Mary Arboit, Joan Waugh's beloved mother, and to Phil Callahan, Gary Gallagher's much-valued friend.

NOTES

1. There has been far more scholarly attention to dissent and disaffection in the Confederacy than in the United States. This phenomenon seems to stem, at least in part, from a belief that the losing side must have experienced greater internal conflict. Much of the story of political, social, and economic turmoil north of the Potomac and Ohio rivers remains to be explored.

2. Recent titles include Drew Gilpin Faust's *This Republic of Suffering: Death and the American Civil War* (New York: Knopf, 2008), Gary W. Gallagher's *Causes Won, Lost, and Forgotten: How Hollywood and Popular Art Shape What We Know about the Civil War* (Chapel Hill: University of North Carolina Press, 2008), Joseph T. Glatthaar's *General Lee's Army: From Victory to Collapse* (New York: Free Press, 2008), and James M. McPherson's *Tried by War: Abraham Lincoln as Commander in Chief* (New York: Penguin, 2008); forthcoming titles include Bill Blair's *With Malice Toward Some: Treason and Loyalty in the Civil War Era*, Stephanie McCurry's *Confederate Crucible: The Disfranchised and the Political Transformation of the Civil War South*, and Joan Waugh's *U. S. Grant: American Hero, American Myth*. James Marten's essay also represents part of a larger work in progress.

Wars within a War

Women Numerous and Armed

Gender and the Politics of Subsistence in the Civil War South

⊰ STEPHANIE McCURRY ⊱

The Confederate war ripped like an earthquake through the foundation of southern life. Its impact registered in every domain from the high reaches of the central state to the intimate recesses of the household. Transformation is the essential characteristic of war, if only because the calling in of long-standing obligations fundamentally changes the citizen's relationship to, and expectations of, the state. In the Confederate war, the claims of the state reached proportions rarely matched in the history of modern nations, reached far past the ranks of white men called upon to serve, to their dependents, the women, children, and slaves who made up the unfranchised mass of the southern population. It is not too much to say that the war forged a new understanding of the relationship between citizens, subjects, and the state, that it forged a renegotiation of the social contract. For those who were not parties to the original contract—including white women citizens governed in the household state—the impositions and openings it created were especially historic. When war was done neither the idea of the people nor that of the government was the same.[1] ✶

One consequence of war was the reconfiguration of southern political life, and particularly the way power on the home front shifted along gender lines, as white women emerged into authority and even leadership on a range of issues that lay at the very heart of popular politics in the Civil War South. Historians have routinely cited the evidence of women's new participation without analyzing its meaning for southern political life.[2] And yet the content of the archives itself testifies to a fundamental shift in the very terms and practices of political representation in the Civil War South.[3] For the materials register not only the penetration of the state but also the rearrangement of household relations, local political networks, and modes of communication. Indeed, they capture the existence of a whole set of new, war-borne political identities, individual and collective, chief among them, I would propose, that of the "soldier's wife." There were new issues in Civil War politics but there were also new players.

These are developments, I rush to say, that had nothing to do with feminism or the conscious pursuit of equal rights for women. There was no political movement in the usual sense, no national organization, and no membership or other institutional records to make our work easy.[4] Rather, these developments are about the state, about the newly intimate and fraught relationship between government authorities, citizens, and subjects. The latter group included those household dependents — white women — whom the government had previously been content to access through the authority of their husbands. The political developments immediately at issue therefore concern southern white women, the vast majority of them from yeoman, poor white, or urban laborer households, pushed into the uncertainty of political practice by the deep disruption of their family and community life in the war.[5]

Their politics are not easily read through our usual lexicon of women's "concerns." For historians have typically defined southern women's politics in one of two ways, assessing them either in relation to their support for women's rights and women's suffrage (the feminist or women's history framework) or for Confederate nationalism (the southern or Civil War history framework). But it was not, I would suggest, in the categorical assertion of their rights as citizens or their contribution to the military defeat of the Confederacy that soldiers' wives politics consisted.[6] They did not make predictable claims about women's rights or citizen's rights, in fact did not much speak a language of rights at all. And they did not align themselves clearly for or against the Confederate cause, in fact did not much speak a language of nationalism at all.[7] It was, rather, their engagement in the deliberative culture of the community and, above all, the actions they took to shape public — even military — policy in their own interests that their politics consisted, and which constituted the assertion of a historically new political identity. By politics, then, I mean something different, more basic, about the organization of political life: about the practices of the deliberative culture; about political identities, circuits of power and authority within localities, discourses of qualification, empowerment, and entitlement; and about the relationships that developed between the state in its various forms and the citizens and subjects it claimed to represent and rule. By politics, in other words, I mean historical process and not just outcomes.

If there had ever been a sense that women were outside politics (and there had), that kind of thinking was obliterated by the shocking events of

1863. Then, in a wave of food riots, soldiers' wives impressed the possibilities of their politics on a shocked nation. Spectacular the riots were, and numerous. At least a dozen violent attacks (there are rumors of more) on stores, government warehouses, army convoys, salt works, railroad depots, and granaries were mounted by mobs of women, numbering from twelve to three hundred and more, armed with navy revolvers, pistols, repeaters, bowie knives, and hatchets, and they were all carried out in broad daylight in the space of one month between the middle of March and the middle of April 1863: a Confederate spring of soldiers' wives' discontent. The events were stunning in their boldness, organization, violence, and not least the shrewdness of the rioters' management of public opinion. For whatever the mayors and editors might say, the public simply assumed that the mobs were composed of soldiers' wives — as if prior developments had prepared them for the actions on the streets — as indeed, I would argue, they had.

There has been no lack of attention to these events. The food riots, the most dramatic and well-known episodes of Confederate women's history, have drawn the interest of historians sporadically over the years and invited comparisons to other like events in early modern history. Social historians tend to read them as the disaffection of the Confederate poor; cultural historians as public expressions of a deep customary idea of the common good.[8] Rich as these readings may be, they miss what is to me most striking about the riots: the deep context, clever politicking, strategic thinking, and collective organization they involved, and the political leadership and mass participation of women they announced. The food riots are thus not just social phenomena, arising organically out of the immiseration of war. They are manifestly political events — a highly public— expression of soldiers' wives mass politics of subsistence — events in an American, southern, and Civil War women's political history we are only now beginning to write.

BY THE BEGINNING of the war it was a public article of faith that the government had entered a new social contract with soldiers for the support and protection of their families. By the end of the first summer, that contract was already shaping local and state politics and transforming the tax burden on citizens. Initially Confederate officials did not imagine any new relationship with the wives. The political relationship was with the soldier whose dependents they now understood as objects of protection under the state's care: "Let them be adopted as the children of the State," the Mississippi governor said of the soldiers' wives and children.[9] In that sense, the state creation of a class of "soldiers' wives" reframed, rather than challenged, female citizen's political status as dependents.[10] As the web of relations between the state and citizens daily thickened, politics remained exclusively an affair of men; in 1861 and 1862, citizen men conducted the negotiations over what the people could sustain. In the early days of the war, when one spoke of the relations between citizens and the state, citizens meant citizen men. The pattern was so old it was hardly noticeable.

It was not long before the hoary gender patterns of American republicanism showed signs of strain. First, some men began to cite service to soldiers' wives in seeking exemptions from service. By 1862, in the face of official skepticism, they had to produce the evidence, moving through neighborhoods, petitions in hand, to collect women's signatures. Now women, preferably soldiers' wives, were required to authenticate men's claims on the mercy of the state.

But more fundamental change was under way in Confederate politics as white women, including poor rural ones, began to take matters into their own hands. By early 1863 an angry and sustained encounter between soldiers' wives and the state had taken shape. The patterns are quite striking. In the antebellum period women's communications with officials were few and far between. But with the war, the necessity of citizens' communication with state officials increased exponentially, and a growing portion of it was from women. In 1861 and 1862 women sent in only a trickle of the petitions war governors received. But by 1863 the number had increased significantly, and by 1864 the number authored by women or by men and women together overmatched those authored simply by men. While harder to quantify, a similar pattern pertains with the various secretaries of war.[11] Those documents thus serve as an index to a new politics, a surprising archival record of the collective public voice of poor white southern women in the Civil War. Go to any archive, open any box of wartime governors' papers or letters to the secretary of war, check any of the books kept by clerks of county courts or agents of local relief associations, and you will find them: barely literate, angry, sometimes threatening letters — not a few either, but masses of them — to Confederate "big men," signed by soldiers' wives.[12] What these documents represent is evidence that white southern women had found a means of self-representation, a way to intervene in the making and changing of their world, a strategic and effective kind of political agency.[13]

But the terms of that new self-representation are telling. Confederate women never could claim the name of citizens. On that account, the weight of the past was just too great. "This Constitution was made for white men — citizens of the United States," Thomas R. R. Cobb of Georgia had proclaimed in November 1860. In that sense it only seemed to reflect the common sense of the matter when, in petitioning their governor in 1863, a group of men and women from Bullock County, Georgia, divided their signatures neatly into two columns: "Citizens Names" and "Soldier Wives Names."[14] Soldiers' wives did not make their claims under the sign of citizen.

But conventional as it might seem, and disempowering, "soldiers' wives" was, in fact, a new identity and one, strangely enough, replete with possibilities. When Margaret Smith moved to get relief for herself and her neighbors she grasped at the possibilities, and in doing so introduced the basic elements of a new politics of subsistence that, by early 1863, poor Confederate women were bringing into being. "We hav seen the time when we could call our Littel chilren and our Husbun to our tables and hav a plenty and now wee have Becom Beggars and starvers an now way to help ourselves," Smith began, poignantly invoking yeoman women's loss of a customary household independence as a consequence of the Confederate army's manpower policy. But Smith knew more than need. Like most soldiers' wives' petitions to governors, hers took an explicitly dialogic form (to borrow James Scott's helpful term), invoking an official promise of protection only to turn it directly back on the state. "[A]n you our govner of north carlina has promust the soldier that thare familieys shod sher of the Last," she reminded Governor Zebulon Vance, quoting back to him, almost verbatim, words he had used in a recent proclamation to the people of North Carolina, "and wee think it is hie time for us to get help in our time of need." Smith's sense of entitlement, though new, was firm. So Margaret Smith called in the soldiers' debt, on behalf, she noted carefully, "of ourselves all the Soldiers Famieleys and Soldiers wives in Dudley desstrict, the righters as Sign thare name."[15] It was hardly a robust claim to the rights of citizens, but sacrifice clearly had its political uses — especially to non-elite women like Smith who turned it into a useful collective identity and claim of entitlement on the state.

For poor Confederate women to become soldiers' wives involved an act of deliberate, impressive, and highly strategic self-creation. Elite women never saw the use in it. They spoke the language of protection. All women did. "I claim the protection of our governor with the conviction that you will do all in your power for our relief," a Mrs. Letitia Page of Gloucester County, Virginia, wrote her governor, John Letcher, confidently in late 1862. Many planter women who wrote state officials sought protection from enslaved laborers, requesting the redeployment of military units or the detail of particular men "to manage and assist in controlling our slaves." But they did not speak, or identify, as soldiers' wives: "Mrs. Let Page," "Mrs. David Shipp," "Mrs. C. Clark," and the "Ladies" signed off, adding no social signifier except marital status.[16]

But when Mary Tisinger and her neighbors in Upson County, Georgia, petitioned their governor, Joseph Brown, for the detail of some man in the service, they delineated the substance of protection in strikingly different terms than elite women and they carefully identified themselves as soldiers' wives. The undersigned "are the wives and widows of deceased soldiers and mothers of soldiers in the Confederate Army," Tisinger and the other women specified in the opening line of their petition. "[A]ll of your Petitioners are very poor and dependent, there are only a few slaves in the neighborhood not exceeding four or five . . . that during peace or before the war your petitioners were dependent on white labor for support." With the male population of the neighborhood all in the army, "we are now," they said, "without protection or any one to gather our little crops of fodder or go to mill for us." Without help, they said bluntly, they would starve. For Tisinger and her neighbors, it was thus the absence of slaves — not their numerous presence — that rendered them in dire need of protection. So if yeoman and poor white women made their demands on the state, like ladies, in the sanctioned language of protection, it is nonetheless clear that they claimed protection, not from slave men but from the sole burden of producing subsistence. Mary Tisinger signed first, "Mary Tisinger with 6 chilrin, soldier wife." Mary Stilwell signed after her, "Mary Stilwell soldiers widow 6 children." Mary Taylor signed too, "mather of solder [unreadable] children." So did Sarah Kersy, "the mother to too soldiers," Elizabeth Kimbalt, "One syster and Brother died in the Army," and so on down the list. Each woman who signed — there were twenty-three of them — specified her identity in terms of the family relation to men in military service and the sacrifice made to the cause. For women identified as "soldiers' wife" (or sometimes just "sw," so obvious was the shorthand), sacrifice was grounds for entitlement, the soldier's wife a critical new identity in relation to the state.[17]

The patterns and class difference thus emerge, and with them the outlines of poor white women's new wartime politics. Elite women, self-identified as "ladies, interpreted the substance of protection out of their historical experience of sexual inviolability and leisure from labor. But yeoman and poor white women, self-identified as soldiers' wives, defined protection in relation to what marriage and coverture had meant to them, as white women in small and often poor farm households in the slave South, and in relation to the new legitimacy their husband's military service conferred. "You no that Wimman and children cannot cradle and mow," one distraught man wrote from wheat-growing western North Carolina. "I have worked as hard as some of the rich men's darkeys," a North Carolina woman put it, "and din make much."[18] Elite women might speak as south-ern ladies or particular rich men's wives. But non-elite women spoke spe-cifically as soldiers' wives, discerning in the historical moment a political possibility that had never existed in the past, not, at least, for women of their class, in their region, in their lifetimes.

By 1863 government officials were beset with demands from soldiers' wives. It was not, surely, the most promising of identifications. "Wife" had always been a category of exclusion, virtual representation, and sacrifice, and "soldiers' wife" seemed likely only to compound its effects.[19] Soldiers' wives were defined by their men's military service; the women never ob-scured that fact. But as they cast it, the sacrifice and the entitlement were clearly theirs. "To think that my loved one had gone and suffered and died in defense of those who were at home living in plenty and they could feel so indifferent about the wants of his family," one woman agonized. They are so "close harted it was moe than any ackeing heart could bear." We are owed more for the sacrifice of our men, the women collectively said. Of that much they were sure. "[W]e have given our sons and husbands and brothers to the batle field," Sarah Halford and her neighbors bluntly put it, "an after so much we hav done," we have been preyed upon by the agents of our own government.[20] *We* have given our men, after *we* have done so much, they said again and again when demanding relief. Indeed soldiers' wives claimed the sacrifice of their men as their own unmatched contri-bution to the cause. They brandished it as their calling card, turning the sacrifice of their men into a legitimate claim on the state's protection and resources.

Developments in the American South during the Civil War thus speak directly to the transformative possibilities, not so much of war itself, but of the cultural environment it creates. The Confederate war was not the only one in which a public emphasis on sacrifice created openings women man-aged to convert into political claims. In World War I Britain, a new public rationale of service and sacrifice (associated with a volunteer army) cre-ated political opportunities that perceptive and not-too-principled femi-nists successfully converted into the vote, earned, as they put it, "by the blood of our sons." In the North during the American Civil War, leaders like Elizabeth Cady Stanton and Susan B. Anthony harbored real hope that they could do the same. But in the South, where no such women's movement existed—where there was no antislavery movement to nurture it—no such fulsome claims to citizenship were possible.[21] Had not the Confederate Band of Brothers formed precisely to prevent such upstart imaginings? Yet even there, in the perfected republic of white men, the war provided astute women opportunities to unsettle fixed conceptions of political belonging as part payment for their sacrifice to the nation. By the middle of the war—self-identified as soldiers' wives—poor white southern women had emerged as a salient new constituency in Confederate political life.

AS THE GROUNDS of a collective political identity, the soldier's wife was a quintessentially southern figure, as much a product of the draft as her soldier husband. It was clear on the face of it that soldiers' wives were a creation of the Confederate state. In fact, as a social group they were an index to the rapid process of state formation under way in the Confederate States of America. Their very existence attested to the new power and reach of the central state, to its intrusiveness and proximity, and to the structural problems faced by the slave republic at war. For in contrast to the Union, which took sons and brothers while sparing husbands (and where the soldier's mother was enshrined as the representative figure for purposes of welfare), the Confederate War Department adopted a policy that exempted virtually no one.[22] With 40 percent of its adult male population enslaved and unavailable for military service, Davis and his various secretaries of war had no choice but to dig ever deeper into the ranks of the male citizenry, mobilizing an estimated 75–85 percent of the nation's adult white men (in contrast to the Union's 50 percent).[23] It was, to say the least, a considerable flexing of federal muscle, a wholly new conception of the power of the central state, and one that required the strongest measures of bureaucratic expansion.[24] The women who described a rural landscape literally stripped of men did not exaggerate.

By 1863 soldiers' wives were legion in the Confederate states. As the central state added new taxation policy—the infamous tithe of April 1863—it thickened immeasurably the network of extraction and bureaucracy within which ordinary citizens were enmeshed.[25] In August 1863, one Alabama man estimated that there were "about one thousand government agents" in this state "under the new system of taxation and purchasing for the army."[26] For people used to a very small government presence in their lives, this was all a tremendous shock. Women suffered under—and protested—the onslaught. Whether it was the tax-in-kind man, the conscript officer, or military units impressing as they went, soldiers' wives had to contend with "the government" as never before. The state was not simply out there, it was in there — inside every household. So if women were still wives, defined by the household and marriage, by 1863, in the grip of a newly powerful state, *that* was itself a measure of radical change. It was not so much that poor white women emerged voluntarily out of the recesses of the household into public life during the war, as that the state came barging in their front door, forcing them into a relationship they had never sought but could hardly refuse.

The particular circumstances of the Confederate war and of Confederate state formation are clearly evident in the content of the politics soldiers' wives forged. For the nexus of issues they agitated — from the government's manpower policies, insufficiency of soldiers' wages, government prices for women's work, inadequacy of relief, injustice of federal taxes, impressment, and monetary policy to name the main ones — were as comprehensive as the struggle to sustain life itself. Together they constituted what I call a "politics of subsistence." That politics took shape on the farms and in the laborer's households of the rural, small town, and urban South as poor white women struggled to scrape out subsistence absent the labor or wages of husbands and grown sons. Increasingly, soldiers' wives saw themselves as the victims of a systemic (not personal) injustice — of a government policy that was literally consuming their substance. They said as much in thousands of letters written to the officials they held responsible. Soldiers, many of them privates earning $11 a month, pressed their commanders and civilian officials about the desperate conditions of their wives and children. But the women proved increasingly likely to fight their own battles. Up from the farmsteads, workshops, settlements, country towns, and busting Confederate cities came a tidal wave of protest and resistance, much of it from women in their newly useful identity as soldiers' wives.

Indeed it is not too much to say that the emergence of soldiers' wives as a force in Confederate politics represented a significant rerouting of power and authority on the home front, and, at least for the duration of the war, a striking realignment of state-citizen relations. For even as women spoke specifically as soldiers' wives, and thus in a gendered voice, they spoke increasingly on behalf of the men of their class, taking leadership on a range of social justice issues at the heart of popular politics in the Confederacy. By the spring of 1863, women's claims on the government had not only increased in volume; they had also become the main vehicles for demands on state officials, expressive of local knowledge and political opposition. "As gustic [justice] belongs to the people," one woman memorably put it, "let us have it."[27] Poor white women's outraged demands for consideration in the making of government policy, and insistence on negotiating for themselves, are arguably unprecedented, certainly in southern, and perhaps in American, history.[28]

Martha Coletrane, a North Carolina soldier's wife, exemplifies the pattern. "Dear Sir," she began her letter to Governor Vance in late 1862, "this is a grate undertakeing for me as I never wrote to a man of authority before." But Coletrane, political novice, wasted no further time on niceties. Necessity requires me to write, she told Vance, getting right down to business, "as we are nonslave holders in this section of the state [and] I hope you and our legislatur will look to it and have justice done our people as well as the slaveholders." It was quite an opening. Like most of the people who wrote their governors, Coletrane had a specific, personal objective bearing on the condition, as she put it, of her family. She wanted to keep her husband out of the army now that the conscription law had recently been extended to capture men, like him, aged thirty-five to forty-five years old. "Without my husband we are a desolate and ruined family," was how she put it. But Coletrane did not request a personal exemption for her husband. Instead she went after the policy itself, presuming to instruct Vance on his deportment in relation to the Confederate Congress, a body, as she well knew, heavily (to the tune of 95 percent of delegates) dominated by slaveholders. "Hold the rane in your own hands," she lectured Vance, "and do not let the confederate congress have the full sway over your state[.] I appeal to you to look to the white cultivaters as strictly as congress has to the slaveholder." Leave the older men as home as reserves, she advised, "to support their families," instead of sweeping them into the army as the new federal law required. "The nonslave holders," "the white cultivaters" — Coletrane articulated a politics of subsistence that spoke not just for her, or for the needs of the women, but for their whole class. "We trust in God and look to you for help four our poor children so no more," she closed.[29] Sole author, Martha Coletrane nonetheless spoke for an imagined community of soldiers' wives. There was a world of political change in that "we."

The wave of food riots, all apparently organized and led by women, that surged through the Confederate states in the spring of 1863 riveted public attention on soldiers' wives and on their claims for justice for the Confederate poor. But the food riots have a deep backstory, one not often told. It consists of a multitude of attempts by poor women like Martha Coletrane to alert their leaders to the vast gulf between their means and the price of subsistence, to convey their mounting rage at those who profited from their immiseration — the speculators, or big men, as they often put it — and to demand policy that met the government's basic obligation to support soldiers' dependents. Soldiers' wives' politics of subsistence took increasingly collective, organized, and confrontational forms even before the street demonstrations of late March and April 1863. Shocked as they were, state officials could hardly say they had not been put on notice.

Political danger loomed, not least in the easy way in which poor white women spoke in the collective voice — for "soldiers' wives," nonslaveholders, or more generally for the poor. But the collective identity was not simply metaphorical. It is not easy to figure out how rural soldiers' wives organized their written protests, but the possibilities for collective organization were quite real. Clerks in government offices confronted with documents signed by hundreds of women must have wondered about the political backstory. I know I do. Did some one carry the petitions around the neighborhood? Write them up at local meetings of women? Did they hire agents to collect the signatures? The more than 500 women who, in 1863, signed "A Petition of the Women of North Carolina" wanted it known that they had not used an agent. But 522 women from the area around Rockingham signed it, lining up their names in columns under the headings "Soldiers Widows Mother" and "Wives Daughters Sisters Friends." The body of the petition was a searing indictment of planter speculators: "Men who promised our Husbands, sons, and brothers when they volunteered to do much to supply their places now leave us prey to the merciless speculators and extortioners who have monopolized the produce of the county." "This is the voice of the women of North Carolina appealing to the chief executive of our state for justice and protection." Vance, they said, should sue for peace. "Let this horrid war end," they closed.[30] The voice is stunning in its clarity, the numbers involved more stunning still. It is difficult to imagine 500 southern women doing anything together before the Civil War. It took more than a small amount of coordination to produce such a document — and a small sea change to produce the sensibility it evinced.

Where did such documents come from? There was no national organization of soldiers' wives with state or local branches organizing a petition campaign in the Confederate South. But there was clearly something we might regard as an ad hoc local mobilization of women repeated in hundreds of settlements. For the coordination required to produce those huge petitions and even their smaller counterparts suggests a prior process of political organization by poor white women hardly customary in that political culture. It also suggests that the groups of women (mobs) who coalesced in various parts of the South in 1863 and 1864, and that drew press attention mostly during food riots, had their basis in a broader local process expressed far more commonly in written protests than out-of-doors actions.

It is not always easy to tell where one political form left off and another began. Women whose sense of the social contract had been violated were formidable enemies.[31] In reading the masses of threatening letters pouring into governors' mailboxes and to the secretary of war one gets the sense of options being entertained — tried on — in ordinary conversation in neighborhoods across the Confederate states. Two women, writing in November 1862, concluded a typical account of how "women cant make support for ther familys" by warning that "the women talk of Making up Companys going to try to make peace for it is more than human hearts can bear." What did they mean by companies? Were those idle threats? One North Carolina woman was arrested for a letter threatening the life of a grist mill owner whose mill was attacked four months later by a posse of armed women, some related to the state's most notorious deserter band.[32]

In Virginia, where the largest food riot would break out, there is no evidence of prior warning in women's letters to the governor.[33] John Letcher was not perceived as a sympathetic figure by the women who took to the streets. But in North Carolina, where Zebulon Vance had performed his part as the protector of the poor soldiers' wives, and where county clerks had already written him about the negligence of magistrates and destitution of the women, everything in the governor's letter bags alerted him.[34]

And then there was this, an anonymous letter that landed on Vance's desk exactly six weeks before the wave of food riots broke out in nearby Salisbury, North Carolina, from "a company" of women (their term) in Bladen County who called themselves "Reglators." The term, which the women misspelled, was calculated to place the authors in the state's long (formerly male) tradition of rural justice and direct action — and most especially evoked the celebrated Regulator movement of the Revolutionary War era. Purloined by a group of women, it startled all the more, spoke of a new present in a traditional history of dissent. They would have corn at $2 a bushel or they would seize it, the women informed Vance matter-of-factly in the opening line. "The time has come that we the comon people has to hav bread or blood and we are bound boath men and women to hav it or die in the attempt." The letter bore all the hallmarks of rural soldiers' wives protests expressed in hundreds, maybe thousands, of other letters written in the southern states by the end of the war. But the cry of bread or blood — which would echo eerily across the CSA in a rash of riots a few weeks later — was new. Like Margaret Smith and countless others, the Reglators laid out the crisis of subsistence that soldiers' wives faced: the erosion of household independence with the conscription of their men; the impossible equation between privates' pay and the prices planter

speculators demanded for food; the need for the state to set prices in the interest of the poor. But to that they added a far more radical view of the war as a species of class warfare, a conspiracy by the rich to complete the expropriation of the poor men's farms on which they had long planned. "The idea is that the slave ownes has the plantation and the hands to rais the bred stufs," they explained to Vance, "and our people is drove of in the war to fight for big mans negro and he at home making nearly all the corn . . . and then because he has the play in his own fingers he puts the price so as to take all the solders wage for a fiew bushels an them that has worked hard, was in living circumstances with a good litle homestid and other thing conventient for there well being will be credited until the debt will take there land and every thing they have and then they will have to rent thure lands of them lords."[35]

The politics of subsistence clearly yielded some radical ideas, in diagnosis but also in the agenda for action. For the Reglators put Vance on notice of their willingness to use violence if political solutions failed. Vance could either take them out of the Confederacy or set a fair price on corn. But if he failed, they warned, then they would take matters into their own hands. If it was not enough that poor white women had come to speak for the people, to advance their collective demands for justice, this group was prepared to assume the final male prerogative and impose their will by force of arms. "Sir," they told Vance, "we has sons, brothers an husbands now fighting for the big mans negro and we are detirmined to have bread out of their barns or we will slaughter as we go."[36] Violence, or so they said, was part of the political repertoire of soldiers' wives.

The Reglators' letter eerily predicted the violent action carried out in Salisbury six weeks later. The conditions were suspiciously similar, as if the Reglators wrote the script for the Salisbury crowd. That they had not speaks all the more powerfully to the quotidian context of poor white women's politics of subsistence in North Carolina and other states about which we know less. Nothing in the record ties the Reglators to events in Salisbury. But a year later, in another starving spring, five women were tried and sentenced to jail terms for forcibly opening and seizing food from a government warehouse in Bladensboro, North Carolina. It was the Reglators.[37]

The American Civil War represents a striking contravention of the usual social prescriptions against female violence. And although there is a long tradition of rough justice to which we might look to understand Confederate developments, southern charivari had not been particularly a female tradition. So although such behavior had been known in other times and places, the women who took to the public highways in 1863 armed with pistols and hatchets could hardly have felt buttressed by some long ago precedent in another country and century.[38] No, the context for southern women's Civil War violence was more immediate and local: a mass movement of women, empowered as soldiers' wives, largely contained to nonviolent protest—and an emboldened minority who crossed the line from threats to violent direct action.

THE FOOD RIOTS. Richmond was the biggest but not the first. First was Atlanta, on March 16, 1863, the next day Salisbury, North Carolina; then Mobile, Alabama; Petersburg, Virginia; probably a copycat, as was Richmond on April 2.[39] "Bread or blood," the Richmond women notoriously shouted—a trademark cry already seen in Regulators' written threats and on the banners of Mobile's "army of women" (as one participant described them) waved in their rough procession through city streets.[40]

Everything about the riots in Atlanta and elsewhere shows the connections between violent new developments and the local political culture of Confederate soldiers' wives. In Atlanta, the fifteen or twenty women who collected "in a body" and proceeded to sack provisions stores began and finished with speeches to the merchant and the public about the "impossibility of females in their condition" paying the asking price for the necessaries of life.[41] It was clear that everyone adjudicating the Atlanta riot (editors, local elites, the broad public) knew—assumed even—that the rioters were "the wives and daughters of soldiers families" and readily conceded the legitimacy of their claims. Even the mayor and city council, though denouncing the action, moved speedily to provide more aid "for the relief of soldiers' families," "the result," one editor plainly admitted, "of the recent women's raid in this city."[42] Though criminal, the women's actions were effective.

In Salisbury, North Carolina, just the next day, when another mob of forty or fifty women mounted armed attacks on about seven merchant establishments, the same broad context was in evidence. There the perpetrators justified their action in precisely the language soldiers' wives ordinarily used in their petitions to governors and secretaries of war. As Governor Vance struggled to respond, Mary Moore, a member of the mob (and perhaps the leader), appealed to him, notwithstanding the violence, on behalf of the rioters "for protection and a remedy of these evils." Her sense of legitimacy was keen. "We Governor are all soldiers' wives or mothers," she began her appeal, "our Husbands and Sons are now separated from us by the cruel war not only to defend their humbly homes but the homes

SOUTHERN WOMEN FEELING THE EFFECTS OF REBELLION, AND CREATING BREAD RIOTS.

This famous northern image of the bread riot in
Richmond, Virginia, accurately suggests that non-elite,
armed women played a major role in the event. *Frank
Leslie's Illustrated Newspaper*, May 23, 1863.

and property of the rich man." She admitted that they had stolen food
and money at gunpoint—23 barrels of flour, 2 sacks of salt, half a barrel
of molasses, and 20 dollars in cash—but cast the riot as the seizure only of
what was rightly owed to the people, whose claims it had fallen on them,
the women, to enforce. "Now Sir, this is all we have done" she finished.[43]
Moore's defense of Salisbury women's mob action was thus more matter-
of-fact than defiant, and all the more extraordinary for it. It confidently
tapped an idea about the social contract with soldiers and their wives that
went deep in popular political culture, and it expressed a sense of entitlement that was clearly historic. What was owed to soldiers' wives? As in
Atlanta, few argued with the women's view.

　　After Atlanta and Salisbury, came riots in Mobile, Alabama; Petersburg, Virginia; and Macon, Georgia—five or more in the space of two weeks.[44] Then Richmond, then more. It was a strikingly coherent series of events, each organized and pulled off locally, as far as we know, yet so closely spaced, so similar in pattern there was wild speculation about the connections. By the time the wave of springtime riots crested in Richmond, conspiracy theories abounded. "That they are the emissaries of the Federal Government it is . . . difficult to doubt," ventured the *Richmond Daily Examiner*. Such seemingly connected and highly organized events were far beyond the capacity of mere women. This had to be the work of professionals: the all-purpose Yankee operatives resurrected for the occasion.[45]

In its respect for the level of organization achieved, the conspiracy theory speaks powerfully to the political capacity of women. For as the evidence accrued—a result of the Richmond city government's decision to pursue criminal charges against the rioters—the Confederate public (and now we) learned about the leadership, recruitment, prior mass meeting, preparations, and collective discipline of women that culminated in the riot on Richmond's streets during the morning of April 2.[46] In other riots there are suggestions of prior organization—the way women (whether twelve or fifty) just materialized "in a body" at a particular, apparently pre-designated time and place with banners, slogans, and speeches at the ready. But in Richmond there is no question. The sheer numbers—an estimated 300 women followed by a crowd that amounted to more than a thousand—defied any possibility of spontaneous eruption,[47] and the evidence that emerged at trial confirmed it.

Richmond puts to rest all questions about Confederate women's political ability. Shocking as it surely was to many, what came out in court testimony was indisputable evidence that the riot on April 2 was a highly organized event, in the planning for at least ten days. Moreover, despite widespread assertions that men were the instigators, it was, in fact, the work of one Mary Jackson, soldier's mother, farm wife, and huckster in meat in Richmond's Second Market. Mary Jackson and about 300 women had together planned and pulled off the biggest civilian riot in Confederate history.[48]

The riot offers a stunning portrait of poor white women's mass political mobilization. Recruiting apparently began around March 22, with Jackson organizing "a meeting of the women in relation to the high prices." Jackson's networks were rural as well as urban, and she worked them all. In addition to women in the market where she worked and at government clothing factories in town, witnesses reported a stream of women coming in from Henrico, Hanover, and New Kent counties on the day before the riot; at least one from a distance of eleven miles. More than 300 women turned up on April 1 for the meeting in the Belvidere Baptist Church on Oregon Hill, where the riot was planned. "All were women there except two boys," one witness, a Mrs. Jamison, explained. "The object of the meeting" she told the court, "was to organize to demand goods of the merchants at government prices and if they were not given the stores were to be broken open and goods taken by force." By all accounts, it was a rowdy meeting. Jackson was clearly in command; indeed, in a stunning assumption of male authority and violation of fundamentalist practice, she "went up into the pulpit" to address the meeting and to issue instructions about how the demonstration was to proceed. She said "she didn't want the women to go along the streets like a parcel of heathens," one woman testified later, "but to go quietly to the stores and demand goods at government prices and if the merchants didn't grant their demand to break open the stores and take the goods." Jackson apparently told them to meet the next morning at 9:00 A.M., to leave their children at home, and to come armed.[49]

Unusual and violent as the riot was, Jackson and the women who planned and executed it were products of the same political culture and politics of subsistence as the mass of Confederate soldiers' wives—Jackson literally so. John B. Jones, a clerk in the War Department (part of whose job was to vet the petitions of soldiers' wives and mothers to the secretary of war) and an eyewitness to the riot, said he recognized Mary Jackson from her "frequent application at the war office for the discharge of her son." Before Mary Jackson took to the streets, in other words, she had been one of the mass of ordinary petitioning Confederate women. Her strategy for the riot suggests as much. For in insisting that rioters first make an offer of government price for the goods they planned to seize from speculators—and in first seeking an audience with the governor to air their grievances before heading out to the streets (an inspired bit of political choreography)—she and the others showed their deep investment in the ideas and practices of the white women's wartime political culture.[50] The women had guns but, like the crowds in Atlanta and Salisbury, also a public relations strategy.

Still, violence was planned for from the beginning. Jackson was seen with a bowie knife and six-barreled pistol as she left the market on the morning of the riot. When the mob surged out of the western gates of Capitol Square up onto Ninth Street, marching silently as Jackson had instructed, the women were heavily armed with domestic implements and the rejected contents of an old armory: axes and hatchets, "rusty old horse pistols, clubs, knives, bayonets stuffed in belts, and specimens of the home-made knives with which our soldiers were wont to load themselves down in the first part of the war," as one witness put it.[51] For a good two hours they wreaked havoc on the streets of Richmond, targeting known speculators, smashing their way into stores with hatchets and axes, looting at gunpoint and loading stolen goods onto wagons they impressed on the street. Many of the women eventually arrested were caught on top of those wagons driving off their haul or in possession of it in working-class neighborhoods and farms in and around the city. At least twelve stores were looted before the public guard was called out and, threatening to fire on the rioters, managed to restore order. Those caught in the subsequent dragnet included otherwise unknown women who distinguished themselves in the fray, among them Mary Duke, a soldier's wife left at home with four children while her husband served in Lee's army. But the authorities also got the ringleaders, including Mary Jackson, there to the bitter end, picked up around noontime in a mob of women trying to break into a store, still un-bowed, brandishing a bowie knife, shouting, yes, "bread or blood."[52]

There would be at least six other riots in 1863, and as in Atlanta, Salisbury, and Richmond, they played out in violent form the politics of subsistence that soldiers' wives had forged.[53] In all of them, too, women's anger was turned as much against government officials as against merchants and planters, had as much to do with the inadequacy of welfare as with speculation. That, as it turned out, was one of the key elements and critical policy implications of the women's riots and the larger politics out of which they grew. And it is the chief measure of its efficacy in Confederate politics and policy. For it was really only in response to the riots that local, state, (and to a lesser extent) federal officials undertook a systematic reform and extension of the traditional antebellum system of delivering relief.[54]

"The great question in this revolution is now a question of *bread*," Governor Joseph Brown of Georgia declared in opening a special session of the legislature he had called for just nine days after the Atlanta riot. Georgia and a number of other southern states would go on to build welfare systems on a scale, in terms of budget and administrative commitments, unprecedented in the history of the two North American states. Nothing in the Union appears to compare. Georgia alone spent as much in one year as Massachusetts did during the whole war. Not so much a reflection, as one historian has put it, of Brown's "overriding concern for the little man," the expansion of state welfare was, more precisely, a political response to the mobilization of yeoman and poor white women in that and other states of the Confederacy. As in North Carolina, where the new law of 1863 was titled "Act for the Relief of the Wives and Families of Soldiers in the Army," and where millers (in Orange County) received instructions to distribute government corn "First to soldiers' wives at six dollars a bushel" and only then "to other needy persons," the new welfare systems were built, quite literally, in the image of the soldier's wife.[55]

There was in the Civil War South a world of political communication and organization we do not know much about. To recapture it is to provide a long-missing context within which to understand the food riots, the spectacular examples of violent direct action the poor white women's political culture yielded. Combined with other developments in the political history of the Civil War South — especially in the new relation of the state to its enslaved subjects — it emerges as part of a much larger argument I am trying to make: that southern men and women, enslaved and free, had some considerable experience of a big state by the time their leaders stacked arms at Appomattox, and that fundamental political change arrived in the American South before — not just with — Confederate military defeat.[56]

NOTES

1. In its general argument this essay, and the book it is extracted from, builds on the work of Raimondo Luraghi, Emory M. Thomas, and Richard Bensel, all of whom stress the revolutionary nature of the Confederate state. Where it differs is in the focus on the unfranchised as key parties in and to the transformation of political life in the Confederacy during the Civil War and, particularly, in the focus on women and gender in that process. See Raimondo Luraghi, *The Rise and Fall of the Plantation South* (New York: New Viewpoints, 1978); Emory M. Thomas, *The Confederacy as a Revolutionary Experience* (Englewood Cliffs, N.J.: Prentice-Hall, 1971) and *The Confederate Nation: 1861–1865* (New York: Harper and Row, 1979); and Richard Franklin Bensel, *Yankee Leviathan: The Origins of Central State Authority in America, 1859–1877* (New York: Cambridge University Press, 1990).

2. For example, Paul Escott and Armstead Robinson routinely use letters from yeoman and poor white women to state governors and the various secretaries of war without noticing that they are from women — they assimilate them to the suffering poor more generally — and thus without noticing the changed patterns of political communication they confirm. See Paul D. Escott, *After Secession: Jefferson Davis and the Failure of Confederate Nationalism* (Baton Rouge: Louisiana State University Press, 1978), "The Moral Economy of the Crowd in Confederate North Carolina," *Maryland Historian* 122 (Spring/Summer 1982): 1–17, and "Poverty and Governmental Aid in Confederate North Carolina," *North Carolina Historical Review* 61 (October 1984): 462–80; Armstead L. Robinson, *Bitter Fruits of Bondage: The Demise of Slavery and the Collapse of the Confederacy, 1861–1865* (Charlottesville: University of Virginia Press, 2005).

3. Here I refer to the increasing proportion of correspondence to public officials — governors, the secretary of war, the Confederate president — by women, which is especially noticeable after 1862.

4. I think, for example, of the contrast with the women's antislavery petition campaigns organized by antislavery societies in the northern states in the antebellum and Civil War period. See Susan Zaeske, *Signatures of Citizenship: Petitioning, Antislavery, and Women's Political Identity* (Chapel Hill: University of North Carolina Press, 2003).

5. The idea of women pushed into political practice is informed by a reading of Begoña Aretxaga, *Shattering Silence: Women, Nationalism, and Political Subjectivity in Northern Ireland* (Princeton, N.J.: Princeton University Press, 1997), 61 and throughout.

6. For the former see especially Bell Irvin Wiley, *Confederate Women* (Westport, Conn.: Greenwood, 1975) and more recently George C. Rable, *Civil Wars: Women and the Crisis of Southern Nationalism* (Urbana: University of Illinois Press, 1989), and Drew Gilpin Faust, *Mothers of Invention: Women of the Slaveholding South in the American Civil War* (Chapel Hill: University of North Carolina Press, 1996); for the latter see Anne Firor Scott, *The Southern Lady: From Pedestal to Politics, 1830–1930* (Chicago: University of Chicago Press, 1970).

7. There is no doubt that poor white women's politics in the Civil War South was part of a larger stream of disaffection on the Confederate home front, which most historians link to the collapse of Confederate nationalism. But the terms of that debate, now long-standing and polarized, are too binary and reductive, I would argue, to illuminate much about poor white women's Civil War politics. It is not only that most of that debate (Victoria Bynum excepted) misses entirely the matter of poor white and yeoman women's new salience in Confederate politics. It is also that, as I see it, the key issue is not the nation but the state, less about affective ties to the nation than about response to the demands of the state. My interest thus lies not in taking sides in the nationalism debate but in trying to gauge the changed political identities, networks, and circuits of authority that underlay the emergence of soldiers' wives as a political force in the Confederate states. It is worth pointing out that in the long-standing association of women and Confederate nationalism (its symbols, rituals, and commemoration) in the literature, no one has yet tackled the issue of class and gender; arguments usually proceed exclusively in reference to elite, slaveholding women. Whether yeoman or poor white women forged a particular identification with the nation, whether they participated in the ceremonies of flag making and presenting that preoccupied elite women in the first year of the war, for example, still remains an open question.

The literature is obviously large, but for a sample on nationalism, pro and con, see Escott, *After Secession*, and Gary W. Gallagher, *The Confederate War* (Cambridge, Mass.: Harvard University Press, 1997). For a rare focus on poor white women see Victorian Bynum, *Unruly Women: The Politics of Social and Sexual Control in the Old South* (Chapel Hill: University of North Carolina Press, 1992). The literature on women and Confederate nationalism goes back to Bell Wiley, but see especially the more recent Faust, *Mothers of Invention*, and Anne Sarah Rubin, *A Shattered Nation: The Rise and Fall of the Confederacy, 1861–1868* (Chapel Hill: University of North Carolina Press, 2005).

8. For the social historians see especially Paul D. Escott, "The Cry of the Sufferers: The Problem of Welfare in the Confederacy," *Civil War History* 23 (September 1977): 228–40, "Poverty and Governmental Aid in Confederate North Carolina," and *After Se-*

cession; Victoria Bynum, *Unruly Women*; and Michael B. Chesson, "Harlots or Heroines? A New Look at the Richmond Bread Riot," *Virginia Magazine of History and Biography* 92 (April 1984): 131–74. For the cultural historians see especially Drew Gilpin Faust, *The Creation of Confederate Nationalism: Ideology and Identity in the Civil War South* (Baton Rouge: Louisiana State University Press, 1988), 52–57. Here Faust draws especially on E. P. Thompson, "The Moral Economy of the English Crowd in the Eighteenth Century," *Past and Present* 50 (February 1971). Paul Escott also uses this framework in "Moral Economy of the Crowd."

9. See, for example, the language in and provision of *"An Act to Create a Fund for the Support of Destitute Families of Volunteers in the State and for other Purposes, Approved December 16, 1861,"* in *Laws of the State of Mississippi passed at Regular Session of the Mississippi Legislature . . . November and December 1861 and January 1862* (Jackson: Cooper and Kimball, 1862).

10. On gender and citizenship see especially Linda K. Kerber, *No Constitutional Right to Be Ladies: Women and the Obligations of Citizenship* (New York: Hill and Wang, 1998).

11. For the earlier pattern see J. M. Cansler to Governor Brown, February 20, 1862, Buchanan, Harlason County, box 26, General Executive Records, Governor's Incoming Correspondence, Joseph E. Brown, RG 1-1-5, Georgia Department of Archives and History, Atlanta (repository hereafter cited as GDAH). For the later pattern see O. D. Gray and others to Governor Brown, February 18, 1862, Graysville, Ga., box 3, Executive Department, Petitions, RG 1-1, GDAH.

12. The generalization is based on counts in the correspondence and petitions of Governor Brown of Georgia, 1861–65, in GDAH. The patterns in the Secretary of War Papers are based on a one-tenth sample of the microfilm reels of Letters Received, 1861–65, RG 109, National Archives, Washington (repository hereafter cited as NA).

13. The definition of political agency is adapted from Aretxaga, *Shattering Silence*, 8.

14. *Substance of Remarks Made by Thomas R. R. Cobb, Esq., Before the General Assembly of Georgia, November 12, 1860* in Allen D. Candler, ed., *Confederate Records of the State of Georgia* (5 vols., 1909–11; reprint in 6 vols., New York: AMS, 1972), 1:160; A. B. Briggs, Sr., and others to Governor Brown, August 8, 1863, Bullock County, Ga., box 1, Executive Department, Petitions, RG 1-1, GDAH.

15. Margaret Smith and others to Governor Vance, February 4, 1863, Wayne County, N.C., box 162, Zebulon B. Vance, Governors Papers, North Carolina State Archives, Division of Archives and History, Raleigh (repository hereafter cited as NCDAH). For the text of the "promust," see Michael Bollinger to Governor Vance, March 3, 1863, Newton, Catawba County, N.C., box 163, Zebulon B. Vance, Governors Papers, NCDAH. The idea of "dialogic" form comes from James Scott, *Domination and the Arts of Resistance: Hidden Transcripts* (New Haven: Yale University Press, 1990), 92.

16. Mrs. Let Page to Governor John Letcher, November 17, 1862, Gloucester County, Va., series 6, John Letcher Papers, Virginia Historical Society, Richmond; Mrs. David Shipp and others to Governor Joseph Brown, July 21, 1864, Stewart County, Ga., box 3, Executive Department, Petitions, RG 1-1, GDAH; Mrs. C. Clark to Governor Brown, n.d., Riddleville, Washington County, Ga., box 3, Executive Department, Petitions, RG 1-1, GDAH.

17. Mary C. Tisinger and others to Governor Brown, August 15, 1864, Upson County, Ga., box 3, Executive Department, Petitions, RG 1-1, GDAH.

18. J. C. Kenner to Governor Vance, April 18, 1864, and anonymous to Governor Vance,

October 9, 1863, Morgantown, N.C., boxes 176, 170, Zebulon B. Vance, Governors Papers, NCDAH.

19. On marriage and citizenship see Kerber, *No Constitutional Right to Be Ladies*; Nancy F. Cott, *Public Vows: A History of Marriage and the Nation* (Cambridge, Mass.: Harvard University Press, 2000); and Stephanie McCurry, "The Citizen Wife," *Signs: Journal of Women in Culture and Society* 30 (Winter 2005): 1659–70.

20. Unsigned to Governor Vance, August 17, 1864, and Sarah Halford and others to Governor Vance, December 23, 1863, Rutherford County, N.C., boxes 179, 172, Zebulon B. Vance, Governors Papers, NCDAH.

21. On Britain see Nicoletta F. Gullace, *The Blood of Our Sons: Men, Women, and the Renegotiation of British Citizenship During the Great War* (New York: Palgrave Macmillan, 2002). On the North in the Civil War, see Jeanie Attie, *Patriotic Toil: Northern Women and the American Civil War* (Ithaca, N.Y.: Cornell University Press, 1998), and *Proceedings of the Meeting of the Loyal Women of the Republic Held in New York, May 14, 1863* (New York: Phair and Company, 1863). Lori Ginzberg's *Untidy Origins: A Story of Woman's Rights in Antebellum New York* (Chapel Hill: University of North Carolina Press, 2005), while vastly expanding our notion of the political cultures that can nurture feminist and suffrage claims, nonetheless shows how firmly tied it was to antislavery politics of various kinds. On the new context of legitimacy in Confederate culture (and politics) see Faust, *Creation of Confederate Nationalism.*

22. Nina Silber estimates that "up to 70 percent of Union soldiers were unmarried" and that "compared with Southern women, fewer women in the North would have to give up a man to the military, whether husband, son, or brother." Most of those who did, she says, were "probably the mothers or sisters of young enlisted men." This is not to say, of course, that there were not married men in the Union army or soldiers' wives on the Union home front. But if the demands of the state elicited a similar new collective identity and political mobilization of poor women as soldiers' wives in the Union states (as I argue it did in the Confederacy), it is not something yet evident from the secondary literature. It is also worth noting that historians of women in the Union have made much less use of governors' papers and the secretary of war papers than southern historians. It would surely be interesting to know more about the postures non-elite women adopted in their appeals for relief to politicians and public officials. On women in the Union see especially Nina Silber, *Daughters of the Union: Northern Women Fight the Civil War* (Cambridge, Mass.: Harvard University Press, 2005), quotations and figures on 16–17; Elizabeth D. Leonard, *Yankee Women: Gender Battles in the Civil War* (New York: Norton, 1994); Elizabeth Young, *Disarming the Nation: Women's Writing in the American Civil War* (Chicago: University of Chicago Press, 1999); Attie, *Patriotic Toil*; and Judith Ann Giesberg, *Civil War Sisterhood: The U.S. Sanitary Commission and Women's Politics in Transition* (Boston: Northeastern University Press, 2000). Forthcoming work by Frances Clarke and Giesberg will surely advance the discussion.

23. For the estimate of the proportion of enslaved men in the adult Confederate population, see Ira Berlin et al., eds., *Freedom: A Documentary History of Emancipation, 1861–1867*, Series II, *The Black Military Experience* (New York: Cambridge University Press, 1982), 12. For the enlistment figures North and South see Gallagher, *Confederate War*, 28–29, and Silber, *Daughters of the Union*, 16–18. On Confederate conscription see Albert Burton Moore, *Conscription and Conflict in the Confederacy* (1924; reprint, Columbia:

University of South Carolina Press, 1996). In one recent study of enlistment in Virginia, Aaron Sheehan-Dean argues that in the parts of the state controlled by the Confederacy 90 percent of eligible white men served in the army. See Aaron Sheehan-Dean, *Why Confederates Fought: Family and Nation in Civil War America* (Chapel Hill: University of North Carolina Press, 2007), 3. This is not to deny that exemptions were made (occupational ones most commonly) but to point up the unusual level of male mobilization reached in the Confederacy.

24. Political scientist Richard Bensel (*Yankee Leviathan*, 131) calls conscription the most statist policy the Confederate government adopted and the strongest measure of bureaucratic expansion.

25. The April 1863 tax law authorized federal authorities to take one-tenth of everything grown or raised on Confederate farms. See Robinson, *Bitter Fruits of Bondage*, 149.

26. George Lynch to Honorable John A. Campbell, August 17, 1863, Clifton, Wilcox County, Alabama, M437, roll 101, frame 352, Confederate Secretary of War, Letters Received, RG 109, NA. Paul Escott says that the Treasury Department named 1,440 appraisers and that the War Department sent 2,965 agents into every part of the Confederacy to collect the tax. Between July and November 1863, tax-in-kind agents collected in excess of $5 million worth of crops; fully two-thirds was collected in North Carolina, Georgia, and Alabama. See Escott, "Poverty and Governmental Aid in Confederate North Carolina," 472.

27. Sarah Halford and others to Governor Vance, December 23, 1863, Rutherford County, N.C., box 172, Zebulon B. Vance, Governors Papers, NCDAH.

28. The obvious comparison is to the petitions of soldiers' wives in the American Revolution. On this see, for example, Linda Kerber, *Women of the Republic: Intellect and Ideology in Revolutionary America* (Chapel Hill: University of North Carolina Press, 1980). But Kerber does not attribute much political significance to the petition as a political form (she calls it "prepolitical"), mentions only one from non-elite women (Charleston seamstresses), and does not document any particular coherence of women as soldiers' wives. The forms of the state, I would point out, were quite distinct in the revolutionary and Civil War period, and there is no comparable evidence of a collective identity or mobilization of women. The other relevant comparison is to the petitioning campaigns of northern women for the abolition of slavery. On this, see most recently, Susan Zaeske, *Signatures of Citizenship*. But this was a centrally organized campaign, with standardized forms preprinted for submission to Congress, that falls more comfortably into the tradition of bourgeois women's reform activity; they were not making demands for policy change in their own interest, for example, and it was not a political movement of poor women.

29. Martha Coletrane to Governor Vance, November 18, 1862, Randolph County, N.C., box 160, Zebulon B. Vance, Governors Papers, NCDAH.

30. "A Petition of the Women of North Carolina" to Governor Zebulon Vance, n.p, n.d. [October 9, 1863], box 184, Zebulon B. Vance, Governors Papers, NCDAH. The date is identified by the accompanying cover letter, Delphina E. Mendenhall to Governor Vance, October 9, 1863, Jamestown, N.C., box 170, Zebulon B. Vance, Governors Papers, NCDAH. This was one of a handful of petitions (all, predictably, from North Carolina) that suggested clear associations with a peace movement.

31. See, for example, Nancy Vines et al. to Governor Vance, September 6, 1863, Green County, N.C., box 169, Zebulon B. Vance, Governors Papers, NCDAH.

32. Jeptha Clarke and Mrs. Martha A. Painter to Governor Vance, November 8, 1862, Catawba County, N.C., box 160, Zebulon B. Vance, Governors Papers, NCDAH; Indictment of Martha Sheets, February 15, 1866 [the letter in question was dated January 1865], Criminal Action Papers, Montgomery County, N.C., NCDAH.

33. The Virginia Governors Papers for the Civil War period are so consistently bureaucratic in nature that one suspects an archival purging of constituent correspondence, including petitions and letters from women. I thank Joseph Glatthaar for a useful conversation about this. On Virginia during the war, see William Blair, *Virginia's Private War: Feeding Body and Soul in the Confederacy* (New York: Oxford University Press, 1998), and Sheehan-Dean, *Why Confederates Fought*.

34. R. W. Rest, County Court Clerk, to Governor Vance, January 2, 1863, Snow Hill, Green County, N.C., box 161, Zebulon B. Vance, Governors Papers, NCDAH.

35. Anonymous ["Reglators"] to Governor Vance, February 18, 1863, Bryant Swamp P.O., Bladen County, N.C., box 162, Zebulon B. Vance, Governors Papers, NCDAH. On Regulators, see Wayne E. Lee, *Crowds and Soldiers in Revolutionary North Carolina: The Culture of Violence in Riot and War* (Gainesville: University Press of Florida, 2001).

36. Anonymous to Governor Vance, February 18, 1863, Bryant Swamp P.O., Bladen County, N.C., box 162, Zebulon B. Vance, Governors Papers, NCDAH.

37. J. W. Ellis and others to Governor Vance, April 13, 1864, Whiteville, Columbus County, N.C., box 176, Zebulon B. Vance, Governors Papers, NCDAH. For confirmation of the link to the "Reglators," see Bynum, *Unruly Women*, 134.

38. On charivari in the South, see Bertram Wyatt-Brown, *Southern Honor: Ethics and Behavior in the Old South* (New York: Oxford University Press, 1982). On European examples, see Natalie Davis, *Society and Culture in Early Modern France* (Stanford, Calif.: Stanford University Press, 1965). The example of the French Revolution was the one that came most readily to mind to literature observers, but women perpetrators themselves never invoked the comparison. See the image from *Leslie's Illustrated Newspaper* reproduced in Faust, *Creation of Confederate Nationalism*, 53.

39. On Atlanta, see *Atlanta Intelligencer*, March 19, 20, 23, 26, 1863; *Atlanta Southern Confederacy*, March 19, 1863; *Augusta Chronicle and Sentinel*, April 5, 1863; and Paul Lack, "Law and Disorder in Confederate Atlanta," *Georgia Historical Quarterly* 56 (Summer 1982): 171–95. On Salisbury, see Mary C. Moore to Governor Vance, March 21, 1863, Salisbury, N.C., and Michael Brown to Governor Vance, March 18, 1863, Salisbury, N.C., box 163, Zebulon B. Vance, Governors Papers, NCDAH; *Richmond Daily Examiner*, March 27, 1863; Escott, "Moral Economy of the Crowd," 1–17; and Bynum, *Unruly Women*, 125–26. On Mobile, see Harriet E. Amos, "All Absorbing Topics: Food and Clothing in Confederate Mobile," *Atlanta Historical Journal* 22 (Fall–Winter 1978): 17–28.

40. *Richmond Daily Examiner*, April 4, 24, 1863; Amos, "All Absorbing Topics," 23.

41. *Atlanta Intelligencer*, March 19, 20, 23, 1863; on the numbers of rioters see *Atlanta Southern Confederacy*, March 19, 1863. Newspapers say the riot was March 18; Michael Chesson says March 16. (Michael Chesson, "Harlots or Heroines?," 136–37.) Little is written about the Atlanta riot, but see Lack, "Law and Disorder in Confederate Atlanta."

42. *Atlanta Intelligencer*, March 19, 23, 26, 1863. The phrase "wives and daughters of soldiers" was repeated in other papers. See *Jackson Daily Southern Crisis*, March 24, 1863, and *Athens Southern Watchman*, April 8, 1863. The *Atlanta Southern Confederacy*, March

19, 1863, identified the women as workers in government clothing factories and used the episode to rail against government seizures of private property.

43. Mary C. Moore to Governor Vance, March 21, 1863, Salisbury, N.C., box 163, Zebulon B. Vance, Governors Papers, NCDAH. For a description of the riot from one of the merchants attacked, see Michael Brown to Governor Vance, March 18, 1863, Salisbury, N.C., box 182, ibid. For Vance's response, see *Carolina Watchman*, March 23, 1863, quoted in Bynum, *Unruly Women*, 125–26. The Salisbury riot was covered sympathetically in the *Richmond Daily Examiner*, March 23, 1863, and in the *Watchman*; the women were never prosecuted.

44. On Mobile, see Amos, "All Absorbing Topics"; on Macon, see Macon *Confederate*, April 1, 1863 (reprinted in *Atlanta Intelligencer*, April 5, 1863), and *Atlanta Southern Confederacy*, April 24, 1863. The Petersburg riot is mentioned in *Staunton [Va.] Spectator*, April 7, 1863 (article accessed via the Valley of Shadow Project at ⟨http://valley.vcdh.virginia.edu/⟩).

45. *Richmond Daily Examiner*, April 4, 1863.

46. For court proceedings see coverage of *Richmond Daily Examiner* cited below; Louis H. Manarin, ed., *Richmond at War: The Minutes of the City Council, 1861–1865* (Chapel Hill: University of North Carolina Press, 1966); and Chesson, "Harlots or Heroines?"

47. Estimates of the numbers of rioters rely on the eyewitness account of diarist John B. Jones in *A Rebel War Clerk's Diary*, 2 vols. (Philadelphia: J. B. Lippincott, 1866), 1:284. Chesson, "Harlots or Heroines?," 138, follows Jones.

48. From the first, eyewitness accounts of the riot identified Mary Jackson as the organizer and leader. See *Richmond Daily Examiner*, April 4, 1863. By April 15, the same paper observed, "Mrs. Jackson is the reputed prime mover and chief instigator of the riot."

49. Ibid., April 24, 8, 1863; Chesson, "Harlots or Heroines?," 144, 154.

50. Jones's testimony reported in *Richmond Daily Examiner*, April 6, 1863. See his account in Jones, *Rebel War Clerk's Diary*, 1:284–86. For evidence that the women sought an audience with the governor, see the testimony of Colonel Bassett French, *Richmond Daily Examiner*, April 6, 1863, and Mrs. Jamieson (who claimed it was her idea) in the *Examiner* on April 24, 1863.

51. Eyewitness quoted in Chesson, "Harlots or Heroines?," 144; *Richmond Daily Examiner*, April 24, 4, 1863; Jones, *Rebel War Clerk's Diary*, 1:284.

52. *Richmond Daily Examiner*, April 7, 8, 11, 24, 1863. The quotation "bread or blood" is from *Richmond Daily Examiner*, April 4, 1863. On Mary Duke, see Chesson, "Harlots or Heroines?," 165.

53. For one in Savannah, see Turnwold, Ga., *Countryman*, May 3, 1863; for Augusta, Milledgeville, and Columbus, Georgia, see Savannah *Republican*, April 13, 1863, and Turnwold, Ga., *Countryman*, April 21, 1863. On St. Lucah and other sites, see Faust, *Creation of Confederate Nationalism*, 52, and Rable, *Civil Wars*, 108–11.

54. I take this subject up at length in chapter five of my book, tentatively titled *Confederate Crucible: The Disfranchised and the Political Transformation of the Civil War South* (Harvard University Press, forthcoming). There were more riots in 1864 in Bladensboro, North Carolina, and Savannah, Georgia, among other places. But it is interesting to note that, in what was another starving Confederate spring, there was nothing on the scale or

prominence of the year before. I would hazard the suggestion that that owed in part to the way the revision and expansion of the welfare system focused poor women's anger about food and attempts to extract it on those agencies and their local agents.

55. Governor Joseph Brown, *Message of March 25, 1863*, in Candler, ed., *Confederate Records of the State of Georgia*, 2:370. The Georgia legislature appropriated $2.5 million in 1863, $6 million in 1864, and $8 million in 1865. See Peter Wallenstein, *From Slave South to New South: Public Policy in Nineteenth-Century Georgia* (Chapel Hill: University of North Carolina Press, 1987), 105. On Massachusetts, see Richard F. Miller, "For His Wife, His Widow, and His Orphan: Massachusetts and Family Aid During the Civil War," *Massachusetts Historical Review* 6 (2004): 71–107. The historian quoted is Paul Escott, "Joseph E. Brown, Jefferson Davis, and the Problem of Poverty in the Confederacy," *Georgia Historical Quarterly*, 61 (Spring 1977): 65, 69. For the North Carolina law, see *Public Laws of the State of North Carolina Passed by the General Assembly at Its Session of 1862–1863* (Raleigh: Holden and Wilson, 1863), 33–35. For the county corn regulations, see Orange County, Miscellaneous Records, folder 1 (1863), Provisions for Families of Soldiers, 1863–1865, County Corn Regulations, NCDAH.

56. It is not so much the recognition that the CSA was a "big state" that is new. That is a view taken by a number of historians, most notably Emory Thomas and Richard Bensel. It is, rather, the linking of that view not to a history of disaffection and the defeat of the Confederacy, as is usually the case, but to the transformation of southern political culture itself in the war, evident especially in the emergence of a new set of political identities and relations involving the disfranchised (slaves and women). The focus offered here on soldiers' wives as a force in Confederate political life clearly raises new questions about gender, class, and politics in the postwar period, ones not easily answered, it seems to me, by the usual focus in the literature on Confederate commemoration or women's rights and women's suffrage.

Friend or Foe

Treason and the Second Confiscation Act

⊰ WILLIAM BLAIR ⊱

During the American Civil War, many northerners had no problem with considering the Rebels as traitors to the Union. The betrayal of the government by the southern Confederates was one of the most common refrains sounded in newspapers, speeches, private correspondence, and essays. Yet nothing was more complicated than arriving at a practical application of treason. A civil war made it difficult to define the relationship of the Rebels to the U.S. government or to know what to do with the traitors when you got your hands on them. Were they still citizens — insurrectionists who were eligible for the death penalty as prescribed by U.S. statute? Or were they public enemies — the equivalent of foreigners making war with the Union? Could you execute the noncombatants who supported the Confederacy, or did you have to treat them as belligerents, subject to the international rules of war without the possibility of prosecution for treason? More to the point, the conservative nature of the law made treason a tricky thing to employ: it contained legal restrictions that made it difficult to gain a conviction. Plus, the war threw up practical obstacles against prosecution. Ultimately, the best way to use treason might be as the rationale for punishment *outside* of the civil courts, through the seizing of property by executive authority on the basis of a military necessity.

These practical problems of treason come into focus in the debates over the Second Confiscation Act of July 1862. In fact, approaching this act through the lens of treason law and the debate over including this crime reinforces the recent trend among scholars to see the legislation as more moderate or conservative, rather than radical. Congress granted the bill the title of an act to punish treason, yet this vigorous declaration against disloyalty has clouded the complicated intentions behind its creation. It is easy to be misled into thinking that lawmakers intended only to visit a harsher war on the Confederate traitors. It also has been popular to assume several things: that the act signaled a harder turn in the prosecution of the war and punishment of traitors; that it represented the efforts primarily of Radicals; and that it helped push Lincoln toward sterner policies against the enemy. Even studies that acknowledge the strong influence of moderate Republicans tend to privilege the radical perspective and goals whenever assessing the bill's failure. Consequently, criticism of the measure's limitations often falls on Lincoln and the executive department, while overlooking the framers of the law.[1]

The Second Confiscation Act was, in fact, a bill that was not intended to accomplish very much — at least from the standpoint of treason. Admittedly, its provisions did attempt to help the military free slaves of Rebels who fell into the Union's hands. But it was also such a messy and complicated piece of lawmaking, and contained such contradictory passages, that it had little or no chance of punishing traitors. Treason was added to the bill to make it clumsy and hard to implement. The point that has been underappreciated until recently by a few scholars is that it was deliberately constructed that way, with moderate Republicans and like-minded Democrats — not Radicals — dictating its final form. Men who hoped to prevent more revolutionary measures, or at least refused to abandon due process in the courts when dealing with the Confederates, guided the clauses on treason into adoption. Blame for the law failing to achieve radical goals lies foremost with moderate Republican senators such as Orville H. Browning, Daniel Clark, Jacob Collamer, and Edgar Cowan, along with key congressmen from the border region. For a long time, historians have expounded on the impact of the border states in causing Lincoln to move cautiously toward emancipation. It should come as little surprise that the same dynamic held true in the Congress in the summer of 1862.[2]

Why the act has received more attention for its construction by Radicals among general works is difficult to say. Specialists who study the act have exposed the complex and multiple agendas behind the legislation. If anything has masked the deeper story for more general works it is perhaps that most studies have approached the bill from the perspective of the Radicals and the goal to achieve emancipation as a war aim. By coming at the legislation from a different direction — one that begins with the consideration of adding treason as an element — the divided mind of Republicans becomes strikingly apparent. The Second Confiscation Act fit within a larger context in which legislators attempted to define how to treat the enemy who opposed the Union — as friend (citizen) or foe (foreign enemy). Plenty of people wanted to punish the Rebels. And yet lawmakers were equally concerned with whether it was still possible in the summer of 1862 to forge a speedier reconciliation by promising the protection of the courts and the Constitution for the property of the insurrectionists.

Up until the final voting on the bill — when the choice appeared to be between a flawed bill or none — the Radicals worked hard to prevent the provisions for treason from becoming included in the law. They understood what was at stake. Radical senators such as Benjamin Wade, Jacob M. Howard, and Lyman Trumbull feared that putting treason into the bill would limit the legislation's effectiveness. Treason required due process. Its deployment recognized that the people should be treated as citizens, or at least as friendly aliens who were owed a defense through trials. Wade understood that no jury formed in the Confederate states — the place where the crimes against the nation had been committed — would return a conviction for treason. Those who favored adding treason to the law were seen by Radicals, correctly, as trying to contain and limit punishment rather than visit a harder war on Rebels. As Wade bluntly put it, "It is idle and nugatory and vain for us to be here talking about confiscation, unless we are ready to adopt some measure other than that of punishing treason under the Constitution and by the course of the common law, because the moment you go across this river, from here to the Gulf, you can convict nobody, as every one knows."[3]

Wade's ending comment bears emphasizing: everyone *did* know the problem — that treason even under normal, peacetime circumstances was one of the most difficult crimes to prosecute and win a conviction. Only two kinds of actions counted: (1) waging war against the United States or (2) adhering to one's enemies, giving them aid and comfort. The framers created a very narrow definition on purpose. They were reacting against British law that allowed for a more expansive definition of treason. In England one did not even have to mount an actual threat: the law recognized constructive treason, or punishment for people who merely expressed that harm should come to the king. Penalties extended to a person's heirs as a monarch confiscated the lands of offenders. Wives and children could be executed. The framers did their best to prevent these kinds of political prosecutions under the Constitution. They denied to the Congress the authority to define treason to avoid changing the rules to fit a particular political context. They also set the standards of evidence high by requiring the testimony of two witnesses to an overt act to overthrow the government, in order to avoid convictions through hearsay or perjury. Finally, they shielded families from sharing in the punishment by limiting penalties only to the life of the offender, a provision that became especially important during the debate over confiscation in 1862.[4]

Through various early trials, the courts supported the narrow definition of treason with its strong test for evidence. George Washington succeeded in prosecuting the whiskey rebels, but Thomas Jefferson was frustrated in his bid to convict Aaron Burr. Plotting to wage war did not count—the act had to be overt, and verified by two witnesses. During the 1850s, committed Unionists, dough-faced presidents, and conservatives in general tried to use treason to attack the antislavery movement, but they failed to convict participants in the Christiana Riot in 1851 and more than a half dozen members of the free soil government in Kansas in 1856. Prosecutors did succeed in one antislavery show-trial by sending John Brown to the gallows. Yet Brown was charged with treason against the Commonwealth of Virginia, not the United States, and he remains the only person executed for the crime before the Civil War. Consequently, any person even loosely acquainted with legal traditions of the new republic understood that the stars had to align in just the right fashion for the prosecution to win a treason trial.[5]

As the war came, the legal realities surrounding treason, as well as the exigencies of national security, kept reinforcing that the most expedient way to accomplish confiscation, root out treason, and punish Rebels was not through civil courts but through the executive department. The rebellion caused many northerners to favor preemptive strikes against suspected traitors, including the arrests of individuals and the seizing of their property without due process of law. Even assaults on free speech were fair game, with people imprisoned without charges for uttering statements against the government or in support of the Confederacy. As a justification for these arrests, it was common to hear the phrase "treason expressed or implied" or treason "actual and implied" to describe the dangerous behavior. Midway through the war, Lincoln himself articulated the need to conduct arrests without habeas corpus as one of the preventative measures against treason.[6]

Early in the war, northerners used the concern over potential treason to stop the flow of contraband, beginning first with the exchange of information with the Confederate States. Lincoln in June 1861 had declared it illegal to have any intercourse with the Confederate South, whether in goods or mail. Travel was restricted and monitored. Payments for business transactions were held up or confiscated. The executive department stepped up its use of special agents to monitor anyone entering and leaving the country. The courts did get involved, but most often for cases involving the capture of seagoing vessels suspected of containing goods helpful to the Confederacy.

In this context, confiscation quickly became adopted by the administration and its supporters as one of the means for protecting national security. With the First Confiscation Act, however, treason was not the main reason for taking property. When the U.S. Congress passed the legislation on August 6, 1861, the law did not target individuals. It was irrelevant if the owners were citizens or foreigners, or even whether they lived in the North, the South, England, or Mexico. It was only the property's relation to war making that mattered. In fact the property could be "guilty" of helping the rebellion even if the owners were innocent of any intention to overthrow the government. To seize property in this fashion, authorities used in rem proceedings, meaning the owner did not have to be in court or offer a defense. This was the accepted procedure for seizing ships and cargo in admiralty courts, allowing the hearings to proceed even if owners lived beyond the jurisdiction of the courts.[7]

This first act was too limited in its reach and reflected the desire to appease slave owners from the border states. Impoundment and condemnation was supposed to occur in courts whose jurisdiction encompassed where the property was located. But no legal action could be accomplished in the insurrectionary states that contained most of the traitors and most of the contraband helping the Confederacy. As importantly, there were problems for supporters of antislavery in how the act considered slaves. Section four denied the claims of disloyal masters for the return of fugitives or impounded slaves. But because of the need to placate the border states, this portion of the act remained deliberately quiet on the question of emancipation, leaving African Americans seized under the law in a netherworld between slavery and freedom.[8] Critics were fond of observing that this situation placed the government in a position tantamount to owning human beings, or at least functioning as substitute masters.

As mentioned, confiscation did not stop with goods: it also involved what we today call detainees or the temporary seizure of people who did not receive due process. During the first year of war, hundreds of white people fell into this category, seized by authorities and held without benefit of habeas corpus for what were called political arrests, or suspected crimes against the nation-state. Potential or implied treason was used as an excuse to hold suspects while authorities searched their businesses and personal property, seizing some of the latter—especially mail—as contraband. Whisked away to one of the forts near Boston, New York, or Baltimore, the offenders sat without benefit of defending themselves until the government decided to let them go. Usually, release came fairly easily after the suspect took the oath of allegiance and promised to avoid transactions with people conducting insurrection.[9] The arrests by the State Department accomplished a couple of things. They did curtail the correspondence between North and South. And they reinforced the tendency to have activities suspected as being treasonous handled by executive department officials who would arrest first and sort out the circumstances later.

Support for visiting a harder war on the traitors followed partisan lines that intensified late in 1861. By December, some Republicans had given up on the notion that conciliation provided the best strategy and were growing impatient with their president over his unwillingness to mount a stronger campaign against Confederate property. Lincoln's annual address to the Congress had rejected moving more quickly or extensively against property for fear of creating "revolutionary" measures that could end up confiscating the property of loyal people. James C. Conkling, a longtime acquaintance of Lincoln, was disappointed in the president's pledge to follow the constraints of the First Confiscation Act. Conkling hoped that the president would endorse the seizure of southern property based on military necessity, especially when the Congress — as it had the prior spring — had seemed "tainted with treason." Like many Republicans, he had more faith in the executive than in the legislative or judicial branches, which contained important Democratic officials and appointments who continued to influence the course of the war. The Supreme Court, for instance, was still led by Roger B. Taney, and many judges who served in federal courts had been appointed by Democratic presidents. This was one of the reasons why Republicans were eager for the president to exert more executive muscle. Conkling believed that Lincoln could justify the use of military power to preserve the constitution "independent of all Law." Instead, the president seemed too bent on placating the loyal slaveholders and conceding to the Congress the power to establish policy.[10]

At this point in the war, Senator Lyman Trumbull of Illinois stepped forward bound and determined to create a much more penetrating confiscation bill. Trumbull's bill brought together several strands of thinking about the prosecution of the war, all of them linked by a common desire to break the power of the disloyal masters who had bullied the nation with their agitation for slavery's expansion. First, of course, were abolitionists who considered the war would achieve little if it did not include emancipation. A second group supporting confiscation of slaves were more moderate Republicans — people who did not refer to themselves as abolitionists but who came to support taking slaves from Rebels because they saw it as the way to win the war and punish the men who had caused it. This position was fortified by the realization that slaves were being used to dig fortifi-

Senator Lyman Trumbull of Illinois. Library of Congress.

cations and conduct other useful labor for the southern military. A third bundle of support for confiscation involved people who wanted to make the Rebels pay for the war — quite literally. They intended to use the proceeds from confiscation to help the U.S. Treasury and alleviate from northerners the burden from the national debt.[11]

This last, monetary motivation for punishing Rebels was of greater importance than emancipation for a host of northern whites.[12] Congress learned in January 1862 that the Treasury could no longer function on specie alone. It was necessary to create paper money to fund the military. This ran contrary to many sensibilities, and not only the Democrats who believed in small government. Salmon P. Chase, secretary of the treasury and a Republican, was loath to abandon hard money. Even if a currency were created, everyone realized that the next step was a tax bill in order to have the newly minted money make its way back to the government. Francis Lieber, a professor at Columbia College and well-connected Republican, told his friend in the Senate, "Now, my dear Sumner, tax, tax us. Let me state as a positive fact that the People are anxious to be heavily taxed, more so than probably ever in history before. Indeed, without a 150 to 200 million tax bill our Legal Tender law will be a ghost enough to frighten the stoutest man."[13]

The champions of emancipation also recognized the financial problems facing the country. When Joseph Medill, the editor of the radical *Chicago Tribune*, wrote Trumbull in June 1862 about the legislation the Congress should address before adjourning, he listed the tax bill as the number one item, confiscation as second, and emancipation as third. Whether these rankings reflected his order of priorities cannot be said definitively, but that he remembered the tax bill first for such a list suggests that it was an issue of considerable magnitude.[14] Consequently, it should come as no surprise that congressional debate on confiscation — and constituent correspondence — often looked upon the measure as a way to defray the national debt.

On December 5, 1861, Trumbull offered to the Senate his bill for the confiscation of the property of Rebels and giving freedom to the persons they held in slavery. The first section of the bill explicitly targeted people who lived where "the ordinary process of law cannot be served," because they were in rebellion against the United States. Section 2 allowed for the confiscation of slaves but went further than the first act by specifically granting freedom to the African Americans taken from their owners. It also encouraged colonization for those who were emancipated. Section 3 acknowledged the right of the president to direct the military to seize property, especially in areas beyond the jurisdiction of civil courts. This was a section crucial to Trumbull's vision for confiscation — basing it on the executive powers and military necessity. Section 4 established a rebellion fund that would reimburse loyal citizens who had suffered damages in the war. Section 5 allowed loyal people whose property was seized to file claims, providing they did so within sixty days. Section 6 set up the process for seizing the property of Rebels who lived in the Confederacy but who had land, investments, and buildings in the loyal states. Procedures could be conducted in rem or without the presence of the owner. The final section did mention treason, but only to add forfeiture of personal property as a penalty.

The complicated legal phrasing contained revolutionary implications.

The senator had found a way to punish Rebels beyond the reach of loyal courts and to allow for the emancipation of slaves. The best way of doing it was to avoid the usual court system. The property of Rebels that remained in loyal territory — their homes, bank assets, and so on — could be taken through in rem proceedings common for prize cases. Slaves, on the other hand, would be freed through executive power. No due process was required. Practically speaking, Trumbull's law would have little immediate impact on most Confederates because it depended, like the president's later emancipation proclamation, on the advancement of armies into insurrectionary states. Yet once that happened, the bill granted the executive department freedom to define the process, including full power to appoint government agents or the military to seize property.[15] The slaves taken by this bill no longer existed in a limbo but were declared free, even if state laws said otherwise in the border region.

Being a careful attorney, Trumbull scrupulously avoided the charge of treason as a trigger for confiscation, and this is very important to note. He knew this could not be prosecuted. The difficulties were legion in establishing courts in rebellious areas to hear individual cases. "It is manifestly impossible to try a man for treason in South Carolina," he told his colleagues in the Senate. He also was convinced that it was unconstitutional to tie treason to confiscation because it ignored the proscriptions against affecting heirs of offenders. In February Trumbull stated that the bill "is intended to operate upon property, upon things; it does not touch the person at all; and it is only intended to reach the property of Rebels who themselves cannot be reached by judicial process. It does not profess or intend to touch the property of any traitor who can be reached by judicial process."[16]

Trumbull also addressed a critical question that ran hand in glove with issues of treason and property rights: what was the nature of the people fighting against the United States? Were the Confederates citizens of the United States or belligerents of a nation similar to the British? Trumbull had to answer these questions, for they were the way conservatives, moderates, and radicals argued for a prosecution of the war that suited their own vision and political ends. The definition of the enemy involved more than splitting hairs over semantics. First of all, these were people who felt bound to explain themselves constitutionality and legally, even if they were doing their best to get around those provisions and play power politics. Second, all realized that the outcome of the battle for defining friend and foe, or traitors and enemies, had profound repercussions for policy-making, including setting the parameters for the treatment of noncombatants, the procedures for exchanging prisoners, the process of emancipation, and the ability to try Rebels after the war as traitors.[17] The situation posed a fascinating dilemma. If the Rebels were citizens subject to U.S. laws, then they could only be deprived of their property as a punishment for an offence against the government—an offense that had to be adjudicated in court. If the Rebels were enemies, however, they became belligerents belonging to a nation at war with the United States.[18] This raised a further question. If the Confederates were enemies from an independent nation, then did this tacitly recognize the right of secession?

Both ends of the political spectrum eventually arrived at the conclusion that the Confederates were enemies and not citizens, but they did so for vastly different reasons. Radicals wanted to waive constitutional protection for Confederates to open them to a greater range of punishment—especially the loss of their slaves—without having to resort to tedious proceedings in courts. The opposition recognized that it could not keep defending Rebels, so they adopted the argument that the conflict had escalated from a civil war to a war between nations. In this interpretation, the Confederates were owed the protection of the rules of international warfare as defined in the *Law of Nations*, a book compiled in the eighteenth century that was recognized as a leading source for relations between nations and war-making. The two sides thus used the same names to achieve opposite goals. One set of leaders defined the Rebels as enemies to make the seizure of property easier; the other used the same term to make confiscation limited and more difficult.

Trumbull made a further distinction shared by people from all political positions both during and after the conflict—the need to differentiate between the leaders and the led whenever considering punishment. The United States could not prosecute every traitor. It was physically impossible and prevented the Union from achieving its primary goal of reunion. Even people who favored punishing the secessionists to the fullest degree understood the need for some kind of discrimination in applying treason. As Trumbull maintained, "Nobody expects to try for treason the two or three hundred thousand men now in arms against the Government, every one of whom is a legal traitor; but we will give them the rights of belligerents; we will take them as prisoners of war; and when those who have been seduced from their loyalty to the Union shall have them returned to their allegiance, we will release them again." He continued: "But the ringleaders of this rebellion—the instigators of it, the conspirators who set it on foot—will, I trust, be brought to trial for treason, and, if found guilty, be executed as traitors."[19]

Slowly during the winter and early spring of 1862, a keen observer could see the moderate faction of the Senate grinding away at the Confiscation Bill to blunt its revolutionary edge. No moderates admitted as much publicly, although Radicals often accused their Republican brethren of undercutting the measure. It would be a mistake to think that all moderate Republicans acted for the same reasons — or that they were trying to scuttle the bill entirely. Some held real constitutional scruples and even were sympathetic to the government using the rationale of military necessity in order to free slaves. But there is no doubt that they took over the direction of the bill and prevented a more sweeping confiscation act. We can see this co-opting of the bill through a careful reading of the changes in the text, through the speeches of representatives in the *Congressional Globe*, through their voting behavior, and through reactions in the press. Taken together, the evidence reveals the creation of a law intended to have very little impact concerning real estate and personal property, with treason acting as an anchor to hold the ship of state fast against the currents of radicalism.

From January to April, Trumbull's bill went through nearly a half dozen amendments before it emerged as an act "Relating to Treason and Rebellion." April was the first time treason had become part of the title. Previous amendments did show efforts by some representatives to define who was disloyal and subject to punishment. Senator John Sherman of Ohio, for instance, proposed to create five classifications of people whose property could be confiscated. It was clear that he considered political and military leaders to be the most heinous criminals, yet even he did not use the term traitor. The amendment that emerged with treason in April was sponsored by Jacob Collamer, which was particularly telling. Collamer was a moderate Republican from Vermont who voted as part of a bloc of senators who watered down confiscation by throwing in the obstacle of due process. Men like him had not rushed to use treason, but they adopted it when it became apparent that a much sterner confiscation bill would become a reality.[20]

Others who joined Collamer included Senator Edgar Cowan of Pennsylvania and Senator Orville Hickman Browning of Lincoln's home state of Illinois. At first, they spent a great deal of time on the floor of the Senate instructing colleagues on why confiscation would not work. They claimed that the procedure was unconstitutional by convicting people without trial and extending the penalties to heirs, both of which the framers had prohibited. Browning stated, "We must deal with them precisely as we would deal with a foreign nation with which we were at war. And if at war with a foreign nation, the law of nations would forbid us to pass a law to confiscate the property of the private citizens of that nation, or even to plunder them when our victorious army had invaded their country."[21] He believed that once victory came, the government could pass laws of amnesty or try individuals for treason. He did desire one kind of confiscation — that involving slave property. To accomplish this without creating a more radical measure, he distinguished between real property and movable property, and said that different procedures applied to both. Real estate, in his opinion, needed legal procedures to take it and could not be accomplished through in rem. But slaves were a different matter. His particular ingredients for confiscating them were: it should be done by the military, sanctioned by the authority to make war on a public enemy, and target the movable property of disloyal people only.[22]

By early May, so many versions of the bill existed that it was persuasive even to Charles Sumner that it needed to go to a select committee in order to untangle the contradictory elements and create a more coherent law. Proponents of confiscation looked upon this with dismay, however. The committee consisted of only two Radicals who had spoken out strongly in favor of seizing Rebel property. It was packed with moderate men — including Cowan and Collamer — and a couple of Democrats camouflaged as members of the "Union" party, or a fusion of Republicans and Democrats. Trumbull, who was part of the committee, could see no good coming from a committee with such a composition. On May 7, he tendered his resignation.

The surest sign that a group of Republicans attempted to block wholesale confiscation by employing treason came from the mounting disgust of Trumbull as he watched the metamorphosis of his bill. The day before his resignation from the select committee, the senator had argued against adulterating the bill by creating the need for courts to convict people for treason. He wanted little to do with the this process, fuming: "I believe that no bill is worth the paper on which it is written that hesitates to take the property of traitors and Rebels before they are convicted in your courts of justice." He added: "Why, sir, it is because you have got no courts of justice in the South that this war is upon us. It is idle to talk about a judicial tribunal in South Carolina condemning a man for treason before you can touch his property."[23] Wade joined him in opposing measures that resorted to courts of law. "I do not believe that any such sentence as that could ever be executed upon but a small number," he said, adding, "I do not know that it will ever reach any. I do not think my brethren around me here are of opinion that it will reach any."[24]

It dismayed Trumbull that when the select committee dominated by

Maj. Gen. Ambrose E. Burnside taking the gloves off. The mood of the country was turning against conciliation for Rebels in the spring and summer of 1862. *Harper's Weekly*, May 24, 1862.

moderate Republicans finished with its work, the bill contained strong references to treason. Treason and punishment of Rebels had become prominent parts of the title, and the first four sections of the bill dealt with this crime against the nation-state. It was surprising, however, to see that the members had gone even further by watering down the terms for sentencing. The committee had allowed for an alternative to capital punishment. This was within the power of the lawmakers. Although the Constitution did not allow the Congress to set the definition of treason, it did give members the latitude to determine the penalties for the crime. In this case, judges could still order the death penalty; however, the bill also created new options—five years' imprisonment and a fine of $10,000.

This troubled Trumbull and Senator Jacob Howard of Michigan. Trumbull wanted the members to think about the practical implications of what they were doing by allowing judges options for punishment. "Who is to exercise that discretion upon our Jeff Davises, your Beauregards, your Toombses, and the men who have plunged this country into civil war, who have brought all this desolation upon us? Who is to exercise it?" He answered the question himself: "The judges of your courts in the southern States. And do you want to put it in the power of the judge of the district of Georgia, who yet holds his office, as I was informed to-day, and who has probably done no act for which you can impeach him — do you want to put it in his power to say whether he shall fine and imprison Mr. Toombs, or whether he shall make him answer on the scaffold for the atrocious crimes he has committed against this country?" Howard, one of the more radical members of Congress, strongly agreed: "I think that a man who deliberately commits treason against his Government, especially such a government as that under which we live, had justly forfeited his life, and that he ought to lose it, and that it is mere tameness to speak of mercy towards that class of persons; I mean such as have deliberately committed the crime of treason."[25]

Defenders of the bill said optional penalties would do two things: ensure that the law was applied and avoid creating martyrs to the Confederate cause. The man who helped push the bill through was Senator Daniel Clark of New Hampshire. A moderate Republican, he served as the chair of the select committee and explained, "You do not want to hang everybody; you may want to punish, by fine and imprisonment, some men that you do not want to hang; and let me suggest to the Senator from Illinois that if he desires that these Rebels shall be punished, he will be much more likely to punish them by having the alternative punishment in the discretion of the court."[26] Senator Garret Davis of Kentucky chimed in that he thought it would be hard to secure a conviction for capital punishment in his state — that too many people in his border state did not see themselves or the Confederates as committing treason. In fact, they saw opposition to the government as a form of patriotism. Having a lesser penalty, in his view, might increase the possibility of returning a conviction.[27]

What distinguished moderates from their Radical colleagues was a constitutional conservatism that also had one eye on the detrimental impact that confiscation could have for securing peace and rebuilding the nation. They remained hopeful for reunion and saw confiscation as needlessly inciting the enemy by giving them further cause for fighting. As Browning said during one of the longest debates on June 25, "Long experience had already taught the civilized world that undue severity of punishment, instead of preventing and diminishing crime, tended to provoke and increase it."[28] Additionally, they refused to consider the entire Confederacy as consisting *only* of traitors. They shared with Democrats the belief that there were voluntary and involuntary Rebels: southerners who had to follow their leaders or risk losing everything. Consequently, they saw the need for greater discretion in assessing punishment, preferably through the courts. Moderates also did not concede that the states had seceded or failed to exist. They feared that hasty confiscation could jeopardize the first and foremost goal of the war — reunion.

The impact of moderate Republicans becomes even more apparent during last-ditch maneuvers by Radicals to force through a House bill that was much tougher on confiscation than the Senate version. Coming into play during late May, H.R. 471 gave far greater latitude for seizing Rebel property and contained harsh implications for the entire Confederate South. Noticeably absent from the bill was any reference to treason. Section 1 established that virtually all property was affected, including estates, money, stocks, credits, and personal effects. Then it named who was affected: officers in the Confederate military, all representatives in the national or state governments, judges or legislators, former officeholders in the U.S. government, and any Confederate holding property in the North. Section 2 expanded this list by giving everyone sixty days from enactment the chance to declare allegiance to the United States or face seizure of their property just as if it were a prize capture at sea. Unlike Trumbull's first crack at the legislation, the House version dictated that condemnation should occur through a U.S. district or territorial court, but it allowed for easier seizure of movable property by authorizing proceedings in districts wherever this "may be first brought." This left the door open to transporting goods to areas of the Union with sitting courts. Had H.R. 471 become the Second Confiscation Act, most Confederate property was ripe for the picking as long as the owners were in rebellion against the United States. The key lay in the owners' loyalty to the nation rather than how particular goods aided the Confederacy. It was a punitive measure — the kind of action generally decided by a civil court. Yet there was no process for determining the loyalty of individuals and certainly no attempt to allow the accused to mount a defense.[29]

On June 27, as the Senate opened debate on whether to accept the House version, a wonderful moment of clarity emerged from amidst the lengthy quibbling over legal principles. As usual, it was Trumbull who cut to the chase. Several days before, Democratic senator Willard Saulsbury of Delaware had spoken out against any form of confiscation and was especially adamant against considering Confederate southerners as traitors. He reiterated his intention to vote against any confiscation measure yet admitted that he preferred the Senate's bill because it allowed for trial by jury. If he had a choice, he said, he would favor including treason in the bill. Trumbull accused his colleague of trying to substitute a weaker provision for a stronger one and favoring a bill that featured controversial issues such as treason and emancipation in order to weaken support for the legislation.

What Trumbull meant by this was somewhat complicated and again shows the strange nature of these debates. The House bill on confiscation contained no references to slaves or emancipation—a separate bill was going to tackle this volatile public policy. The Senate version, however, did address the controversial subject. As mentioned, it freed slaves who were seized under the act. So here was a conservative senator from a slave-owning state—a man who opposed emancipation as a violation of property rights—rejecting a law that did not include freedom for slaves and accepting one that did. This same bill featured the procedures for treason that Salisbury also had consistently rejected. He was ostensibly following this strange course to create a bill with so many disagreeable elements that it might not pass. Sensing this strategy, Trumbull accused his colleague: "I wanted to bring it out, as I have brought it out by the avowal of the Senator from Delaware that his object in substituting the Senate bill was to get something less efficient than the House bill, and that he intended to oppose any and all confiscation."[30]

The voting patterns confirm that the Democrats were not the only ones hoping to adopt a "less efficient" provision. The conservative border state men, many of whom believed in state rights and slavery, joined with Republicans to push through the punishment of Rebels for treason. As the roll calls came for which version of the bill to enact, a bloc of senators consistently chose the Senate over the House bill. Moderate Republicans typified by Browning, Clark, Collamer, and Cowan kept alive the Senate bill despite their own stated constitutional qualms against using treason as a means of confiscating property. Most of the Radicals fought for the House version. One border state senator followed the pattern that Trumbull had predicted. Senator Davis of Kentucky rejected the House bill, supported the Senate amendments, and then voted against confiscation entirely. Moderate Republicans and these Democrats may have voted similarly, but they did so for different reasons. Democratic legislators reacted against the use of confiscation to achieve emancipation. Republicans were more inclined to endorse freedom for slaves, especially if conducted through the military as a war measure. But they had reunion as a priority and were nervous about letting all forms of property become vulnerable.[31]

When the final vote came, many of the Radicals supported the bill that contained treason. They had come along grudgingly, only after a final effort to push through the House bill that was far stronger. Looking at the final voting on the bill, in fact, is not the way to assess the political alignments on the legislation. It gives an erroneous picture of Republican unanimity and does not reflect how Trumbull, Wade, Howard, and others considered the resulting Second Confiscation Act as horribly flawed and unlikely to realize their goals of punishing the Rebels.

The law that finally emerged thus contained three distinct parts that reflected the varying concerns of the complex factions involved in its construction. The first four sections dealt with treason; sections five through eight covered confiscation; and nine through twelve involved emancipation. It was not the best of legislation — far from it. It was confusing, contradictory, and — as historian Silvana Siddali has wisely observed — "made it relatively easy to emancipate slaves, and difficult (at least, legally) to confiscate any other kind of property." Yet it was better than nothing and at least clarified the military's role in emancipation.[32]

The treason provisions, however, almost killed the act. Lincoln threatened to veto it. The president was like most moderate Republicans in believing that the provisions calling for confiscation as a punishment for treason were unconstitutional. The president had received more than enough advice on this point by members of his party. In early June, Ohio politician Thomas Ewing said the bill was "in my opinion & the opinion of nine tenths of the Bar clearly unconstitutional." Among other things, Ewing opposed "the pretence of proceeding in rem against property." Yet he saw even greater damage coming from a broad assault on property that could fuel resistance by Rebels and result in the destruction of the moderate Republicans' alliance with Democrats, which was known as the Union Republican Party. Pass the bill and he forecast the loss of Radical Republicans and a tilt in the party toward the Democrats. Browning voiced very similar concerns over the partisan repercussions of the act. He visited Lincoln on July 14, expressing his firm opinion that the bill was unconstitutional. Then the senator strongly urged the president to veto the act, saying: "[I]f he vetoed it he would raise a storm of enthusiasm in support of the Administration in the border states which would be worth to us 100,000 muskets, whereas if he approved it I feared our friends could no longer sustain themselves there."[33]

The president framed a veto message that took issue with Congress over the provisions for treason. Two particular areas bothered him — the forfeiture of property rights beyond the offender's life and, to a lesser extent, the loose wording involving the emancipation of confiscated slaves. Concerning the first issue, he specifically mentioned having problems with all parts of the act that resulted "in the divesting of title forever." He was a bit troubled by the in rem proceedings, or the lack of due process for taking property but suggested that might be remedied by giving more time to the accused to respond to the charges. The president, however, left wriggle room for seizing slaves by saying that he understood the Constitution spoke about only real property when restricting forfeitures for life as a penalty for treason. In Lincoln's interpretation, chattel property, or slaves, could be taken even if this denied their service to heirs of the masters.[34]

Congress had not seen this message ahead of time, but word of his position had reached moderate Republicans, sparking a reaction to save the bill. To answer Lincoln's concerns, lawmakers prepared a joint resolution (H.R. 110) that specified that confiscation lasted only during the lifetime of the owner. The Radicals at first bristled at what they considered to be legislative interference by the president and a continuance of conciliation to Rebels.[35] It became clear, however, that they had little choice because they did not have the votes to override a veto. Ultimately, the joint resolution passed but without the support of Trumbull, Wade, and a couple of other Radicals. Sumner supported it because of his faith that it enabled the military to seize property, including slaves, as a military necessity.

Implementation of the legislation has received justifiable criticism from scholars for its limited, conservative reach. One study has noted that the admiralty courts yielded far more income from prize cases: more than $10 million versus a paltry $130,000 for confiscation.[36] Yet it is clear that the inclusion of treason by the moderate Republicans provided much of the reason for the law's weakness. Contemporaries — and not only Republican journals — noticed this when the legislation became law. Newspapers such as the *New York Herald*, a voice for War Democrats in the North, believed the law was filled with conciliation and clemency for Rebels. As Lincoln himself had announced, the act gave Rebels sixty days to return to the Union before any widespread confiscation could take place. It also diminished the penalty for treason, allowing for fines and imprisonment rather than death. The *Herald* added that there were provisions allowing for executive pardons, which made the bill lean further toward clemency. It claimed that the president "still desires to treat our revolted States and their people as within the reach of a magnanimous forbearance." The author did not neglect to sound alarms about emancipation or the possibility of feeding the war fever of the South through such an act, but even here the writer counseled that Lincoln's goal for reunion meant "he very wisely keeps the negro in the background as far as possible."[37]

Other newspapers had cheered what they saw as the crucial change of direction in the legislation during May. The *Boston Daily Advertiser* had noticed the differences between the House and Senate versions, praising the latter for recognizing that "confiscation must be punitive, and that being so, it must depend upon the conviction of the offender." This writer was far more satisfied with the Senate bill, which proceeded more in line with the Constitution by resorting to court hearings to determine guilt. The writer observed that the House bill would have visited far more pain upon the South, reducing millions to pauperism. These actions would have fanned the war flames and threatened reunion. "For our own part, we do not find in that direction the way to the restoration of the peace of the republic."[38]

Republican newspapers tended to agree with the assessment of the new law as lacking teeth but differed over whether this was a good or a bad thing. The *New York Times* cheered passage of the act because it defined the penalty of treason, adding that, judged by the tendencies of other nations, the U.S. version was exceedingly lenient. "It gives the Rebels to understand distinctly the penalties they incur *under the law*, as well as from the sword, by persisting in their rebellion. It gives a definite legal character to these penalties, and affords, for all now engaged in the rebellion, an opportunity to retrace their steps if they desire to do so."[39] Yet the more radical organs found the Senate's Confiscation Act either disappointing or a dead letter. A Cleveland newspaper accurately judged what had happened and who was responsible for watering down the law. In early July, a writer proclaimed, "Confiscation was practically killed yesterday by a union of a portion of the Republicans with the anti-Confiscation men in the Senate, on the milk and water, trial-by-jury bill." The writer correctly expected nothing to pass "so practical as the House confiscation bill which a portion of the Republicans, aided by Saulsbury, Powell, Carlile and others of the school, succeeded in defeating."[40]

Enforcement of the law fell to Attorney General Edward Bates, who typically discouraged prosecutions for treason. Even before the Second Confiscation Act had passed, he had warned district attorneys to be careful when it came to prosecuting people for this high crime against the state. He claimed he was not against doing so but wanted the government to proceed only if conviction were likely. He was looking primarily for the political statement that such proceedings could make and thus wanted quality not quantity in actions. In May of 1862, he told the U.S. district attorney in western Virginia not to prosecute treason unless he was "pretty sure of the proof; for it is better to forego the charge, than be beaten at the trial." But he also did not think trials were the only way to have an impact. Indictments alone could suit quite nicely, if applied strategically. He believed it best "for ulterior purposes" to indict only "distinguished" offenders for treason. If they were beyond reach of the law in Confederate-controlled territory, all the better: the point could be made without risking an unfriendly verdict from jurors or creating martyrs if the government did win a conviction.[41]

Bates applied a similar approach whenever seizing the property of traitors. Early in 1863 he was asked to explain himself to the Congress, when Radical legislators thought he moved too slowly against the property of Judge John A. Campbell, a former U.S. Supreme Court justice who had gone to the Confederacy and left belongings in Washington. His was being prodded to take those personal items, especially the furniture of the justice, through in rem proceedings. Bates explained that even though he could conduct a hearing without the accused being present, he still needed to follow the law and come up with sufficient evidence. "The law is highly penal," he wrote, adding, "and, therefore, in the judicial proceedings, the Courts will take care that the forms prescribed are minutely observed." He then lectured the Congress: "If newspapers were witnesses and public rumor proof, the confiscation of property of thousands of Rebels might be easily and quickly accomplished. But that is not so: The guilty facts must be precisely alleged, and they must be proven by testimony above all legal exception. And this must continue so, until it shall please Congress to alter the method of proceeding."[42] The position of the government in pursuing treason cases underscores that legal authorities understood it was a difficult situation requiring limited application, and not the way to conduct large-scale confiscation of property.

Despite the restrictive nature of confiscation, the bill did mark the last gasp of moderation concerning the treatment of Rebel property. Military seizures of property for its own use were far less contested by northerners and upheld consistently by the courts. Plus, other legislation allowed for clearer ways of taking property with fewer constitutional scruples involved. The Direct Tax Act of June 7, 1862, and the Captured and Abandoned Property Act of March 12, 1863, meant that tax agents followed the army into the South. They calculated land values based on 1861, dumped on a heavy penalty, and used public auctions or government purchase to acquire land when owners who were at war with the government invariably failed to pay the tax. In the end, about $5.1 million changed hands in this way, far more than under confiscation.[43]

In the years ahead, court cases upheld military confiscation and reflected a changing mood over whether Rebels were citizens or enemies. By 1864, the Supreme Court heard a case with the quaint sounding title of *Mrs. Alexander's Cotton*. Maj. Gen. Nathaniel P. Banks's men had seized seventy-two bales of cotton owned by Elizabeth Alexander during the Red River campaign. She filed a claim for reimbursement, which was denied. Her attorneys argued that she had taken an oath of loyalty and that Lincoln's Proclamation of Amnesty and Reconstruction (December 1863) had, in effect, pardoned her. Undoubtedly it did not help her case that she took this oath only several weeks after the military seized her crop. The court ruled against her, with Chief Justice Salmon P. Chase indicating that there were no friends but only foes in a region in rebellion against the United States. He wrote, "[A]ll the people of each State or district in insurrection against the United States, must be regarded as enemies, until by the action of the legislature and the executive, or otherwise, that relation is thoroughly and permanently changed."[44] In effect, by 1864 there was no such thing anymore as an involuntary Rebel—at least one recognized by courts. As long as a state was considered in insurrection, the residents were treated by the courts as enemies whose property was vulnerable to military hands, no matter the actual loyalty of individuals.

Adding treason back to the analysis of the Second Confiscation Act highlights a number of factors. For one, the findings add to the discussion of the president's role in overseeing the process of emancipation. Historians often have portrayed Lincoln as out of step with the radical nature of the Second Confiscation Act, indicating that the Congress was somehow ahead of him on the issue of emancipation.[45] That would be true if the Second Confiscation Act were only the product of Radicals. But it was not. Lincoln was closer in sentiment to the moderate Republicans on the way the Constitution limited certain actions, and he certainly was not opposed to their beliefs that the executive had the power to seize the chattel property of the enemy on the basis of military necessity. And it is clear that without Lincoln's subsequent stand on emancipation the Second Confiscation Act would have been a very stubborn mule to ride in order to achieve freedom for slaves.

Additionally, it was very clear to the friends of abolition that customary legal channels provided uncertain means for punishing the Rebels. It was the executive department, and not the judicial or legislative branches, that offered the best chance to implement freedom for the slaves of the enemy and to ferret out treason before it could rear its head. During the summer of 1862 moderate forces had created a confiscation law that had very little real meat to it concerning treason; however, they reasoned their way out of the constitutional box by allowing, in the latter portions of the act, for the president to free slaves based on military necessity. Eventually, the influence of conciliatory men waned in the face of elections, court appointments, and the changing mood of northerners, who became less inclined to believe in the existence of involuntary Rebels. But in the critical moments of 1862, as the war shifted toward the dual goals of reunion and freedom for slaves, the legislative impulse was still torn between the paths of radicalism and conciliation. Lincoln's later proclamation was, in fact, necessary to set aside ambiguities on what became the government's posture for emancipating slaves without requiring courts to work out individual cases.[46]

Ironically, then, punishment of Rebels during the war was best used outside of the court system. Through arrests and military seizures of property, including slaves, and the holding of suspected traitors without due process the executive branch enforced a looser, more flexible meaning of treason that was more in line with how northern citizens thought about what the Confederate leaders had done. In effect, the practical work of confiscation left the military as the chief arbiter. Because of the peculiarities of our constitutional history, the legal domain was often an obstacle against punishing the Rebels for treason, which was used by the more conciliatory forces in the country who had little intention of prosecuting the crime. And the Radicals? They had to turn their backs on this law in favor of a more expedient method for freeing slaves. In practice, if not in words or beliefs, the North implicitly recognized secession, or at least the Confederacy's existence as an independent nation containing belligerent enemies at war with the United States. Treason with a small "t" was in effect a reality throughout the conflict; but treason with a capital "T" faced strong hurdles against ever being implemented.

NOTES

1. Three recent works on confiscation have noticed how the Second Confiscation Act became watered down by moderate Republicans and Democrats: John Syrett, *The Civil War Confiscation Acts: Failing to Reconstruct the South* (New York: Fordham University Press, 2005), 1; Daniel W. Hamilton, "A New Right to Property: Civil War Confiscation in the Reconstruction Supreme Court," *Journal of Supreme Court History* 29:3 (2004): 254–55 and

The Limits of Sovereignty: Property Confiscation in the Union and the Confederacy during the Civil War (Chicago: University of Chicago Press, 2007); and Silvana R. Siddali, *From Property to Person: Slavery and the Confiscation Acts, 1861–1862* (Baton Rouge: Louisiana State University Press, 2005). For more traditional approaches that consider the measure as part of a hard war or Radical impulses, see David Herbert Donald et al., *The Civil War and Reconstruction* (New York: W. W. Norton, 2001), 281–82; Mark Grimsley, *The Hard Hand of War: Union Policy toward Southern Civilians, 1861–1865* (New York: Cambridge University Press, 1995), 68–70; David Herbert Donald, *Lincoln* (New York: Simon and Schuster, 1995), 364–65; Ira Berlin et al., *Slaves No More: Three Essays on Emancipation and the Civil War* (New York: Cambridge University Press, 1992), 40–41; Eric Foner, *Reconstruction: America's Unfinished Revolution, 1863–1877* (New York: Harper and Row, 1988), 51; and Allan Nevins, *The War for Union: War Becomes Revolution, 1862–1863* (New York: Scribner's, 1960), 145–46.

2. Besides the work of Syrett, Siddali, and Hamilton noted above, a few historians have noticed the split among Republicans and the problems of treason in limiting the effectiveness of the bill. Most welcome is the precise treatment of confiscation by Allan G. Bogue in *The Earnest Men: Republicans of the Civil War Senate* (Ithaca, N.Y.: Cornell University Press, 1981), 226–35. His classification of moderate and Radical Republicans, which appears on p. 98, describes the alignments seen in this study. James M. McPherson has commented on the flaws in the bill, revealing its passages as contradictory and with other problems attorneys could highlight to scuttle the legislation. See his *Battle Cry of Freedom: The Civil War Era* (New York: Oxford University Press, 1988), 500.

3. *Congressional Globe*, 37th Cong., 2nd sess., 1957.

4. For an overview of treason law, see James Willard Hurst, *The Law of Treason in the United States: Collected Essays* (Westport, Conn.: Greenwood Press, 1945).

5. R. Kent Newmyer, *John Marshall and the Heroic Age of the Supreme Court* (Baton Rouge: Louisiana State University Press, 2001), 180; Jean Edward Smith, *John Marshall: Definer of a Nation* (New York: Henry Holt, 1996), 352; Paul Finkelman, "The Treason Trial of Castner Hanway," in *American Political Trials*, ed. Michael R. Belknap (Westport, Conn.: Greenwood Press, 1994), 84–85.

6. After the war, as northerners tried to figure out what to do with the Rebels, Robert Dale Owen looked for restoration of political rights only for Rebels who purged themselves of treason "actual or implied." See his letter of June 21, 1865, in *The Liberator*, July 7, 1865. For Lincoln's views, see his letter to Erastus Corning and Others, June 12, 1863, in Abraham Lincoln, *The Collected Works of Abraham Lincoln*, ed. Roy P. Basler, 9 vols. (New Brunswick, N.J.: Rutgers University Press, 1953–55), 6:260–69.

7. Siddali, *From Property to Person*, 78–79; 12, *Statutes at Large*, 12:319.

8. Siddali, *From Property to Person*, 84–94; Syrett, *Civil War Confiscation Acts*, 10–19.

9. See, for example, the case of Edward B. Wilder in U.S. War Department, *The War of the Rebellion: A Compilation of the Official Records of the Union and Confederate Armies*, 127 vols., index, and atlas (Washington: Government Printing Office, 1880–1901), ser. 2, 2:693–703.

10. For the portion of Lincoln's message on confiscation, see *Collected Works*, 5:48–49; James C. Conkling to Lyman Trumbull, December 16, 1861, Lyman Trumbull Papers, Library of Congress, Washington (repository hereafter cited as LC).

11. See, for example, A. G. Stevens to Lyman Trumbull, December 9, 1861, Lyman Trumbull Papers, LC, and *New York Times*, May 21, 1862.

12. For the financial context, see Siddali, *From Property to Person*, 197–201.

13. Bray Hammond, "The North's Empty Purse, 1861–1862," *American Historical Review* 67 (October 1961): 1–18; Francis Lieber to Charles Sumner, February 18, 1862, box 42, Francis Lieber Papers, Henry E. Huntington Library, San Marino, California.

14. J. Medill to Lyman Trumbull, June 6, 1862, Lyman Trumbull Papers, LC.

15. *Congressional Globe*, 37th Cong., 2nd sess., 942–43.

16. Ibid., 942.

17. McPherson, *Battle Cry of Freedom*, 500.

18. For a discussion of the limitations of definition, see "The Rightful Power of Congress to Confiscate and Emancipate," *The Monthly Law Reporter* (June 1862): 469.

19. *Congressional Globe*, 37th Cong., 2nd sess., 943.

20. Senate Bill 151, *Senate Bills and Resolutions*, 37th Cong., 2nd sess., Library of Congress, A Century of Lawmaking for a New Nation, ⟨http://memory.loc.gov/cgi-bin/ampage?collId=llsb&fileName=037/llsb037.db&recNum=502⟩ (accessed on January 7, 2007).

21. *Congressional Globe*, 37th Cong., 2nd sess., 1137–41.

22. Ibid.

23. Ibid., 1959.

24. Ibid., 1962.

25. Ibid., 2172, 2170 [Howard].

26. Ibid., 2166.

27. Ibid., 2167–68.

28. Ibid., 2920.

29. House Bill 471, May 27, 1862, *House Bills and Resolutions*, 37th Cong., 2nd sess., ⟨http://memory.loc.gov/cgi-bin/ampage?collId=llhb&fileName=037/llhb037.db&recNum=2535⟩ (accessed on January 7, 2007).

30. *Congressional Globe*, 37th Cong., 2nd sess., 2970–71, 2972 [quotation].

31. Ibid., 2995–96, 3006.

32. James G. Randall, *Constitutional Problems Under Lincoln* (New York: D. Appleton), 279 n. 10; Siddali, *From Property to Person*, 165.

33. Thomas Ewing to Abraham Lincoln, June 2, 1862, Abraham Lincoln Papers, LC; Orville Hickman Browning, *The Diary of Orville Hickman Browning*, ed. Theodore Calvin Pease and James G. Randall, 2 vols. (Springfield: Illinois State Historical Library, 1925), 1:558.

34. Abraham Lincoln to Congress, [July 17, 1862], Draft of Veto Message, Abraham Lincoln Papers, LC.

35. *Congressional Globe*, 37th Cong., 2nd sess., 3374–75.

36. Syrett, *Civil War Confiscation Acts*, 58.

37. *New York Herald*, July 28, 1862.

38. *Boston Daily Advertiser*, May 17, 1862.

39. *New York Times*, July 15, 1862.

40. *Daily Cleveland Herald*, July 1, 1862.

41. Edward Bates to Benj. H. Smith, May 7, 1862, Letterbook B, no. 5, vol. 8, entry 10, Records of the Attorney General, RG 60, National Archives, Washington.

42. Edward Bates to Galusha Grow, January 14, 1863, in ibid.

43. Syrett, *Civil War Confiscation Acts*, 107. See also James G. Randall, "Captured and Abandoned Property during the Civil War," *American Historical Review* 19 (October 1913): 66.

44. U.S. Government, *United States Reports: Cases Adjudged in the Supreme Court* (Washington: Government Printing Office, 1865), 69:419.

45. See, for example, Allan Nevins, *The War for the Union: War Becomes Revolution, 1862–1863* (New York: Scribner's, 1960), 146.

46. For this last point, see Siddali, *From Property to Person*, 141.

My Enemies Are Crushed

McClellan and Lincoln

⇥ JAMES M. MCPHERSON ⇤

On September 7, 1862, Maj. Gen. George B. McClellan wrote to his wife exultantly that "my enemies are crushed, silent, and disarmed." What on earth did he mean? Had he won a great battle against the Army of Northern Virginia that has somehow escaped the attention of historians? This was far from the only time that McClellan referred to titanic struggles with his enemies. "I am in a *battle* & must fight it out," he wrote on another occasion. My "bitter enemies . . . are making their last grand attack. I *must & will* defeat them."[1] Abraham Lincoln would have been startled by such bellicose language from McClellan, whom he had compared to "an auger too dull to take hold." McClellan, said the president, was a commander who "would not fight."[2]

Lincoln was right. McClellan's "bitter enemies" whom he had "crushed" in September 1862 were not the Rebels but instead other generals in the Union army and high officials in the U.S. government—Generals John Pope and Irvin McDowell, who had been relieved of command and whose troops had been absorbed into McClellan's Army of the Potomac, and Secretary of War Edwin M. Stanton, who had wanted to cashier McClellan. If McClellan had exerted as much energy and determination in his battles against the enemy army as he did against these supposed enemies in his own army and government, the North might have won the war in 1862.

The strongest language McClellan used against Confederates was "those rascals," while he described his adversaries in the Union Congress, administration, and army as "heartless villains . . . wretches . . . incompetent knaves a most despicable set of men."[3] When Winfield Scott was still general in chief and McClellan's commanding officer in 1861, the thirty-four-year-old McClellan described him as "a dotard" and "a perfect imbecile." He privately ridiculed Lincoln in the fall of 1861 as "nothing more than a well meaning baboon . . . 'the *original gorilla.*'"[4] As for members of Lincoln's cabinet, Secretary of State William H. Seward was "a meddlesome, officious, incompetent little puppy" and Secretary of the Navy Gideon Welles was "weaker than a garrulous old woman."[5] McClellan reserved his greatest animosity for Stanton, who had been the general's confidant and supporter before he became secretary of war in January 1862 and lost faith in McClellan's competence and determination. McClellan made Stanton the scapegoat for the failure of his Peninsula campaign in 1862. The secretary of war, he wrote his wife, was "the most depraved hypocrite & villain" he had ever known. If he "had lived in the time of the Saviour, Judas Iscariot would have remained a respected member of the fraternity of Apostles."[6]

McClellan certainly had powerful paranoid tendencies, but he did not make up this vision of "bitter enemies" out of whole cloth. His sharpest critics were Radical Republicans in Congress and the cabinet — especially the congressional Joint Committee on the Conduct of the War and Secretary of the Treasury Salmon P. Chase as well as Stanton. All of them had once been McClellan backers but had become profoundly disillusioned. After the Army of the Potomac was driven back from Richmond in the Seven Days battles, Senator Zachariah Chandler of Michigan, a leading member of the Committee on the Conduct of the War, wrote privately that "McClellan is an imbecile if not a traitor. He has virtually lost the army of the Potomac" and "deserves to be shot."[7] After McClellan resisted orders to reinforce General Pope with the 6th and 2nd Corps at the second battle of Bull Run on August 29–30, 1862, Stanton wanted McClellan court-martialed and Chase said he should be shot.[8]

How had matters come to such a pass by August 1862? To answer this question, we must go back to the last week of July 1861. Lincoln had called McClellan to Washington after the Union defeat at First Bull Run to become commander of the newly named Army of the Potomac. Fresh from commanding a small Union force whose victories in western Virginia helped put that Unionist region on the path to becoming the new state of West Virginia, McClellan received a hero's welcome in the capital. The press lionized him as a "young Napoleon"; the correspondent for the *Times* (London) described him as "the man on horseback" to save the country; the president of the United States Sanitary Commission said that "there is an indefinable *air of success* about him and something of the 'man of destiny.'"[9]

This adulation surprised McClellan and then went to his head. The day after arriving in Washington, he wrote, "I find myself in a new & strange position here — Presdt, Cabinet, Genl Scott & all deferring to me — by some

strange operation of magic I seem to have become *the* power of the land."
Three days later he went to Capitol Hill and was "quite overwhelmed by
the congratulations I received & the respect with which I was treated."

Congress seemed willing to "give me my way in every thing." McClellan developed what can only be called a messiah complex during these
first weeks in Washington. "God has placed a great work in my hands," he
wrote. "I was called to it; my previous life seems to have been unwittingly
directed to this great end."[10]

But God seemed to place obstacles in McClellan's path. The first of
them was General in Chief Winfield Scott. A hero of the War of 1812 and
conqueror of Mexico in 1847, Scott was America's greatest soldier since
George Washington. Old and infirm by 1861, however, he could work only
a few hours each day while the young Napoleon put in sixteen hours organizing and training his new army. Tension and then conflict between the
old and new military titans soon erupted. McClellan attended a cabinet
meeting on his second day in Washington, to which Scott was not invited.
McClellan bypassed Scott frequently and communicated directly with
Lincoln and other cabinet members—including Seward, even as the general was privately condemning the secretary of state as an incompetent
and meddlesome puppy.

The action that most angered Scott was a memorandum from McClellan on August 8, 1861, sent to both Lincoln and Scott, that highlighted
what turned out to be McClellan's main defect as a military commander—
an alarmist tendency to inflate enemy strength and intentions. The Confederate army in his front only twenty miles from Washington, McClellan insisted, had 100,000 men (their real numbers were about 40,000) and
reinforcements were passing through Knoxville to join them. Washington
was in danger of attack by this huge force, McClellan told Scott (and Lincoln). "Our present army in this vicinity is entirely insufficient for the
emergency," McClellan warned, so he advised Scott to order forward all
troops scattered in other places within reach of Washington to meet this
"imminent danger."[11]

Scott regarded this communication as an insult to his own authority
and his management of the army. He also scoffed at McClellan's estimate of enemy numbers and his fears of an imminent attack. He called
McClellan to his headquarters and apparently dressed him down. At the
same time, Scott asked Secretary of War Simon Cameron to place him on
the retired list—in effect submitting his resignation as general in chief.[12]
Lincoln was upset by this contretemps between his two top commanders.

He stepped into the quarrel between McClellan and the first of his many "enemies"—a task that the beleaguered president would have to repeat many times in the next fifteen months. He persuaded Scott to stay on and persuaded McClellan to withdraw his offending letter. In what passed for an apology, McClellan promised to "abstain from any word or act that could give offense to General Scott or embarrass the President." He also offered his "most profound assurances of respect for General Scott and yourself."[13]

At this very time, however, McClellan was writing privately that the Confederate army in his front now numbered 150,000 men. "I am here in a terrible place," he fumed. "The enemy have 3 to 4 times my force. . . . Genl Scott is the most dangerous antagonist I have . . . a perfect imbecile. . . . He will not comprehend the danger & is either a traitor or an incompetent. . . . The President is an idiot, the old General in his dotage—they cannot or will not see the true state of affairs."[14]

Although Lincoln had managed to defuse a blowup between his two top generals, tensions continued to simmer for the next two months. McClellan persisted in leaving Scott out of the loop of his communications with the president and cabinet. During these months several Republican leaders in Congress, as well as broad segments of the northern press, grew restless as McClellan continued to train his expanding army and to hold impressive reviews but did nothing to advance against the main Confederate army or to prevent the enemy from establishing batteries on the Potomac below Washington to blockade the river. McClellan declined to cooperate with the navy in an expedition to capture these batteries and end what had become a national humiliation by October 1861. When Assistant Secretary of the Navy Gustavus V. Fox informed Lincoln of McClellan's failure to provide troops for this purpose, the president, according to Fox, "manifested more feeling and disappointment than I have seen him before exhibit."[15]

At about the same time, Senator Benjamin F. Wade, soon to become chairman of the Joint Committee on the Conduct of the War, wrote to his colleague Zachariah Chandler of Michigan: "The present state of things must not be suffered to continue. . . . We have vast armies in the field maintained at prodigious and almost ruinous expense. Yet they are suffered to do nothing with the power in our hands to crush the rebellion. . . . We are in danger of having our army set into winter quarters with the capitol in a state of siege for another year."[16] McClellan met with the senators and managed to convince them that he wanted to advance but Scott held him back. They went to Lincoln and pressed him to force Scott out. The president had Scott's earlier request for retirement on his desk; Scott renewed the request, citing continued deterioration of his health.[17]

McClellan was pulling every string he could to get himself appointed as Scott's successor. But the old general wanted that job to go to Henry W. Halleck, author and translator of books on military strategy and history, who like McClellan had resigned from the army in the 1850s to pursue a more rewarding civilian career. Halleck returned to the army in August 1861 with a commission as major general. Scott hoped he could get to Washington from California in time for Lincoln to appoint him rather than McClellan as Scott's successor. But it was not to be. On October 18, Lincoln persuaded the cabinet to accept Scott's request to retire. McClellan learned of this decision from one of his sources in the cabinet — probably Montgomery Blair, but perhaps Chase, a McClellan ally at this time. McClellan wrote to his wife on October 19: "It seems to be pretty well settled that I will be Comdr in Chf within a week. Genl Scott proposes to retire in favor of Halleck. The presdt and Cabinet have determined to accept his retirement, but not in favor of Halleck," who was at sea and would not arrive for another two or three weeks.[18]

On November 1, McClellan achieved his goal: Scott retired and McClellan became the youngest general in chief of United States armies in history — as well as field commander of the Army of the Potomac. Lincoln expressed some concern that "this vast increase in responsibilities . . . will entail a vast labor upon you." "I can do it all," McClellan replied.[19]

Having convinced Radical Republican senators — and perhaps Lincoln also — that it was only Scott's timidity that had kept him on a leash, McClellan now faced expectations that he would advance. But in conversations with the president he immediately began backtracking. In his mind the Confederate forces in northern Virginia now numbered 170,000 (three times their actual size). He reminded Lincoln of what had happened at Bull Run in July when the Union army fought a battle before it was trained and disciplined. The disastrous outcome of a reconnaissance in force toward Leesburg on October 21, when several Union regiments were ambushed at Balls Bluff and Lincoln's friend Colonel Edward Baker was killed, lent legitimacy to McClellan's counsel of caution. "Don't let them hurry me," McClellan urged Lincoln. "You shall have your own way in the matter," the president assured him. But he also warned McClellan that the pressure for the army to do *something* instead of dress parades and reviews was "a reality and should be taken into account. At the same time General you must not fight till you are ready."[20]

McClellan proved to have a tin ear about that ever-present "reality," which the president could not ignore. But the general heard loud and clear Lincoln's counsel not to fight until he was ready. The problem was that he was perpetually *almost* but never *quite* ready to move. The enemy always outnumbered him, and his own army was always lacking something. In response to Lincoln's request, the new general in chief prepared a memorandum stating that "winter is approaching so rapidly" that unless the Army of the Potomac could be increased from its current strength of 134,000 men to 208,000, the only alternative to taking the field "with forces greatly inferior" to the enemy was "to go into winter quarters."[21] Since Lincoln was well aware that the army could not be increased by that much before the end of the year, if ever, his shoulders must have slumped when he read these words. They slumped more as week after week of unusually mild and dry weather slipped by in November and December with no advance in Virginia and no military success anywhere except the capture of Port Royal Bay and the adjacent Sea Islands by the navy.

Lincoln began dropping by McClellan's headquarters or his home near the White House almost daily to consult with him. McClellan grew to resent these visits as a waste of time or an unwanted form of pressure. More than once he hid himself away "to dodge all enemies in shape of 'browsing' presdt etc."[22] On November 13, Lincoln and Seward, along with the president's secretary, John Hay, called unannounced on McClellan at home but learned that he was at a wedding. When the general returned an hour later, the porter told him that Lincoln was waiting to see him. McClellan said nothing and went upstairs to bed. The president and secretary of state waited another half hour before a servant deigned to tell them that the general was asleep. Hay was furious at "this unparalleled insolence of epaulettes." But as they walked back to the White House, Lincoln told him that it was "better at this time not to be making points of etiquette and personal dignity." Significantly, however, from then on Lincoln almost always summoned McClellan to his office when he wanted to talk with the general. After one such occasion four days later, McClellan wrote to his wife that at the White House "I found 'the *original gorilla*,' about as intelligent as ever. What a specimen to be at the head of our affairs!"[23]

About December 1, despairing of any initiative by McClellan, Lincoln drafted a proposal for part of the army to make a feint toward Centreville to hold the enemy in place while two other columns moved south along the Potomac—one by road and the other by water—to turn the Confederate flank and move up the Occoquan Valley to Brentsville southwest of Manassas. On paper, at least, this plan reflected what Lincoln had learned from his recent reading of works on military history and strategy—including one of Halleck's books. Lincoln's plan would avoid a frontal attack on Confederate defenses at Centreville and Manassas, which McClellan claimed were impregnable. The general rejected the plan, however, because he said the enemy's greatly superior numbers would enable him to detach mobile reserves to counterattack and defeat the flanking force.[24]

Meanwhile, the confrontation with Britain over the seizure of James Mason and John Slidell from the British ship *Trent* caused a diplomatic crisis and dried up the sale of bonds to finance the war. Just before Christmas, McClellan fell sick with typhoid fever. Northern morale and Lincoln's own mood plunged to a low point in the first days of the New Year. On January 10 the president dropped in at the office of Quartermaster General Montgomery C. Meigs. "General, what shall I do?" asked Lincoln. "The people are impatient; Chase has no money . . . the General of the Army has typhoid fever. The bottom is out of the tub. What shall I do?" Meigs advised him to assert his prerogative as commander in chief and set in motion a campaign without regard to McClellan, who might not be able to resume duty for weeks.[25]

This counsel echoed similar advice from Attorney General Edward Bates. Except for Lincoln's insistence the previous June that Scott order the army forward toward Manassas—against Scott's judgment—Lincoln had deferred to Scott and then to McClellan on military strategy. The unhappy outcome of the Manassas campaign had sobered the president. With no military training or experience, Lincoln recognized the need to rely on professionals. But the professionals had disappointed him—and now the chief disappointment was ill. Having begun a cram course of reading in military strategy, Lincoln was open to Bates's urging that, "being 'Commander in chief' by law, he *must* command" rather than continue "this injurious deference to his subordinates."[26]

So Lincoln walked out of Meigs's office on January 10 and summoned to his own office two of the Army of the Potomac's division commanders, Brig. Gens. Irvin McDowell and William B. Franklin. The army's senior division commander, McDowell was also the choice of the Committee on the Conduct of the War to replace McClellan. Franklin was one of McClellan's personal friends and protégés. These two seemed an unpromising combination to carry out Lincoln's insistence on action. Nevertheless, the president figuratively knocked their heads together at the meeting on January 10. According to McDowell's notes, Lincoln said that "if General McClellan did not want to use the army, he would like to *borrow* it."[27]

Lincoln ordered the two generals to come up with a plan and to meet the next day with him and Meigs (who would be responsible for logistics) plus several cabinet members.

They came up with two plans. McDowell formulated a short-range flanking movement via the Occoquan River similar to Lincoln's earlier proposal. Franklin sketched out a deep flanking movement all the way down the Chesapeake Bay to Fort Monroe to operate against Richmond via the Peninsula between the York and James Rivers. McClellan had been mulling a similar operation for some time, and Franklin was privy to it— while McDowell and the president obviously were not. Most of those at the January 11 meeting favored McDowell's plan. McClellan got wind of this meeting, probably from Chase, and rose from his sickbed to meet with the same group on the 13th. He refused to reveal his plan to them, stating that he feared a leak. But when he assured Lincoln that he actually *had* a plan and a timetable to carry it out, the president once again deferred to him and adjourned the meeting.[28]

Five days later, Lincoln's confidant, Senator Orville H. Browning of Illinois, wrote in his diary that the president had "expressed great confidence" in McClellan. But when two more weeks went by and matters continued "All Quiet Along the Potomac," as a popular song had it, Lincoln's confidence waned. On January 31 he issued Special Order No. 1 specifying that the Army of the Potomac must move against the enemy at Centreville and Manassas by February 22.[29] As intended, this order forced McClellan for the first time to reveal his plans in detail. Instead of moving via the Occoquan against Manassas, he proposed to take the army 100 miles farther by water down the Potomac and the Chesapeake Bay and up the Rappahannock River to Urbana, Virginia. From there he would have a secure supply base to launch a fifty-mile campaign to Richmond. This move would force the Confederates to evacuate Manassas and retreat south to defend Richmond, which McClellan predicted he might reach before the enemy could get there.[30]

Lincoln was concerned that the Rebels instead might attack Washington before McClellan got anywhere near Richmond. The president posed a set of hard questions to McClellan asking him why his distant-flanking strategy was better than Lincoln's short-flanking plan. Two sound premises underlay Lincoln's questions: first, the enemy army, not Richmond, should be the objective; and second, Lincoln's plan would enable the Army of the Potomac to operate close to its own base (Washington) while McClellan's plan, even if successful, would draw the enemy back to its base

(Richmond) and greatly lengthen Union supply lines.[31] Although McClellan's responses to these questions did not entirely satisfy Lincoln, he again deferred to the general's supposedly superior professional qualifications and reluctantly approved McClellan's plan.

Assembling the shipping and other logistical resources for McClellan's campaign would take several weeks. This was one of the reasons Lincoln had questioned it. "Does not your plan involve a greatly larger expenditure of *time*, and *money* than mine?" he had challenged McClellan. Largely ignoring this question, McClellan set to work with a will to organize the campaign. Meanwhile, other Union forces won a string of victories in Tennessee, North Carolina, Florida, and Arkansas that made the Army of the Potomac's continuing inactivity seemingly more humiliating by comparison.

Ugly rumors began to circulate in Republican circles that McClellan, a Democrat, did not really want to crush the rebellion. McClellan had made little secret of his dislike of abolitionists and Radical Republicans. His closest political associates — including his favorite division commanders in the Army of the Potomac, Fitz John Porter and William B. Franklin — were Democrats who wanted to restore the Union on the basis of something like the Crittenden Compromise that would preserve slavery and the political power of southern Democrats. Some of the generals serving in the Confederate army confronting him "were once my most intimate friends," he acknowledged (privately) in November 1861. McClellan did not want to fight the kind of war the Radicals were beginning to demand — a war to destroy slavery and the planter class and to give the restored Union a new birth of freedom. McClellan wrote in November 1861 to an influential Democratic friend: "Help me dodge the nigger. . . . *I* am fighting to preserve the integrity of the Union. . . . To gain that end we cannot afford to raise up the negro question."[32]

Radical Republican senators Benjamin Wade and Zachariah Chandler had played a significant role in boosting McClellan to the position of general in chief the previous November. Four months had passed, and, in their view, McClellan had betrayed them by doing nothing. They were suspicious of his politics and perhaps half believed rumors of his disloyalty, but the main reason for their conversion from supporters of McClellan to his most vocal critics was the general's military inactivity. On March 3, Lincoln met with members of the Committee on the Conduct of the War. They gave the president an earful of complaints about McClellan. Committee chairman Ben Wade urged Lincoln to remove him from command. If he did so, Lincoln asked, who should replace him? "Why, anybody!" Wade reportedly responded. "Wade," Lincoln supposedly said, "*anybody* will do for you, but not for me. I must have somebody."[33]

Despite Lincoln's deflection of Wade, the president was in fact considering the removal of McClellan. Four weeks had gone by since Lincoln had lukewarmly approved the general's Urbana plan. The army was still in winter quarters. The day after his meeting with the committee, Lincoln told a Pennsylvania congressman that unless McClellan moved soon he would be replaced.[34] Three days later Lincoln summoned McClellan to the White House and told him with unprecedented bluntness that his tenure was short unless he got moving. The president also hinted — perhaps stated openly — that some influential men believed that the real purpose of his Urbana plan was to leave Washington uncovered so the Rebels could capture it. McClellan was outraged, but Lincoln assured the general that he did not believe a word of the rumors. With his tin ear for the political realities of both his and the president's positions, McClellan said that he would resolve any doubts about his Urbana plan by submitting it to a vote of his eleven division commanders and the army's chief engineer officer. They voted eight to four in favor of the plan — not surprising, perhaps, since most of those eight owed their positions to McClellan's sponsorship. Three of the four division commanders with the greatest seniority voted against the plan.[35] Next day Lincoln issued an order organizing the Army of the Potomac into four corps and appointed the four senior generals — including the three who voted against the plan — as the corps commanders. If McClellan failed to get the message, Lincoln added more clarity three days later by relieving McClellan from duty as general in chief because, as commander of an army about to take the field, he could no longer "do it all." For the time being, Lincoln and Secretary of War Stanton would do the job of general in chief.[36]

On the very day that a majority of generals had voted for the Urbana plan, Confederate general Joseph E. Johnston threw a monkey wrench into the operation by withdrawing from the Centreville-Manassas line to Culpeper south of the Rappahannock River, where he was in a position to block McClellan's intention to move toward Richmond. The Union commander immediately led the Army of the Potomac on what he called a "practice march" to the abandoned Confederate works. Northern journalists who accompanied the army discovered that the Confederate defenses were by no means as formidable as McClellan had claimed and the camps had room for only about half as many men as McClellan had estimated.

And several of the heavy artillery redoubts mounted logs painted black rather than large-caliber cannons. These "Quaker guns" caused McClellan much embarrassment. Already doubtful of his estimates of enemy numbers and strength, Lincoln and Stanton never again gave credibility to the general's perpetual complaints of inferior numbers. Johnston's retreat compelled McClellan to shift his proposed flanking movement all the way to Fort Monroe at the tip of the Virginia Peninsula. This time all four corps commanders voted for the plan, and Lincoln reluctantly approved — provided McClellan left behind sufficient force to protect Washington. The general promised to do so but failed to consult with Lincoln about what constituted a sufficient force. After he departed for the Peninsula, McClellan sent back a memorandum summarizing the units he had left to defend the capital. Lincoln and Stanton soon discovered that the number of these troops was considerably less than McClellan had stated, so the president held back McDowell's corps. Thus began a prolonged and increasingly bitter controversy in which McClellan blamed the government for failing to support his campaign against an enemy whose numbers he consistently inflated by a factor of two or three.

The details of the Peninsula campaign are beyond the scope of this essay. But a little of the flavor of controversy is suggested by Lincoln's letter of April 9 to McClellan. At a time when 70,000 Union troops had already arrived and deployed before Confederate defenses behind the Warwick River south of Yorktown held by only 17,000 enemy soldiers, McClellan decided that the enemy's position was too strong to attack and began preparing a siege with heavy artillery. An exasperated Lincoln wrote to him:

> [Y]ou will do me the justice to remember I always insisted, that going down the Bay in search of a field, instead of fighting at or near Manassas, was only shifting, and not surmounting, a difficulty — that we would find the same enemy, and the same, or equal, intrenchments at either place. The country will not fail to note — is now noting — that the present hesitation to move upon an intrenched enemy, is but the story of Manassas repeated. . . . It is indispensable to *you* that you strike a blow. . . . I have never written you, or spoken to you, in greater kindness of feeling than now, nor with a fuller purpose to sustain you. . . . *But you must act.*[37]

McClellan seemed constitutionally unable to act, only to *react*. His response to Lincoln's urging of an attack was to write his wife: "I was much tempted to reply that he had better come & do it himself."[38] McClellan yielded the initiative to the enemy, especially after Robert E. Lee became commander of the Army of Northern Virginia on June 1. McClellan's list of "enemies" in his own government and in the northern press grew longer as he blamed others but never himself for the failure of the Peninsula campaign. In the middle of the Seven Days battles, on June 28, he sent a telegram to Stanton that concluded with these words: "I have lost this battle because my force was too small. . . . [The] Government has not sustained this army. . . . If I save this army now, I tell you plainly that I owe no thanks to you or to any other persons in Washington. You have done your best to sacrifice this army."[39] Shocked by the two concluding sentences, the head of the War Department telegraph office recopied the dispatch without them before sending it on to Stanton, so he and Lincoln never saw these sentences. Nevertheless, they were well aware that Stanton had become McClellan's chief whipping boy and that some of that hostility spilled over to the president himself. After Lincoln had given his consent to the Peninsula plan in March, McClellan had written to a prominent Democrat: "The President is all right—he is my strongest friend." But now, three months later, he wrote to his wife that "Honest A[be] has again fallen into the hands of my enemies."[40]

After McClellan retreated to the James River in the Seven Days battles, Lincoln called Henry W. Halleck from the West to become general in chief. McClellan added Halleck to his list of enemies when he advised Lincoln to withdraw the Army of the Potomac from the Peninsula to reinforce Maj. Gen. John Pope's newly created Army of Virginia southwest of Washington. Pope also joined the list. McClellan predicted that Pope would be "badly thrashed" by Lee, "Very badly whipped he will be & ought to be—such a villain as he is ought to bring defeat upon any cause that employs him."[41]

These startling sentiments help explain why McClellan resisted repeated orders from Halleck to rush the 6th and 2nd Corps of the Army of the Potomac to Pope's aid during the second battle of Bull Run. Lincoln was shocked by McClellan's actions. He "wanted Pope defeated," the president told his private secretary.[42] But through thick and thin, soldiers in the Army of the Potomac remained fiercely loyal to McClellan. Even those in the Army of Virginia preferred him to Pope. When Maj. Gen. Ambrose E. Burnside turned down Lincoln's offer of command of the Army of the Potomac, Lincoln felt he had no choice but to retain McClellan in command of that army and to merge the Army of Virginia into it.

The president was painfully aware that both armies were "utterly demoralized." McClellan was the only man who could "reorganize the army and bring it out of chaos," Lincoln said. He "has the army with him . . . [and] we must use the tools we have. There is no man . . . who can . . . lick these troops of ours into shape half as well as he. . . . If he can't fight himself, he excels in making others ready to fight."[43]

Events of the next two months confirmed Lincoln's judgment. As the Army of Northern Virginia invaded Maryland, McClellan did reorganize the two armies into one and lick them into shape. He also prepared them to fight, which they did at South Mountain and Antietam on September 14 and 17, respectively. When McClellan telegraphed an exaggerated report of his victory at South Mountain, Lincoln wired back congratulations and added: "Destroy the rebel army, if possible."[44] But when the president learned that McClellan had held back his reserves at Antietam instead of exploiting potential breakthroughs because he feared a counterattack by an enemy whose numbers he inflated by a factor of three, and that he had not renewed the attack on September 18 but instead let the enemy escape across the river, Lincoln again evinced disappointment. The president visited the army during the first four days of October to pump some energy and aggressiveness into McClellan. When Lincoln returned to Washington, he had Halleck send an order to McClellan that any other general would have considered peremptory: "Cross the Potomac and give battle to the enemy. . . . Your army must move now while the roads are good." But McClellan stayed north of the Potomac for almost three more weeks. In a letter whose sentiments surely echoed Lincoln's, Halleck expressed enormous frustration: "I am sick, tired, and disgusted," he wrote. "There is an immobility here that exceeds all that any man can conceive of. It requires the lever of Archimedes to move this inert mass."[45]

Lincoln finally gave up on "tardy George." On November 7 he removed him from command and appointed a reluctant Ambrose Burnside to replace him. Lincoln explained his decision to John Hay: "I peremptorily ordered him to advance. . . . He kept delaying on little pretexts of wanting this and that. I began to fear he was playing false — that he did not want to hurt the enemy. I saw how he could intercept the enemy on the way to Richmond. I determined to make that the test. If he let them get away I would remove him. He did so & I relieved him."[46]

Seventeen months and three commanders of the Army of the Potomac later, Lt. Gen. Ulysses S. Grant, who had also learned that it seemed to require the lever of Archimedes to move that army, asked cavalry commander James H. Wilson: "What's wrong with this army?"[47] Wilson did not have any good answers. If Grant had asked Lincoln this question, the president might accurately have replied that McClellan had created the army in his own image, and even Grant would find it a hard job to overcome that legacy.[48]

NOTES

1. George B. McClellan to Mary Ellen Marcy McClellan, (hereinafter Ellen), September 7, 1862, February 26, 1863, McClellan Papers, Library of Congress, Washington (repository hereafter cited as LC). All citations of McClellan's letters and reports will be to the original sources. These documents are also published in a superbly edited collection, George B. McClellan, *The Civil War Papers of George B. McClellan*, ed. Stephen W. Sears (New York: Ticknor and Fields, 1989), and can be found there by the appropriate date.

2. Francis Preston Blair to Montgomery Blair, November 7, 1862, in William E. Smith, *The Francis Preston Blair Family in Politics*, 2 vols. (New York: Macmillan, 1933), 2:144; Orville Hickman Browning, *The Diary of Orville Hickman Browning*, ed. Theodore Calvin Pease and James G. Randall, 2 vols. (Springfield: Illinois State Historical Library, 1925), 1:563 (entry of July 25, 1862).

3. McClellan to Samuel L. M. Barlow, July 25, 1862, Barlow Papers, Huntington Library, San Marino, California [repository hereafter cited as HL]; McClellan to Ellen, July 31, 1862, October 11, 1861, McClellan Papers, LC.

4. McClellan to Ellen, August 8, October 11, November 17, 1861, McClellan Papers, LC.

5. McClellan to Ellen, October 11, 1861, McClellan Papers, LC.

6. McClellan to Ellen, July 13, 22, 1862, McClellan Papers, LC.

7. Chandler to his wife, July 11, 6, 1862, quoted in Bruce Tap, *Over Lincoln's Shoulder: The Committee on the Conduct of the War* (Lawrence: University Press of Kansas, 1998), 124, 122.

8. Gideon Welles, *Diary of Gideon Welles*, ed. Howard K. Beale, 3 vols. (New York: W. W. Norton, 1960), 1:93–102 (entries of August 31, September 1, 1862); Salmon P. Chase, *The Salmon P. Chase Papers*, ed. John Niven, 5 vols. (Kent, Ohio: Kent State University Press, 1993), 1:366–68 (diary entries of August 29, 30, 31, September 1, 1862).

9. William Howard Russell, *My Diary North and South*, ed. Fletcher Pratt (New York: Harper and Brothers, 1954), 240 (entry of July 27, 1861); Allan Nevins, *The War for the Union: The Improvised War, 1861–1862* (New York: Scribner's, 1959), 269.

10. McClellan to Ellen, July 27, 30, Aug. 9, Oct. 31, 1861, McClellan Papers, LC.

11. U.S. War Department, *The War of the Rebellion: A Compilation of the Official Records of the Union and Confederate Armies*, 127 vols., index, and atlas (Washington: Government Printing Office, 1880–1901), 11(3):3–4 (set hereafter cited as *OR*; all citations to ser. 1 unless otherwise noted).

12. McClellan to Ellen, August 8, 1861, McClellan Papers, LC; Scott to Cameron, August 9, 1861, in *OR* 11(3):4.

13. McClellan to Lincoln, August 10, 1861, Abraham Lincoln Papers (Robert Todd Lincoln Collection), LC.

14. McClellan to Ellen, August 8, 9, 14, 16, 19, 1861, McClellan Papers, LC.

15. U.S. Congress, Joint Committee on the Conduct of the War, *Report of the Joint Com-*

mittee on the Conduct of the War, 8 vols. (Washington: Government Printing Office, 1863–66), vol. 2, part 1 (*The Army of the Potomac*), 241 (set hereafter cited as *JCCW*).

16. Wade to Chandler, October 8, 1861, in Russel H. Beatie, *Army of the Potomac: McClellan Takes Command. September 1861–February 1862* (New York: Da Capo, 2004), 25–26.

17. McClellan to Ellen, October 26, 1861, McClellan Papers, LC; Scott to Simon Cameron, October 31, 1861, in *OR*, ser. 3, 1:538–39.

18. McClellan to Ellen, October 19, 1861, McClellan Papers, LC.

19. John Hay, *Inside Lincoln's White House: The Complete Civil War Diary of John Hay*, ed. Michael Burlingame and John R. Turner-Ettlinger (Carbondale: Southern Illinois University Press, 1997), 30 (entry dated "November 1861").

20. Ibid., 25, 29 (entries of October 10, 26, 1861).

21. McClellan to Simon Cameron, undated but probably October 31, 1861, in *OR* 5:9–11.

22. McClellan to Ellen, October 31, 1861, McClellan Papers, LC.

23. Hay, *Inside Lincoln's White House*, 32 (entry of November 13, 1861); McClellan to Ellen, November 17, 1861, McClellan Papers, LC.

24. "Memorandum to George B. McClellan on Potomac Campaign," circa. December 1, 1861, in Abraham Lincoln, *The Collected Works of Abraham Lincoln*, ed. Roy P. Basler, 9 vols. (New Brunswick, N.J.: Rutgers University Press, 1953–55), 5:34–35.

25. "General M. C. Meigs on the Conduct of the Civil War," *American Historical Review* 26 (January 1921): 292.

26. Edward Bates, *The Diary of Edward Bates, 1859–1866*, ed. Howard K. Beale (Washington: Government Printing Office, 1933), 218, 220 (entries of December 31, 1861, January 3, 1862).

27. Minutes of the meeting written by McDowell, in William Swinton, *Campaigns of the Army of the Potomac* (New York: Charles B. Richardson, 1866), 80.

28. Ibid., 79–85.

29. Browning, *Diary*, 1:525 (entry of January 18, 1862); Lincoln, *Collected Works*, 5:115.

30. McClellan to Edwin M. Stanton, February 3, 1862, in *OR* 5:42–45.

31. Lincoln to McClellan, February 3, 1862, Lincoln, *Collected Works*, 5:118–19.

32. McClellan to Samuel L. M. Barlow, November 8, 1861, Barlow Papers, HL.

33. Several versions of this anecdote exist; this one from Helen Nicolay, in *Lincoln's Secretary: A Biography of John G. Nicolay* (New York: Longmans, Green, 1949), 149, is evidently based on recollections by her father, who may have been present at the meeting. See also Tap, *Over Lincoln's Shoulder*, 113.

34. James H. Campbell to his wife, March 4, 1862, in Don E. Fehrenbacher and Virginia Fehrenbacher, eds., *Recollected Words of Abraham Lincoln* (Stanford, Calif.: Stanford University Press, 1996), 76.

35. Stephen W. Sears, *To the Gates of Richmond: The Peninsula Campaign* (New York: Ticknor and Fields, 1992), 3–9; *JCCW*, vol. 2, pt. 1:270, 360, 387.

36. Lincoln, *Collected Works*, 5:149–50, 155.

37. Ibid., 185.

38. McClellan to Ellen, April 8, 1862, McClellan Papers, LC.

39. *OR* 11(1):61.

40. McClellan to Samuel L. M. Barlow, March 16, 1862, Barlow Papers, HL; McClellan to Ellen, June 22, 1862, McClellan Papers, LC.

41. McClellan to Ellen, August 10, 1862, McClellan Papers, LC.

42. Hay, *Inside Lincoln's White House*, 37 (entry of September 1, 1862).

43. Welles, *Diary*, 1:113 (entry of September 7, 1962); Hay, *Inside Lincoln's White House*, 38–39 (entry of September 5, 1862).

44. Lincoln to McClellan, September 15, 1862, Lincoln, *Collected Works*, 5:426.

45. Halleck to McClellan, October 6, 1862, *OR* 19(1):72; Halleck to Hamilton R. Gamble, October 30, 1862, *OR*, ser. 3, 2:703–4.

46. Hay, *Inside Lincoln's White House*, 232 (entry of September 25, 1864).

47. James H. Wilson, *Under the Old Flag*, 2 vols. (New York: D. Appleton and Co.), 1:400.

48. For a recent exploration of McClellan's military leadership that emphasizes the importance of the general's political beliefs, see Ethan S. Rafuse, *McClellan's War: The Failure of Moderation in the Struggle for the Union* (Bloomington: Indiana University Press, 2005).

Profile in Leadership

*Generalship and Resistance in Robert E. Lee's First Month
in Command of the Army of Northern Virginia*

⊰ JOSEPH T. GLATTHAAR ⊱

"I wish his mantle had fallen on an abler man, or that I was able to drive
our enemies back to their homes," Robert E. Lee informed his daughter-
in-law Charlotte on June 2, 1862. Although Lee wrote with the obligatory
modesty, he was not alone in doubting his ability to accomplish the task.
His friend Gen. Joseph E. Johnston had just suffered a serious wound in a
battle that failed to drive the Union forces away from the capital of Richmond. Two days later, President Jefferson Davis tapped Lee as the army
commander, with the objective of driving a larger Federal command from
the gates of Richmond.[1]

Scholars and Civil War enthusiasts have devoted their attention to
the ensuing battles later that month called the Seven Days, in which Lee
and his newly dubbed Army of Northern Virginia drove the Federal army
twenty miles back and avoided a large-scale siege that most likely would
have resulted in the fall of Richmond. Yet what Lee executed in the inter-
vening weeks was one of the most brilliant turnarounds in American military history. With the Rebel army's back to Richmond and powerful resistance in and out of the army to his leadership, Lee implemented a plan so
comprehensive that it altered his army's culture. He dictated changes in
behavior among officers and enlisted men that paved the way for improvements in combat and husbanded valuable resources. While not wholly successful in changing army culture to meet his own desires, he did alter it
enough to enable the army to extend its ability to fight for almost three
more years. The fact that he did so in the face of strong objections and resistance demonstrates his unusual leadership talents.

Lee came from the Old Army, where he had built a great reputation.
Few men of his age could compete with his pedigree. The son of Revolutionary War hero "Light Horse" Harry Lee, he descended from one of
the most powerful families of Virginia. Although his family fell on hard

times as his father's career degenerated and he squandered family wealth, young Robert made a name for himself at West Point, graduating second in the class of 1829. He entered the Corps of Engineers, where he continued to impress those around him. Young Lee also took time to marry the daughter of George Washington Parke Custis, which linked him to General Washington. In the Mexican War, Lee served on Maj. Gen. Winfield Scott's handpicked staff. Time and again, Lee proved that he was a man of great courage and sound judgment, emerging from the war with the best reputation of all the junior officers in the Regular Army. With Commanding General Scott as his patron, Lee enjoyed choice assignments and, by mid-nineteenth-century army standards, rapid promotion for a field officer. Appointed superintendent of West Point, he vacated his position before his term of service officially ended to take over as lieutenant colonel of the newly created 2nd U.S. Cavalry, which Secretary of War Jefferson Davis stocked with choice officers. At the time, Edmund Kirby Smith, who also earned a promotion to join the same regiment, called Lee "the most accomplished officer and gentleman in the army." By early 1861, Lee received promotion to colonel and regimental commander. Not long before, he had led the party that crushed John Brown's raid on Harpers Ferry and gained national notoriety. In the midst of the secession crisis, Scott offered Lee command of the principal field army, which he declined to join with his native Virginia. Endowed with a brilliant mind, and a stickler for education, Lee was a man of rare talents. As Prussian military officer and observer Justus Scheibert noted of Lee, "he made the impression not of a soldier, but of a man of affairs."[2]

By the time of the Civil War, Lee's reputation had preceded him to the point that volunteers anticipated he would be the mastermind of the Confederate victory. A Virginia cavalryman called Lee "my beau ideal of a military chief," despite "the sternest expression of countenance I ever saw." Two months later, a Tennessean described a visit by Lee to his command. "He is a fine looking old fellow," recorded the twenty-one-year-old, "weighs about 160 lbs Heavy set full breasted Keen Dark Grey Eye Heavy *Mustache*." Lee, he concluded, "has a commanding military bearing." In time, his hair would gray, and he would grow his trademark "whiskers as white as cotton."[3]

Yet within certain circles, there was an undercurrent of doubt about Lee. By May 1861, after observing Lee at close hand over the previous six years, Edmund Kirby Smith had come to the conclusion that he lacked the ability for large-scale command, describing his selection to head Virginia forces as "unfortunate." Smith, like numerous others, was put off by Lee's slowness to come to a decision. Sam Melton, who served on Brig. Gen. Milledge L. Bonham's staff and had a very favorable impression of the Virginia general, informed his wife in May 1861 that Lee "is a splendid officer; slow — too slow, but thoroughly accomplished." In a letter that has become almost famous for its misreading of the man, South Carolina governor Francis W. Pickens announced to Bonham just before First Manassas, "The truth is Lee is not with us at heart, or he is a common man, with good looks, and too cautious for practical Revolution." Even Lee's trusted staff member, Walter H. Taylor, complained later in the war to his future bride about Lee's slowness to arrive at a decision. "He is too undecided," Taylor grumbled, "takes too long to firm his conclusions."[4]

What these supporters and early critics confused or blurred, however, was the distinction between caution and thoroughness. Lee liked to gather all the information and ruminate on the facts before implementing a course of action. While he could make snap judgments, and did so during the war, he knew that instant decisions were more likely to be wrong decisions. The caution that these individuals perceived and criticized was in fact the process of decision-making of a mature thinker trying to solve complicated problems. Slow to decide on a course of action, Lee formulated bold plans and implemented them even more boldly.

Lee's greatest strength as a military commander stemmed from his mastery of the operational art of war — the ability to use military forces in campaigns or major operations to achieve strategic goals in a theater of war. Over the course of three and a half decades of military service, Lee had sharpened his skills as a campaign planner through experience and study. In short, he could see how each command related to another, and how he could employ various pieces in combination to achieve success or influence the situation a hundred miles away or more. Lee had an uncanny talent for anticipating movements of the enemy. Lee also understood that the Confederacy would fight almost always against a superior force. The only way it could compensate for the imbalance was to throw all its strength into each fight. Troops held out of battle in reserve were wasted power.[5]

But for Lee, as for other military leaders throughout history, army command was a learned science and art. Time would prove that few could master the necessary transition; Lee was an exception. In the prewar army, he had never led more than a regiment, and it would take time to make the leap to army command. Like other soldiers in the war, he would have to learn on the job, and those harsh lessons usually cost lives and sometimes territory. As Lee quickly witnessed firsthand, the Rebel public and its soldiery often had unreasonable expectations and were unforgiving in failure.

In Lee's first major command in the field, he had to coordinate three separate columns in the rugged terrain of western Virginia. Lee's plan was too complicated, particularly with inexperienced subordinates in mountainous country and under poor weather conditions. With his command mired in mud, Lee could not deliver a powerful blow, and eventually his command retreated.

Fueled by excessively optimistic tales in the newspapers as the campaign was unfolding, soldiers and civilians alike reacted as if Lee had committed some monstrous and irreversible blunder. Newspapers and the public howled over Lee's incompetence. Edward A. Pollard, a Richmond newspaperman and sharp critic of the Davis administration, determined, "The most remarkable circumstance of this campaign was, that it was conducted by a general who had never fought a battle, who had a pious horror of guerrillas, and whose extreme tenderness of blood induced him to depend exclusively upon the resources of strategy, to essay the achievement of victories without the cost of life." A student at West Point when Lee was superintendent, Ben Allston reported to his father that people called Lee a "dirt dauber" (a small insect that leaves a soiled trail in its wake). "Slow he unquestionably is, and he has disappointed a host of friends," Allston asserted, "but he is there in command & must be upheld, until we find one who we are sure will do better than he has done." South Carolinian Alexander C. Haskell, a family friend of the Lees, described to his mother satirical sketches he had seen of Lee, "with a double barrel spy glass in one hand, and a spade in the other reconnoitering the position of the enemy." The caption read, "to retreat a little & throw up fortifications, the instant he set eyes upon them." Haskell commented, "This is unjust to a fine officer, but it does somewhat exhibit his very cautious policy."[6]

At the time, Lee responded privately to his critics with a twinge of sarcasm. "I am sorry, as you say, that the movements of our armies cannot keep pace with the expectations of the editors of the papers," he commented to his wife. Still, those vicious attacks surely must have hurt, and they unquestionably damaged Lee's reputation to the point that Davis decided to send Lee away from Richmond. The defense of Charleston and coastal South Carolina, Georgia, and Florida was unquestionably an important mission, and the job did require engineering skills, but surely there were more essential duties for one of five full generals in the Confederacy.

Davis must have realized that the only way he could save what was left of Lee's reputation was to send him away from Richmond and let the frenzy die out.[7]

Away from the Richmond fishbowl, Lee succeeded to the point that when Davis recalled him to Richmond for consultation and then placed him in charge of "military operations in the armies of the Confederacy," a soldier in the 14th South Carolina Infantry, defending his native state, confessed to his wife, "I am very sorry for it, for I had more confidence in him than in all other Generals together." The *Charleston Mercury*, a venomous anti-administration paper if ever there was one, applauded Lee's elevation. In the aftermath of several Confederate failures, the editors expected a prompt turnaround. "Under Lee's prudent management we expect that our affairs will soon begin to look brighter."[8]

Yet memories back in Virginia were long, and noncombat achievements in South Carolina, Georgia, and Florida altered few opinions. "The appointment of Genl Lee as chief military advisor of the Presdt. looks like a fatal mistake," Thomas Preston of Johnston's staff commented. Lee's "traits of mind" would prove more problematic than they were the previous year, he predicted. "May God in mercy protect us." Catherine Edmondston, a North Carolinian and unusually perceptive diarist, held nothing but contempt for Lee. "He is too timid, believes too much in masterly inactivity, finds 'his strength' too much in 'sitting still,'" she recorded. Even Lee's counterpart on the Union side, Maj. Gen. George B. McClellan, rejoiced when he thought that Lee, in his new position, would replace Johnston as field commander. "I prefer Lee to Johnston—," he elaborated to Lincoln, "the former is *too* cautious & weak under grave responsibility—personally brave & energetic to a fault, he yet is wanting in moral firmness when pressed by heavy responsibility & is likely to be timid & irresolute in action."[9]

On June 1, Davis relieved Lee "temporarily" from his duties as military adviser to take command of the Confederate forces in Eastern Virginia and North Carolina. Lee had no intention of acting as a temporary caretaker. He served at the pleasure of the commander in chief, and in every assignment, he would do his utmost to succeed. In mid-March 1862, when Davis called him back to Richmond as his military adviser, Lee conveyed that same sense of duty to his wife. "It will give me great pleasure to do anything I can to relieve him and serve the country," he explained to her, "but I do not see either advantage or pleasure in my duties. But I will not complain, but do my best." As the new army commander, he would shape it and fight it as he saw best, and he would continue to do so until Davis relieved him.[10]

Lee's initial mission was obvious: He had to drive the Union forces away from the Confederate capital. Of all the Rebel cities, Richmond was the one the fledgling nation could least afford to lose. It was the nation's capital, a symbol of the independent Confederacy, and a major industrial and transportation hub. Its capture by the Yankees would require the defenders to fall back to southwest Virginia and abandon most of the state, uncovering huge areas of agriculture, livestock, and citizens to Union control.[11]

Immediately, Lee began placing his imprimatur on the army. From his vantage point as Davis's chief military adviser, he had exposure to the military needs and mobilization capacity of the entire Confederacy, certainly better than Johnston or any other army commander. Lee also knew how and to what degree southerners could contribute to the nation's defense.

From his days as head of Virginia forces early in the war, his visits to the front, and most of all his service in South Carolina, Georgia, and Florida, Lee developed a feel for the men under his command. He understood what motivated his troops because he shared a commitment to the same cause. A southerner through and through, Lee possessed the same southern values that were ingrained in his soldiers. Like most southern whites, he endorsed the institution of slavery and particularly enjoyed its benefits as a slave owner during his time in Virginia. As a southern white male, he fully understood the great value that culture placed on honor and courage. Society demanded that its men act aggressively in war, particularly one in which hearth, home, rights, and dignity were at stake. Lee knew that he and his subordinate officers would have to harness and exploit that spirit of aggressiveness to offset Union superiority in manpower and equipment. Yet Lee also realized that certain vital wartime duties did not come readily to southerners, that southern culture did not promote these qualities or the execution of certain vital tasks. He and his fellow commanders would have to compel them to perform those critical assignments, which on the surface ran counter to their cultural upbringing but would promote victory and save lives. "The victories of the enemy increase & Consequently the necessity of increased energy & activity on our part," he wrote back in February. "Our men do not seem to realize this, & the same supineness & Carelessness of their duties Continue. If it will have the effect of arousing them & imparting an earnestness & boldness to their work, it will be beneficial to us. If not we shall be overrun [*sic*] for a time, & must make up our minds to great suffering." He then concluded with the powerful words, "All must be sacrificed to the country." In order to win, the troops and the larger society from which they came must exhibit a level of discipline and sacrifice that few had known in peacetime.[12]

Lee's first act included the establishment of a new name for his forces. While Davis or others occasionally referred to the primary field force as the Army of Northern Virginia, the name never stuck. In Lee's first announcement as the new commander, Special Orders No. 22 on June 1, he informed the troops that he was certain "every man has resolved to maintain the ancient fame of the Army of Northern Virginia and the reputation of its general," Joseph E. Johnston. He adopted the name fully, and in time, the Army of Northern Virginia became synonymous with Lee.[13]

Within days of taking over as the new army commander, Lee sought to improve the health, comfort, and well being of his troops. He established and enforced routines for the distribution of provisions and required division commanders to scrutinize the requisitions of subordinates. Johnston's staff was not particularly adept at administering, and that neglect of procedure and paperwork filtered down the chain of command, resulting in sloppiness, occasional neglect, and a squandering of precious resources. Rations arrived so infrequently that men in the Orange Battery resorted to trapping rats, soaking them in clear water overnight, and frying them for breakfast the next day. By insisting on proper procedures, Lee hoped to ensure that no soldiers wanted for food and basic supplies and that the army cut down on wastage. He complained to the quartermaster general that "This army has with it in the field little or no protection from weather" and arranged for small fly tents for the men. He also circulated directives to all officers to pay attention to the "health and comfort of the men under command, and spare unnecessary exposure and fatigue," so that everyone was ready for the ensuing battle. Lee even authorized whiskey rations, at the discretion of division commanders, "when deemed essential to the health of the men, from inclemency of the weather or exposure in the swamps." Together, these efforts at improving the quality of life of soldiers would boost morale. They would also have the residual effect of building confidence in officers who must lead them into battle. Officers who cared well for their troops, who ensured they had adequate clothing, supplies, and equipment, earned a higher standing with the men.[14]

At the same time, Lee called on officers and men to be vigilant in their efforts to conserve valuable materiel, knowing the difficulty of procuring replacement items. Lost or damaged supplies hindered the war effort severely. "The increasing difficulty in replacing them," he directed four days after taking charge, "makes greater watchfulness and care necessary in their preservation." One week later, he rebuked his command for squandering specific resources. The quartermaster had issued 800,000 tents during the past year, many of which soldiers had destroyed or discarded carelessly. "The means of supply are becoming more limited while the demand continues great," he warned.[15]

When fundamental items like barrels started to run short, Lee ordered his troops to recycle them, rather than allocate valuable manpower to chopping trees, planing lumber, and building new barrels. Even more critical was the wastage of ammunition, a great Confederate concern throughout the war. Soldiers carried packages of cartridges in their pockets and unintentionally damaged them. Only when entering combat should soldiers carry ammunition in their pockets. He ordered ordnance sergeants to collect and send to Richmond damaged cartridges for recycling and to inspect troops to guarantee compliance.[16]

Damage and destruction of public property injured the cause. On his daily rides, Lee explained, he "observed with concern in passing through Camps, too much disregard to the proper preservation of public property." He was "firmly convinced that our success is mainly dependent upon the economical and proper appropriation of public property at all times." Compared to their northern enemy, Confederates had very little margin for error. To win, they must learn to husband resources.[17]

Lee deemed intelligence as critical to success. He instructed subordinate officers to accumulate as much information as possible on the enemy force in the immediate vicinity, to prepare better to receive attacks and to guide the army in striking a blow against it. Confederates scoured northern newspapers for information and units so that they could gage Federal strength accurately. At the same time, Lee requested that the secretary of war see to it that newspapers kept certain movements out of print. Security, the Virginian understood, worked both ways.[18]

Lee's predecessor, Johnston, had taken no steps to prepare detailed maps of the Virginia Theater. As soon as Lee took command, the policy changed. Chief Engineer Walter H. Stevens installed Albert H. Campbell as head of the Commission of Engineers and Draughtsmen, with the duty of preparing maps that showed "the R.Rds.[railroads] Stage Farm Rds, Water Courses, Woods, Clearings, farm houses, Ponds, Marshes, & Commanding Elevations." It would take time to complete maps with this level of detail, and none would influence the outcome of the battle for Richmond, but detailed maps would provide valuable information for future operations.[19]

Lee also sent cavalry commander James Ewell Brown Stuart on a re-connaissance around the Union left flank to determine its vulnerability for attack. In flamboyant style, "Jeb" Stuart rode completely around Mc-Clellan's line, destroying supplies, seizing prisoners, causing mayhem, and gathering priceless information, convincing Lee that his battle plan was sound.[20]

To prevent Federals from strengthening their lines, Lee adopted an aggressive approach. As a trained engineer, he knew that it would be almost impossible for the Federals to haul huge guns over the soft, often muddy earth along the Peninsula and the Chickahominy River. They would have to ship them to the front by the York River Railroad. Lee sought the construction of a huge, iron-plated, mounted gun — similar to something the navy might employ — to shell the railroad and prevent large cannons, massive amounts of ammunition, and even provisions from reaching the front. Until the gun arrived, the army commander directed his sharpshooters and artillerists to pester the enemy as much as possible, as "enemy work parties must be arrested." Any effort to prevent the Federals from digging better trenches and approaches and forwarding weapons and supplies would save Rebel lives and perhaps aid in successful operations.[21]

While Rebel marksmen and gunners impeded Union progress, Lee decided he must employ his other troops in building and improving their works, yet he was challenging a naive cultural perspective on warfare. "Our people are opposed to work," the general alerted the commander in chief in words reminiscent of his predecessor Johnston. "Our troops, officers, Community & press, All ridicule & resist it." It was the very means by which McClellan was closing in on Richmond. "Why should we leave to him the whole advantage of laborers," he wondered. "Combined with valor fortitude & boldness, of which we have no fair proportion, it should lead us to Success." After describing how the Romans combined fortifications and fighting so skillfully, he then concluded, "There is nothing so military as labour, & nothing so important to our army as to Save the lives of its soldiers." Three days into his command, he ordered each division to assign 300 men to work under the supervision of engineer officers to dig earth-works, make sharpened logs called abatis, and build other obstructions and fortifications. Soldiers resented the labor; Lee did not care. Trenches and works would save Rebel lives and multiply combat power, which the Confederates badly needed to offset substantial Union manpower and equipment superiority. In addition to the work details, he required division commanders to see to it that officers and men "strengthen their positions in the most perfect manner with redoubts, barricades, abatis, rifle pits, &c.,

so that everyone had a hand in the manual labor." By mid-June, jotted an officer in his diary, "the whole front is one rifle pit, & many little redoubts." The trenches, so described a soldier to his wife, had a banquette or ledge about two to three feet off the bottom, so that soldiers could walk freely in the trench, completely protected from rifle fire, and then step up to shoot at the Yankees. As an added precaution, Lee laid out plans for another line of works farther to the rear. He saw to it that the secretary of war impressed one in every four slaves from five counties to the west to build more works in safer locations near Richmond.[22]

Richmond teemed with soldiers who were absent from their units, and straggling and wandering off had reached epidemic proportions. According to D. H. Hill, "There are hundreds and thousands of skulkers, who are dodging off home or lying a round the brothels[,] gambling saloons & drinking houses of Richmond." Lee directed Stuart to send a company of cavalrymen each day to scour the capital in search of absent troops, and to coordinate with the provost marshal there. On one raid, the horsemen netted large numbers of soldiers who were attending the theater in Richmond. "I am glad they were caught in no worse place than the Theatre," Maj. Gen. John Bankhead Magruder, a general who knew a bit about theatrics himself, consoled Hill. "Men who in times like these can have a stomach for amusement must necessarily make good fighters." Yet, much to Hill's chagrin, clashes of authority between the cavalry and the provost marshal in Richmond failed to halt the flow, and troops continued to sneak out of camp and into Richmond for theater and less culturally elevating activities.[23]

In the battle of Seven Pines, an ugly problem resurfaced: soldiers abandoned their posts to seek ammunition, to plunder, or from fear, and thus reduced the critical number of men who fired their weapons. Various commanders tried to halt the practice, but it was Lee who took charge. To check the flagrant straggling and plundering, and to keep troops with their commands, Lee ordered each regimental commander to create a provost guard, consisting of a lieutenant, a noncommissioned officer, and ten privates. He also directed that "No Officer is authorized to withdraw his command from its position in line of battle to procure ammunition," a problem that appeared all too frequently at Seven Pines. Division commanders were to enforce this and to see that ammunition was brought forward to the troops.[24]

All the while, Lee kept Davis informed of what he was doing and what he planned to do. The day after Davis placed Lee in command officially, he had asked the general, "Please keep me advised as frequently as your engagements will permit of what is passing before and around you." Lee needed no prodding. Having spent months and months at Davis's side, he knew the president wanted his subordinates to keep him informed. Lee did just that, and the level of industry he exhibited, the attention to important details, comforted Davis, giving the president the sense that he had a general in command who would really take charge. To his wife, Davis elaborated, "Lee is working systematically[,] cooperating cordially and the army is said to feel the beneficial effect of it."[25]

Others were not so optimistic. Since February, the Confederacy had suffered setback after setback. Out west, Federal soldiers had punctured the Confederate cordon with the capture of Forts Henry and Donelson. The Rebels not only lost an entire field command at Donelson, but they also had to abandon Nashville, the capital of Tennessee, to the Yankees. The retreat stopped in northern Mississippi. Confederate forces regrouped and launched a counterstrike at Shiloh that nearly drove the Yankees into the Tennessee River, but Federal reinforcements helped them sweep the field. The Rebel army commander, Gen. Albert Sidney Johnston, was killed in action on the first day of battle. By the end of May, Corinth, Mississippi, an important railroad junction, fell into Yankee hands. Farther south, along the Mississippi River, a Union naval and land force captured New Orleans, the largest city in the Confederacy. Back east, a Yankee expedition seized coastal islands in North Carolina, and overwhelming Union numbers had compelled the principal field command in Virginia to retreat to within view of the Richmond spires. When Johnston finally attacked, his commanders bungled the plans. Uncoordinated yet aggressive strikes dented but could not break the Union line. If not for Stonewall Jackson and his brilliant successes, whipping three separate Federal commands, preserving most of the Shenandoah Valley for the Confederacy, and detaining troops that could have gone to McClellan's army around Richmond, the cause might have appeared utterly hopeless.

After the command fiasco at Seven Pines, William Preston Johnston, the president's aide and the son of Albert Sidney Johnston, grumbled to his wife, "The trouble is we have *no Generals*." With Lee now in command of the army, his spirits buoyed a bit. Young Johnston believed Lee possessed patience, administrative ability, absolute integrity, and an unshakable commitment to the Confederacy. His disadvantage was that he neither knew the officers so well, nor did they know him. "I hope more from him, than I did from Johnston," he admitted. Though providing no ringing endorsement, Johnston nonetheless retained some faith in Lee.[26]

After conferring with Lee on June 1, Brig. Gen. William N. Pendleton, the chief of artillery, revealed his pleasure with the new army commander. "I liked very much his tone & bearing in the conference I had with him the evening before last," Pendleton penned his wife two days later. "His head seems clear & his heart strong." Lee had two great problems, the clergyman-turned-general explained to his wife. He must shield Richmond and then whip McClellan and the Yankees. Unfortunately, protection of Richmond imposed considerable restrictions on Lee's options to defeat the Federals. "Few men have ever borne a greater weight than that which now rests upon his shoulders," Pendleton conveyed solemnly.[27]

Others, however, expressed lingering doubts about Lee as a field commander. A knowledgeable staff officer jotted in his diary, "One week since real fighting ceased & Genl Lee took command—not so sanguine of our defeating McClellan as when he first came up." The following week, an acerbic D. H. Hill offered the same old refrain. "Genl Lee is slow and cautious," he complained to his wife.[28]

The flurry of reforms and duties impressed few other people in or out of the army. Not many even mentioned Lee's appointment in letters and diaries. Those who did grumbled over the manual labor, affixing Magruder's old nickname "King of Spades" to Lee but otherwise saying little about him, his appointment, or his changes in the army. Rare was the soldier like Pvt. Samuel Oakey, who, after three weeks under his new commander, was convinced this one was better. "General Lee is more vigilant than Johnson was," he alerted his cousin. "Lee wont give up an inch of ground to the Enemy without contesting it."[29]

Soldiers fixated on the trenches as a sign that Lee would only engage the enemy on the defensive. Still embracing a naive sense of honor and combat, the notion of fighting behind fortifications did not sit well with them. "The very idear of two large armys only separated by a small stream to be entrenching themselves is out of the question," jotted Capt. Robert G. Haile of the 55th Virginia Infantry. "I go in for their meeting each other in open ground and fight it out and be done with it."[30]

Civilians seemed even less impressed with Lee and his approach to warfare. Catherine Edmondston, from a North Carolina slaveholding family, offered no kind words for Lee. "I do not much like him, he 'falls back' too much," she commented. After listing his failures in Western Virginia and South Carolina, Edmondston jabbed at him, "His nick name last summer was 'old-stick-in-the-mud.' There is mud enough now in and about our lines, but pray God he may not fulfill the whole of his name." Mary Chesnut, the well-connected South Carolina diarist, recorded, "Lee is King of Spades. They are all once more digging for dear life." She believed the Confederacy's only hope was Stonewall Jackson conjuring up some of his magic. Like so many southerners, she thought fighting behind earthworks and frequent retreats cut the heart out of the soldiers. "Our chiefs contrive to dampen and destroy the enthusiasm of all who go near them. So much entrenching and falling back destroys the morale of any army," she pinpointed. "This everlasting retreating, it kills the hearts of the men."[31]

In confirmation, John Moncure Daniel, editor of the *Richmond Examiner*, drew upon his poison pen to express his dismay at the way Lee handled the crisis. "As for this city," he spit sarcastic venom, "if its fate depends on a game in which '*spades are trumps*,' played by two eminent hands of the old army, each knowing every thing that the other knows, there is no doubt but that the Confederate Government will, sooner or later, be spaded out of Richmond." Even the editors of the *Richmond Enquirer*, a wartime paper that seldom criticized the government, believed the "instincts and genius of the Southern troops" were "peculiarly suited to attack." So virulent were the sentiments, and so obstinate were those claims, that Davis feared the worst: "Politicians, Newspapers, and uneducated officers have created such a prejudice in our army against labor that it will be difficult until taught by bad experience."[32]

Lee had another way in mind. What neither the civilians nor the soldiers knew was that Lee had done all this with the intention of assuming the offensive. He oversaw the provisioning and improved the comfort of troops so that they would enter the campaign well rested. He husbanded resources for the fight and gathered intelligence to plan his attack. By harassing the enemy, he attempted to keep their works from being completed, and he drew together the maximum number of men for the fight. He dug fortifications not so much to counter McClellan's advance but to free up large numbers of soldiers for an attack while a small portion of the army held Yankees at bay.

On June 25, Lee hurled 65,000 troops, including forces from the Shenandoah Valley, against the Union right flank while 25,000 men in trenches held a force over three times as large at bay. Day after day, Lee's men hammered the Federals back from Richmond, until their retreat halted some twenty miles away, on the James River and under the protection of Union gunboats. Coordination and initiative failed his subordinate commanders, and the Union army had escaped destruction. Lee had wracked up larger casualties, but he and his men had saved Richmond.

Soldiers accorded the general full credit. Several days into the fight, Maj. Gen. Lafayette McLaws announced to his wife, "General Lee is rapidly regaining, if he has not already regained entirely, the confidence of the Army and the people as a skillful and even a dashing officer. The criterion in military matters is success, and up to this hour the combinations of General Lee have been of the most marked, decided, and successful. You cannot imagine how gratifying is the feeling to Soldiers to know that their Chief is Competent to all position." A Virginia soldier echoed those sentiments. "It was consummate generalship that drove McClellan from his fortifications," he insisted to his wife, according full credit to Lee for the triumph. Troops attached no blame for the heavy Rebel losses to the army commander. "General Lee has certainly won his laurels," a Texan attested to the folks at home. "The plan of the campaign was certainly well conceived, and it was not Genl. Lee's fault that it was not well executed."[33]

During the course of the campaign and for almost two weeks after it ended, a newspaper reader would have been hard-pressed to discover that Lee had much to do with the fight. Newspapers covered subordinate commanders, particularly Jackson and his sweep from outside the Shenandoah Valley against the Union flank. The *Augusta Constitutionalist* even reported Jackson as the "principal command of our army." When a story in Atlanta's *Southern Confederacy* under the headline "'The Masterly Strategy and Generalship of Commanders of the Confederate Army'" mentioned Lee, it barely paid notice to him, and when it did, the writer gave equal credit to the absent, wounded Joe Johnston, who received top billing. The *Charleston Mercury*, which had sung Lee's praises some months earlier, targeted the Virginian, claiming the "blundering manner in which he [the enemy] was allowed to get away, the desultory way in which he has been pursued . . . are facts, we fear, not very flattering to the practical generalship of General LEE."[34]

Yet in the ensuing days and weeks, Lee emerged as the hero of the hour. Sometimes slow to admit their criticisms had been misplaced, newspapers came around to praise Lee. In the Richmond print, it took a letter of grievance from an author under the pseudonym "Justice" to challenge the earlier negative coverage. "Justice" complained to the *Richmond Enquirer* that he noticed "in certain quarters a disposition to ignore the fact that we owe, in an eminent degree, our recent great victory to General Lee, and to ascribe to others the praise justly due to his admirable and successful strategy." Clearly, it had a shaming effect. That same day, the *Enquirer* admitted: "The result of the conflict thus far is a splendid tribute to the capacity of our Commanding General Robert E. Lee. Henceforth his name is as immemorial as history can make a man. The facts when analysed, as we hope soon to be better able to do, will display a combination of strategy, prudence, vigor, and sagacity in planning the attack, that have rarely been equaled in the history of military operations." The *Richmond Dispatch* trumpeted the victory as "without parallel in the annals of warfare." Lee received no such praise. On July 2, the *Richmond Whig* repeated the letter of "Justice" and responded tepidly, "But with Lee against McClellan, and Southern troops against Northern, we may safely and sanguinely await the final issue." By July 10, the *Whig* referred to the "splendid operation of Gen. Lee on the Chickahominy." Then, nearly two weeks after the publication of the "Justice" letter, on July 14, the editor of the *Whig* came around to accord Lee his due. He informed his readership that numerous civilians had skillfully manipulated the story of Confederate successes and failures, boosting the standing of their favorites and denigrating the reputations of others. Lee was a particular target. "Disparagement, sarcasm and ridicule have made him the mark of many a flying arrow," the paper explained. "Now comes his reward." Lee took the helm with Yankees at the gates of Richmond, and he quietly formed his plan of action and stayed the course, despite doubts and criticism. "He has amazed and confounded his detractors by the brilliancy of his genius, the fertility of his resources, his energy and daring," opined the editor. "He has established his reputation forever, and has entitled himself to the lasting gratitude of his country." Lee, who had "met injustice without a murmur, now seems to almost hide from praise."[35]

The image of McClellan's massive army, cowering under the protection of Yankee gunboats, elicited delight across the Confederacy and restored order to the southern universe. The Confederate people had anticipated such great achievements from its soldiers but instead had suffered a steady string of setbacks at the hands of those characterless Yankees. A siege would surely have resulted in the fall of Richmond, and without the Confederate industrial hub and the symbol as the nation's capital, secessionists could not have prosecuted the war for very long. In just thirty days, Lee had completely altered the fortunes of the Confederacy. As Cpl. James Adair of the 8th Georgia Infantry explained to his newspaper audience in Atlanta's *Southern Confederacy*, in words that would ultimately anticipate widespread sentiments in Confederate states, "At many times we were in the midst of showers of shot and shell, from which escape seemed impossible. I tried to put my trust in God and Gen. Lee. The former had the power to protect us from the shafts of death hurled at us by the enemy, while the latter led us through Yankee camps, driving back, capturing thousands of Yankees and their 'baggage.'"[36]

More than just defeat the Union army, Lee had begun to alter army culture and to win the hearts and minds of the officers and men. In a war in which Confederates sought to punish Union invaders until the northern public became discouraged, the Confederacy would have to endure great sacrifices and husband precious resources. Neither Lee's predecessors in command nor his subordinate officers and men understood that. By implementing his changes, Lee was able to prepare the soldiers better for campaigns, free up troops for risky maneuvers (which became his trademark), and stretch limited resources to sustain an army in the field that could wage war for three years longer against overwhelming odds. All along the way, he encountered resistance within and without the army. That first month was one of the greatest feats of large-scale leadership in American history.

NOTES

1. R. E. Lee to [Charlotte Lee], June 2, 1862, no collection, Virginia Historical Society, Richmond (repository hereafter cited as VHS).

2. E. K. Smith to Mother, October 20, 1855, Edmund Kirby Smith Papers, Southern Historical Collection, University of North Carolina, Chapel Hill (repository hereafter cited as SHC); Justus Scheibert, *Seven Months in the Rebel States*, ed. William Stanley Hoole (Tuscaloosa, Ala.: Confederate Publishing Company, 1958), 39.

3. D. H. Hill to Wife, June 6, [1861], Daniel Harvey Hill Papers, U.S. Army Military History Institute, Carlisle, Pa. (repository hereafter cited as USAMHI); James Keith to Mother, June 7, [1861], Keith Family Papers, VHS; William P. Parker diary, August 16, 1861, William P. Parker Papers, Washington and Lee University; Frank [Barron] to Annie, May 20, 1864, Barron Papers, Fredericksburg and Spotsylvania National Battlefield Park, Fredericksburg, Va. (repository hereafter cited as FSNBP).

4. E. K. Smith to Mother, May 10, 16, 1861, R2, Edmund Kirby Smith Papers, SHC; Sam to Wife, May 29, 1861, Samuel Wicliffe Melton Papers, University of South Carolina, Columbia (repository hereafter cited as USC); F. W. Pickens to Bonham, July 7, 1861, Milledge Luke Bonham Papers, USC; Walter Taylor to [Bettie], March 4, 1864, Walter H. Taylor Papers, Norfolk Public Library.

5. See Jay Luvaas, "Lee and the Operational Art: The Right Place, the Right Time," *Parameters* (Autumn 1992): 2–18, for a marvelous introduction to Lee and the operational art.

6. Edward A. Pollard, *The First Year of the War* (New York: Charles B. Richardson, 1863), 168; Ben Allston to Father, December 9, 1861, R. F. W. Allston Papers, South Carolina Historical Society, Charleston; A. C. Haskell to Mother, January 22, 1862, Alexander C. Haskell Papers, SHC; *Richmond Enquirer*, September 20, 1861, p. 1, col. 3.

7. R. E. Lee to Wife, October 7, 1861, quoted in Robert E. Lee Jr., *Recollections and Letters of General Robert E. Lee* (1904; reprint, Garden City, N.Y.: Garden City Publishing, 1924), 51; R. E. Lee to [Charlotte], December 25, 1862, Lee Family Papers, VHS; Douglas Southall Freeman, *R. E. Lee: A Biography*, 4 vols. (New York: Scribner's, 1934–35), 1:598.

8. General Orders No. 14, WD, A & IGO, March 13, 1862, Orders Received by 15th Virginia Infantry, December 1861–April 1862, RG 109, National Archives, Washington (repository hereafter cited as NA); [Andrew Wardlaw] to Wife, March 12, 1862, Civil War Miscellaneous Collection, USAMHI; *Charleston Mercury*, March 11, 1862, p. 1, cols. 3–4, March 17, 1862, p. 1, col. 3; Davis to Lee, March 2, 1862, in U.S. War Department, *The War of the Rebellion: A Compilation of the Official Records of the Union and Confederate Armies*, 127 vols., index, and atlas (Washington: Government Printing Office, 1880–1901), ser. 1, 6:400 (set hereafter cited as *OR*; all subsequent references to ser. 1); Freeman, *R. E. Lee*, 1:605–31.

9. Tho S Preston to Wife, March 28, 1862, Preston-Davis Papers, University of Virginia, Charlottesville (repository hereafter cited as UVA); Catherine Ann Devereux Edmondston, *"Journal of a Secesh Lady": The Diary of Catherine Ann Devereux Edmondston, 1860–1866*, ed. Beth Gilbert Crabtree and James W. Patton (Raleigh: North Carolina Division of Archives and History, 1979), 169 (entry for May 6, 1862); McClellan to Lincoln, April 20, 1862, in George B. McClellan, *The Civil War Papers of George B. McClellan: Selected Correspondence, 1860–1865*, ed. Stephen W. Sears (New York: Ticknor and Fields, 1989), 244–45.

10. R. E. Lee to Mary, March 14, 1862, in Lee, *Recollections and Letters*, 66–67.

11. John H. Reagan, *Memoirs: With Special Reference to Secession and the Civil War* (1906; reprint, Austin, Tex.: Pemberton Press, 1968), 139; Josiah Gorgas, "Extracts from my notes written chiefly soon after the close of the war," 1, 6, 19–21, 24–25, 31, 33–35, Gorgas Family Papers, University of Alabama, Tuscaloosa; Edward Porter Alexander, *Fighting for the Confederacy: The Personal Recollections of General Edward Porter Alexander*, ed. Gary W. Gallagher (Chapel Hill: University of North Carolina Press, 1989), 512.

12. R. E. Lee to Son, February 23, 1862, Markham Papers, Museum of the Confederacy, Richmond, Va. (repository hereafter cited as MC). For Lee on slavery and slave ownership, see Emory M. Thomas, *Robert E. Lee: A Biography* (New York: W. W. Norton, 1995), 72, 173, 177–78, 183–84, 273–74; and Michael Fellman, *The Making of Robert E. Lee* (New York: Random House, 2000), 54–75.

13. General Orders No. 15, A & IGO, October 22, 1861, in *OR* 5:913–14; Special Orders No. 22, HQ, June 1, 1862, in *OR* 11(3):569. Lee called it the Army of Northern Virginia in Special Orders No. 4, HQ, Richmond, Va., April 5, 1862, Special Orders, Virginia Forces, April 29, 1861–May 30, 1862, RG 109, NA.

14. Lee to Myers, June 10, 1862, General Orders No. 68, HQ, Dept. of No. Va., June 14, 1862, Circular, HQ, June 10, 1862, in *OR* 11(3):585–86, 599, 588; Henry J. Mugler diary, May 30[?], 1862, Henry J. Mugler Papers, Virginia, vol. 13, FSNBP; General Orders No. 63, HQ, Dept. of No. Va., June 5, 1862, M921, roll 11, frames 172, 174, General and Special Orders and Circulars Issued, Army of Northern Virginia (hereafter cited as GSOCI), RG 109, NA.

15. General Orders Nos. 64, 67, HQ, ANV, June 5, 12, 1862, M921, roll 1, frames 172, 174, GSOCI, RG 109, NA.

16. General Orders No. 68, HQ, Dept. of No. Va., June 14, 1862, in *OR* 11(3):599. Earlier in the campaign, Magruder complained of a "wasteful expenditure of ammunition," as did Lee. (See General Orders No. 177, HQ, Army of Peninsula, April 9, 1862, Orders Received, 15 VA; and General Orders No. 28, HQ of the Forces, June 20, 1861, Virginia Forces, RG 109, NA.)

17. General Orders No. 66, HQ, Dept. of No. Va., June 8, 1862; General Orders No. 67, HQ, Dept. of No. Va., June 12, 1862, M921, roll 1, frames 173–74, GSOCI, RG 109, NA.

18. Circular, HQ, June 10, 1862, Lee to Stuart, June 11, 1862, Lee to Randolph, June 11, 1862, in *OR* 11(3):588, 590–91; Alexander, *Fighting for the Confederacy*, 68–69.

19. Stevens to Campbell, June 9, 1862, in Richard W. Stephenson, "General Lee's Forgotten Mapmaker: Major Albert H. Campbell and the Department of Northern Virginia's Topographical Department," *North & South* 8 (March 2005): 66, 69; Davis enclosure, February 18, 1865, in *OR* 47(2):1306.

20. H. L. P. King diary, June 15, 1862, Thomas Butler King Papers, SHC; Ch. Friend to Wife, June 15, [1862], Blanton Family Papers, VHS; AAR of Stuart, June 17, 1862, in *OR* 11(1):1036–40.

21. Circular, HQ, June 10, 1862, Lee to Stevens, June 5, 1862, Lee to Gorgas, June 5, 1862, Lee to Mallory, June 21, 1862, Minor to Lee, June 24, 1862, in *OR* 11(3):588, 574, 610, 615. By June 24, the navy provided an iron-plated, rifled 32-pounder, with 200 shells.

22. Lee to Davis, June 5, 1862, R. E. Lee Papers, United States Military Academy; General Orders No. 62, HQ, Dept. of No. Va., June 4, 1862, M921, roll 1, frame 167, GSOCI, RG 109, NA; Circular, HQ, June 10, 1862, A & IGO, June 13, 1862, in *OR* 11(3):588, 597; H. L. P. King diary, June 14, 1862, Thomas Butler King Papers, SHC; W. S. Grady, July 12, 1862, Henry Woodfin Grady Papers, Emory University, Atlanta, Ga.; Jno. T. Smith to Cic. Heath, June 20, 1862, Smith-Johnson Papers, MC; Longstreet to Hill, June 13, 16, 1862, D. H. Hill Papers, Library of Virginia, Richmond.

23. General Orders No. 63, HQ, Dept. of No. Va., June 5, 1862, in *OR* 11(3):576–77; D. H. Hill to Wife, June 10, 1862, Daniel Harvey Hill Papers, USAMHI; J. B. Magruder to Hill, June 13, 1862, Letters Sent, Right Wing of Army of Northern Virginia, RG 109, NA; John [Scurry] to Sarah, June 19, 1862, John G. Scurry Papers, Gilder Lehrman Collection, Morgan Library, New York City.

24. General Orders No. 68, HQ, 1st Div., 1st Corps, June 2, 1862, General Orders & Circulars, Gen. W. H. C. Whiting's Command, February–July 1862, RG 109, NA; General Orders No. 10, HQ, Longstreet's Div., June 2, 1862, James Longstreet Papers, MC; Special Orders [no number given], HQ, Longstreet's Division, June 3, 1862, Bryan Grimes Papers, North Carolina Department of Archives and History, Raleigh; Circular, Inspector General's Office, Dept. of No. Va., June 9, 1862, William N. Pendleton Papers, SHC; General Orders No. 63, HQ, Dept. of No. Va., June 5, 1862, M921, roll 1, frame 170, GSOCI, RG 109, NA; *Augusta Constitutionalist*, July 2, 1862, p. 2, col. 2.

25. Davis to Lee, June 2, 1862, in *OR* 11(3):569; Davis to Varina, June 19, 1862, War Department Collection of Confederate Records: Confederate Papers Relating to Citizens or Business Firms ("Citizens File"): Davis, Jefferson, box 20681, RG 109, NA.

26. Wm. Preston Johnston to Wife, June 1–2, 1862, Mason Barret Collection, Tulane University, New Orleans, La.

27. W. N. Pendleton to Darling love, June 3, 1862, William N. Pendleton Papers, SHC.

28. D. H. Hill to Wife, June 16, 1862, Daniel Harvey Hill Papers, USAMHI; H. L. P. King diary, June 8, 1862, Thomas Butler King Papers, SHC.

29. Samuel to Cousin, June 22, [1862], John Oakley Papers, Duke University, Durham, N.C.

30. Robert Gaines Haile Jr., *Tell the Children I'll Be Home When the Peaches Get Ripe:*

The Journal and Letters of Robert Gaines Haile, Jr., ed. Robert M. Tombes (Richmond: Tizwin, 1999), 39–40.

31. Edmondston, *"Journal of a Secesh Lady,"* 189 (entry for June 8, 1862); C. Vann Woodward, ed., *Mary Chesnut's Civil War* (New Haven, Conn.: Yale University Press, 1981), 387. The absence of comments in soldiers' letters and diaries on Johnston's wounding and Lee's elevation and work is striking.

32. *Richmond Examiner*, June 10, 1862, in John M. Daniel, *The Richmond Examiner During the War* (New York: Arno, 1970, reprinted from 1868 edition), 56; *Richmond Enquirer*, June 17, 1862, p. 4, col. 1; Jefferson Davis to Varina Davis, June 11, 1862, Jefferson Davis Papers, MC.

33. McLaws to Wife, June 28, 1862, McLaws Papers, SHC; John T. Thornton to [wife], July 4, 1862, John T. Thornton Papers, UVA; Thos. J. Goree to Mother, July 21, 1862, in Thomas Jewett Goree, *The Thomas Jewett Goree Letters, I*, ed. Langston James Goree (Bryan, Tex.: Texas Family History Foundation, 1981), 164.

34. *Augusta Constitutionalist*, June 28, 1862, p. 2, col. 1; *Atlanta Southern Confederacy*, July 10, 1862, p. 2, cols. 2–3, July 11, 1862, p. 2, col. 2; *Charleston Mercury*, July 8, 1862, p. 1, col. 2. A scan of the Richmond newspapers, which were a primary source for other newspapers around the Confederacy, demonstrates how little press Lee received.

35. Justice to Editors of the Enquirer, n.d., *Richmond Enquirer*, July 1, 1862, p. 2, col. 2, and editorial, p. 2, col. 1; *Richmond Dispatch*, July 2, 1862, p. 1, col. 1; *Richmond Whig*, July 2, 1862, p. 1, cols. 1–2, July 10, 1862, p. 1, col. 1, July 14, 1862, p. 1, cols. 1–2.

36. Soldier Jim to *Atlanta Southern Confederacy*, July 25, 1862 (published July 31, 1862), in William B. Styple, ed., *Writing & Fighting from the Army of Northern Virginia* (Kearny, N.J.: Belle Grove, 2003), 121.

In Your Hands That
Musket Means Liberty

African American Soldiers and the Battle of Olustee

⊰ J. MATTHEW GALLMAN ⊱

The battle of Olustee — or Ocean Pond — was fought on February 20, 1864, about ten miles east of Lake City, Florida, and about forty-five miles north of Gainesville. In the grand military narrative of the Civil War, it was a minor battle culminating a failed Union operation in northern Florida. The original plan, proposed by Maj. Gen. Quincy A. Gillmore, commander of the Department of the South, and approved by President Abraham Lincoln, combined an array of economic and political objectives. The idea was to send a small force into northern Florida to cultivate Unionist support, liberate (and enlist) slaves, cut off Confederate supply lines, and perhaps acquire some of the state's stores of cotton and timber. On February 7 a division of Union troops under Brig. Gen. Truman B. Seymour captured Jacksonville, in the northeast corner of the state, and prepared to move westward. On the 20th, Seymour's command of about 5,500 men — including three regiments of black troops — faced 5,000 Confederates under Brig. Gen. Joseph Finegan at Olustee. The terrain was flat, marshy, dense with thin grass and weeds, and broken by stands of pines. Ocean Pond limited movement to the north. The tracks of the Florida, Atlantic, and Gulf Railroad ran on an east-west axis along the southern edge of where the armies met.

From the standpoint of the invaders, the best that could be said of Olustee is that it did not go as badly as it might have. In the early afternoon, Union cavalry encountered Confederate pickets in advance of Finegan's prepared entrenchments. At about 2:00 P.M. the 7th Connecticut Infantry moved forward with some artillery, driving the Rebel pickets back toward Olustee, but as they did, the superior Confederate force threatened to flank and overwhelm the Federals. As the Connecticut troops fell back around 3:00 P.M., the 7th New Hampshire Infantry and the 8th U.S. Colored

Troops moved forward, with the 7th taking the right flank. In the chaos of the moment, orders became garbled and the men from New Hampshire fell apart soon after they arrived, leaving the 8th USCT isolated and facing a superior Confederate force. Within twenty minutes Col. Charles W. Fribley, the 8th's commander, fell mortally wounded. Soon the black regiment was also in retreat, and the Union's situation had become precarious.

Seymour had already sent three New York regiments to the right to support the panicked Connecticut troops. Now, as the 8th fell back and the Union artillery was in danger of capture, Seymour called up his remaining reserves. Several miles to the rear, Col. James Montgomery commanded a brigade of two African American regiments, the 54th Massachusetts Infantry and the 1st North Carolina Colored. The two African American regiments rushed into the fray, with the North Carolinians moving to the right and the 54th shielding the 8th on the left as they retreated. The fighting raged as daylight faded, and Seymour ordered his men to abandon the field. Most of the Union soldiers made a safe return to Jacksonville. Still, the losses were heavy. The Union suffered 1,861 killed, wounded, and missing; the Confederacy reported 961 casualties.[1]

Although a minor episode in the larger military narrative of the Civil War, Olustee figures more prominently in the wartime history of African American soldiers. Their story illuminates how the history of the Civil War is — in a variety of ways — a story of fundamental similarities amongst diverse people, and at the same time a narrative defined by crucial differences, both demographic and ideological, sometimes revealed in unexpected and ironic ways.

Scholars of Civil War soldiers can be simultaneously splitters and lumpers. Thus, the military historian may speak of a particular "fighting regiment" as contrasted with another that was prone to cowardice or poor discipline. But many Civil War historians have noted the fundamental commonalities in attitude, motivation, and experience bridging the two armies, producing bonds that would facilitate postwar reconciliation among veterans. In these broad discussions, the African American soldier commonly stands to the side, the subject of separate monographs and collections but rarely interwoven into that master narrative — and with good reason. The multiple steps that led to the inclusion of black men in the Union army are a distinctive story. Once in uniform, African American soldiers endured unequal treatment from government officials, a skeptical reception from their white comrades, and threats of execution or enslavement at the hands of their enemies. And even where scholarly questions might span white and black soldiers, the evidence inhibits the analysis.

Archives are packed with white soldiers' letters and diaries, but few black soldiers left behind such private writings.[2]

For many Americans, knowledge of the USCT comes from the movie *Glory* (1989), the exciting tale of the 54th Massachusetts from enlistment to the heroic and tragic assault on Fort Wagner in July 1863. As Civil War movies go, *Glory* is recognized as a superb piece of work, albeit one told largely through the eyes of the regiment's charismatic white commander, Col. Robert Gould Shaw. The film's audiences received an excellent sense of military action, even though the filmmakers tinkered a bit with some of the minor details. Moreover, tens of thousands of viewers learned quite a bit about black troops during the Civil War and the multiple inequalities that the 54th faced.

Yet *Glory* seems intent on injecting as much diversity as possible into this single regiment. The result is an interesting cross-section of personality and human experience slowly blended together to produce a cohesive fighting unit, reminiscent of any number of old war movies. Viewers watch as the highly educated, culturally sophisticated man trains and fights alongside the illiterate laborer, the angry ex-slave, the grizzled elder statesman, and a host of men of varied backgrounds who seemingly share only race in common. While this portrayal gave audiences a taste of the diversity among the 180,000 African American men who served in the Union army, it overstated the range within the 54th. As the first regiment of northern black troops, it represented the best and the brightest of the sons of northern black elites. Eighty percent were born as free men. The bookish character Thomas Searles — played by Andre Braugher — was probably close to the norm, rather than the charmingly peculiar aberration suggested by the film.[3]

Those who have seen *Glory* will recall that the film did portray one other USCT regiment, providing a stark comparison with the disciplined men of the 54th. In June 1863, Shaw and his men joined Colonel Montgomery and the 2nd South Carolina Infantry in a brief sortie to Darien, Georgia, where Montgomery ordered the sacking of the town. The 2nd was composed of freedmen, and under the cynical Montgomery they are thoroughly undisciplined, to the disgust of Colonel Shaw and his men.[4] The filmmakers might have presented this scene as a contrast between the unruly behavior of the recently enslaved men of the 2nd and the higher ethical standards of the free-born men of the 54th, but — in keeping with the narrative focus on Colonel Shaw — the cinematic emphasis is really on the two white commanders. Shaw and Montgomery articulate different perspectives on what the Union can reasonably expect from black men in uniform. Montgomery is a devout abolitionist, but he has a limited respect for his men, and treats them accordingly; Shaw has greater hopes and expectations. Thus, the moviegoer is left to conclude that the 2nd and the 54th behaved differently at Darien because their white commanders approached their tasks differently.

Turning from film back to history, what information is available about the three regiments of African American troops who fought at Olustee? The first into the fray were the 8th U.S. Colored Troops. Recently recruited in eastern Pennsylvania and trained at Camp William Penn just outside of Philadelphia, the 8th was under the command of Colonel Fribley. Prior to Olustee, the regiment had seen no action. The 1st North Carolina—which had been re-designated the 35th USCT on February 8, 1864—was another relatively green regiment. Recruited along the eastern seaboard of Virginia, North Carolina, and South Carolina the previous summer and mustered in on June 30, the men of the 1st were freedmen who had made the dramatic transition from slavery, to freedom, to military service. Prior to the Florida invasion, the 1st had been engaged in siege operations outside Charleston, but they had yet to see any serious action. They were commanded by James Beecher, the brother of Harriet Beecher Stowe and Henry Ward Beecher, but Beecher was on leave that February and command had passed to Lt. Col. William N. Reed.[5]

The 1st went into battle alongside the 54th Massachusetts, part of a two-regiment brigade commanded by Colonel Montgomery. The 54th, alone among the three black regiments at Olustee, marched across Florida with the confidence of a veteran regiment. Although *Glory* left the filmgoer with the impression that the charge on Fort Wagner had decimated the 54th, the veteran regiment had survived the disastrous assault, assembled new recruits anxious to join a celebrated unit, and returned to battle. The 54th was commanded by Col. Edward N. Hallowell, a Philadelphian who had survived his wounds at Fort Wagner and rejoined his regiment after a brief recuperation.

Many characteristics and experiences forged a bond among these three regiments, making it logical for any observer or chronicler to treat them as a unit. Thirteen months after Abraham Lincoln issued the revolutionary Emancipation Proclamation, the 1st N.C., 8th USCT, and 54th Massachusetts represented a revolution on the battlefield: a significant presence of armed black men. The soldiers of the U.S. Colored Troops, of which these three regiments represented a small contingent, were collectively a part of at least two sorts of revolutions. First, they were invaluable new recruits at a time when the Union sorely needed reinforcements. As historian Joseph T. Glatthaar has argued, the addition to Union military forces of 180,000 men — arriving on the scene when they did and swelling the Union ranks on strategically vital battlefields — helped ensure a northern military victory.[6] They were not merely symbols but critical soldiers in the Union cause, helping turn the tide in a war that had become a battle over slavery. The North's black regiments became revolutionary actors as soon as they donned blue uniforms. By fighting alongside white men and against white enemies, black soldiers destabilized a host of assumptions about race and manhood. In this sense, too, the African American soldiers shared a common bond that transcended their diverse histories and circumstances.

While they were collectively changing the military terrain and recasting the nation's racial landscape, the USCT troops also shared the common bond that came from shared discrimination and injustice. Whatever the conditions of their birth or the terms of their enlistment, black soldiers were forced to endure a litany of insults and humiliations at the hands of their government: they fought under white commissioned officers, routinely drew assignments more as laborers than warriors, and received the poorest equipment and lower wages than the thirteen dollars a month paid to white infantrymen.

In all these senses the African American soldiers at Olustee were fundamentally similar to each other, and fundamentally different from their white comrades. But that is only part of the story. Several characteristics distinguished the regiments of the USCT. Three traits come to mind, all of which were represented among the black regiments that fought at Olustee. First, the Union's African American troops hailed from many parts of the country. The 54th Massachusetts was distinctive in that the original recruits came from across the North and the Border States, but when the regiment sought to replenish its depleted ranks after Fort Wagner, it turned to New England: 80 percent of the 286 new men hailed from either Massachusetts or Vermont.[7] The men of the 8th came largely from eastern Pennsylvania. The 1st North Carolina originated along the eastern coast of South Carolina, North Carolina, and Virginia. The African American regiments at Olustee were further differentiated by their level of training and combat experience. At one end of the spectrum was the 54th Massachusetts, which was a truly veteran regiment. On paper the 1st North Carolina was a fairly experienced regiment, but in fact its members had had little opportunity to fire their weapons in anger. The Pennsylvanians were an extraordinarily green regiment. The Florida invasion was their first campaign. Although the three black regiments at Olustee had confronted similar barriers, they—just like white Civil War regiments—marched into battle with very different levels of experience.

A further trait that separated the Union's black regiments, and also distinguished them most powerfully from their white brethren, was the array of circumstances and motivations that lured them into uniform. White volunteers left behind a wealth of letters, providing insight into the forces that led them to enlist and enabled them to endure years of warfare. Although each man responded to his own personal impulses, various patterns do emerge. When they enlisted, Civil War soldiers were following the dictates of both masculinity and ideology. War presented an opportunity to demonstrate manhood, and the failure to fight called that manhood into question. But the initial volunteers were not simply following paths determined by culture or testosterone. Their letters—both North and South—revealed a deep commitment to nation and cause.[8] By the third year of the war, the mix of motivations had shifted. New white recruits responded to the persuasive lure of high bounties or the threat of conscription. Other men offered their services as paid substitutes, serving in the place of draftees. Perhaps bounty men and substitutes also embraced the Union's core values, but they required the additional financial incentives to act on those impulses.

What about those black men who chose to shoulder a weapon? The three regiments at Olustee represent distinct points on a spectrum—or really multiple spectrums—as defined by geography, chronology, and servitude. For the men at the extreme poles—the 54th and the 1st—the decision to fight might have come rather naturally and even easily. The 54th's recruiters drew on that pool of the North's free black men who felt most compelled to strike a blow against the South and the slaveocracy. For freedmen along the Carolina coast, the impulse to fight their former masters must have been even more powerful. Moreover, for ex-slaves who sought economic autonomy and a modicum of independence, soldiering represented the best of a limited range of options.[9]

In contrast to the 54th Massachusetts and the 1st North Carolina, the 8th U.S. Colored Troops occupied the geographic center. The 8th mustered in for training at Camp William Penn, outside of Philadelphia, on December 4, 1863, nearly ten months after Massachusetts governor John Andrews received permission to recruit the North's first regiment of black men, and four and a half months after the 54th Massachusetts led the charge at Fort Wagner. What made these Pennsylvanians join the Union army? The most willing African American recruits had already enlisted in the previous months. In fact, the 54th Massachusetts had an entire company recruited in Philadelphia, and Philadelphia men appeared in most of the other companies of the 54th and 55th Massachusetts.[10] For those African Americans who had not been swept up in the previous winter's war fervor, there was ample reason to remain on the sidelines. By the war's third year, the northern economy was prospering and jobs were fairly plentiful. And when the men of the 8th enlisted, the Pennsylvania recruiters for the USCT had not yet begun to offer bounties to black volunteers.

Moreover, despite the much-celebrated Emancipation Proclamation, northern black men had every reason to conclude that this was still not their war. At home they endured a host of legal, political, and institutional indignities delivering the daily message that African Americans were not equal partners in the nation. In a particularly disturbing ironic twist, when the wives and loved ones of Philadelphia's black soldiers tried to ride the city's streetcars out to Camp William Penn, the conductors refused to let them sit in the covered section, requiring instead that they ride standing on the cars' open platforms. Many women preferred to walk the miles to the training camp rather than enduring the insult to their womanhood.[11] If their lives on the home front were not sufficient to convince them that this was not their fight, by the fall of 1863 northern black men knew that the Union army hardly promised to be a haven of racial equality. Whereas the men of the 54th had had reason to believe that they were entering a new world of racial equality, or at least equal compensation and treatment, by the time the 8th mustered in, all understood that black men were not going to enjoy equal treatment from the Union army, and if captured they were liable to face harsh treatment at the hands of their enemies.

What made these later waves of northern black men enlist? Although few personal papers have survived, there are ways to gain a sense of what spoke to these prospective recruits. By examining newspaper editorials, public speeches, and recruiting broadsides, the historian can piece together a portrait of the considerations that shaped decision-making among Pennsylvania's black men in the fall of 1863.

It would perhaps surprise many modern observers to learn that Civil War Philadelphia had a substantial middle-class black community, with a dense web of institutions and organizations. Black Methodists turned to Philadelphia's *Christian Recorder*, a weekly organ of the AME Church, for information and commentary on current events.[12] When the war first broke out, many northern blacks — including three companies of Philadelphians — jumped at the chance to offer their services, but the *Christian Recorder* repeatedly dissented from this martial spirit. "To offer ourselves for military service *now*, is to *abandon self-respect and invite insult*," the paper advised.[13] In those first months of the war, Frederick Douglass shared this skepticism. "Nothing short of an open recognition of the Negro's manhood his rights as such to have a country equally with others would induce me to join the army in any capacity," he told a friend.[14]

By February 1863 the terrain had shifted. Lincoln's Emancipation Proclamation had not only turned the Union army into an agent of liberation, but it had also opened the door to the extensive arming of black troops. On February 14, the *Christian Recorder* ran an editorial about "Colored Soldiers," asking "Will They Fight? Should They Fight?" In answer to the first question, the paper declared that anyone familiar with the history of black Americans should know that they had never "failed to show their courage when the hour and place has come." The second question was a bit more complicated. Before they enlist, the paper asserted, black men "should . . . know whether they are to have all the rights and privileges of other citizens in every state of the Union, and receive as much compensation for their services as any other soldier according to their rank in the army."[15] If the *Recorder* still had doubts, Douglass had already cast his lot with the Union cause, promising the government that "we are ready, and only ask to be called into this service." Before long, Douglass had signed on as a military recruiter for the 54th Massachusetts, calling on "Men of Color" to "fly to arms and smite with death the power that would bury the government and your liberty in the same helpless grave."[16]

Within a few months, black men had begun to demonstrate their valor on the battlefield, putting more pressure on the northern black leadership. In May 1863, the *Recorder* reprinted a series of resolutions passed by the AME Church during its annual conference in Philadelphia. Having witnessed the exploits of "those men of color, our brethren, acquaintances, and friends" on the battlefield, the conference formally resolved that "the great political interests of the colored people of these United States are at last thrown into the balances of military equity" and that "no pains be spared by us at home to advance the general interests of our soldiers in the field." The AME Church and the *Christian Recorder* were now squarely behind the black military effort.[17]

But although the door was now open to black troops, the Philadelphians' frustrations were not over. On June 17, 1863, in the midst of a local fervor over Robert E. Lee's invasion of Pennsylvania, a company of black Philadelphians offered their services for defense of the state. At first it seemed that the government had accepted this new step in an ongoing revolution: city military officials sent the black recruits on to Harrisburg. But that is as far as they got. The Union army promptly sent the volunteers home in disgrace, refusing their patriotic services while white Philadelphians failed to respond to the crisis.[18]

Meanwhile, Pennsylvania's white Unionists had come around to the idea that the North should recruit black troops. The following week, several hundred leading Philadelphians petitioned Secretary of War Edwin M. Stanton for authority to recruit three new black regiments. Stanton quickly granted permission, and the city's Supervisory Committee for Recruiting Colored Regiments swung into action, supported by the efforts of Maj. George L. Stearns, the state's new recruiting commissioner for U.S. Colored Troops. The proposed terms of enlistment underscored the fact that these new fighting men — like their black comrades already in the field — were not going to receive equal treatment. The Supervisory Committee could enlist three new regiments of three-year volunteers, but unlike white enlistees in 1863, these new men would not receive bounties, and whereas white infantry recruits could count on thirteen dollars a month, these men would get ten dollars a month, and up to three dollars of that could be paid in clothing. If the men of the 54th had reason to feel misled, these new Pennsylvania recruits would know precisely where they stood.[19]

As it happened, young Cincinnati journalist Whitelaw Reid was in Philadelphia when word of the new recruiting drive reached the city. Reid reminded his readers of Stearns's impressive credentials as an abolitionist. The Boston merchant had supported radicals in Kansas and helped fund John Brown's raid on Harpers Ferry. But Reid pointed out that the gentlemen behind this new initiative were cut from different political cloth. These men were "not Abolitionists" or "Free Soilers," and in fact they were "scarcely . . . Republicans" at all but rather "Union men" intent on "calling out a valuable element of their military strength, for relieving . . . the burdens of their white population." "What a change!" Reid remarked. "Scarcely six months ago, to advocate the arming of negroes was to horrify all the respectable conservatives in the Union party." But now abolition had become "an accepted fact" and the recruiting of black men "no longer a theory or an experiment" but a policy embraced by the conservative leadership, "in Philadelphia, at least."[20]

While Philadelphia's pragmatic white Unionists calculated that black soldiers could fill recruiting quotas while helping win the war, the city's black leadership saw the turn of events as an important challenge and opportunity. With the secretary of war's authorization in hand, more than fifty prominent African Americans gathered to draft and sign a grand proclamation, addressed to the North's "Men of Color!" "Now or Never!"

it declared, "This is our golden moment. The Government of the United States calls for every able-bodied colored man to enter the army for the three years' of service, and join in fighting the battles of liberty and Union. A new era is open to us," they effused. The committee reproduced the proclamation as a broadside to be distributed across the city, and as a spectacular eight-foot banner that hung outside the Supervisory Committee's Chestnut Street offices.

This extraordinary proclamation, whose signers included Thomas Dorsey, Octavius V. Catto, Frederick Douglass, and William Forten (the father of young diarist Charlotte Forten), merits some close examination. By this point in the war, northern citizens had grown accustomed to exuberant recruiting posters. Most in the genre combined patriotic and martial imagery with relatively few words, calling on young men to serve their country while sharing in the glory of war. By mid-1863 recruiting posters had already begun to include promises of considerable bounties and other financial inducements. Some sought to convince white men that voluntary enlistment on their own terms was preferable to conscription. But the men of the Supervisory Committee relied on extended rhetoric rather than simple patriotic imagery. The broadside included nearly 700 words of text.

Several themes ran through this fascinating proclamation, but one core message remained paramount. The fifty-five signers spoke directly to their target audience's sense of manhood. In fact, the word "manhood" appears six times in the text, and terms like "man," "men," "manly," and "freemen" appear another fourteen times. The message was clear. For generations black Americans had suffered the humiliations of slavery and abuse. "Our manhood has been denied, our citizenship blotted out, our souls seared and burned, our spirits cowed and crushed, and the hopes of the future of our race involved in doubts and darkness." Now the Civil War, and the U.S. government, had provided them with the opportunity simultaneously to strike a blow at a hated enemy and prove their manhood to a skeptical nation. In making the case, the authors played every card at their disposal to challenge the manhood of those young men who had not yet enlisted. A host of immigrant races had already proven their valor on the battlefield they noted. "If we are not lower in the scale of humanity than Englishmen, Irishmen, white Americans, and other races, we can show it now." And this was not merely a matter of black men in comparison to white men. Recently freed slaves, they noted, had already demonstrated their heroism on battlefields like Port Hudson and Milliken's Bend. "If they have proved themselves heroes, cannot we prove ourselves men? Are freemen less brave than slaves?"

Certainly wartime appeals to manhood and masculinity are hardly surprising. But traditionally — and particularly during the Civil War — that rhetoric was cast in the language of individualism. Military service presented the young man with the opportunity to demonstrate his personal honor, heroism, and fundamental manhood, to himself and his larger society. But in the "Men of Color!" broadside the manhood in question was collective. The words "our," "we," and "us" appear no less than fifty times in this proclamation. "Our manhood" is in question, and "we" must answer the call, they said. Either that, or admit that "freemen" are indeed "less brave than slaves" and "lower in the scale of humanity" than even Irishmen.

The signers understandably couched their argument in the most positive terms, stressing why young black men should cast their lot with the Union cause rather than contemplating the many arguments against participation in an army in which they would be treated like second-class citizens. But near the close they hinted that negative arguments were in the air. "Stop at no subterfuge," they warned. "Listen to nothing that shall deter you from rallying for the army."

Meanwhile, the Supervisory Committee reserved Philadelphia's National Hall for a grand recruiting rally on July 6, 1863. The mass meeting could hardly have come at a more dramatic moment. Three days earlier Robert E. Lee's Army of Northern Virginia suffered a disastrous loss at Gettysburg, and on July 4 Union commander Ulysses S. Grant captured the vital city of Vicksburg on the Mississippi River. Suddenly the war was going well for the Union, but none of these developments changed the status of black soldiers in the field or of black citizens at home. It would be up to the evening's three speakers to make the case to both the patriotic and the skeptical.

The first to ascend the platform was local congressman Judge William D. Kelley. An abolitionist and friend of the local black community, Kelley began his address by building upon the themes of manhood. "Are you content to spend your lives as boot-blacks, barbers, [and] waiters . . . when the profession of arms . . . invites you to acknowledged manhood, freedom and honor?" he asked. After two hundred years of oppression, the war had "opened the way for the Africo-American to prove his manhood to the world." But while the broadside spoke to a collective black male identity, Judge Kelley seemed to speak directly to individuals, challenging each man to grasp the moment and assert his own manhood and thus elevate his station in life. As if to reinforce that point, Kelley next turned his attention to the "old men," "mothers," and "girls" in the audience. Fathers should threaten to "disinherit and denounce" sons who "prove cowards"; mothers should demonstrate that they are ready to match white women in their sacrifices; and girls should make it clear that they would "rather marry the wooden leg and empty jacket sleeve of a war-torn hero" rather than a handsome coward.

Military service might promise the glories of manhood and future elevation, but what about the persistent realities of an unequal present? Here the congressmen made no grand promises, but instead he turned to the "white men and women" in the audience and called upon them to flood Congress with petitions "demanding" equal pay and pensions for these brave black soldiers. Meanwhile, they should ensure that black widows and orphans would be cared for if their menfolk fell in battle. Kelley's appeals were met with choruses of "Yes, we will" from his white listeners, effectively assuring the predominantly black audience that their claims would not be forgotten. He closed his remarks with a passionate declaration that "the negro is the 'coming man' for whom we have waited" and that the fate of the nation rested in his hands. The congressman took his seat to "Tremendous and long-continued cheering."

As the applause died down, the audience turned their attention to the next speaker, Anna Elizabeth Dickinson. Only twenty years old, the Philadelphia Quaker had already established an impressive reputation as a radical orator and patriot. The child of abolitionists, Dickinson had impeccable credentials as an advocate for black rights. Now she had a delicate rhetorical task: how to cajole African American men into uniform, knowing full well that she was asking them to accept a poor deal.[21]

Dickinson took Gettysburg as her starting point. No black troops had fought there, but she argued that Union fortunes had shifted because the nation had embraced emancipation and started arming black men. In the past, she noted, black civilians had been used to assist the nation's military causes, but only with "their brains contracted; their souls dwarfed; their manhood stunted." Now, finally, the people had declared that "we have wronged you enough" and the time had come to "stand aside and let you fight for your own manhood, your future, your race." Dickinson admitted that the nation needed the black soldier to win the war, but at the same time she could not ask them to step forward on those grounds alone. To do so, she said, would cause her to blush with shame. How could she answer the obvious question: If you need us, "'why don't you give us the same bounty, and the same pay as the rest?'" "I have no answer to that," she admitted, as the room erupted in cheers.

Instead of asking black men to fight for a white cause, Dickinson tried to argue that the war was indeed "a war of the races, of the ages." True, equal pay and bounties "are good: liberty is better," she declared. Unequal treatment is bad, "slavery is worse." Although her listeners might reasonably "hesitate because you have not all, [y]our brothers and sisters in the South cry out, 'Come to our help, we have nothing.'" In her rousing conclusion, Dickinson called on her audience to seize the opportunity and claim the gains dangled before them: "The black man will be a citizen, only by stamping his right to it in his blood. Now or never! You have not homes! — gain them, You have not liberty! — gain it. You have not a flag! — gain it. You have not a country! — be written down in history as the race who made one for themselves, and saved one for another." Once again, the published accounts reported that the speaker left the platform to "immense cheering."

The evening's final speaker was none other than Frederick Douglass, the eloquent ex-slave and frequent spokesman for the African American community. Douglass had long since thrown his energies into black enlistment, and in fact two of his sons served in the 54th Massachusetts. But it was one thing to tour the North encouraging young men who were predisposed to the fight, and quite another thing to make the case to the reticent and the skeptical. Although Kelley and Dickinson had strong credentials as allies to the African American community, they still spoke across a racial divide. How would Douglass cast his arguments?

Like Dickinson, Douglass opted to confront the elephant in the room: the unequal pay and bounties offered to black soldiers. He promised to be "plain and practical" in his remarks. There were, he reasoned, two views to take on the subject: the "narrow view" and the "broad view." The narrow view would emphasize the obvious fact that men who are all risking their lives should receive equal compensation and treatment, regardless of their race. Douglass readily acknowledged the justice in the argument. But the man who took the broad view would recognize that the wisest path to "manhood, equal rights and elevation, is that we enter this service." The act of fighting would be "ennobling" to the black race, and was thus worth the intermediate humiliations of salaries and bounties.

Stepping away from those narrow material concerns, Douglass asked his audience to consider the two sides that were "today face to face" in the bloody conflict. The question, he insisted, should be "which is for us, and which is against us?" Even if one could argue that the Federal government was not fully invested in making the war about slavery, Douglass pointed out that the Confederacy was dedicated to protecting and expanding slavery. Moreover, whereas the Union cause may have appeared indifferent to slavery two years earlier, Douglass pointed to ample evidence that the worm really had turned and the North was moving toward emancipation, citizenship, and racial justice. And in picking up the themes of the "Men of Color" broadside, Douglass announced, "The opportunity is given us to be men. . . . Once let the black man get upon his person the brass letters U.S.; let him get an eagle on his button, and a musket on his shoulder, and bullets in his pocket, and there is no power on the earth or under the earth which may deny that he has earned the right of citizenship in the United States."

Finally, in echoing Dickinson's arguments, Douglass told his listeners that northern whites would likely win the war and abolish slavery without their help. If they wanted future equality and citizenship, "this is no time for hesitation." Indeed, black men received lower wages, had been denied black commissioned officers, and had previously been spurned by Pennsylvania's recruiting officers. But if they hoped for a happier future, they must set aside those past grievances and have faith in a changed future. "Young men of Philadelphia," he declared, "you are without excuse. The hour has arrived, and your place is in the Union army. . . . In your hands that musket means liberty."[22]

At first the combination of patriotic editorials, enthusiastic broadsides, and passionate rhetoric struck a responsive chord among eastern Pennsylvania's African Americans. Many of those who had been spurned in mid-June now stepped forward to join the new regiments, and hundreds of other young men followed suit. By the end of July these recruits had filled the first of the three proposed regiments, and in August the 3rd USCT left Camp William Penn for South Carolina, where they would join the 54th Massachusetts in the assault on Fort Wagner. Two months later the 6th USCT headed south from Philadelphia. But local recruiters worried that the flow of African American volunteers had slowed to a trickle. In September, African American Jacob A. White reported that "recruiting is dull at present." The following month barely half a company of new recruits reported to Camp William Penn. In fact, the city finally agreed in mid-December—not long after the 8th mustered in—to offer $250 bounties to black volunteers, thus following a strategy already widespread in white recruiting.[23]

Even though the men of the 8th USCT shared many fundamental characteristics and concerns in common with their comrades in the 54th Massachusetts and even the 1st North Carolina, the timing of their recruitment and the arguments used to cajole them into uniform underscore fundamental differences. Those men who agreed to enlist at the end of 1863 weighed the arguments that their service would further the interests of black Americans and the multiple challenges to their collective manhood against nagging doubts that accompanied realities in a racially segregated northern society and continuing reports of unequal treatment experienced by their brothers in arms. In fact, shortly after speaking in Philadelphia, a frustrated Douglass temporarily abandoned his recruiting efforts because of the combined weight of discriminatory Union practices and Confederate threats to execute black prisoners.[24]

What made these men hang back in the recruiting frenzy of June and early July, but then step forward in November or December? No doubt these volunteers, like white recruits, responded to a host of entirely personal considerations. Perhaps family members heeded the advice of Judge Kelley and exerted pressure on individual young men. Or, conversely, maybe some had to convince their loved ones that enlistment was the right path or at least the time was right. Still, it seems reasonable to conclude that these men were collectively more reticent about the cause — or the role of black men in that fight — than those Philadelphians who rushed to join the 54th, or even the men who jumped at the chance to join the 3rd USCT several months earlier. If the various recruiters knew their intended audience, which seems likely, it follows that the men who joined the 8th were a particularly contemplative lot. Prior appeals to national patriotism or vengeance against the slaveholding aristocracy had failed to reach them; the martial enthusiasm of blue uniforms and brass bands had not found its mark. Until the Supervisory Committee began offering bounties, the practical arguments for enlisting were not persuasive, or at least no more so than they had been months earlier. The arguments that spoke to those men who enlisted in late 1863 called for a subtle weighing of variables and considerations. They should relent and sign up *despite* all the good reasons not to because in the long run their sacrifice would yield important gains for black Americans. Something in that message struck a nerve, tilting the balance in favor of marching off to war. And so they found themselves wearing the same uniform as the veterans of the 54th Massachusetts and the freedmen of the 1st North Carolina.

The 8th left Camp William Penn for Hilton Head, South Carolina, on January 16, 1864. In South Carolina they worked on entrenchments and other fortifications, sometimes alongside the 54th. The 54th's Cpl. James Henry Gooding was impressed with the raw newcomers. "Some say that the 54th has a rival," he reported to the readers of the New Bedford *Mercury*, "the 8th U.S. regiment is indeed a splendid organization, and I may add that no regiment in the department can boast a more healthy-looking, martial bearing body of men."[25] Before long both regiments were ordered farther south to Florida, where they would join in the occupation of Jacksonville.[26] On February 20, they found themselves marching west from Jacksonville toward Lake City as part of General Seymour's excursion across northern Florida. With the 54th and 1st bringing up the rear under Colonel Montgomery, the untested 8th had the honor of being the first black regiment in the Union column. Thus when the 7th Connecticut faltered that afternoon, Seymour turned to the green Pennsylvanians. It was hardly an ideal opportunity to learn the art of war. When the 8th rushed forward, many still wore their knapsacks and half carried unloaded weapons; the regiment's first sergeants had no opportunity to discard their sergeant's sashes, making them inviting targets for enemy rifles. If that was not hard enough, shortly after the 8th arrived on the scene, the 7th New Hampshire to their right dissolved in a morass of confused orders, hostile enemy fire, and sheer panic.[27]

Contemporary accounts from the battlefield tell a horrific tale. Lt. Oliver Willcox Norton reported that the 8th successfully "formed a line under the most destructive fire I ever knew." Regimental surgeon Dr. Alex P. Heichold noted that they "wavered at first, but soon recovered themselves, and then commenced the struggle for life and death." Both white observers credited the 8th with almost astonishing bravery for such untried men. Dr. Heichold pointed out that the regiment had "but little practice in loading and firing" and few had ever heard a cannon's roar. As Norton put it, they "could stand and be killed" but they had little chance of taking any toll on the enemy. When the word finally came to withdraw, their inexperience became even more costly, as the retreating regiment gathered in frightened clumps, becoming the perfect target for deadly enemy fire. Even as casualties mounted and Colonel Fribley fell mortally wounded, most of the men of the 8th responded bravely—although largely ineffectually—throughout the crisis. As one Confederate officer put it, "they stood killing d——d well, but they didn't hurt us much."[28]

When the 54th and the 1st appeared on the scene at the double-quick, the narrative changed dramatically. Capt. Luis F. Emilio recalled that his comrades in the 54th rushed into the fray with the ironic battle cry, "Three cheers for Massachusetts and seven dollars a month!" The veterans of Fort Wagner formed a battle line with dispatch and opened fire, effectively

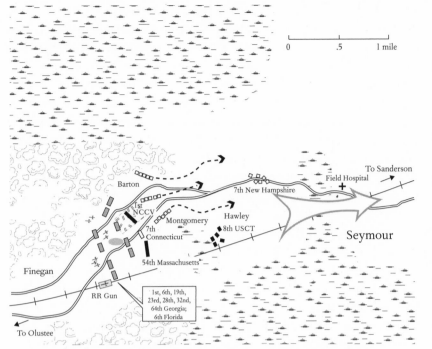

Battle of Olustee, February 20, 1864. From Richard M. Reid's *Freedom for Themselves: North Carolina's Black Soldiers in the Civil War Era.*

saving the day for the disorganized Union forces. A correspondent to the *Boston Journal* reported that they "fought like tigers"; the 54th's Capt. James W. Grace agreed that "no regiment fought like it." Meanwhile, according to a *Philadelphia Press* account, the 1st North Carolina arrived "with a yell on the double-quick," cheered on by their white comrades in the 47th New York Infantry. The 1st's Capt. J. S. Croft, who took over for the fallen Colonel Reed, was proud to recall that his men earned "the warmest praises" from all observers. A variety of contemporary accounts shared this assessment.[29] In his account of his failure, General Seymour acknowledged that "the colored troops behaved credibly—the Fifty-fourth Massachusetts and First North Carolina like veterans," in stark contrast to several white regiments, most notably the 7th New Hampshire.[30]

Seymour's comments are telling, both in his praise of his black troops and in the distinctions that he drew amongst his men. The 8th, 54th, and 1st all behaved bravely, no doubt demonstrating their manhood to all who cared to contemplate the issue. The real differences on the battlefield, and in the way the white observers commented on the scene, had little to do with racial politics. True, the men from Massachusetts adopted a battle cry that pointedly reminded their white comrades that while they were good enough to die for the cause, they were apparently not good enough to be paid the same as the men they were saving. But the irony of their timely appearance and heroic performance was more complex than that. On this battlefield, with its motley assortment of green troops, draftees, and bounty men, the 54th and the 1st behaved "like veterans" because that is precisely what they were. In that moment the Union soldiers from New York, New Hampshire, and Connecticut were probably less concerned with the niceties of racial prejudice and more focused on the fact that the men in the blue uniforms arriving from their rear seemed to know precisely what they were doing. If they were aware that one USCT regiment was composed of the sons of some of northern black America's leading families, whereas the other black regiment was made up of recently freed slaves, those hugely significant sociopolitical realities were presumably lost in the confusion. Meanwhile, the intrepid men of the 8th USCT surely demonstrated that "free men" were every bit as brave as "slaves," but they also illustrated that on the battlefield other differences took a back seat to experience. They had mastered the art of dying well, but little else.

If in the hail of bullets Union soldiers really lost track of racial difference, that color-blind moment would not last long. The men from Colonel Montgomery's brigade helped make the difference between a disastrous rout and an orderly retreat, but Olustee was still a Union defeat. As they fled from the scene, Seymour's men had to confront a new set of grim realities. The Confederacy had threatened to enslave or execute captured USCT troops and their white officers, and Union soldiers were well aware of rumored battlefield atrocities where Rebels had killed black troops on the battlefield rather than taking them as prisoners. With the Union army in retreat, various black soldiers and their white comrades stepped forward to keep the wounded black troops from Confederate hands. Dr. Heichold insisted that wounded USCT troops be given priority in the ambulances, reasoning that white soldiers would fare better at the hands of Confederate troops. Meanwhile, a small detail of men from the 54th who had been held in reserve during the battle stepped forward to cover the retreat. When the men of the 54th discovered several boxcars of wounded left behind in Baldwin — about halfway between Olustee and Jacksonville — they secured ropes to cars and bodily dragged their fallen comrades to safety.

Despite these efforts, numerous postbattle accounts — written by both Union and Confederate soldiers — reported the battlefield execution of wounded USCT soldiers. By one estimate, as many as fifty men were killed after the fighting stopped. Seven months earlier Frederick Douglass had urged Philadelphia's young men that "in your hands that musket means liberty." After the battle, when wounded white soldiers had generally abandoned their weapons, black men clung to their rifles even when they could no longer march. As a sergeant major in the 8th observed, wounded men came "into camp with their arms and equipments on, so great was their endurance and so determined were they to defend themselves till death." On more than one occasion, wounded black men died rather than accept capture and execution.[31]

The USCT regiments at Olustee suffered heavy casualties. The two veteran regiments survived with the least damage. The 54th lost 13 men killed, 62 men and 3 officers wounded, and 8 men missing. The 1st lost 2 officers and 20 men killed, 8 officers and 123 men wounded, and 77 men missing. The untested 8th fared the worst, with 48 men and Colonel Fribley killed, 8 officers and 180 men wounded, and 1 officer and 72 men reported missing.[32]

In 1863 the men of the 8th had hesitated to enlist when their brothers in the North and South had jumped at the chance. By wavering they had illustrated the fundamental concerns that divided northern blacks. By finally enlisting before bounties had been added to the mix, they demonstrated that their decisions were probably not dictated by pragmatic financial concerns. It was as if they had collectively subscribed to the arguments articulated by the *Christian Recorder* the previous February. Of course, the black man would fight if circumstances warranted it, but reasonable men could — and did — disagree about whether he should fight.[33] Finally, in February 1864 they demonstrated that their reticence had not been from a lack of manhood or courage. They fought bravely, even though they had little sense of the art of war. In both their bravery and their ineffectiveness, the 8th USCT illustrated a fundamental point about the differences among Civil War soldiers. Whatever distinctive traits divided one regiment from another in the paths they took to war, once the shooting started, experience mattered more than race, or geography, or ideology.

That leads to one final irony. Although they did not enlist until months after the battle of Gettysburg and saw no action until February 1864, the 8th participated in considerable combat over the next fourteen months. They fought at Fair Oaks, the Bermuda Hundred, Chaffin's Farm, and Hatcher's Run, and saw heavy duty throughout the siege of Petersburg, finally joining in the chase of the Army of Northern Virginia to Appomattox Court House in April 1865. By the end of the war, the regiment had lost 4 officers and 247 men to mortal wounds and disease, with another 245 men wounded and 72 captured or missing. After the war, the 8th was honored as one of the celebrated "Three Hundred Fighting Regiments" of the Civil War.[34]

NOTES

1. On the campaign and battle see George F. Baltzell, "The Battle of Olustee (Ocean Pond), Florida," *Florida Historical Quarterly* 9 (April 1931): 199–223; Arthur Bergeron, "The Battle of Olustee," in *Black Soldiers in Blue: African American Troops in the Civil War Era*, ed. John David Smith (Chapel Hill: University of North Carolina Press, 2002), 136–49; Noah Andre Trudeau, *Like Men of War: Black Troops in the Civil War, 1862–1865* (Boston: Little, Brown, 1998), 129–55; Robert P. Broadwater, *The Battle of Olustee, 1864: The Final Union Attempt to Seize Florida* (Jefferson, N.C.: McFarland, 2006); Stephen E. Woodworth and Kenneth J. Winkle, eds., *Oxford Atlas of the Civil War* (New York: Oxford University Press, 2004), 218–20; Luis F. Emilio, *A Brave Black Regiment: The History of the 54th Massachusetts, 1863–1865* (1894; reprint, Cambridge, Mass.: Da Capo, 1995), 148–85; and *Christian Recorder*, March 12, April 2, 9, 1864. For a superb website on the battle of Olustee, see ⟨http://extlab1.entnem.ufl.edu/Olustee/⟩.

2. For the leading treatments of African American soldiers in the Civil War, see Benjamin Quarles, *The Negro in the Civil War* (1953; reprint, New York: Da Capo, 1979); Dudley Taylor Cornish, *The Sable Arm: Black Troops in the Union Army, 1861–1865* (1956; reprint, Lawrence: University Press of Kansas, 1987); James M. McPherson, *The Negro's Civil War* (1965; reprint, New York: Vintage, 2003); Joseph T. Glatthaar, *Forged in Battle: The Civil War Alliance of Black Soldiers and White Officers* (New York: Free Press, 1990); Ira Berlin, "The Black Military Experience, 1861–1867," in Ira Berlin, Barbara J. Fields, Steven F. Miller, Joseph P. Reidy, and Leslie S. Rowland, *Slaves No More: Three Essays on Emancipation and the Civil War* (New York: Cambridge University Press, 1992); Smith, ed., *Black Soldiers in Blue*; and Trudeau, *Like Men of War*. In his prize-winning study of the motivations of Civil War soldiers, James M. McPherson read "at least 25,000" soldiers' letters and 249 diaries. McPherson reports that black men made up only 1 percent of his sample of Union soldiers. See McPherson, *For Cause and Comrades: Why Men Fought in the Civil War* (New York: Oxford University Press, 1997), pp. viii–ix, 11–12. For a recent treatment of Union soldiers from North Carolina, including the 1st North Carolina Colored Infantry (35th USCT), see Richard M. Reid, *Freedom for Themselves: North Carolina's Black Soldier in the Civil War Era* (Chapel Hill: University of North Carolina Press, 2008).

3. On the 54th, see Emilio, *Brave Black Regiment*, and Peter Burchard, *One Gallant Rush: Robert Gould Shaw and His Brave Black Regiment* (New York: St. Martin's Press, 1965). On *Glory*, see Martin H. Blatt, "Glory: Hollywood History, Popular Culture, and the Fifty-Fourth Massachusetts Regiment," in *Hope and Glory: Essays on the Legacy of the Fifty-Fourth Massachusetts Regiment*, ed. Martin H. Blatt, Thomas J. Brown, and Donald Yacovone (Amherst: University of Massachusetts Press, 2001), 215–35.

4. For a discussion of the actual episode, see Trudeau, *Like Men of War*, 73.

5. On the 1st North Carolina, see ibid., 114.

6. Joseph T. Glatthaar, "Black Glory: The African-American Role in Union Victory," in *Why the Confederacy Lost*, ed. Gabor S. Boritt (New York: Oxford University Press, 1992), 133–62.

7. Edwin S. Redkey, "Brave Black Volunteers: A Profile of the Fifty-Fourth Massachusetts Regiment," in Blatt, Brown, and Yacovone, eds., *Hope and Glory*, 22–23.

8. See McPherson, *For Cause and Comrades*.

9. For discussions of these divergent attitudes toward black recruitment, see David W. Blight, *Frederick Douglass' Civil War: Keeping Faith in Jubilee* (Baton Rouge: Louisiana State University Press, 1989), 148–74; James M. McPherson, *The Struggle for Equality: Abolitionists and the Negro in the Civil War and Reconstruction* (Princeton, N.J.: Princeton University Press, 1964), 202–4; McPherson, *Negro's Civil War*, 29–35, 175–85.

10. Frank H. Taylor, *Philadelphia in the Civil War, 1861–1865* (Philadelphia: The City, 1913), 187.

11. *Christian Recorder*, December 26, 1863; Philip A. Foner, "The Battle to End Discrimination Against Negroes on Philadelphia's Streetcars: (Part I) Background and Beginning of the Battle," *Pennsylvania History* (September 1973): 261–90.

12. McPherson, *Negro's Civil War*, 51.

13. *Christian Recorder*, April 27, 1861; J. Matthew Gallman, *Mastering Wartime: A Social History of Philadelphia During the Civil War* (New York: Cambridge University Press, 1990), 45.

14. Blight, *Frederick Douglass' Civil War*, 99. Blight cites Douglass to Samuel J. May, August 30, 1861, in Philip S. Foner, ed., *The Life and Writings of Frederick Douglass*, 5 vols. (New York: International Publishers, 1950), 3:158–59.

15. *Christian Recorder*, February 14, 1863.

16. Frederick Douglass, "Address Delivered in New York," February 6, 1863, in Frederick Douglass, *The Frederick Douglass Papers*, ed. John W. Blassingame, Series One, 5 vols. (New Haven, Conn.: Yale University Press, 1985), 3:569; Blight, *Frederick Douglass' Civil War*, 159.

17. *Christian Recorder*, May 23, 1863.

18. Taylor, *Philadelphia in the Civil War*, 188; Gallman, *Mastering Wartime*, 46–47.

19. *Address of the Hon. W. D. Kelley, Miss Anna E. Dickinson, and Mr. Frederick Douglass, at a Mass Meeting, Held at National Hall, Philadelphia, July 6, 1863, for the Promotion of Colored Enlistments* (Philadelphia: n.p., 1863), 1, 8, African American Pamphlet Collection, Library of Congress, Washington; Gallman, *Mastering Wartime*, 47.

20. *Cincinnati Gazette*, June [?], 1863, miscellaneous scrapbook, Anna Elizabeth Dickinson Papers, Library of Congress, Washington. This dispatch from "Agate" (Whitelaw Reid) is dated June 22, 1863.

21. On Dickinson's life, see J. Matthew Gallman, *America's Joan of Arc: The Life of Anna Elizabeth Dickinson* (New York: Oxford University Press, 2006).

22. *Address of the Hon. W. D. Kelley, Miss Anna E. Dickinson, and Mr. Frederick Douglass*, 2–7.

23. By the end of the war, eleven regiments of African American soldiers had been trained at Camp William Penn. See Taylor, *Philadelphia in the Civil War*, 189–90; Jeffry D. Wert, "Camp William Penn and the Black Soldier," *Pennsylvania History* 46 (October 1979): 335–46; Frederick M. Binder, "Pennsylvania Negro Regiments in the Civil War,"

Journal of Negro History 37 (1952): 383–417; Gallman, *Mastering Wartime*, 47–49; Jacob A. White to Joseph C. Bustill, September 8, 1863, *Journal of Negro History* 11 (January 1926): 85; and *Christian Recorder*, August 1, 1863.

24. Blight, *Frederick Douglass' Civil War*, 167.

25. Virginia M. Adams, ed., *On the Altar of Freedom: A Black Soldier's Civil War Letters from the Front* (Amherst: University of Massachusetts Press, 1991), 109–10.

26. For a firsthand account by a musician with the 8th USCT, see William P. Woodlin diary, The Gilder Lehrman Institute of American History, New York City.

27. Broadwater, *Battle of Olustee*, 7–33; Taylor, *Philadelphia in the Civil War*, 191; Trudeau, *Like Men of War*, 137–42; Edwin S. Redkey, ed., *A Grand Army of Black Men* (New York: Cambridge University Press, 1992), 41; *Christian Recorder*, April 16, 1864.

28. Trudeau, *Like Men of War*, 143; Bergeron, "Battle of Olustee," 146; Glatthaar, *Forged in Battle*, 145; *Christian Recorder*, March 12, 1864. Praise for the 8th USCT was not universal. Some men from the 3rd Rhode Island Artillery blamed the 8th for failing to support their battery. See Broadwater, *Battle of Olustee*, 93–96.

29. Trudeau, *Like Men of War*, 145–47; Adams, ed., *On the Altar of Freedom*, 114; Broadwater, *Battle of Olustee*, 123, 127; Emilio, *Brave Black Regiment*, 163.

30. Cornish, *Sable Arm*, 268–69.

31. Trudeau, *Like Men of War*, 150–52; Redkey, ed., *Grand Army of Black Men*, 42; *Christian Recorder*, April 9, 16, 1864. Arthur Bergeron notes that while there were a few atrocities, "no wholesale massacre of the blacks occurred" (Bergeron, "Battle of Olustee," 144). Robert Broadwater accepts the estimate that roughly fifty wounded black soldiers were executed after nightfall. See Broadwater, *Battle of Olustee*, 141–43.

32. Baltzell, "Battle of Olustee (Ocean Pond), Florida."

33. *Christian Recorder*, February 14, 1863.

34. Taylor, *Philadelphia in the Civil War*, 191.

With Malice toward Both

Abraham Lincoln and Jefferson Davis in Caricature

⊰ HAROLD HOLZER ⊱

In the fall of 1856, the British news weekly *London Punch* published an extraordinary caricature commenting rather presciently, it turned out, on American politics. It depicted supposedly prototypical northern and southern men fighting violently for dominance. "North" was shown holding "South" in a chokehold, the "South" brandishing a dagger and a cocked pistol, with a whip menacingly tucked into his belt for good measure, probably to remind viewers of the latent weapon of slave labor. There is no doubt about the meaning of this image. It suggested that North and South were about to destroy each other, or die trying.

The year 1856 was the height of fame for Chang and Eng, the "original" Siamese twins who were connected by a thick flap of tissue at their midsections, so it is no surprise that the trend-conscious *Punch* artist showed his two symbolic characters similarly bound to each other—and thereby to the Union—through just such a lifeline. It was a clever artistic device. But what makes this caricature extraordinary is the physical appearance of the two symbolic figures who represent their respective regions. The year of its publication was 1856. Abraham Lincoln was then still a regional, not a national, celebrity. He had been photographed only once in his life, and was certainly unknown to London's artists. Jefferson Davis was arguably more famous—he was then serving as secretary of war in the cabinet of President Franklin Pierce—but he was hardly yet the living embodiment of Dixie. Yet the "twins" in this cartoon bear an uncanny resemblance not so much to each other but to the two political leaders who would later come—in the realms of political life and political caricature alike—to personify their respective sections of the country. Anyone looking at this cartoon five years after its publication would have sworn that the two protagonists battling each other in *Punch* in 1856 were none other than Jefferson Davis and Abraham Lincoln.

Printmaker unknown, *The American Twins, or North and South.*
Woodcut engraving, published in *London Punch*,
September 27, 1856. Author's collection.

In some ways, Lincoln and Davis actually did look rather alike. Both
Kentucky-born presidents had thin physiques and high cheekbones, and
before long, both wore beards as well: Lincoln, a full set of luxuriant whiskers that he gradually trimmed down during his White House years to
little more than a goatee; and Davis, conversely, a goatee that he later
allowed to blossom into full whiskers. Theirs would not be a Jefferson-
Adams, or Lincoln-Douglas battle of caricatured physical opposites. But
unlike Davis, Lincoln was not a handsome man, and in their early wartime
photographs one British observer saw worlds of difference. "Without relying too much on physiognomy," former and future member of Parliament
Alexander J. Beresford-Hope wrote with distaste, "I appeal to the *cartes de
visite* of both Lincoln and Davis, and I think all who see them will agree
that Jefferson Davis beards out one's idea of what an able administrator

and a calm statesman should look like better than Abraham Lincoln, great as he may be as rail-splitter, bargee, and country attorney."[1]

Whatever their physical shortcomings, few leaders ever gave cartoonists greater gifts with which to work. Davis, prim, aristocratic, tight-lipped, and sour, almost cried out to be caricatured. Lincoln, a giant scarecrow in a swallow-tail coat, hair usually wildly unkempt—resembling "the offspring of a happy marriage between a derrick and a windmill," in the words of one satirical campaign biography from 1864[2]—seemed almost born for caricature, although his famous sense of humor probably left many people with the impression that he was on to the joke himself and laughed at the results as hard as anyone. Looks notwithstanding, as several 1860 campaign cartoons implicitly suggested in humorously hyperbolized portraits of a long-limbed Republican galloping to victory in that year's "political race," Lincoln had staying power: he literally had "legs," both as a politician and the subject of caricature.

And while Jefferson Davis would soon appear alongside—and in bareknuckles opposition to—Lincoln in political cartoons, it was the less-famous Lincoln who was introduced to the picture-hungry public first, in abundantly produced, widely circulated pictorial lampoons that flooded the country that fall. Candidate Lincoln did no public campaigning, but prints acted as ubiquitous surrogates, effectively introducing, and often exaggerating, both his attributes and liabilities. Davis did not campaign either. But that was because the new Confederate States of America held no national election that year. Jefferson Davis was selected at a convention, not by a vote of the people. Thus, at first he inspired nothing like the thick trail of cartoons that ushered candidate Lincoln into prominence. Caricatures were products of the same roiling political culture that also inspired torchlight parades, noisy rallies and widely attended speeches, and as much as 80 percent turnout of eligible white male voters—many of whom bought cartoons that celebrated their favorites and assailed their rivals. Those conditions never existed in the Confederacy.

With his giant frame and backwoods origins—which inspired cartoonists to portray him in homespun clothes—Lincoln could seem bigger than his rivals, sometimes bigger than life. His roots in manual labor also provided cartoonists an irresistible idea for a standard prop: the signature tool of his fabled frontier trade. For years, the onetime rail-splitter would be shown in cartoons wielding a log rail to suppress his rivals, carrying the biggest bat, for example, in a symbolic baseball game.[3]

But rail-splitter symbolism could be used against him, too, to illustrate Democratic charges that the Republicans of 1860 frustratingly emphasized

Lincoln's log-cabin origins in order to divert public debate from contentious issues like slavery. In other words, Republicans "used" the rail, as at least one cartoon charged, to keep abolitionists like Charles Sumner from letting the proverbial cat (in this case a not-so-subtle black cat representing "the spirit of discord") "out of the bag."[4]

"Scat," an alarmed *New York Times* editor Henry J. Raymond shouts in an extended voice box caption typical of these lampoons, "or our fat will all be in the fire." Lincoln, who declares that he thought the cat was "safely bagged at Chicago," site of the nominating convention, now worries there will be "old scratch to pay, unless I can drive her back again with my rail." In a similar vein, the cartoon *The Great Exhibition of 1860* reduced him to the role of compliant organ grinder's monkey astride a rail hobbyhorse. In this cartoon the symbol was now turned against Lincoln to ridicule him: a lock secured to his mouth to prevent him from straying from Horace Greeley's party line of silence, with William Seward hovering in the background unable to restrain the squirming, "irrepressible" infant symbolizing the concealed slavery question. Seward, the author of the controversial "irrepressible conflict" doctrine so alarming to the slaveholding South, and Greeley, the *New York Tribune* editor who championed the Republicans, were depicted often in 1860 campaign cartoons as threatening surrogates who would surely ascend to power in a Lincoln administration.

As *The Rail Candidate* admitted in yet another print, the rail prop eventually became the "hardest stick I ever straddled"—implying he was equally complicit in his party's disingenuous campaign of diversion. The August 1860 *Comic Monthly* print *The Rail Ould Western Gentleman* reduced him to a scarecrow, his frame comprised entirely of crude log rails. Visible disturbingly nearby lurk bombs representing the planks of the Republican Party platform, about to detonate the rails piled on his flatboat. Here was yet another denunciatory reminder that perpetuating an admiring emphasis on Lincoln's hardscrabble youth could not much longer keep explosive issues out of the presidential campaign.

Frequently present—barely beneath the surface—in many of these early cartoons was the incendiary issue of race. Just as Chang and Eng had achieved earlier fame as sideshow curiosities in the 1850s, the new decade saw showman P. T. Barnum similarly exploit a childlike African as a so-called "man monkey" he named "the What Is It?" and displayed at his famous museum, promoting him, though half human and half brute, as "playful as a kitten and every way pleasing interesting *and* amusing."[5] Evidence that the milieu of the political cartoon was not much different from that of the sideshow came when Currier and Ives ingeniously placed the

Barnum sideshow attraction beside Lincoln for a crude anti-Republican campaign print. Delighted by his presence, the candidate blithely declares that he feels "fortunate . . . that this intellectual and noble creature should have been discovered just at this time, to prove to the world the superiority of the Colored over the Anglo-Saxon race," adding: "He will be a worthy successor to carry out the policy which I shall inaugurate." It was inevitable that the most vitriolic 1860 cartoons suggested that Lincoln was using his frontiersman persona to mask his plan to elevate African Americans to equal status. Hiding a "nigger" in a woodpile of his own making, in a particularly racist example of this mean-spirited cartoon genre, he declares, "Little did I think when I split these rails that they would be the means of elevating me to my present position."

It is no wonder that Frederick Douglass soon went on record complaining about the campaign's many ugly examples of "cowardly disclaimers and miserable concessions to popular prejudice against the colored people."[6] Make no mistake: these cartoons were no laughing matter. They were designed to incite genuine fear. But anti-Lincoln campaign cartoons were *not* created by Lincoln's enemies. They were churned out by the commercially motivated publishing industry itself, feeding a seemingly insatiable appetite for caricature that was as old as the Republic itself, and growing exponentially as new technologies made possible their quick publication and widespread distribution.

In assessing these political relics, it is important always to keep in mind precisely what they meant and did not mean in their own time: exactly where they appeared, who purchased them, and how they were used. The answer to the last question is: we do not fully know. What we do know is that there were two types of political caricature in mid-nineteenth-century America: one might call them bound and unbound. The bound variety ran in illustrated periodicals—like the *London Punch, Harper's Weekly*, and *Frank Leslie's Illustrated Newspaper*—and in more obscure titles like *Phunny Phellow Comic Monthly* and the long-forgotten New York paper *Momus*, named for the Greek god of mockery and censure.[7] These cartoons were plentiful, timely, and impermanent. They were made to exist for a week or at most a month, only until the next issue rolled off the press. They were ephemeral and disposable.

Not so the unbound variety, the separate-sheet prints that proliferated in 1860 and beyond. These were lithographed display items, meant to last—not forever perhaps—but, printed on stiff paper, they were certainly more durable than the work that appeared on brittle newsprint. They were created by well-established picture publishers like Currier and Ives of New

York, the most prolific of them all. But more so than newspaper cartoons, which after all were meant for the family homes of their subscribers, they featured vulgar and ribald imagery: characters who stomped on such sacred symbols as the American flag, thumbed their noses at each other, drank whiskey, fought with their fists, and sometimes dressed as women or concealed minstrelish African Americans. They fit perfectly into the brawling world of politics, but they were certainly not meant for the home.

Their proliferation, however, did not mean that their publication was part of an organized campaign by either or both parties. In fact, throughout the campaign Currier and Ives issued vitriolic pictorial attacks not only on Lincoln but also on his opponents,[8] and leavened their catalog by offering flattering portraiture of candidates Douglas and Lincoln as well.[9] In perhaps the most striking example of their nonpartisan publishing policy, Currier and Ives published two contradictory rail-splitter cartoons that year. One showed Lincoln, clad in a Wide-Awake outfit, riding his rail triumphantly to the White House, the embodiment of the American dream — the living personification of the idea, as Lincoln himself would put it a few months later, "that *all* should have an equal chance" in a country dedicated to advancing "the condition of the honest, struggling, laboring man."[10] Yet with equal conviction, Currier and Ives presented him in an altogether different version of the scene riding that same rail to the "Lunatic Asylum," abetted by radical abolitionists, suffragettes, criminals, Mormon free-love advocates (one of whom confesses she regards Lincoln with a "passionate attraction"),[11] socialists, pickpockets, idlers, and of course crudely drawn African Americans. Republicans could choose one print, and Democrats the other.

As such cartoons demonstrate, Lincoln was never the cartoon publisher's exclusive butt of ridicule. Lampoons of the day more accurately reflect how much the nineteenth-century American public liked its politics laced with humor. Pictorial humor was part of the political culture, and had proliferated at least since 1804, when a cartoonist named James Akin showed Thomas Jefferson as a prairie dog vomiting gold coins to finance the secret purchase of West Florida.[12] In the decades that followed, printmakers did not choose favorites: they provided caricature for all tastes, beliefs, and prejudices, as long as there were customers to buy them. Their motive was profit, not propaganda. And by functioning as equal-opportunity abusers, it is possible that they reflected the public debate more than they influenced it. Lithographed cartoons, more so than woodcut newspaper caricatures, were designed to appeal to unwavering partisans of one candidate or the other, not necessarily to make new converts.

For a long time, historians had difficulty explaining how customers originally used these separate sheet cartoons. Nineteenth-century Americans left few clues about their popularity, except by preserving many copies. One priceless glimpse of their impact was discovered in a British newspaperman's account of an autumn 1860 visit to New York, which he found "seething with excitement," fueled in part by political images. "[A]ll the way up Broadway," he reported, "the windows of the palatial shops" are "full of election caricatures. Bookstalls in the railroad stations," he reported, "teaze me with portraits of 'the railsplitter.'" At "local printshops," the reporter saw cartoons of "a gaunt Abe Lincoln trying to ford the Potomac" in one window, and "Douglas being flogged by his mother for associating with the naughty 'Nebraska Bill'" in the other. Here, too, was "Abe Lincoln spouting from a platform of rails, under which grins a half-concealed nigger."[13] In Boston, similarly, newspapers would later notice "satanic" and "malicious" political cartoons that similarly "attracted crowds at the shop windows" during high political season. Everywhere, the reporter concluded, "advertisements meet your eye of this inflammatory kind."[14]

But shop windows were only points of sale. Cartoons did not merely decorate stores; they were also purchased in bulk for distribution by or display in political clubs. They were slapped up in taverns[15] and pasted mischievously to publicly visible walls and fences (modern political operatives call this practice "wildposting" or "sniping," and it is still in use, though restricted by many municipal codes). Popular prints were meant "for solace, for ornament, [and] for parade," in the revealing words of one period auctioneer.[16] Of course, bawdy cartoons were not meant to ornament homes; they were precisely the kind of pictures that could be toted in raucous political parades typical of the period, as historian Mark E. Neely Jr. has discovered. They were popular without ever being quite respectable. "Wretched in design, scandalous in character and offensive of good taste and correct sentiment" according to one Philadelphia newspaper, ". . . it is surprising that public decency does not at once set the seal of condemnation on them."[17] The public never did, though the political cartoons of 1860, designed to earn money for nonpartisan publishers but capable of exacerbating partisan intransigence, did little to soften the positions that led to Lincoln's sectional victory that election day. Nor did they ameliorate the secession crisis that followed, which inspired the first prints of Jefferson Davis. Not yet a national figure, Davis was seen in one post-election Currier and Ives print as but one southern United States senator unwilling to compromise to save the "dis-United States."

And—to use Lincoln's phrase—"the war came."[18] At first, with the market sated with Lincoln caricature, printmakers looked for inspiration to the military, which, like politics, was a man's world that tolerated taste-

lessness. So not surprisingly, one of Jefferson Davis's earliest appearances in a Civil War–era cartoon came in Currier and Ives' *The Old General Ready for a Movement*, showing Union commander Winfield Scott, looking younger and more formidable than the very old general he had actually become, squatting over a foxhole latrine and waiting for Jeff Davis to flee his hiding place and into his noose.[19] In truth, Davis and his Confederacy would prove much harder to snare than the general, and Lincoln, first believed.

Unlike his Union counterpart, Davis came to office armed with a military reputation left over from the Mexican War, lending credibility to stories—exaggerated as they turned out to be—that in July 1861 he appeared on the Bull Run battlefield in uniform to turn defeat into victory for the Confederacy.[20] Thus it was understandable that northern image-makers came to believe that as Union troops fled back to Washington, Jefferson Davis, the literal Confederate commander in chief, loomed impressively on the hills above, earning credit for the unexpected triumph. So one print suggested.[21]

In the inevitable war of caricature that ensued, Lincoln at first hurt his case by the manner of his own flight to Washington. After a ten-day-long journey from Springfield to his inauguration, during which Lincoln appeared publicly on a daily basis delivering countless speeches, his alarmed friends learned of a suspected assassination plot awaiting him in Baltimore and convinced the president-elect to cancel a scheduled public carriage ride through town. To avoid detection, Lincoln was even persuaded to abandon his signature stovepipe hat and frock coat, don a cloak and soft cap, and pass from one downtown railroad station to another in the dead of night. He did so "without being recognized by strangers," as Lincoln himself put it later, "for I was not the same man." To one friend, he predicted: "I reckon they will laugh at us."[22]

That proved an understatement. After newspapers mocked his so-called "Underground Railroad" Journey, one southern journal calling it a "disgraceful act" by "a country clown" that "had made many converts in the ranks of Secessionists,"[23] *Vanity Fair* mockingly welcomed *The New President of the United States* in a cartoon that showed him covered from head to foot in impenetrable disguise, wearing a tasseled military cloak and a beribboned Scottish tam. That same day, *Harper's Weekly* contributed a hilariously elaborate report of its own on *The Flight of Abraham*, a multi-

Adalbert Volck, *Passage Through Baltimore*. Etching, Baltimore,
1861. Later published in "V. Blada's" *War Sketches*.
Author's collection.

panel cartoon that took the frightened president-elect from the alleged
midnight alarm that woke him with the news of the threat to his life, to his
first meeting with outgoing president James Buchanan, with Lincoln still
quaking from the experience.[24] And one of Baltimore's own artists, Adalbert Volck, mocked the hapless president-elect hiding in a baggage car,
recoiling in horror at the mere sight of a black cat.[25] These wildly exaggerated assaults would eventually abate, but the suggestive Scotch cap, originally an abolitionist symbol, would remain a fixture in Lincoln caricature

for years — gaining equal prominence with the log rail — and serving as a constant reminder of the worst fate that could befall a new president confronting the daunting secession crisis: the charge of cowardice.

It is little wonder that early wartime prints depicted Lincoln as anything but a formidable military figure. He was unable, in one print, to quell the weak rebellion with his outdated hunter's shotgun, in another unconvincingly relying on his trusty rail to do battle with Jeff Davis, now, and often thereafter, dressed in exaggerated plantation regalia that emerged as a staple of his own caricatured image. But the print, *I Am Glad I Am out of the Scrape* exists only in a single known proof copy deposited for copyright by Cincinnati lithographer Carl Anton on May 24, 1861. It was never produced in quantity. Nor was Adalbert Volck's image of the new commander in chief as a latter-day Don Quixote, with Maj. Gen. Benjamin F. Butler as his Sancho Panza, not just tilting against windmills but also tellingly riding past a broken-down rail fence, no doubt to suggest to viewers how far the mighty self-made man and his claims to fame had fallen.

Although Volck may well have been the most brilliant caricaturist of the Civil War, his very talent and sophistication invite delusions about his impact. No scholar has found evidence of how many copies Currier and Ives churned out for each of its titles, but we can surmise how *few* copies Volck produced. That is because all his etchings were issued privately and secretly, and distributed only to a handful of his fellow Confederate sympathizers in Baltimore.[26] To risk further distribution might have increased the artist's influence but also would have exposed him to arrest in Union-controlled Maryland. All caricatures were not created equal. Those that remained unseen were as silent as proverbial trees falling in abandoned forests. Modern viewers must constantly ask themselves: who saw these pictures? How were they used? Great as they were, Volck's deft cartoons influenced few when they were first created, finding their way into the literature only after the war ended. Their influence has been routinely overstated ever since.

Surviving northern-made prints from 1861 and 1862 strongly suggest that as contemptuously as the region viewed its own president's military credentials, it regarded Davis's with grudging respect and some fear. He might be dismissed as a traitor consorting with a Prince of Darkness, who lauds him a "fit representative of our realm." But even when shown trampling disrespectfully on the American flag, Davis seemed more than vaguely threatening. It was probably with a contempt born of apprehension that one printmaker offered a trick print that on one side showed Davis going off to war — and on the other side, held upside down, returning

Carl Anton, *I Am Glad, I Am out of the Scrape!*
Proof copy of a lithograph, Cincinnati, 1861. Library of Congress.

in humiliation. *Punch*, by comparison, appeared so confused by what it concluded was the ambiguous tone of Lincoln's first inaugural address that it depicted the new president simultaneously as a god of war and a lady of peace. Nor did the cartoonists let Lincoln forget his Baltimore humiliation. One example, a sheet-music cover called the *Abe-Iad* showed him fleeing from a feebly launched, harmless-looking cannonball, wearing his Scotch tam and cloak disguise to reinforce his cowering image, his long legs now seeming to carry him comically in the opposite direction from that in which caricatures had portrayed him racing to victory just a few months earlier.

But this print, too, came out of Baltimore in 1861, and however clever such early efforts, Union forces occupying the city quickly silenced that city's anti-Lincoln image-making except for Volck's efforts underground. New Orleans fell to the Union by 1862, and nascent Confederate print publishing died out there, too, under threat of censorship.[27] For the rest of the Civil War, the only notable and widely available pictorial commentary on Lincoln would come from Union soil.

That is, after the shaky debut, and quick descent, of the sole pictorial response from the Confederacy: a doomed periodical called the *Southern Illustrated News*. Most publishers of separate-sheet prints in Richmond were assigned after 1861 to such "official" publishing as war maps, stamps, and currency, leaving the ill-fated newspaper with scant supplies and a shallow pool of artists. Conceived to rival New York weeklies like *Harper's* and *Leslie's*, the *News* did not publish its maiden issue until late September 1862. Thereafter, it managed only a tiny output of anti-Lincoln caricature. Its frequent, importuning advertisements for engravers are easily explained in view of the amateurish caricatures its resident contributors usually offered its readers: Lincoln as a puppet-master, for example, trading one hapless general for another; as a schoolmaster patiently instructing his duncelike students — both good ideas poorly executed that moreover indicate that the paper did not even know by 1862 that Lincoln had worn whiskers for a year. An occasional flash of brilliance from the paper, like *I Wish I Was in Dixie*, depicting Lincoln as a wistful balladeer longing for conquest despite McClellan's failed 1862 invasion, were the exception, not the rule. But it offers a hint of what might have been had the *Southern Illustrated News* been able to continue publishing throughout the war.[28]

Not surprisingly, the weekly reserved its most vicious assaults for emancipation, the dreaded culmination of all the warnings about racial upheaval so provocatively offered in the campaign cartoons of 1860. Once he issued the proclamation in September 1862, Lincoln was routinely shown — just as Davis had been portrayed at the outbreak of rebellion — not only consorting with the Devil, but in one case, unmasked as the Devil himself. In another such cartoon, the railsplitter meets his fate on another gallows made of split rails, a Lincoln done in by his own symbolism. Davis was not spared either. He was simultaneously portrayed in precisely the same way in the North: as a traitor deserving execution. The quality of newspaper engravings differed, and the South, its printmaking capitals occupied or diverted, was unable to compete at all in the realm of separate-sheet poster cartoons. But viewers in both sections for a time were treated to a similar message: the opposing president was satanic, treacherous, and fit to be hanged.

Of course, Presidents Lincoln and Davis never encountered each other during the war. Cartoonists, however, made certain that they came face to face on paper. The body of caricature showing the two leaders together is small but rich (one *London Punch* cartoon, for example, casting them as gladiators; another showing them as homely seductresses in drag, trying to coax John Bull out of neutrality; and yet another, as opponents in a high-stakes, winner-take-all game of billiards).

Printmaker unknown, *Masks and Faces: King Abraham before and after Issuing the EMANCIPATION PROCLAMATION*. Woodcut engraving, published in *Southern Illustrated News*, Richmond, Virginia, November 8, 1862. The New York Public Library; Astor, Lenox, and Tilden Foundations.

Politics, like war and sports, was a realm for males only at the time, and along with the pool hall, one of the most irresistible motifs of American caricature was the males-only boxing ring, in which Democrats and Republicans, northerners and southerners, had been doing inconclusive symbolic battle for a generation. It offered a solution to the perennial problem of how to portray the protagonists entertainingly. Cartoonists routinely placed Lincoln and Davis in manly combat. In one such boxing cartoon, Lincoln batters Davis to a pulp but demands unconditional surrender: the Confederate president must cry "uncle" to end the bloodshed.

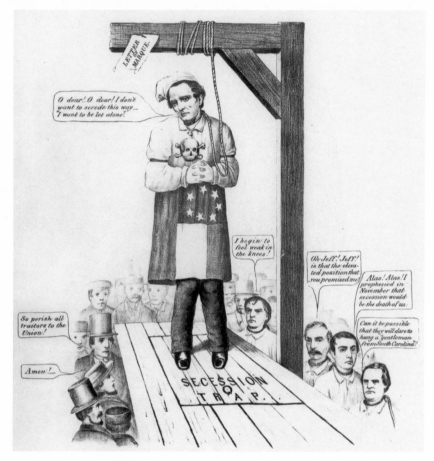

Currier and Ives, *Jeff Davis, On His Own Platform, as the Last "Act of Secession."*
Lithograph, New York, 1861 (also published as *Jeff Davis, on the Right Platform*).
Library of Congress.

In such battles between pugilists, in part because they were published in the Union, Lincoln enjoyed a decided edge, leaving Davis "deeply humiliated" in one such Currier and Ives print. Bare-knuckle boxing in its day was as vaguely disrespectable as political cartoons; so they made a good match, no pun intended.

Did Jefferson Davis ever see or chuckle at an anti-Lincoln caricature in the *Southern Illustrated News* or elsewhere? We have no evidence that he did—in fact it is rather hard to imagine—but we should not be at all surprised that the Lincoln family owned an anti-Davis cartoon. Just as the Union victory at Gettysburg had inspired Lincoln to write a piece of rhyming doggerel about Robert E. Lee's failed invasion, now the president—or

Ben Day, *Caving in, or a Rebel "Deeply Humiliated."* Lithograph, published by Currier and Ives, New York, ca. 1862. Library of Congress.

perhaps his children — obtained a copy of *"How Happy Could I Be With Either,"* an 1863 carte de visite cartoon showing a grim-looking Davis, his pants patched and his toe protruding from his old shoe, glumly regarding a sign announcing the Confederate surrender at Vicksburg and retreat from Gettysburg.[29]

This is not to suggest that wartime northern patriotism liberated Lincoln from pictorial criticism; quite the contrary. He was still routinely vilified for such failings as sacrificing thousands of war dead (only to be reminded of one of his little jokes), or swallowing up new conscripts to fight on to save the Union. And while emancipation gave Lincoln an image comeback of sorts in some quarters — a new opportunity for the old railsplitter to use his axe, one print applauded, to break the backbone of rebellion (a monster trained and controlled by Davis) — not every cartoonist concurred. To Baltimore's subterranean Adalbert Volck, one of the few artists of the day with an undisguised political agenda, however limited his reach, emancipation was a pact with the Devil, written with ink supplied by Satan himself.

Election seasons always triggered an increase in the business of caricature—and 1864 proved no exception, war notwithstanding. If the election would go on, so would the rowdy tradition of political caricature. This presidential race, for the first time, unleashed caricature generated directly by a political operation. The provocative cartoon sheet *Miscegenation*, which warned of a national future in which whites would become servants and blacks members of society, was commissioned by the Democratic newspaper the *New York World*. The paper had only recently been shut down by the Lincoln administration and had a score to settle.[30]

Lincoln knew of and outfoxed the paper's insidious campaign to spread the falsehood that the president embraced race mixing,[31] and he left no record that he was perturbed by its pictorial predictions of dire consequences that would follow an abolitionist triumph. Yet one cartoon in the series likely got under his skin—*The Commander in Chief Conciliating the Soldier's [sic] Votes on the Battle Field*—which gave visual accompaniment to the *World*'s libelous report that Lincoln had once asked Ward Hill Lamon to sing comic songs amidst the carnage of the Antietam battlefield. That fiction so infuriated Lamon that he composed a heated refutation. Urging caution, Lincoln wrote out his own, calmer draft rebuttal, but like several of the famous letters he wrote chiefly to let off steam, the president ultimately decided that it ought not to be sent.[32] Still, the episode surely struck a nerve, just as the picture likely did when it fueled the controversy.

Although he was not a candidate himself in the campaign between Lincoln and George B. McClellan, Jefferson Davis emerged in cartoons as a principal player in the 1864 contest between the Republican president and his Democratic challenger. That year's campaign cartoons also reminded voters that most printmakers would still play both sides of the political street. On the one hand, for example, Currier and Ives included Davis among an ignominious pro-McClellan quartet—the other three being New York's former secessionist Mayor Fernando Wood, Copperhead Ohio congressman Clement Laird Vallandigham, and "Jeff's friend" Satan— holding aloft the Democrats' rotted party platform and its two-faced nominee. Yet with equal fervor and skill, the commercially motivated New York firm depicted McClellan as a peacemaker in another cartoon, struggling manfully to keep Lincoln and Davis from tearing the country apart.

At the same time the New York publishers offered their various audi-

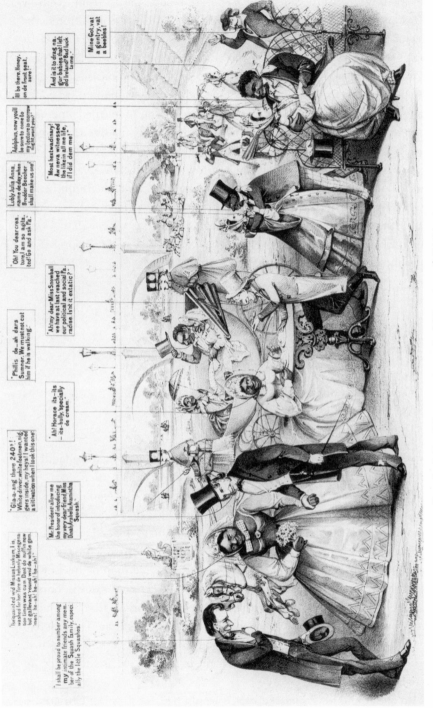

Bromly & Co., *Miscegenation or the Millennium of Abolitionism*.
Lithograph, published by *New York World*, 1864. Library of Congress.

ences straightforward campaign posters for both the Lincoln–Andrew Johnson and McClellan–George H. Pendleton tickets, they offered the cartoon *"Your Plan and Mine?,"* asking voters to choose one. One of its panels showed McClellan offering an olive branch to a tattered Davis, who, in turn, subjugates a black Union soldier; and, for comparison, another showed Lincoln forcing Davis into "unconditional submission," to which Davis replies in unlikely capitulation: "I beg of you to let me come back into the Union & not to punish me too severely for my madness and folly." Specifically targeting the all-important military vote was the print *The Soldier's Song*, a scathing pictorial reminder that election day offered a choice between "Unionism" and "Copperheadism." As if the blunt image of Davis as a snake coiled around a palmetto tree wasn't vitriolic enough, the print offered an anthem, too, complete with an appeal that "every Union Family in the Land preserve a copy . . . as a token of disapprobation and contempt for Home Traitors":

> When the bold American Eagle
> That old serpent shall lay low,
> The young vipers will "skedaddle,"
> No more their puny heads to show.
>
> When their master "Jeff" has fallen,
> They will h[a]unt the hills and woods,
> Any where to hide themselves,
> Their wives, children, and their goods.

As it happened, the verses presaged Davis's ignominious skedaddling future (a future that would soon be vivified in caricature).

Lincoln's worst nightmare—a McClellan victory that would have sent him packing from the White House, as illustrated in a Currier and Ives cartoon (Scotch tam back on his head for the flight)—turned out instead, in *Frank Leslie's Illustrated Newspaper*, to be a bad dream for Jefferson Davis, suddenly transformed into a white-bearded old man by his unwelcome guest. "Is that you still there LONG ABE?" Davis cries out in horror. "Yes," Lincoln replies, armed with the "latest Union majorities." He adds: "And I'm going to be FOUR YEARS LONGER." By Christmas "Little Jeffy" was still sleeping, and Santa Lincoln, again dominating the cartoon genre, was magnanimously wondering which gift to leave in Davis's stocking: an olive branch or a sword.

No one would have guessed that it would be Lincoln's last Christmas. The cartoonists' predictions notwithstanding, he would not be there "four

Currier and Ives, *"Your Plan and Mine."* Lithograph, New York, 1864. Library of Congress.

Jeff Davis's November Nightmare. Published by
Frank Leslie's Illustrated Newspaper, December 3, 1964.
The Lincoln Museum, Fort Wayne, Indiana.

years longer." In fact, he had little more than five months to live, and martyrdom would carry him beyond the reach of caricature. But Davis's nightmare was just beginning. That election year, a St. Louis printmaker suggested in the uncanny *Jeff Wants to Get Away* that Davis would soon try to escape advancing Union forces by relying on a blackface disguise to evade his pursuers. The reality proved even more humiliating for the Confederate president. Lincoln had entered the presidency in disgrace, memorably portrayed by cartoonists as a coward in disguise. Now, in a piece of unexpected historical irony that artists only dreamed about, Jefferson Davis *exited* the presidency in precisely the same way: in disgrace and disguise as well. And northern printmakers rushed to seize the opportunity. Female regalia, imposed occasionally during the Lincoln-Davis caricature "rivalry" to disparage both men, now became the exclusive costume of one.

The story is familiar: when Union troops caught up with Davis in flight in Georgia, his wife threw her raincoat over his shoulders should he need to keep warm on his escape. Or so the president and his wife always insisted — Mrs. Davis pointedly defending her action by snidely adding, "I would have availed myself of a Scotch cap and cloak . . . to avert from him the awful consequences of his capture."[33]

The consequence to Davis's reputation was devastating. Just as reporters and cartoonists had rushed to exaggerate Lincoln's Baltimore disguise, so also northern cartoonists, beginning in *Frank Leslie's Illustrated Newspaper*, conceived of a cowardly Davis hilariously fleeing in his wife's dress. With extraordinary speed and inventiveness, separate sheet cartoon echoes flowed relentlessly off the presses, along with carte de visite photo cartoons of *Jeff in Crinoline* for family albums, and sheet-music covers illustrating *Jeff in Petticoats* ditties for the parlor piano.

Typical products portrayed "The capture of Jeff Davis," a "so-called President in Petticoats," "Our erring sister caught at last," or the "Chas-ed Old Lady of the Confederacy," cartoons that transformed the once-proud president a laughingstock across the North, skedaddling clumsily to the last ditch in his wife's dress, or reducing "Southern chivalry" to hoopskirts as his captors laugh mockingly. Davis's humiliation knew no pictorial bounds. Cartoons displayed him in drag on a gallows with the ghost of John Brown, himself a hanging victim once considered too controversial to be depicted in pro-Union prints, now as his ironic executioner. Another showed Davis hurled over a cliff to the underworld, his dagger and stolen gold scattering as he heads down to hell — where, in yet another print, he meets legendary traitor Benedict Arnold and, still wearing women's clothes, declares: "I have come home."

Davis's image experienced an upward turn when he was manacled at Fort Monroe, a restraint he resisted with enough energy to restore his manhood and emerge from his brief imprisonment as something of a living martyr to the Lost Cause. This modest iconographical comeback would be abetted by northern printmakers eager to compete for a reopened southern market. Only a few months after gleefully reducing the Davis image to tatters, they began rehabilitating him with handsome portraiture that, since 1861, Confederate publishers had been unable to provide and northern ones had been unwilling to print or distribute. The anti-Davis output continued, but straightforward portraits restored some equilibrium. Commercialism trumped patriotism, just as it traditionally overrode partisan politics.

Lincoln's image, once as strongly buffeted by pictorial assault as enhanced by pictorial praise, ascended. His death even prompted *Punch* to

The only true Picture of the Capture of Jeff. Davis, from the account furnished by Col. Pritchard of the 4th. Mich. Cavalry:

Jack and Gill went up the hill / To fetch a pail of water / Jack fell down and broke his crown, / And Gill came tumbling after.

The nasty mean Yankee / wont even let poor friends / my poor mother going / to the well for a / na go to the well for a / bucket of water.

O Gentlemen! it's only / my poor mother-going / to the well for a / bucket of water

I think the United / States government / could find something / better to do, than to / be hunting down / women and children.

Varry tame! she's the / Bearded Lady', saying / around town." Where's / Barnum?

Why Corpral! She's a / regular old Shanghai. / look what long Boots / and spurs she's got.

Hallou., Boots and Spurs / on a Woman." drop that / bucket and hook it. or I'll / drop you quicker than a / Duck tumbli can slide down a / Duck lunch can slide down a / Barnum's windpipe.

Jeff. Davis Caught at Last. Hoop Skirts & Southern Chivalry. "I think the United States Government could find something better to do," states a dagger-wielding Davis attired in women's clothing, "than to be hunting down women and children." Author's collection.

Oscar H. Harpel, *Finding the Last Ditch.*
Running the "Head" of Secession "into the Ground."
Lithograph, Cincinnati, 1865. Library of Congress.

recant all its past visual criticism with a poignant depiction, *Britannia Sympathises with Columbia.* As a sure sign that laughter would no longer intrude on Lincoln's reputation, the cartoon was accompanied by a serious poetic apology composed by the very author of the coarse English comedy that Lincoln was enjoying at Ford's Theatre when he was killed. Tom Taylor's "The 'Scurril Jester's' Recantation" purported to speak for all who had lampooned Lincoln while he lived.

> My shallow judgment I had learnt to rue,
> Noting how to occasion's height he rose,
> How his quaint wit made home-truth seem more true,
> How, iron-like, his temper grew by blows. . . .
>
> The Old World, and the New, from sea to sea,
> Utter one voice of sympathy and shame.[34]

Sympathy and shame evolved into sanctification. Lincoln the object of pictorial ridicule vanished. Lincoln as revered national hero emerged to take his place. It is notable that the figure of Uncle Sam, who earlier cartoons depicted as resembling George Washington, ended up looking more like Abraham Lincoln. To the victors belong the spoils, in iconography as in all else, and Lincoln's image went on to become a staple of twentieth-century cartoons, present in ghostly form to guide Woodrow Wilson or Franklin D. Roosevelt through challenging times of their own, or to manifest national mourning at the loss of another murdered president, John F. Kennedy.[35]

In short, Lincoln became a monument, literally so in the background of an 1881 cover print in the comic periodical *Puck*, published to mock the publication that year of Jefferson Davis's memoirs. Davis, depicted in ragged boots, tattered bonnet, and all that is left of his notorious 1865 disguise — a metal hoop — hawks his "history of treason" like a pathetic street peddler, still clutching his omnipresent bag of stolen Confederate treasure. Reduced to a dissolute symbol of secession and slavery, Davis had survived the war only to outlive his ability to compete with the late United States president in caricature and cartoon. The caption to this picture made its postwar assessment all too plain: "A Dead Hero and a Live Jackass."[36] The Lincoln and Davis images had evolved in opposite directions.

What might the image-makers have said had the tables been turned? That question cannot be answered with certainty, but Lincoln's death won for him the battle of iconography; in reverential prints he lived on in eternal nobility, as if he had never been caricatured at all. Davis remained, for the most part, the traitor hanging from a sour apple tree. But his downfall occurred not only because the North won the war and Lincoln became its final casualty. Years earlier, Baltimore's pro-Confederate, anti-Lincoln pencils had been stilled, just as they were silenced in occupied New Orleans, while in Richmond, potentially rich satire vanished when its artists were conscripted into the Confederate armed forces, or assigned to government publishing. American memory might be somewhat different had paper, ink, artists, and the city of Baltimore remained in the Confederacy, and had David Glasgow Farragut's Union naval flotilla not captured New Orleans in 1862. But of course, cartoonists had never made Lincoln the sole object of derision.

Yet another stubborn myth deserves debunking. For generations, some historians have insisted that in life, Lincoln was singled out for particularly vicious caricature: parodied, vilified, attacked, and defamed like no other American.[37] In truth, Lincoln was as often praised as he was pillo-

T. A. Wales, *A Dead Hero and a Live Jackass.* Woodcut engraving,
published by Keppler and Schwartzmann for *Puck*, New York,
June 22, 1881. Courtesy Roger Bridges.

ried. The same publishers who showed him as a buffoon also softened his
homely features in handsome portraits — it was business, after all, not politics. Lincoln's opponents, whether Douglas or Davis or McClellan, were
subjected to equally harsh treatment when they, too, tickled the cartoonists' fertile imaginations. The legend of the nobly suffering Lincoln, attacked unfairly by the artists of his day, deserves at long last to perish from
the earth.

Perhaps Lincoln said it best: To paraphrase one of his most endearing
letters, cartoons were nothing more and nothing less than "a fair specimen
of what has occurred to me through life" — or to others in the business of
politics, too. As he once put it, "I have endured a great deal of ridicule
without much malice; and have received a great deal of kindness, not quite

free from ridicule. I am used to it."[38] His contemporaries were used to it as well, and their constituents embraced the ridicule with malice toward all and charity for none.

NOTES

1. Belle Becker Sideman and Lillian Friedman, eds., *Europe Looks at the Civil War* (New York: Orion, 1960), 33. Beresford-Hope later co-founded the *Saturday Review*. The quotation is from a series of lectures he delivered on the American Civil War in 1861.

2. *Only Authentic Life of Abraham Lincoln, Alias "Old Abe,"* 1864, reprinted in Stefan Lorant, *Lincoln: A Picture Story of His Life*, rev. ed. (New York: W. W. Norton, 1969), 230.

3. Currier and Ives did so, for example, in *The National Game. Three "Outs" and One "Run,"* published in 1860. See Frank Weitenkampf, *Political Caricatures in the United States* (New York: New York Public Library, 1953), 124.

4. See, for example, *Letting the Cat Out of the Bag!!*, in the collection of the Library of Congress, and illustrated in Bernard F. Reilly Jr., *American Political Prints, 1766–1876: A Catalog of the Collections in the Library of Congress* (Boston: G. K. Hall, 1991), 439.

5. From the caption to an advertising print promoting the Barnum exhibit, *Barnum's Gallery of Wonders No. 26[:] What is It?—Or "Man Monkey . . . ,"* published by Currier and Ives, New York, ca. 1860, original copy in Gerald Le Vino Collection, Museum of the City of New York.

6. *Douglass' Monthly*, December 1860, quoted in Philip S. Foner and Yuvall Taylor, eds., *Frederick Douglass: Selected Speeches and Writings* (Chicago: Lawrence Hill Books, 1999), 416.

7. For the best study of these newspaper cartoons, see Gary L. Bunker, *From Rail-Splitter to Icon: Lincoln's Image in Illustrated Periodicals, 1860–1865* (Kent, Ohio: Kent State University Press, 2001).

8. See, for example, the anti-Lincoln *Abraham's Dream*, copyrighted on September 22, 1864, and the pro-Lincoln *Your Plan and Mine*, registered on September 28, 1864, Copyright Records, Southern District of New York, September 1864–December 1864, Rare Book Room, Library of Congress, Washington.

9. See Harold Holzer, "How the Printmakers Saw Lincoln: Not-So-Honest Portraits of 'Honest Abe,'" *Winterthur Portfolio* 14 (Summer 1979): 148–49, and Harold Holzer, Mark E. Neely Jr., and Gabor Boritt, *The Lincoln Image: Abraham Lincoln and the Popular Print* (New York: Scribner's, 1984), 27–44.

10. Abraham Lincoln, *The Collected Works of Abraham Lincoln*, ed. Roy P. Basler, 9 vols. (New Brunswick, N.J.: Rutgers University Press, 1953–55), 4:240, 204.

11. An argument has been made that this print also ended the brief flourishing of anti-suffrage caricature. See Gary L. Bunker, "Antebellum Caricature and Woman's Sphere," *Journal of Women's History* 13 (Winter 1992): 37.

12. Reilly, *American Political Prints*, 10.

13. Author unknown, "Election-Time in America," *All the Year Round* 103 (April 13, 1861): 67, copy in the Lincoln Museum, Fort Wayne, Indiana. Historian Matthew Noah Vosmeier was the first to study and publish this material. See Vosmeier, "'Election-Time in

America': An Englishman's View of Popular Politics During the 1860 Campaign," *Lincoln Lore*, nos. 1832, 1833 (October, November 1991).

14. Catharina Slautterback, "Charles Sumner and Popular Prints in the Election of 1862," *Imprint* 29 (Autumn 2004): 13–15. The observations were made two years after the Lincoln presidential campaign of 1860, but they indicate that the same methods for promoting and displaying caricature — and the same responses — were demonstrated in a Senate campaign. Slautterback quotes the Boston *Commonwealth*, September 27, 1862, and the *Liberator*, December 5, 1862.

15. Glenn C. Altschuler and Stuart M. Blumin, *Rude Republic: Americans and their Politics in the Nineteenth Century* (Princeton, N.J.: Princeton University Press, 2000), 198.

16. Catalogue of Banks, Platt & Co., New York, quoted in Georgia B. Barnhill, "The Making and Collecting of Prints in New York, 1825–1861," *Imprint* 28 (Spring 2003): 28.

17. *Philadelphia Public Ledger*, October 4, 1864, quoted in Mark E. Neely Jr., *The Boundaries of American Political Culture in the Civil War Era* (Chapel Hill: University of North Carolina Press, 2005), 36.

18. From Lincoln's second inaugural address, March 4, 1865, in Lincoln, *Collected Works*, 8:332.

19. See Mark E. Neely Jr. and Harold Holzer, *The Union Image: Popular Prints of the Civil War North* (Chapel Hill: University of North Carolina Press, 2000), 26.

20. Charles C. Jones Jr., for example, told his father on July 24, 1861, that Davis was "leading the center column on that fearful day." See Mark E. Neely Jr., Harold Holzer, and Gabor S. Boritt, *The Confederate Image: Prints of the Lost Cause* (Chapel Hill: University of North Carolina Press, 1987), 15.

21. The lithograph by an unknown printmaker, benignly titled *The Battle of Bull's Run*, is in the Library of Congress collection.

22. Benson J. Lossing quoted in Don E. Fehrenbacher and Virginia Fehrenbacher, eds., *Recollected Words of Abraham Lincoln* (Stanford, Calif.: Stanford University Press, 1996), 306; Norman Judd quoted in ibid., 272.

23. *Baltimore Sun*, February 25, 1861; *Charleston Mercury*, February 24, 1861.

24. *Vanity Fair, Harper's Weekly*, March 9, 1861.

25. Volck's etchings were published under the pseudonym V. Blada in portfolios titled *Comedians and Tragedians of the North* and *Sketches from the Civil War in North America* (Baltimore: privately published, ca. 1862, 1863), original copies in the Maryland Historical Society, Baltimore.

26. The subject is treated in Neely, Holzer, and Boritt, *Confederate Image*, 44–54.

27. Ibid., 3.

28. The New York Public Library owns a complete set of the periodical, which began publishing irregularly in 1864 and soon thereafter ended its run.

29. Lincoln's poem, "Gen. Lees invasion of the North, written by himself," is in the John Hay Library, Brown University, Providence, R.I. The cartoon carte of Davis is in the Lincoln Family Album collection of The Lincoln Museum, Fort Wayne, Indiana.

30. Henry J. Maihafer, *War of Words: Abraham Lincoln and the Civil War Press* (Washington: Brassey's, 2001), 174–75.

31. For Lincoln's response to the *Miscegenation* hoax — an effort to elicit his praise for a book purporting to be a serious call for racial integration — see David E. Long, *The Jewel of Liberty: Abraham Lincoln's Re-Election and the End of Slavery* (New York: Stackpole,

1994), 168–69, 172–77. Long also offered much insight into the role that cartoons played in that campaign.

32. Ward Hill Lamon, *Recollections of Abraham Lincoln, 1847–1865* (Chicago: A. C. McClurg, 1895), 144–47.

33. Varina Davis, *Jefferson Davis: Ex-President of the Confederate States of America. A Memoir* . . . , 2 vols. (New York: Belford, 1890), 2:641. Jefferson Davis's own defense, from his memoirs, was reprinted on pp. 638–40 of Mrs. Davis's work. For a perceptive treatment of the episode, see Nina Silber, "Intemperate Men, Spiteful Women, and Jefferson Davis," in Catherine Clinton and Nina Silber, eds., *Divided Houses: Gender and the Civil War* (New York: Oxford University Press, 1992), 283–305.

34. Lincoln as *The Federal Phoenix* appeared in *Punch* on December 3, 1864; *Britannia Sympathises with Columbia* on May 6, 1865, complete with the Tom Taylor eulogy in verse, "The 'Scurril Jester's' Recantation." Both engravings were by John Tenniel, who achieved his greatest fame that same year, 1865, as illustrator of Lewis Carrol's *Alice's Adventures in Wonderland.*

35. See "Lincoln and Wilson Facing the Storm," *Philadelphia Press*, reprinted in *Cartoons Magazine*, 1918, in Barry Schwartz, *Abraham Lincoln in the Forge of National Memory* (Chicago: University of Chicago Press, 1992), 233; "That's nothing, Franklin; you ought to read what they said about me," n.d., in William D. Pederson and Frank J. Williams, eds., *Franklin D. Roosevelt and Abraham Lincoln: Competing Perspectives on Two Great Presidencies* (Armonk, N.Y.: M. E. Sharpe, 2003), 9; and Bill Mauldin's "Weeping Lincoln," *Chicago Sun-Times*, November 1963, in Merrill D. Peterson, *Lincoln in American Memory* (New York: Oxford University Press, 1994), 327.

36. Roger A. Fischer, *Them Damned Pictures: Explorations in American Political Cartoon Art* (North Haven, Conn.: Archon, 1996), 181.

37. See, for example, Rufus Rockwell Wilson, ed., *Lincoln in Caricature* (New York: Horizon Press, 1953), vi; or Lorant, *Lincoln*, 182.

38. Lincoln to James H. Hackett, November 2, 1863, in Lincoln, *Collected Works*, 6:559

Walt Whitman's Real Wars

⊰ STEPHEN CUSHMAN ⊱

In the first few pages of Walt Whitman's little book *Memoranda During the War*, which carries on the cover of at least one copy of its privately printed first edition the gold-lettered words "WALT / WHITMAN'S / MEMO-RANDA / OF THE WAR / Written on the Spot / in 1863–'65" and shows on its title page the publication date "1875–'76," appears this passage:

> Future years will never know the seething hell and the black infer-nal background of countless minor scenes and interiors, (not the few great battles) of the Secession War; and it is best they should not. In the mushy influences of current times the fervid atmosphere and typical events of those years are in danger of being totally forgotten.[1]

As his critical jab at the "mushy influences of current times" clearly re-veals, Whitman did not write this prophetic passage on the spot during the years 1863–65. Instead, the tone of this mini-jeremiad suggests that he wrote it in the later 1860s, when he was also working on his sweeping indictments of postwar mushiness in *Democratic Vistas*, the first part of which appeared in 1867, or in the early 1870s. He prepared his *Memoranda* for publication (much of the book first appeared in articles published dur-ing 1874 in the New York *Weekly Graphic*) at a moment when the title of Mark Twain's and Charles Dudley Warner's *The Gilded Age* (published 1873 but dated 1874) was giving the "current times" an enduring nick-name.

Whitman's lament about the ignorance and amnesia of the future com-bines with his anger at the present to express a passionate commitment to memory, loyalty, patriotism, and nationalism, about which much re-mains to be said.[2] But for the moment let us complicate our sense of Whit-man's commitment, or his expression of that commitment, by looking at a later version of this same passage, now no longer in the first few pages of *Memoranda During the War* but shifted to the last pages of the Civil

War section of his autobiographical *Specimen Days & Collect*, published in 1882. In this later version the passage reads:

> Future years will never know the seething hell and the black infernal background of countless minor scenes and interiors, (not the official surface-courteousness of the Generals, not the few great battles) of the Secession war; it is best they should not — the real war will never get in the books. In the mushy influences of current times, too, the fervid atmosphere and typical events of those years are in danger of being totally forgotten.[3]

Although even the minor differences between these two passages — the lowercase "war" and the insertion of "too" — invite productive commentary, let us pass to the two large differences, both of which could point to Whitman's experiences in the late 1870s and early 1880s as also a reader rather than solely a writer of Civil War history. The first large difference, the dismissive reference to "the official surface-courteousness of the Generals," could reflect Whitman's assessment of any number of recently published texts, among them the writings by generals for the first numbers of the *Century Illustrated Monthly Magazine*, which began publication in 1881, or the letters and reports of generals collected and published in *The War of the Rebellion: A Compilation of the Official Records of the Union and Confederate Armies*, the first volume of which appeared the year before.

But it is over the second large difference, the insertion of the famous clause "the real war will never get in the books," that I would like to linger, since this often-quoted statement, which appears in many treatments of the Civil War that have little or nothing to do with Whitman, and which now serves as the title for an anthology of Civil War writings by well-known American authors, usually passes unexamined by those who quote it. What does Whitman mean by this provocative, peremptory pronouncement? What can such a statement mean, and what has it come to mean to us? What does it tell us about his sense of the Civil War or the memory of that war? And what does it tell us about his own little Civil War book, *Memoranda During the War*?

At least one of Whitman's readers, who also happens to be an eminent historian of Civil War memory, argues that Whitman's prophecy has proven to be flat-out wrong: "Contrary to Whitman's famous prediction, the 'real war' would eventually 'get into [*sic*] the books' because historians and writers have learned so much in the twentieth century about unearthing and telling the stories of real people."[4] I take this statement, which comes from David Blight's prize-winning *Race and Reunion* (2001), to be basically an accurate one about the development of historiographic methodologies in the twentieth century, although it tends toward tautology (we represent the real war in books by representing real people's representations of the real war), and it takes at face value the slippery term "real." Admittedly, the dictates of pragmatism, whether historical or philosophical, discourage us from subjecting every word we use to intensive analysis, but since this particular word, "real," and the phrase it inhabits, "real war," necessarily push us toward the heart of any discussion of the Civil War and memory, a little more rigor would seem to be in order.

So let us consider various ways of reading and hearing Whitman's statement. The first might go this way: *the real war will never get in the books because there is no such thing as the real war*. In considering the statement this way, we are free to practice whatever brand of epistemological skepticism we hold dearest, whether a poststructuralist version that derives from Jacques Derrida, or an American pragmatic version that derives from Ralph Waldo Emerson, or an ancient Greek version that returns us to Democritus, Protagoras, Gorgias, Pyrrho, and others. According to one or more of these views, we could not know the real war or could not communicate that knowledge in books, or we could communicate that knowledge in books but only in ways that show the knowledge to depend on language that is itself nothing but an endlessly self-referential construction. Although Whitman had a healthy skeptical streak, as we see in the small poem "Are You the New Person Drawn toward Me?" with the ominous final line "Have you no thought O dreamer that it may be all maya, illusion?," his statement is not that of someone who does not believe in something called "the real war"; it is the statement of someone who does and who associates the real war with seething hells and infernal backgrounds, as well as with countless minor scenes and interiors, which by implication he himself has witnessed.[5] Furthermore, if all Whitman meant by his famous statement is that he did not believe that we could know anything to be real, he would perhaps have been saying something profound about human existence but also at some point something rather trivial about the Civil War as a particular instance of human existence.

A second way of reading and hearing Whitman's pronouncement would assume that in fact there is such a thing as the real war, and it would go something like this: *the real war will never get in the books because it is too huge and cannot be contained in any one book and will still exceed all the books we might ever write*. According to this view, which I admit comes closer to my own than the extremely skeptical one, the real war consists of nothing less than every event, thought, feeling, or trace in perception, imagination, memory, writing, photography, painting, draw-ing, music, monumental sculpture, ceremonial commemoration, reenact-ment, artifactual materiality, landscape, and the environment leading up to and away from the years 1861 to 1865, and only a limitless, omniscient repository could contain it all. The corollary of this view would be that all books about the war, as well as a good many others not explicitly about it, whether good or bad, earnestly truth-telling or deliberately falsifying, con-tain some metaphysically charged particle of the real war. Ontologically dazzling as such a notion may be, and welcome as it may be to those of us still deeply engaged in writing books about the war, finally this way of reading and hearing Whitman's statement, by expanding it to include so much, eventually dilutes and also trivializes it.

A third possible reading, a much more specific and less comprehensive one, takes its cue from the clause to which Whitman has attached his state-ment about the real war, the clause "and it is best they should not," refer-ring to future years never knowing the real war. Read or heard this way, Whitman's statement would seem to refer to the tastes and mores prevail-ing among writers, publishers, and readers in the United States in the late nineteenth century, as though he were saying the real war was rated X, whether for violence or obscenity or thoughts and emotions too hard to reconcile with loyalty, patriotism, and nationalism, so it is best for the mushy, timid, squeamish future that it stick to books about the war rated G or perhaps PG. If Whitman meant something along these lines, his readers might recognize the analogy between his sense of something hidden and unspeakable about the war, on the one hand, and something hidden and unspeakable about his own sexuality, on the other. For whatever reason or reasons, Whitman would be making an elaborate show of protecting his vulnerable readers from truths he implies they cannot bear at the same time that he unmistakably announces the existence of such truths. This way of reading or hearing Whitman's statement does not exclude either of the two already mentioned, but it does justify David Blight's contradiction of that statement. Since the second half of the nineteenth century, the tastes and mores of writers, publishers, and readers have changed con-siderably, and especially after the wars of the twentieth century, we are much more grimly aware of seething hells and infernal backgrounds in war than Whitman's readers were, and we are much more likely to write and read books testifying to that awareness.

Whitman's famous statement may have meant and continue to mean all these things and more at different times, both to him and to his readers, but in moving now to the heart of the matter for this discussion, I want to suggest one last possibility, which again does not necessarily exclude any of those already discussed. To hear this possibility we need to imagine momentarily shifting rhetorical emphasis from "the *real* war will never get in the books," where most quotations of the statement seem to place it, to "the real war will never get in the *books*," as opposed, say, to the photographs, in which so many early viewers naively believed the real war could be gotten. In other words, what happens when we begin to listen to Whitman's statement not as one about the Civil War, and its real or unreal versions, but as a writer's statement about books and bookmaking? On one level, this reading once again would seem to trivialize Whitman's statement, since, after all, very little that is real gets in books because books are mostly abstracted representations of reality. When they talk about food, they do not serve food one can really eat. When they talk about rain, they do not cause rain to fall on ground that needs it. When they talk about war, they do not maneuver armies and fight battles and bury the dead and hospitalize the wounded.

But on another level, both for Whitman and for all subsequent makers of books about the Civil War, this is precisely the point. Since no book includes real war, how does one go about making a book that most persuasively appears to include real war? What are the rhetorical conventions of sentence- and paragraph-building, argument-arranging, evidence-presenting, and conclusion-drawing that mark one book's verbal abstraction of war as more authentic than another's? To what extent do these conventions vary with specific genres, differentiating the poem from the novel, from the memoir, from the doctoral dissertation in Civil War history, and to what extent do the conventions transcend generic boundaries? In the remainder of this discussion what I am going to be arguing is that in *Memoranda During the War* Walt Whitman carried out various prose experiments in writing Civil War history; that those experiments have as their common aim the production of an illusion or appearance of reality; that, despite several failures, at many moments in *Memoranda* his experiments are powerfully successful; that his statement about the real war not getting in the books is disingenuous when it comes to his own, in which he developed, if not pioneered, new verbal conventions for representing real war; and that at least two of the conventions he developed still characterize much Civil War historiography and by extension many of the ways in which the Civil War gets remembered in writing.

The first convention that marks Whitman's attempts at representing real war is neither one he pioneered nor one that characterizes professional Civil War historiography, and that is the convention of prominent first-person narration that tends repeatedly toward self-referentiality and self-description. Consider this parenthetical insertion, which appears almost a quarter of the way into *Memoranda*:

> (In my visits to the Hospitals I found it was in the simple matter of Personal Presence, and emanating ordinary cheer and magnetism, that I succeeded and help'd more than by medical nursing, or delicacies, or gifts of money, or anything else. During the war I possess'd the perfection of physical health. My habit, when practicable, was to prepare for starting out on one of those daily or nightly tours, of from a couple to four or five hours, by fortifying myself with previous rest, the bath, clean clothes, a good meal, and as cheerful an appearance as possible.) (18; 30)

In subsequently transposing this paragraph to *Specimen Days*, Whitman decided to drop the parentheses and give this casual aside, first inserted after a paragraph describing the wounds and death of Amer Moore, 2nd U.S. Artillery, the distinction of its own section and title, "My Preparation for Visits" (*PW*, 51–52).

This paragraph, which we can use to label what we might call Whitman's convention of personal presence, belongs to the genre of autobiography, a term that, according to the *Oxford English Dictionary*, the poet Robert Southey coined in 1809. That this term for "the writing of one's own history" should have appeared in English during the heyday of Romanticism, when exaltation of the individual self and imagination was the order of the day, makes perfect sense and perhaps confirms the worst suspicions of those inclined to roll their eyes at what they think of as Whitman's insufferable Romantic egotism. After all, they might argue, how can we take seriously the history of someone who constantly shifts the focus from the war he wants to depict to himself and his own personal habits? For that matter, how can we excuse the bad taste of someone who allows descriptions of his ablutions, sartorial regimen, and diet to intrude on our response to a description of a young man shot in the head and paralyzed from the waist down?

For Whitman, representing the real war and representing himself remain inseparable through *Memoranda During the War*, and their inseparability produces many extraordinary moments, such as the one in a section dated "Aug. 12" (1863) in which he describes seeing Lincoln "almost every day" (22; 39) and then gives us this memorable pair of sentences: "They pass'd me once very close, and I saw the President in the face fully, as they were moving slow, and his look, though abstracted, happen'd to be directed steadily in my eye. He bow'd and smiled, but far beneath his smile I noticed well the expression I have alluded to" (24; 41). Of course it is not just Lincoln's gaze that looks into Whitman's eye but the reader's as well, so that a passage about Lincoln ends up being a passage about Lincoln's wordless connection with Whitman, our narrator.

Whitman's insistence on his own personal presence also emerges in second-person addresses to his "Reader dear" (32; 56) and in his experiments with second-person pronouns more generally, of which sections called "An Army Hospital Ward" and "Death of a Wisconsin Office" offer prime examples. In these sections, which are not, in my opinion, among the most effective in *Memoranda*, though they are not the worst failures either, Whitman casts himself in the role of guide, playing Virgil to our Dante, as he leads us into the other world of the hospitalized wounded: "Let me specialize a visit I made. . . . Let us go into Ward 6. . . . You walk down the central passage. . . . You may hear groans. . . . Look at the fine large frames. . . . Look at the patient and mute manner of our American wounded, as they lie in such a sad collection" (11–12; 18–19; ellipses added). This kind of stagy presentation has affinities with both fiction and nineteenth-century journalism, two other genres Whitman also worked in, the latter much more than the former, and it clearly demonstrates an attempt to authenticate his narrative by, first, appearing to take the reader with him into a zone traveled only by authorized personnel and, second, by establishing his authority as guide on whom a subordinate reader depends. In experimenting with this approach, Whitman exploits one of the grammatical distinctions of English, as opposed to French or German, since in English the second-person pronoun "you" does double duty, meaning both "you" and "one," the latter quickly shading toward "I," so that "one walks down the central passage" really means "I walk down the central passage." In these second-person experiments Whitman not so subtly manipulates these multiple possibilities to lead his reader toward his own loyal, patriotic, and nationalist affirmation of the special qualities of "our American wounded."

Before we dismiss the convention of personal presence as, among other things, altogether different from the current procedures of Civil War historiography, we would do well to remember a few points. One is that the classical antecedents of historical writing show how in the beginning autobiography and history often had much in common, as many moments in, for example, Xenophon's *Anabasis* make abundantly clear. Although Xenophon talks about himself in the third person, his story of the fifteen-hundred-mile retreat after the Battle of Cunaxa in 401 B.C. is also in fact the story of Xenophon himself, after he has been chosen to lead the march from Persia. A second point is that although a dissertation committee would be likely to take a dim view of work that included many passages like the one in which Whitman talks about bathing and dressing and eating before he goes to the hospitals, it is also true that at least one recent version of Civil War memory, that embodied in Tony Horwitz's popular *Confederates in the Attic* (1998), depends heavily on the convention of personal presence, using first-person pronouns on nearly every page.

But it is a third point that bears more directly on the discussion at hand. To judge Whitman's experiments with the convention of personal presence harshly is to forget how closely we now identify the personal with the real. Personal details, personal revelations, personal anecdotes: the high value we put on these phenomena, on their power to establish the real texture of a particular narrative, reflects the converging legacies of the Reformation, the Enlightenment, Romanticism, and, most recently, psychoanalysis. Although extensive talk about oneself would amount to unprofessional behavior in writing about the Civil War now, we have little use, as either scholars or general readers, for narratives of the war in which personal details, about civilians or combatants, are absent. David Blight's contradiction of Whitman confirms this point. During the twentieth century, writers of history got much better at telling the real stories of real people, or, to put it another way, the personal stories of people who did not make the headlines. Although they did not necessarily need Whitman's example to make this improvement, we can test the power Whitman generates by means of the personal in ways that anticipate much to come in the twentieth century, by considering a passage from *Memoranda* in which the personal is absent:

> Such, amid the woods, that scene of flitting souls — amid the crack
> and crash and yelling sounds — the impalpable perfume of the
> woods — and yet the pungent, stifling smoke — shed with the radi-
> ance of the moon, the round, maternal queen, looking from heaven
> at intervals so placid — the sky so heavenly — the clear-obscure up
> there, those buoyant upper oceans — a few large placid stars beyond,
> coming out and then disappearing — the melancholy, draperied night
> above, around. . . . . . . [*sic*] And there, upon the roads, the fields, and
> in those woods, that contest, never one more desperate in any age or
> land — both parties now in force — masses — no fancy battle, no semi-
> play, but fierce and savage demons fighting there — courage and scorn
> of death the rule, exceptions almost none. (15; 25)

This highly wrought paragraph, which consists of nothing but grammatical fragments lacking a main verb to produce a single complete sentence, appears in a section headed "May 12 — A Night Battle, over a week since." Whitman opens this section, which runs more than three pages, by recurring to a by-now-familiar theme: "We already talk of Histories of the War, (presently to accumulate) — yes — technical histories of some things, statistics, official reports, and so on — but shall we ever get histories of the *real* things?" (13; 22). Dropped in the version of "A Night Battle" that appears in *Specimen Days* (*PW*, 45), this questioning sentence appears to be the ancestor of the famous clause about the real war never getting in the books.[6] The italicizing of "real" signals the charge this question has for Whitman, and after one of his idiosyncratic seven-dot ellipses, he implicitly proceeds to answer the question by undertaking the narration of "part of the late battle of Chancellorsville," narration that includes the paragraph above.[7]

At least one of Whitman's recent readers, writing for the *New Republic*, finds this paragraph quite moving: "Why did such scenes cut me so deeply?" she muses after quoting the version from *Specimen Days* through "draperied night above, around," a version that drops the initial "Such" and "the round, maternal queen," while inserting "silently and languidly" between "coming" and "out."[8] The answers to her question, which arises in the course of thoughts about the beautiful weather in New York on September 11, 2001, could be many, but they could not include the reality or authenticity of Whitman's account of the night battle at Chancellorsville. Although scholars and critics of Whitman have let the accuracy of this account pass unexamined, his narration of the night of May 2, 1863, substitutes nothing but well-worn literary conventions for the authenticity of personally witnessed scenes, and as a result it falls embarrassingly short of written representation worthy of the real war.[9]

To begin with, Whitman's account shows a very dim grasp of who did what where at Chancellorsville.[10] True, even many participants in the battle would still have had a similarly dim grasp only a week afterward, but they presumably would have known to which units they belonged and whether or not they were involved in combat. Among Whitman's more glaring errors, which he had more than ten years to correct and which may have come from garbled newspaper reports or his own imperfect listening to soldiers' stories, on which he often relied, are the location of divisions of Sedgwick's 6th Corps in burning woods around Chancellorsville on May 2 (14; 24), when in fact Sedgwick's Corps was still at Fredericksburg, and the assignment to the 2nd Division of the 3rd Corps, led, according to Whitman, by "Hooker himself" (15; 26), of an advance actually carried out by David Birney's 1st Division. Whitman also shows no sense of the limited scale of Birney's advance, which resulted in 196 casualties, many of them from friendly fire (an unpleasant detail Whitman does not mention in "A Night Battle" or anywhere else in *Memoranda*). Although Whitman insists the midnight attack planned by 3rd Corps general Dan Sickles, who goes unnamed in "A Night Battle," was "quite a general engagement" (14; 23) with "both parties now in force" (15; 25), in fact it was evidently small enough to pass unnoticed by Edward Porter Alexander, who was on the spot "hunting out our line of battle in the woods from the extreme right to the extreme left" and whose account of Whitman's night battle occupies only two sentences: "Several times during the night there occurred false alarms on the enemy's line. There would be a musket shot or two, & then several, & then whole brigades would fire tremendous volleys in our direction, & I would get behind a tree & wait for them to quiet down."[11]

The one detail that Whitman gets right, and the one that obviously enchanted him in the writing of his account, is the detail about a large moon casting bright light over Chancellorsville on the night of May 2.[12] Alexander notes the moonlight, too, as do many other participants in the battle. But although the moonlight may have been a real feature of the battle of Chancellorsville, where its efficacy in the thick woods of the Wilderness remains doubtful, it proved to be the undoing of Whitman's attempt at writing the history of "real things," since it seduced him into the stock literary conventions and motifs of romance and sentimentality. That such conventions and motifs are operating with little restraint in Whitman's account shows clearly in his use of one of the stalest images in poetic treatments of battle, that of blood on grass: "the red life-blood oozing out from heads or trunks or limbs upon that green and dew-cool grass" (14; 24). Of many contemporary examples of the same image, let one, housed in an iambic tetrameter couplet from Mary Hunt McCaleb's *Lenare: a Story of the Southern Revolution, and Other Poems* (1866), suffice: "Their rigid forms now cold in death, / Their hearts' blood crimsoning the heath."[13] Even if Whitman had invented this image, however, it still betrays ignorance of the distinct conditions of flora in the Wilderness, or of woods in general, since grass has a hard time growing where dense second-growth forest dominates.

Returning to the paragraph above, which has moved at least one reader so deeply, we can use manuscript evidence and our own ears to confirm that the only reality present in Whitman's account is the reality of poetic form. In its autograph manuscript version the sentence that became "Such, amid the woods, that scene of flitting souls — amid the crack and crass and yelling sounds" reads, "And that was war, and such its scene of flitting souls that night, that beauteous gorgeous night," which recast into lines reads as perfectly regular iambic verse many people would not associate with the founding father of American free verse:

> And *that* was *war*, and *such* its *scene*
> Of *flitt*ing *souls* that *night*,
> That *beaut*eous *gorg*eous *night*.[14]

The iambic imperative governs the final version as well, both in *Memoranda* and in *Specimen Days*. And that was war? Probably not. But it was certainly Whitman's literary substitute for war when he had nothing personal to go on. The literary fraud of "A Night Battle" then culminates in a fulsome fantasy about the death of an unknown soldier, "the Bravest Soldier," who crawls off to die in a secluded spot, undiscovered by burial squads (16; 27), a fantasy quite likely inspired by that other notorious fraud on the same subject, Alexander Gardner's fictional caption about the staged photograph subsequently published in *Gardner's Photographic Sketch Book of the Civil War* (1866) as "Home of a Rebel Sharpshooter, Gettysburg, July 1863," a photograph in a book Whitman, given his love of the new medium, must have known.[15]

Painful as it is for those who admire Whitman to acknowledge the fraud of "A Night Battle," especially when he himself presents it as his contribution to histories of real things, doing so clears the way for describing the genuine achievements of *Memoranda*, achievements that anticipated much we now take for granted in the writing of Civil War history and the perpetuation of Civil War memory. The first of the two achievements on which I want to focus for the rest of this discussion is that of representing the war from the bottom up rather than the top down. We have already noted the dismissive references to "the official surface-courteousness of the Generals" and "technical histories of some things, statistics, official reports, and so on," but now we can consider Whitman's alternative to such things. As though reacting against his own excesses, he immediately follows "A Night Battle" with the names (or initials) of specific men and their conditions, beginning with "Thomas Haley, Co. M, Fourth New York Cavalry — a regular Irish boy" and continuing through Amer Moore, who precedes Whitman's self-description in what became "My Preparation for Visits." Along the way we come upon this passage:

In one bed a young man, Marcus Small, Co. K, Seventh Maine — sick with dysentery and typhoid fever — pretty critical, too — I talk with him often — he thinks he will die — looks like it indeed. I write a letter for him home to East Livermore, Maine — I let him talk to me a little, but not much, advise him to keep very quiet — do most of the talking myself — stay quite a while with him, as he holds on to my hand — talk to him in a cheering, but slow, low, and measured manner, talk about his furlough, and going home as soon as he is able to travel. (17; 29)

Although the authority of personal witness and presence informs this passage, we should guard against naively accepting it as nothing but raw material "written on the spot." Compared to the stylistic excesses of "A Night Battle," the simple, informal, understated rhetoric has the trustworthy sound of ordinary reality, but in fact this low-voltage style also represents a verbal experiment, one that succeeds where the other fails. What Whitman actually wrote in his notebook, and whether or not he wrote it at Small's bedside or sometime after this visit we cannot know, is this: "ward C bed 25 Marcus M Small co K 7th Maine Cynthia C Small East Livermore Androscoggin co Maine Sept 17) father Dr Wm B Small took sick about 4 weeks in reg hos — has diarrhea."[16] Somehow the diarrhea mentioned in the notebook entry has worsened into dysentery and typhoid fever in the *Memoranda* passage, which focuses on Whitman's ministrations to the Maine soldier, among them his sustaining of the fiction that Small will recover and return home, when, according to both patient and visitor, the death of the former looks much more likely. Particularly noteworthy here is the description contained in "talk to him in a cheering, but slow, low, and measured manner," a description both of Whitman's self-consciously adopted verbal manner with Small and, by implication, of his self-consciously adopted manner with his reader, for whom he slows and measures his language with commas, rhyme, and alliteration.

To argue that even Whitman's most real representations of the real war also involve verbal tailoring is not really the point, however. Anyone who has ever written a second draft of any representation of reality has also tailored that reality. Instead, the point is that Whitman's experiment in the passage about Marcus Small involves not simply the presentation of some details and the withholding of others, or not simply the mannered measuring of sentences and parts of sentences; it involves the selection of such a passage at all, a passage that surely anticipates, if I read him correctly, what David Blight calls "telling the stories of real people." Marcus

Small? A real person with real parents, a real hometown, a real company and regiment, a real bed, and real illness. His story? That he thinks he will die, that he looks "pretty critical," that he cannot write a letter home for himself, that Whitman visits and talks with him. What Whitman leaves unsaid here is an assumption that he would share with Blight: telling the story of this real person in a single short paragraph is as much a part of getting the real war in his book as telling the story of a night battle at Chancellorsville, which he never witnessed. In fact, considering that the story of the night battle at Chancellorsville is the only one of its kind in *Memoranda* (unless we include the extended account of Lincoln's assassination, which Whitman also did not witness), whereas passages like the one about Marcus Small recur throughout, we may reasonably conclude Whitman came to believe that getting the real war in a book depended more heavily on telling the stories of real people than on imagining battle descriptions.

Whitman was not the only person who told the stories of real people between the 1860s and the 1870s or 1880s, when the generals began publishing so many stories told from the top. Much to his chagrin, Louisa May Alcott anticipated Whitman with her *Hospital Sketches*, published in 1863, and Sam Watkins, subsequently the representative Confederate private for Ken Burns, obviously shared a commitment to telling the stories of real people in *"Co. Aytch": A Side Show of the Big Show*, based on newspaper articles that appeared in 1881 and 1882. But what distinguishes Whitman from these two examples, and what marks him as a pioneer in the formation of Civil War memory, is his refusal to accept that the stories he tells are merely side shows of the big show. Whether that refusal merely confirms his egotism or instead reflects a radically innovative reassessment of what Civil War history is and what Civil War historiography should do, the fact remains that any subsequent historian who has worked under the assumption that getting the real war in books necessitates focusing also on black soldiers or common white soldiers or enslaved army servants or plantation mistresses or small farmers or female factory workers or members of various immigrant or ethnic groups in different roles and capacities follows Whitman and extends his method.

To be sure, Whitman's experimentation includes hedges and disclaimers that occasionally sound like Watkins, as when the former suggests, "The present Memoranda may furnish a few stray glimpses in that life and into those lurid interiors of the period, never to be fully convey'd to the future" (5; 7), and the latter echoes, "I only give a few sketches and incidents that came under the observation of a 'high private' in the rear ranks of the rebel army."[17] A few stray glimpses, a few sketches and incidents, nothing too comprehensive or ambitious. But then Whitman can also make statements that neither Alcott nor Watkins ever would, statements such as "I now doubt whether one can get a fair idea of what this War practically is, or what genuine America is, and her character, without some such experience as this I am having" (25; 43). Contemporary Civil War historians may wince at the notion of something called "genuine America," but the general trend of their work since the Civil War centennial shows that the collective activity of representing the war, and of publishing those representations, confirms Whitman's doubt that we can afford to dispense with the stray glimpses of individuals in our efforts to arrive at some sense of what the war practically was.

We have seen that Whitman's *Memoranda During the War* experiments with the convention of personal presence. We have seen that his achievement in the book relies in part on the convention of opposing the top-down narrations of courteous generals, in ever-widening circulation, with the bottom-up narrations of ordinary people, people whose importance to the writing of Civil War history he asserts with a strenuous outspokenness ahead of his time. Now let us turn finally to a third convention, that of claiming to represent the general with the particular. As we can quickly appreciate, this convention follows closely from the second, since it is a very short step from saying the real war involves the lives of ordinary people to saying this particular ordinary person represents ordinary people in general. Many of Whitman's best readers have recognized that *Memoranda* takes as one of its central concerns the problem of how to represent the war, which some then abstract into the problem of how to represent in general. In the process of this abstraction, a few have argued that Whitman carries out his representation by substituting the part for the whole, which literary people call synecdoche.[18] But this description of Whitman's practice is not quite adequate. In substituting *head* for a bovine in the phrase *two hundred head of cattle*, one is substituting a significant part of that bovine for the whole creature, who will not be going anywhere without its head. But when Whitman "specializes" (11; 18) one of the soldiers he visits, Thomas Haley or Amer Moore or Marcus Small, it does not necessarily follow that this specimen soldier is truly representative.

This, of course, is the point. Although Whitman would like to convince us that a given "specimen," which comes from the Latin verb *specere*, meaning "to look at," and claims etymological kinship with "spectacle" and "spectacles," is a true synecdoche, a true substitution of a representative, important part for the whole, in fact his spectacles may be, if not rose-colored, then certainly tinted red, white, and blue. When he claims that "the Common People" are "emblemised in thousands of specimens of first-class Heroism" (4; 5–6), or when he describes a soldier as "a typic one" (16; 27), he is not merely substituting a recognizable part for the whole, such as *head* for the bovine attached to it. Instead, he is urging his readers to accept a given sample as emblematic or typical. Such urging belongs to the realm of argument, if not propaganda, rather than to the realm of rhetorical substitution practiced by poets and orators. Without doubt the armies of both North and South included thousands of specimens of first-class heroism, for example. But without doubt they also included thousands of specimens of cowardice, and yet in his imaginative account of the night battle at Chancellorsville Whitman himself tells us that he chooses to ignore these: "(We hear of some poor fighting, episodes, skedaddling on our part. I think not of it. I think of the fierce bravery, the general rule)" (14; 23).

What is "the general rule"? How does it relate to the "real" war? At this point, memory traditions, along with contested definitions and expressions of loyalty, patriotism, and nationalism, come sharply into the foreground. In the course of *Memoranda During the War* Whitman makes some sweeping statements on the basis of the specimen soldiers he visits and describes, statements such as, "It may have been odd, but I never before so realized the majesty and reality of the American common people proper," and this realization "fell upon me like a great awe" (29; 50–51). Even more extreme, especially coming from a man who never left North America, is the unsettling pronouncement he encases in parentheses, "(The Americans are the handsomest race that ever trod the earth)" (52; 93). Other readers of *Memoranda* have commented on the reconciliationist impulse of the book, as Whitman is careful to include both white northerners and white southerners under the heading "American," but none, to my knowledge, has pointed out Whitman's deliberate tampering with his specimens, his suppression of certain samples in order to produce his emblems and types of what he calls the general rule.

In the closing pages of *Memoranda*, before the lengthy notes that come afterward, Whitman summarizes his experiences in the Washington hospitals with some statistics: "During my past three years in Hospital, camp or field, I made over 600 visits or tours, and went, as I estimate, among from 80,000 to 100,000 of the wounded and sick, as sustainer of spirit and body in some degree, in time of need" (55–56; 100–101). He also tells us that he went among "the black soldiers, wounded or sick, and in the contraband camps" (56; 101). It is not clear if these visits or tours among black soldiers are included in the total of six hundred, but what is clear is that Whitman's list of hospitals—Finley, Campbell, Carver, Lincoln, Emory, Harewood, Mount Pleasant, Armory Square, Judiciary (27; 46–47)—does not include, for example, the L'Ouverture Hospital for black soldiers, located in Alexandria, despite his claim, "I am in the habit of going to all, and to Fairfax Seminary, Alexandria" (26; 45). More to the point, even if Whitman did visit black soldiers in L'Ouverture Hospital, he does not give his readers a single specimen of a black soldier anywhere in *Memoranda*. This omission does not come as a large surprise to anyone familiar with Whitman's views on race, which tended to reflect his identification with white workingmen in Brooklyn and Manhattan and led him to decry slavery on economic grounds, rather than on moral or spiritual ones. For Whitman the chief evil of slavery lay in the competition of black slave labor with white wage labor, not in any philosophical problems it posed.[19] Given this view, many will find the exclusion of black soldiers from Whitman's specimens predictable.

More surprising is his treatment of foreigners fighting in the Civil War. To make the arithmetic easy, we can take Whitman's upper estimate of a 100,000 soldiers visited and calculate that if 90 percent of these were Union and 10 percent Confederate, then he should have encountered approximately 22,000 foreigners fighting for the North and 1,000 fighting for the South.[20] Even if he encountered a higher percentage of Confederates, and consequently fewer foreigners, the arithmetic still suggests that he would have visited thousands and thousands of foreign-born men, and yet *Memoranda* is conspicuously lacking in specimens of them. At one point early in the book, Whitman confronts this issue head-on, claiming that the soldiers are "far more American than is generally supposed—I should say nine-tenths are native born" (18; 31). Although much closer to true for the Confederate army than the Union, even this low estimate would yield visits with eight to ten thousand foreigners, only one of whom appears among his "typic" soldiers. In the first few pages we encounter "M. de F., of the Seventeenth Connecticut," who is "an intelligent looking man, has a foreign accent, black-eyed and hair'd, a Hebraic appearance" (9; 14). But this soldier, identified elsewhere as Maximilian de Fisheur, turns out to be a lone exception to the general rule of *Memoranda*, depending on whether we read Thomas Haley, described as "a regular Irish boy" (16; 27), as Irish-born or of Irish descent.[21] All we have to do is listen to the last names of other soldiers mentioned in Whitman's published works—Holmes, Giles, Lilly, Boardman, Haskell, Wilber, Miller, Mahay, Monk, Elliott, Brooks, Smith, Sawyer, Cunningham, Farwell, Babbitt, Byrd, Morgan, Williams—

and to consider the omission of, for example, Henry Thurer ("Wants to see a German Lutheran clergyman") and John Grundke ("German") to hear that for Whitman the general rule of specimen cases tended to include white soldiers of Anglo-Irish-Scottish descent and to exclude others.

Although we might feel considerable dismay at the manipulation behind Whitman's would-be synecdoches, we should be careful not to settle for pointing out the mote in his method while ignoring the beam in our own. If no historical writer can get all of the real war in a book, it follows that all books about the war, even the most ambitiously comprehensive, must proceed by a method of sampling bits and pieces of its reality. Some of these samplings acknowledge their incompleteness straightforwardly, as Sam Watkins's book does, although that book also contains enough irony to make readers suspect that its author has a higher opinion of his "few sketches and incidents" than he lets on. But other books, though they necessarily proceed by sampling, adopt a much different strategy and proceed not merely by sampling but by making large claims for the significance of a particular sample, the representativeness of that sample, and the contribution of this sample to an understanding of the real war. In other words, they follow Whitman rather than Watkins.[22]

Well of course they do, the response might go; how could they do otherwise? But this question simply reveals the extent to which Whitman's method, which writes from the bottom up while making large claims about the real war based on the asserted representativeness of a particular sampling or specimen of the war, has become naturalized into invisibility by subsequent Civil War historiography, especially in the latter part of the twentieth century. As a matter of fact, books about the war could proceed in many different ways. They could, for example, make no large claims at all, simply presenting instead their specimens, as photographs without captions do. They could abandon the rhetoric of argument and persuasion, along with theses to support, evidence to interpret, conversations to summarize and intervene in. What would such books look like? How would they fit into our picture of professional historiography? Would they no longer be books at all? Would these alternatives quickly move us beyond the technology of printed books into the realm of electronic archives and digital projects? The answers to such questions are not immediately apparent.

What is apparent is that despite what he says about the relation of real war to books, Whitman developed a method of representing the war that many subsequent books employ. To say that these subsequent books follow Whitman is not to make a claim about the influence of *Memoranda*

During the War on later writers, not to use "follow" in the sense of what disciples do in relation to their master. Since Whitman's book appeared in a very limited, privately printed first edition, such a claim would be irresponsible. It is unlikely he had many followers among the first members of the American Historical Association, founded a few years after the publication of *Memoranda*. But to say that much subsequent Civil War historiography, particularly the kind that focuses on telling the real stories of real people, as opposed to the general-centered narratives Whitman criticizes in his little book, follows him in another sense is to make a claim about the history of Civil War history, and through that history a claim about Civil War memory. It is to say that before Whitman published his articles, the first of which appeared in the *New York Times* in February 1863 (*PW*, 296), and then his little book about the war, people writing about the wartime lives of those who were not generals, whether they wrote in letters or diaries or newspapers, did not make the same large claim Whitman made in the same large way in which he made it, often implicitly, sometimes explicitly, that my story and the stories of people around me are as real a part of the real war as any general's story. Some might wish for Whitman to be more humble, especially those unfamiliar with "Song of Myself" and other poems in *Leaves of Grass* (1855; 1891–92), but few twenty-first-century students of the Civil War now would say he is wrong. Humble or not, he got there first, and establishing an accurate history of Civil War history requires saying so.

NOTES

1. University of Virginia Special Collections has two copies of Whitman's *Memoranda During the War* (Camden, N.J.: Author's Publication, 1875–76), in which this passage appears on p. 5. The copy with gold letters on its cover is inscribed "Lou Whitman / from Walt." (Louisa Whitman was the wife of Whitman's brother George, a veteran of the 51st New York Infantry.) A facsimile of this book was published by Applewood Books, Boston, in 1990, and the pagination is the same as the original. A more recent edition is *Memoranda During the War*, ed. Peter Coviello (New York: Oxford University Press, 2004), in which this passage appears on p. 6. Subsequent references to *Memoranda* will appear parenthetically in the text and give the page number in the original edition, followed by that in Coviello's.

2. For persuasive recent discussion of nationalism in *Memoranda*, see Coviello's introduction, especially pp. xl–xlvii. For my own discussion of Whitman's complicated brand of patriotism, see Stephen Cushman, "Whitman and Patriotism," *Virginia Quarterly Review* 81 (Spring 2005): 163–77.

3. Walt Whitman, *Prose Works 1892*, vol. 1 (New York: New York University Press, 1963), 116. Subsequent references to this edition appear in the text as *PW*. *Specimen Days &*

Collect was originally published by Reese Welsh and Company (later David McKay) in Philadelphia in 1882.

4. David Blight, *Race and Reunion: The Civil War in American Memory* (Cambridge, Mass.: Harvard University Press, 2001), 19.

5. *Leaves of Grass: A Textual Variorum of the Printed Poems*, vol. 2, ed. Sculley Bradley, Harold W. Blodgett, Arthur Golden, William White (New York: New York University Press, 1980), 382.

6. A transcription of the manuscript draft of this sentence, originally headed "May 2 — '63," appears in *Notebooks and Unpublished Prose Manuscripts*, vol. 2, ed. Edward F. Grier (New York: New York University Press, 1984), 921: "We talk of the Histories of our Union War, (which have already begun to accumulate, many volumes, both sides and a few partially good ones)."

7. That here Whitman himself italicizes "real" obviously supports readings of "the real war will never get in the books" that implicitly do the same, but it does not preclude the insights we generate from shifting the emphasis, for the sake of this discussion, to "books."

8. Rochelle Gurstein, "On Weather," *The New Republic Online* (post date July 20, 2005). See ⟨http://www.tnr.com/doc.mhtml?i=w050718&s=gurstein072005⟩.

9. Among the most significant works that include material on or discussion of Whitman and the war are Daniel Aaron, *The Unwritten War: American Writers and the Civil War* (New York: Knopf, 1973); Robert Leigh Davis, *Whitman and the Romance of Medicine* (Berkeley: University California Press, 1997); Daniel Mark Epstein, *Lincoln and Whitman: Parallel Lives in Civil War Washington* (New York: Ballantine, 2004); Betsy Erkkila, *Whitman the Political Poet* (New York: Oxford University Press, 1989); Charles I. Glicksberg, ed., *Walt Whitman and the Civil War* (Philadelphia: University of Pennsylvania Press, 1933); Justin Kaplan, *Walt Whitman: A Life* (New York: Simon and Schuster, 1980); Kerry C. Larson, *Whitman's Drama of Consensus* (Chicago: University of Chicago Press, 1988); Walter Lowenfels, ed., *Walt Whitman's Civil War* (New York: Knopf, 1961); John Harmon McElroy, *The Sacrificial Years: A Chronicle of Walt Whitman's Experiences in the Civil War* (Boston: David R. Godine, 1999); Roy Morris Jr., *The Better Angel* (New York: Oxford University Press, 2000); David S. Reynolds, *Walt Whitman's America: A Cultural Biography* (New York: Vintage, 1995); Timothy Sweet, *Traces of War: Poetry, Photography, and the Crisis of the Union* (Baltimore: Johns Hopkins University Press, 1990); and M. Wynn Thomas, *The Lunar Light of Whitman's Poetry* (Cambridge, Mass.: Harvard University Press, 1987), which contains insightful remarks about the theatricality of the Chancellorsville "set piece" (213–15).

10. For details about the battle, I have relied on Stephen W. Sears, *Chancellorsville* (Boston: Houghton Mifflin, 1996), 300–302.

. 11. Edward Porter Alexander, *Fighting for the Confederacy: The Personal Recollections of General Edward Porter Alexander*, ed. Gary W. Gallagher (Chapel Hill: University of North Carolina Press, 1989), 206.

12. See *Notebooks and Unpublished Prose Manuscripts*, 2:533, for Whitman's entry for May 3, 1863: "Hooker's advance still fighting glorious nights — soft fine full moon" (space in original).

13. Excerpted in Lee Steinmetz, ed. *The Poetry of the American Civil War* (East Lansing: Michigan State University Press, 1991), 228. Originally published 1960.

14. The manuscript shows that Whitman canceled and revised words and phrases on his

way to producing the iambic pattern. See "Fragment from the manuscript of 'Memoranda During the War,'" #3829-ac, Special Collections, University of Virginia, Charlottesville.

15. See Alexander Gardner, *Gardner's Photographic Sketch Book of the Civil War* (1866; reprint, New York: Dover, 1959), plate 4 (no page number), and William A. Frassanito, *Gettysburg: A Journey in Time* (New York: Scribner's, 1975), 186–92.

16. *Notebooks and Unpublished Prose Manuscripts*, 2:615.

17. Sam R. Watkins, *"Co. Aytch": A Side Show of the Big Show* (1882; reprint, New York: Macmillan, 1962), 19.

18. See, for example, Sweet, *Traces of War*, 48, and Coviello, introduction, *Memoranda*, xliv.

19. See Cushman, "Whitman and Patriotism," 170.

20. For help with these percentages, I am grateful to Gary Gallagher, who directed me to James M. McPherson's *Battle Cry of Freedom: The Civil War Era* (New York: Oxford University Press, 1987), 606 n. 31, and *Ordeal by Fire: The Civil War and Reconstruction*, 2nd ed. (New York: McGraw-Hill, 1992), 357. McPherson cites Ella Lonn's *Foreigners in the Confederacy* (Chapel Hill: University of North Carolina Press, 1940), 200–240, especially 200 and 218–20. These sources give figures of 24 percent for foreign soldiers in the Union army and 9 or 10 percent in the Confederate. In correspondence Gallagher explained that he differs slightly from McPherson, preferring a figure of 25 percent for foreign soldiers in the Union army.

21. In connection with this and the following sentences, see Glicksberg, *Walt Whitman and the Civil War*, 148–54.

22. One example is Charles Royster's *The Destructive War: William Tecumseh Sherman, Stonewall Jackson, and the Americans* (New York: Knopf, 1991). Although he chooses to focus on two important generals rather than on ordinary soldiers, Royster explains in the opening paragraph of his short preface that his book, which deals primarily with "the scale of destruction to which the participants committed themselves," gives "particular attention" to Sherman and Jackson because for "large numbers of their contemporaries these men epitomized the waging of successful war by drastic measures justified with claims to righteousness." By rationalizing his samples as epitomes, while avoiding any language qualifying or questioning the representative value of his samples as epitomes (such as the qualification that the war in the East became much more destructive a full year after Jackson died), Royster adopts a method closer to Whitman's magnification of significant specimens than to Watkins's more qualified presentation.

Hollywood Has It Both Ways

*The Rise, Fall, and Reappearance of
the Lost Cause in American Film*

⊰ GARY W. GALLAGHER ⊱

Hollywood's engagement with the Civil War has featured strikingly different portraits of the Confederacy. The Lost Cause narrative, refined by former Confederates in the postwar era, flourished in films for nearly half a century. Much of its success grew from Hollywood's two most popular and influential Civil War–related films — *The Birth of a Nation*, director D. W. Griffith's silent-era blockbuster released in 1915, and *Gone with the Wind*, producer David O. Selznick's treatment in 1939 of Margaret Mitchell's hugely successful novel. Between them, the films grossed approximately two billion dollars when adjusted for inflation; they also exposed generations of Americans to strongly positive depictions of the Confederacy and the slaveholding South, as well as to hostile treatments of Reconstruction. In 1965, *Shenandoah* marked a turn away from Lost Cause cinematic conventions, and the appearance of *Glory* in 1989 ushered an emancipation narrative to center stage. Since the early 1990s, the Lost Cause has steadily receded in film — just as Lost Cause symbols such as the St. Andrew's Cross battle flag have retreated from the public sphere in the United States. The appearance of *Gods and Generals* in 2003 showed that a major Hollywood production could still embrace much of the Lost Cause tradition, but *Cold Mountain*'s release a few months later suggested that the Lost Cause probably had not turned a corner toward renewed cinematic acceptance.[1]

Although there was no *official* Lost Cause interpretation, an examination of several recurring themes will set up this essay's exploration of films. Lost Cause advocates presented slavery as peripheral to the decision for secession and to the establishment of the Confederate nation. Where they engaged slaves and slavery, they did so with an eye toward proving that African Americans had demonstrated loyalty to their masters amid the war's upheaval. The Lost Cause also cast the war as a hopeless effort, highlighting the white South's huge sacrifice—human and material—in the face of overwhelming northern military power that spread destruction throughout the Confederacy. Defeat thus brought no loss of honor; indeed, former Confederates claimed they had waged an honorable struggle for the constitutional high ground against a massively powerful and vindictive foe.

Robert E. Lee stood at the center of much Lost Cause literature. Because he had contended against odds as great as two-to-one, Lost Cause warriors could cast Lee and his soldiers as stalwart heroes engaged in a valiant but doomed fight. Slavery need not intrude on this landscape of martial honor, and the martyred "Stonewall" Jackson, a deeply religious and personally idiosyncratic subordinate of undeniable talent, usually stood at Lee's right arm. The emphasis on Lee and his army gave precedence to military events in Virginia and the rest of the Eastern Theater, with Gettysburg as an interpretive dividing point. That battle took on much greater importance in Lost Cause writings than it had enjoyed during the conflict. It also supplied an alternative explanation for the loss of the war. James Longstreet's sulking behavior at Gettysburg, asserted many Lost Cause writers, had denied Lee victory and the South its independence. This argument gave an especially bittersweet tinge to the Pickett-Pettigrew assault of July 3 as a transcendent Lost Cause example of southern courage—the hugely important "High Water Mark of the Confederacy." Beyond Lee's battlefields, the Lost Cause generally overlooked contentious debates on the home front to depict a united Confederate people waging a determined resistance against brutal Yankee oppressors. Women often received extravagant praise as the staunchest Confederate partisans, joining gallant soldiers and loyal slaves in a vision of dauntless Confederate resistance.[2]

Two other preliminary observations are in order. In seeking evidence of the Lost Cause tradition, I understood that Hollywood's overriding goal is to provide entertainment that will earn profits. Studios, producers, and directors seldom have a didactic purpose. They focus on plots and characters that create and sustain dramatic momentum, often purchasing the film rights to successful novels such as *Gone with the Wind*, *The Killer Angels*, and *Cold Mountain*. Yet films undeniably teach Americans about the past. It is likely that more people have formed perceptions about the Civil War from watching *Gone with the Wind* than from reading all the books written by historians since Selznick's blockbuster debuted in 1939.

The Birth of a Nation represented the first full-scale cinematic exploration of America's great national bloodletting. With Thomas F. Dixon's
noxiously racist novel *The Clansman* as its guiding text, Griffith's story of
war, reunion, and Reconstruction wholeheartedly embraces Lost Cause
themes.[3] The Old South, epitomized by the courtly Dr. Cameron and his
family in South Carolina, features a social structure "where life runs in
a quaintly way that is to be no more." The "kindly master" of Cameron
Hall presides over a world populated by loyal slaves and genteel white
people. The Camerons send three sons to war—a "mother's gift to the
cause"—and two of them die. They also contribute their material wealth,
willingly accepting hardship and proudly wearing old clothes. Late in the
war, tattered Confederate soldiers find "parched corn their only rations."
Griffith's use of Col. Ben Cameron, the one son not killed in the war, and
his soldiers to highlight Confederate privations and sustained courage fits
nicely within the Lost Cause interpretive framework. The film also portrays a southern home front menaced by hordes of U.S. soldiers. Griffith
focuses considerable attention on William Tecumseh Sherman's operations
in Georgia during 1864. "While women and children weep," proclaims one
of the silent film's explanatory panels, "a great conqueror marches to the
sea." After watching images of dislocation and loss on the Confederate
home front, coupled with those of great sacrifice on the battlefield, many
early-twentieth-century viewers could understand Griffith's sense of the
"agony which the South endured that a nation might be born."

Between 1915 and 1949, *The Birth of a Nation* played to large audiences
throughout the United States. Its racist message prompted outrage in some
places outside the old Confederacy, as when a reviewer in the *New Republic* pronounced it an "aggressively vicious and defamatory" spectacle that
amounted to "spiritual assassination." Yet the film generated its largest
profits in northern and western cities, where patrons likely were dazzled
by Griffith's technical skill and masterful staging and little bothered by
his racism. Burns Mantle, drama critic for the *New York Daily News*, addressed this phenomenon in noting an "element of excitement that swept
a sophisticated audience like a prairie fire in a high wind."[4]

Gone with the Wind ended *The Birth of a Nation*'s reign as the most
impressive and profitable cinematic expression of the Lost Cause. David O.
Selznick's epic almost certainly has been the single most powerful influence on American perceptions of the Civil War. It remains part of the cultural landscape through repeated airings on television, its canonical char-

Confederate battle flag against a background of soldiers wounded in fighting at Atlanta.
This image from *Gone with the Wind* links the scale of Confederate sacrifice directly
to the most famous symbol of the struggle for southern nationhood. Photofest.

acters and scenes available for comparison with recent films. *Gone with
the Wind* echoed *The Birth of a Nation* in many ways. It opens with an
embellished version of Griffith's tribute to a "quaintly," doomed southern
way of life: "There was a land of Cavaliers and Cotton Fields called the Old
South. . . . Here in this pretty world Gallantry took its last bow. . . . Here
was the last ever to be seen of Knights and their Ladies Fair, of Master and
of Slave. . . . Look for it only in books, for it is no more than a dream remembered. A Civilization gone with the wind." Scarlett O'Hara, the film's
heroine, and, for most of the Civil War part of the film, Rhett Butler, its
dashing leading man, admittedly do not fit Lost Cause stereotypes, each
being too self-absorbed to care about the fortunes of the Confederacy. Yet
the film as a whole adheres closely to the Lost Cause narrative.

Gone with the Wind's white South strives mightily and suffers griev-
ously in pursuit of Confederate nationhood — parts of the Lost Cause narrative, it is worth noting, did not stray far from the historical record. The
human toll receives sustained attention. Many of the O'Haras' friends and
neighbors die in the war, and a memorable scene depicts wounded soldiers at Atlanta's railroad depot. Fifteen hundred extras fill the screen as

the longest and highest tracking shot to that point in film history affords graphic evidence of the war's grisly toll. A flapping Confederate battle flag, dominating the foreground when the camera reaches its highest point, reminds viewers of the cause for which these men risked their lives.[5]

Most of the white civilians in *Gone with the Wind* express devotion to the Confederacy. Melanie Wilkes exemplifies the model of patriotic womanhood. Impeccably ladylike, she willingly parts with material goods, including her wedding ring, and literally takes up a sword when confronted by one of Sherman's scavenging soldiers at Tara. At the other end of the social spectrum, brothel madam Belle Watling donates money to the soldiers' hospital, observing that she is "a Confederate like everybody else." Even the cynically materialistic Rhett Butler has a conversion experience on the road to Tara after Atlanta falls. "I am going, my dear, to join the army," he tells an incredulous Scarlett after watching exhausted Confederate soldiers trudge by: ". . . I'm a little late, but better late than never." *Why* is he going, she asks. "Maybe its because I've always had a weakness for lost causes, once they're really lost," he answers. "Or maybe, maybe I'm ashamed of myself. Who knows?"

The Lost Cause preoccupation with Union manpower and resources stands out in several parts of the film. In a scene with Scarlett at Christmas in 1863, Ashley Wilkes, home from Lee's army on furlough, observes: "Oh, Scarlett, my men are barefooted now, and the snow in Virginia is deep. When I see them, and I see the Yankees coming and coming, always more and more. . . ." Sherman and his army reprise their role from *The Birth of a Nation*. D. W. Griffith's "great conqueror" returns as the "Great Invader," whose legions form an "oncoming juggernaut" spreading terror and devastation among Confederate noncombatants. A montage of endless lines of Union soldiers set against a background of flames suggests the irresistible, faceless Union power so important to Lost Cause writers. Scarlett's journey from Atlanta to Tara reveals Sherman's impact on the Georgia countryside. She passes ruined farms and plantations littered with military detritus and carcasses of dead animals that invite attention from circling vultures.

Selznick's film avoids the more inflammatory racial politics of *The Birth of a Nation* by emphasizing a reciprocal loyalty between the principal African Americans characters and their owners.[6] As the fight for Atlanta enters its last phase, Scarlett engages Big Sam and three other field hands from Tara in a conversation that bristles with Lost Cause meaning. A scene that lasts but a few moments conveys white devotion to the Confederacy, slaves' loyalty to their owners, and slaveholder concern for the bondsmen's welfare. Scarlett hails the slaves, escorted by a mounted Confederate officer, as they march out to dig defensive works. Big Sam reports that Scarlett's father, ever the loyal Confederate, complained because a bad knee prevented his fighting for the Confederacy. Mr. O'Hara's willingness to help the cause weakened a bit when he opposed sending the slaves to Atlanta, "But your Ma says the Confederacy needs us, so we'se gwine to dig for the South." As the column of laborers begins to move, Big Sam reassures his owner's daughter: "Good-bye, Miss Scarlett. Don't worry, we'll stop them Yankees." "Good-bye, Big Sam," she answers with some feeling: "Good-bye, boys. If any of you get sick or hurt, let me know." The original Lost Cause writers could not have improved on these tender expressions of affection between slaveholder and slaves.

Although *Gone with the Wind* marked the apogee of Lost Cause influence in Hollywood, the succeeding twenty-five years yielded a number of major films that handled the Old South and the Confederacy gently. Two examples, among many possible candidates, are *Santa Fe Trail* (1940), which deals with sectional tensions in the late antebellum years and adopts a staunchly pro-southern stance, and *The Horse Soldiers* (1959), director John Ford's treatment of a Union cavalry raid that imagines a Confederacy of loyal slaves and gallant Confederates caught up in a doomed struggle.

Shenandoah signaled a shift in Hollywood's relationship with the Lost Cause. Released in January 1965, six months after congressional passage of the Civil Rights Act of 1964, it shuns glorification of the plantation South and, most tellingly, places slavery at the center of the Confederate war. The film stars Jimmy Stewart and focuses on the nonslaveholding family of Charlie Anderson, who live on a prosperous five-hundred-acre farm in Virginia's Shenandoah Valley. The film's anti–Lost Cause tenor emerges early when one of Charlie's sons remarks that as Virginians the Andersons cannot ignore the war. Charlie responds by asking if the sons want to own slaves. No, they reply. "Now suppose you had a friend that owned slaves and suppose somebody was going to come and take them away from him," continues Anderson. "Would you help him fight to keep them?" The sons say they would not, with one explaining, "I don't see any reason to fight for something that I don't believe is right, and I don't think that a real friend would ask me to."

The film also abandons Hollywood's earlier model of black servility. In one scene, a teen-aged slave named Gabriel watches a Union patrol capture Boy, Anderson's youngest son. Boy instructs Gabriel to tell Mr. Anderson what happened, whereupon a black Union soldier breaks in: "You don't have to tell his pa nothin.' You're free." Gabriel seizes the opportunity, shows up later in the film as a U.S. soldier. Just as previous films had grossly exaggerated the degree to which slaves remained loyal to their masters, so also does *Shenandoah* distort historical reality by showing integrated U.S. military units—both the one that captures Boy and the one in which Gabriel serves. This shift from loyal or childlike slaves to black and white soldiers in the same regiments suggests how far *Shenandoah* moved beyond Hollywood's well-worn conventions for black characters in Civil War stories.

HOLLYWOOD TURNS AWAY FROM
DIXIE . . . THE LOST CAUSE IN CRISIS

Shenandoah proved to be the last major Civil War film until *Glory*'s appearance in 1989 opened a fourteen-year period that yielded *Gettysburg* (1993), *Sommersby* (1993), *Ride with the Devil* (1999), and, as already noted, *Gods and Generals* and *Cold Mountain* (both 2003). The years that separated *Glory* from *Gods and Generals* and *Cold Mountain* witnessed increasingly negative treatment of the Lost Cause. Although Confederates function as a mostly faceless, indistinct foe opposing the 54th Massachusetts Infantry and other U.S. units in *Glory*, one scene would greatly unsettle any Lost Cause advocate. On a rainy night during the initial period of training, Col. Robert Gould Shaw informs the soldiers of the 54th that if captured they will not be treated as prisoners of war. They will be returned to slavery and their white officers executed—an unequivocal reminder that the Confederacy was determined to preserve slavery and adamantly opposed to any U.S. policy that promised freedom.

Taken in chronological turn, the five films that followed *Glory* chart Hollywood's eroding sympathy for Confederates, their slaveholding society, and their war. Several Lost Cause elements stand out in *Gettysburg*, which translated Michael Shaara's Pulitzer Prize–winning novel *The Killer Angels* to the screen.[7] Most obvious is the idea that the battle represented a dramatic moment when the Confederacy could have established its independence. It falls to Brig. Gen. Lewis A. Armistead, one of Maj. Gen. George E. Pickett's brigade commanders, to establish the battle as the Confederacy's moment of decision. "They are all willing to make the supreme sacrifice to achieve victory here," he remarks about his soldiers just before the Pickett-Pettigrew assault on July 3, "the crowning victory and the end of this war." Joshua Lawrence Chamberlain, the film's Union hero during fighting on Little Round Top on July 2, agrees that Confederate independence hangs in the balance: "I think if we lose this fight," he states before the fighting begins, "we lose the war."[8]

The film also parallels Lost Cause writers in lavishing attention on generalship and questions of responsibility for the Confederate defeat. The roles of Robert E. Lee and James Longstreet receive full exposition, but they sometimes depart from Lost Cause models. Extensive attention to Lee leaves no doubt about his importance, and in one scene his soldiers erupt in a spontaneous expression of admiration — shaking their weapons, shouting their loyalty, and reaching out to touch him — that Lost Cause adherents would savor.[9] But overall Lee is tired and ill and strangely passive, seemingly resigned to leaving everything to God even before the battle opens. Longstreet, in contrast, functions as a modern warrior who knows the value of defensive fighting and repeatedly urges Lee to abandon offensive tactics. The sulking subordinate so often sketched in Lost Cause literature makes no appearance. Indeed, most viewers likely would conclude that Longstreet is the better general and Lee a noble anachronism with little understanding of how to fight an enemy whose weaponry renders frontal assaults suicidal.[10]

Scenes involving Confederate motivation relegate the institution of slavery to the margins, allowing characters to voice Lost Cause attitudes. In one, a visual homage to Winslow Homer's iconic painting titled *Prisoners from the Front*, Tom Chamberlain, Joshua's younger brother, asks three captured Confederates why they fight. A Tennessee yeoman responds: "I don't know about some other folk, but I ain't fightin' for no darkies one way or the other. I'm fightin' for my rights [pronounced 'rats']. All of us here, that's what we're fightin' for." Why can't the North just "live and let live?" wonders the Tennessean.[11] Up the chain of command, Brig. Gen. James L. Kemper, a Virginia politician commanding a brigade in Pickett's division, similarly denies the importance of slavery. "What we are fighting for here," he tells the British observer A. J. L. Fremantle, "is freedom from what we consider to be the rule of a foreign power. . . . That's what this war is all about." In a conversation on the morning of July 2, Lee and Longstreet agree that they resigned their U.S. commissions only because they could not countenance fighting against their families. On another occasion Longstreet tells Fremantle, "We should have freed the slaves, then fired on Fort Sumter." This last quite astonishing observation has no basis in historical fact but seeks to emphasize Longstreet's modern sensibilities, raising a crucial question: why fire on Fort Sumter if the slaves are already free?[12]

Robert E. Lee (Martin Sheen) and James Longstreet
(Tom Berenger) take their ease in *Gettysburg*. Neither character
exhibits devotion to the Confederacy in the film. Photofest.

A centerpiece of Lost Cause celebrations of Confederate gallantry and manhood, the Pickett-Pettigrew assault unfolds in a sequence that lasts about as long as it took Lee's infantry to traverse the undulating ground between Seminary Ridge and Cemetery Ridge on July 3. During the massive bombardment preceding the advance, a scene behind General Armistead's line establishes ties between Confederates and their Revolutionary War forebears. Armistead chats with the inquisitive Englishman Fremantle, pointing to officers descended from Patrick Henry and other Revolutionary patriots. Former Confederates who tried hard after the war to portray themselves as the true inheritors of the Revolutionary tradition surely would like this scene. They also would appreciate director Maxwell's detailed treatment of the attack itself. Panoramic shots of attacking formations dotted with battle flags, close-ups of the grisly human toll exacted by Union artillery and musket fire, and a climactic final surge that carries a few hundred Confederates through the northern defensive line create a feeling of desperate courage against intimidating obstacles. General Kemper falls with a ghastly wound and General Armistead with a mortal one, joining masses of their nameless infantrymen sacrificed in the name of their cause.

But precisely what cause is it? Along with its characterizations of a passive Lee and a highly admirable Longstreet, *Gettysburg* contradicts Lost Cause tradition in one other important way. There are innumerable Confederate flags in evidence but no sense of Confederate nationalism animating soldiers in the Army of Northern Virginia — many of whom in 1863 would have described the army as the embodiment of their *nation*. Time and again southerners celebrate their states, as when Armistead tells Fremantle on July 3: "We are all sons of Virginia here." Lee and Longstreet address this topic in several scenes. On the morning of July 2, Longstreet remarks that his loyalty lies with his home state and his family — a sentiment with which Lee concurs. That night Longstreet confides to Armistead his suspicion of all political causes: "My only cause is victory." Following the bitter failure on July 3, Lee and Longstreet talk beside a flickering fire. "If this war goes on," Lee mutters, "and it will, it will, what else can we do but go on you and I? Does it matter, after all, who wins? Is that ever really the question? Will Almighty God ask that question in the end?" Former Confederates certainly asked that question after the war, and the historical Lee cared passionately about Confederate independence. He functioned throughout the war as an ardent nationalist, as did many of his subordinates and men who served in Confederate ranks. *Gettysburg* would have it otherwise.[13]

Released the same year as *Gettysburg*, *Sommersby* takes a decidedly less tolerant stance toward the Confederate cause.[14] Set in the early postwar period, it shifts Daniel Vigne's *The Return of Martin Guerre* (1982) from sixteenth-century France to Tennessee in 1865–66. As the story unfolds following Jack Sommersby's return from the war, it takes on a post–civil rights movement tone. Black characters play a major role, and not as the loyal retainers so dear to Lost Cause hearts. Throughout the story, Jack Sommersby manifests implausibly enlightened views about race. One important scene conveys the positive tenor of his racial attitudes — as well as the very racist postures of his ex-Confederate neighbors. Jack proposes to a mixed crowd of black and white people in a town meeting that they grow tobacco. He will give them a piece of land, tools, and fertilizer, and they will keep half of the profits. When he pays off the mortgage on his farm, moreover, they can buy their plots of land at a fair price. He is a thoroughly sympathetic character who hopes former slaves will participate fully. An incredulous African American named Joseph asks whether "coloreds and all" can join in. Jack says yes. The other white people are taken aback, murmuring that they won't work that way. "I ain't livin' next to no niggers," rasps one woman. In these and other scenes dealing with race, Jack and his wife, Laurel, find themselves opposed by former Confederates.

Jack envisions a biracial community in which shared economic want trumps race. He calls for collective action. In order to purchase seed and other supplies to make the tobacco crop, the community must pool its resources. Black people and white people contribute watches, valuables, or whatever they can muster. An old black man gives a piece of pottery, and Joseph offers some beautiful carved ivory. As Jack leaves to get the seed, Joseph, an old black woman, Laurel, and Laurel's son all wave good-bye. Several community action sequences follow, with black and white people stepping off beds for seedlings while the music swells and their children play together. They eventually harvest the crop and cure the tobacco.

The film closes with a courtroom sequence during which Jack is tried for murder. His black friends join Laurel in rallying around him despite knowledge that he is not her husband but a man named Horace Townsend, a look-alike who spent time in Yankee prison with the real Jack Sommersby and determined to take his place. Jack confronts one racist neighbor during the trial, insisting that the man agreed to testify only to prevent Sommersby from "selling land to a colored man, who would then be a property owner on a level with citizens like yourself." The neighbor turns to the judge, played by James Earl Jones, calling him a "nappy-headed son-of-a-bitch." "In two years when the Yankees are gone," the witness hisses, "you will be in the field where you belong." The courtroom scene provides no clue about *why* the Sommersbys differ so radically from their white neighbors regarding race. Whatever the answer to that unspoken question, and no matter how anachronistic Jack's and Laurel's behavior toward black neighbors within the context of early postwar Tennessee, the film's repudiation of the Lost Cause tradition is unequivocal and powerful.[15]

Ride with the Devil deals with another unsavory dimension of the conflict and neatly sidesteps the major pitfalls inherent in making a modern film about Confederates.[16] Director Ang Lee shows how to explore a proslavery society that nearly destroyed the United States without alienating critics and much of his potential audience. He adopts a two-part approach: first, show racism and brutality on both sides; and second, create a violent tapestry in which the principal characters stand aloof from politics and ideology, dealing in human terms with disruptive events and manifesting enlightened attitudes about slavery and race. An opening text accurately sets the film's turbulent stage: "On the western frontier of Missouri, the American Civil War was fought not by armies, but by neighbors. Informal gangs of local southern *bushwhackers* fought a bloody and desperate guerrilla war against the occupying Union army and pro-Union *Jayhawkers*. Allegiance to either side was dangerous. But it was more dangerous still to find oneself caught in the middle." The film includes large doses of vicious behavior by Union and Confederate soldiers, murders of pro-Confederate and pro-Union civilians, and almost casual savagery on both sides.[17]

The protagonists are Confederate guerrillas Jacob "Jake" Roedel, Jack Bull Chiles, George Clyde (who makes "Yankee killing as entertaining as greasing a gander"), and a free black man named Daniel Holt. This diverse quartet departs conspicuously from *Gone with the Wind*'s Lost Cause catalog of Confederate types. No grand planters, cultured ladies, or honor-bound regular army officers populate the film. Jake's parents are Unionist Germans, but his friendship with Jack's family has made him "as southern as they come." Jack's family lives in a comfortable two-story brick house — not a mansion like Tara or Twelve Oaks — and own some slaves. Clyde and Holt grew up together, with Clyde part of a slaveholding family targeted by Kansas Jayhawkers.

A film charged with racial tensions among both Union and Confederate figures labors to portray a believable bond among the four Confederate guerillas. The men transcend nineteenth-century racial boundaries in ways that seem highly unlikely but probably are necessary in a film about Confederates released in 1999 and directed by Lee. Early on, viewers learn that Holt killed three Kansas Jayhawkers who came after Clyde. Now other Yankees want to settle accounts with Holt "real bad." Clyde sums up the relationship succinctly: "He's not my nigger. He's just a nigger who I trust with my life every day and every night, that's all." Late in the film, Holt tells Jake that Clyde had bought his freedom. Jake initially voices doubts about Holt, remarking that "a nigger with guns is still a nervous thing to me." The two gradually become close friends and the film's principal male characters. Although they cannot be dismissed as mere action "buddies," they do function in ways typical of that stock Hollywood type.

After the men's relationships have been established, they meet a young widow named Sue Lee Shelley. A pro-Confederate Missourian, she falls in love with and has a child with Jack and eventually marries Jake. Sue Lee also must accept Holt, whom she initially identifies as a slave rather than one of the guerrillas. The four men are spending the winter on a farm owned by the family of Sue Lee's dead husband. During her first visit to a small dwelling they have built into a hillside, Holt walks in. "What's he doing here, inside?" she asks. "Ma'am, this nigger's with me," answers George Clyde, "His name is Holt." "Wouldn't he be more useful off in a field plowing?" she responds. No, says Clyde, he is "one nigger I wouldn't try to hitch behind a plow." Sue Lee soon acknowledges Holt as one of the guerrillas, allowing her entry into what has become an even more implausible group.

Having dealt with the problem of race among his leading characters, Lee carefully defines them as "good" Confederate guerrillas. They all participate in bloody encounters, and the body count of innocent civilians and Union and Confederate guerrillas rapidly mounts. Jack and his father, George Clyde, Jake's Unionist father, and Sue Lee's former father-in-law are among the slain. But the good guerrillas are easily identifiable among more loathsome comrades who exhibit repellant racism and a willingness to kill indiscriminately. One of the bad guerrillas casually mentions that some units are "scalping every nigger they can find," glances at Holt, and adds, "except, of course, our own." A crucial sequence depicts the sack of Lawrence, Kansas, on August 21, 1863, by Confederate guerrillas under William Clarke Quantrill. Quantrill's raid, which left approximately 150 men and boys in Lawrence dead, ranks among the war's notable atrocities, a brutal mission of retribution aimed at punishing the town for its role in the long-standing contest over slavery in the territories. In Lee's rendering of the event, bad guerrillas are personified by a cold-eyed killer named Pit Mackeson. They murder unarmed men in front of their terrified families, burn the school, and ransack businesses and homes. Jake and Holt refuse to participate in the slaughter. Their behavior raises doubts in Mackeson, who threatens Holt and later wounds Jake before leading his own band on a rampage of robbery and plunder.

The guerrillas in *Ride with the Devil* operate in a world little concerned with national allegiance. Although viewers know in a general way that the guerrillas favor a southern way of life dependent on slavery, no character takes the time to explain precisely what the Confederacy means to them. Jake and Holt discuss motivation in a crucial scene toward the end of the film. Why had they fought as Confederate guerrillas? What had been their *cause*? Holt's had been his friend George Clyde, with whom he stood when Yankees killed Clyde's family. Jake, similarly, had supported Jack

During the raid on Lawrence, Jake Roedel (Tobey Maguire) confronts racist Confederate guerrilla who threatens Daniel Holt (Jeffrey Wright). The scene fosters a sense of the improbable comradeship that unites Roedel and Holt across racial lines. Photofest.

after Yankees brutalized the Chiles family. Thus did a former slave and the son of pro-Union German parents find themselves fighting against the United States. Neither is really a Confederate. Their causes are personal, and when George Clyde and Jack Chiles are killed, Holt and Jake are free to cast off their nominal Confederate association. The film ends on a note of racial harmony between men who had been caught up in, but ideologically unconnected with, a bloody war between the Confederacy and the United States.

Sommersby and *Ride with the Devil* strongly suggested that Hollywood would no longer rely on durable Lost Cause themes in exploring the Confederate experience. Perhaps the exploits of Confederate soldiers fighting for their beleaguered cause, attractive white characters who unabashedly embrace and sacrifice for the slaveholding republic, and loyal slaves who help keep the home front functioning had been banished for good.

So it seemed until 2003, when *Gods and Generals* highlighted the resiliency of the Lost Cause tradition.[18] Directed by Ron Maxwell, whose credits included *Gettysburg* a decade earlier, this film served up a hearty helping of Lost Cause fare. It also triggered a contentious debate among reviewers and historians that recalled, in more subdued form, the reactions to *The*

Birth of a Nation and *Gone with the Wind*. *Newsday* dismissed the film as a "shameless apologia for the Confederacy as a divinely inspired crusade for faith, home and slave labor." The *Boston Globe* thought "it insults the sensibilities of anyone not clinging to rosy memories of the slave-era South." The *Washington Post* charged that the film was "clearly intended as something of a Confederate Honor Restoration Project, in which the men of the South are cut loose from the weight of slavery's evil and portrayed as God-fearing, patriotic, noble and heroic." Academic critics also weighed in. "*Gods and Generals* brings to the big screen," wrote one, "the major themes of Lost Cause mythology that professional historians have been working for half a century to combat."[19]

Maxwell countered that such criticism amounted to nothing but political correctness. Asked what would entice a multiethnic American audience to a story that "treats Confederate figures with dignity," he remarked: "The truth! . . . Jackson was a Union man. Lee and Jackson were both uncomfortable with slavery. But that is not what their war was about. . . . Virginia was their home. They would fight for their home. . . . There are some things in my picture over which some historians might differ, but there are no lies or outright distortions in it. And 'political correctness'? Never!" Dennis Frye, a historian who worked closely with Maxwell on the film, supported the director. "Making history a reality is Ron Maxwell's passion," wrote Frye. "Generating *good* history from Hollywood is his indefatigable mission." The *American Enterprise* seconded Frye's opinion in a staunchly supportive review that declared the film "an American masterpiece about the most myth-laden, destructive, and regenerative episode in American history." This reviewer observed that Maxwell understood "just how startling it will be for an audience to see Southerners presented as men who believe they are fighting a defensive war against Yankee imperialists."[20]

A "prequel" to *Gettysburg* based on Jeff Shaara's novel of the same title, *Gods and Generals* touches almost every Lost Cause base. To a greater degree than the book, Maxwell's screenplay makes Stonewall Jackson the central character, and its handling of slaves and slavery also departs significantly from Shaara's text. The film sympathetically explores Confederate motivations for secession and features Robert E. Lee and Jackson as a brilliant and devout command team. Combat sequences center on the battles of First Bull Run, Fredericksburg, and Chancellorsville—all Confederate victories and the last two showcases for the talents of Lee and Jackson against much larger U.S. armies. It links Confederates to the Revolutionary generation and takes pains to explain that Confederates fight to defend home and hearth. Although the film also portrays Union characters, Confederate generals and civilians dominate the narrative. More than forty minutes pass before the first U.S. soldiers appear to serve as an amorphous foe vanquished by Confederates at First Bull Run. No Federal soldier has a speaking part until Joshua Chamberlain's entrance nearly an hour into the film.[21]

Lee and Jackson shoulder the burden of explaining Confederate motivations. In a scene at the Virginia secession convention, a speaker denounces Abraham Lincoln and evokes the example of George Washington and Lee's father, Revolutionary hero Henry "Light Horse Harry" Lee, in tendering command of the state's forces. "Profoundly impressed," Lee accepts and vows to devote himself to "the service of my native state, in whose behalf alone I will ever again draw my sword." Shortly after Virginia secedes, Jackson tells his brigade of Shenandoah Valley soldiers that the North precipitated the sectional crisis just as Great Britain forced a crisis on their ancestors. "We will never allow the armies of others to march into our state and tyrannize our people," affirms Jackson. In a subsequent conversation with cavalry officer James E. B. Stuart, Jackson refers to Yankees as "violators of our homes and firesides." More than a year later, before the battle of Fredericksburg, Lee makes the same point more fully. "There is something that these Yankees do not understand, will never understand," he says while gazing across the Rappahannock River toward Ferry Farm, where George Washington was born. "You see these rivers and valleys and streams, fields, even towns?" he asks with emotion in his voice. "They are just markings on a map to those people in the War Office in Washington," but for Lee and Confederates they are birthplaces, burial grounds, and battlefields where their ancestors fought: "They are the incarnation of all our memories and all that we are, all that we are."

Most vocal about their loyalty to Virginia at the outset, Lee and Jackson soon become ardent Confederates. Everything they prize about Virginia becomes exemplified by the Confederacy. In this vein, Jackson directly ties the Confederate attempt at nation building to that of the revolutionary generation when, in taking leave from his first command, he alludes to "this, our second war of independence." Jackson also lectures a member of his staff about the relative nobility of the Union and Confederate war efforts. "If the Republicans lose their little war" and suffer defeat in the next round of elections, he observes, they will simply return to their homes "fat with war profits." But if Confederates fail to achieve victory, "we lose our country. We lose our independence. We lose it all." Former Confederate writers could not have offered a more invidious comparison of the two causes. That same winter, Lee toasts southern women, without whose bravery and fortitude southern soldiers would lack the strength to "defend the Confederate cause."

Lee's toast reflects the film's portrayal of Confederate slaveholding women and other civilians as self-sacrificing patriots. In an early scene in Fredericksburg, young men leaving for the army receive a flag and assurances from their mother, Jane Howison Beale, that everyone on the home front will support them. Mrs. Beale also remarks with an air of acceptance that many men will fall before true freedom comes to the Confederacy. Another scene suggests support for the Confederacy across class lines. Common soldiers bid their wives good-bye and brothers exchange parting words as mechanics, yeoman farmers, and working-class men hurry to join their units. During the bombardment of Fredericksburg in December 1862, women and children show pluck as they become refugees, trudging across a winter's landscape to the safety of Confederate military lines. Stonewall Jackson commends the courage of women and children left to fend for themselves, calling for execution of deserters in part because they have betrayed the trust of loyal civilians.

Treatment of African American characters stands as the film's most controversial dimension. One of the Beale family's house slaves named Martha sets the overall tone. Although a bit more complex than Mammy in *Gone with the Wind*, Martha shares a similar bond with her owners. She wishes her young masters well with kisses and a brief embrace when they ride off to war in their new Confederate uniforms. As the Union's Army of the Potomac approaches before the battle of Fredericksburg, Martha thinks primarily of the white family's safety. "We got to get you and dem children out of here in a hurry," she tells her mistress. "We'll all leave together," replies Jane Beale: "I will not leave you to the mercy of those blue devils." "Miss Jane," comes the reply, "you know they are not going to be bothering us colored folks." If she stays, adds Martha, the Yankees likely will not plunder the house. After the Federal shelling on December 11, during which the black and white members of the household seek shelter in the cellar, the Beales leave in an ambulance — after Jane and Martha embrace. Federals arrive soon thereafter and meet Martha in the front yard. "Is this your master's place?" inquires a soldier. "This is my place," she answers. "Sorry to bother you, Ma'am," reply the soldiers, who spare the Beale property without expressing a hint of surprise that a black woman

Stonewall Jackson (Stephen Lang) offers Jim Lewis (Frankie Faison)
the job as his cook in *Gods and Generals*. Photofest.

would own such a fine home. After the battle of Fredericksburg, Federals
use the Beale house as a hospital, which gives Martha an opportunity to
deliver a mixed message of loyalty to the Beales and a yearning to be free:
"I love them people you done chased from this house. I'se known them
most all of my life. The Beales is good people. Mister General, I'se born a
slave, and I wants to die free. Lord knows I wants to die free, and I want
my children to be free. Heaven help me. And God bless you all."[22]

Two scenes between Stonewall Jackson and Jim Lewis, his black cook,
match *Gone with the Wind* in establishing a sympathetic relationship
across racial lines. The first occurs when Jackson meets Lewis in 1861. "I
understand you are from Lexington," says the general. "You come highly
recommended to me, Jim." Lewis replies: "Lexington is my home, General, same as you'rn. If I could do my share in defendin' my home, I'll be
doin' the same as you." "If you love your country, fear the Lord, and have
no trouble getting up at four in the morning, the job is yours," says Jackson.
Lewis takes the assignment — eager, apparently, to help defend his home
and his "country" against Federals who pose an unexplained threat to him
and other black people in Lexington.

Later in the film, after a long day's march, the two men look forward
to a Confederacy without slavery. Under a star-studded night sky, the
mounted Jackson looks skyward and asks God "to watch over Jim Lewis's

family, over his friends, his loved ones wherever they may be." Lewis says, "Lord, I know you sees into the hearts of all men just like you sees into the heart of old Jim Lewis." The camera focuses on Jackson, his eyes closed, as Lewis talks. "And Lord, I know . . . there be no hidin' from your truth and your ever-watchful eye." "Amen," says Jackson. "How is it, Lord," continues Lewis, ". . . a good Christian man like some folks I know can tolerate dey black brothers in bondage? How is it, Lord, you don't just break dem chains? How is it, Lord? My heart is open and achin', and I wants to know." Caught up in Lewis's questions, Jackson takes over: "Lord, speak to us, speak to your children, speak to Jim Lewis and Thomas Jackson, your humble and obedient servants. Speak to all of us. Our hearts *are* open. Lord, you show us the way, we will follow." Lewis and Jackson both say "Amen." Then the slaveholding general raises the possibility of freedom: "Jim, you must know that there are some officers in this army who are of the opinion that we should be enlisting Negroes as a condition for freedom. General Lee is among them." Lewis acknowledges rumors about this "'round the camp." "Your people will be free, one way or t'other," asserts Jackson, the "only question is whether the southern government will have the good sense to do it first and soon and in so doing seal a bond of enduring friendship between us." "That what they says, General," allows Lewis without a trace of sarcasm or irony. "God's plan is a great mystery," concludes Jackson: "It will be revealed to us."[23]

As far as testimony from the time reveals, this last episode between Jackson and Lewis has no basis in fact. Nor does the historical record suggest that Jackson manifested any active opposition to slavery. He probably believed that God would settle the question in time and that mortals should refrain from tampering with divine intentions. Why, then, construct the exchange with Jim Lewis? It seems a gratuitous Lost Cause gesture calculated to recast the nineteenth-century Jackson for a modern audience. Maxwell conceded that modern viewers might find it hard to understand the scenes with Lewis and Martha Beale. But Lewis "stayed with Jackson as long as he lived, out of loyalty to him as a man," and Martha Beale, "a real historical figure," is "treated with respect" in the film.[24]

As already noted, Maxwell proudly touted the accuracy of his film. "Perhaps the most powerful aspect of the motion picture *Gods and Generals*," he wrote in a book published as a companion to the film, "is the fact that the story is true."[25] Indeed, apart from the imagined scenes between Jackson and Lewis, the treatment of Confederates generally hews closely to the historical record. Maxwell's attention to feelings of Confederate nationalism on the part of Lee and other characters certainly makes sense. Lee and Jackson were very religious and gifted commanders who won victories against long odds. Although the Confederacy suffered from internal tensions of various kinds, most civilians supported the war despite widespread suffering. Civilian and military leaders often praised the steadfastness of Confederate women, and letters and diaries include myriad references to the war as a fight for home and against northern coercion. Some slaves probably exhibited loyalty, or at least experienced complex emotions, regarding their masters. The problem in *Gods and Generals* is one of balance—what Maxwell left out in creating his tapestry of valiant Confederate officers and citizens at war. What about the thousands of slaves who ran away to Union lines? Or those who sullenly went about their business but hoped for U.S. success? What about slavery as a precipitant of secession and war? Or white citizens unhappy with the Confederacy? The list of questions could go on and might include this: who would guess that a film so celebratory of Confederates at war could be released in 2003?

As if on cue later in 2003, *Cold Mountain* offered a striking counterpoint to *Gods and Generals*.[26] Based on Charles Frazier's best-selling novel and directed by Anthony Minghella, it tells the story of a Confederate deserter's Odysseus-like trek home to North Carolina from the Virginia battlefront. Many reviewers praised it, as when *USA Today* gushed: "In its vivid depiction of tragedy, waste and the plundering of a generation, Anthony Minghella's epic . . . is the equal of any Civil War movie ever made." Slightly less enthusiastic, the *Washington Post* lauded the "subtly spectacular craftsman Anthony Minghella" and termed *Cold Mountain* "one of those films that might be called 'complete.'" An academic reviewer noted various factual errors but applauded Minghella's bringing to the screen so "unflinching a portrayal of the bleak and unsettling realities" of a Civil War experienced by "thousands of hardscrabble Southern men and women who lived through it." The *New York Times* liked the film's showing that "the Civil War, like World War II, empowered a generation of women."[27]

Taking a dramatically different position from Maxwell, Minghella stressed that neither historical accuracy nor the Civil War especially concerned him. "The film is not a history lesson," he stated. "It doesn't exist to stand in for a study of a real event. Rather, it tries to cast light on some circumstances which surround any war. . . . If I thought I was making a Civil War film, then I wouldn't have taken this project on." Hoping to explore characters "caught up in tensions they often don't understand," he simply used the Civil War as a setting. Yet he also noted, "I mired myself

Ada Monroe (Nicole Kidman) and Inman (Jude Law) shortly before he leaves to fight for the Confederacy. In earlier scenes, she had mocked his decision to join the army and expressed relief at escaping from slaveholding society in Charleston. Photofest.

in Civil War books"—an odd expenditure of time in light of his other comments.[28]

Cold Mountain can best be understood as a feminist antiwar film that turns almost every Lost Cause convention on its head. Virtually all white southern women in the film are either indifferent to or deeply against the war. A few examples will illustrate this point. Just before the war, in a scene much like one at Twelve Oaks in *Gone with the Wind*, a man bursts into church and announces secession. "We got our war!" a young man shouts. Amid much whooping and hollering, other men exclaim: "We got our war! We got it! We got it! It's about time!" Ada Monroe, the film's slaveholding heroine, says derisively to Inman, the nonslaveholding male protagonist, that now he has "his" war. A short time later she asks if Inman is enlisting. "If there is a war, we'll all fight," he answers. Did he get a tintype made, she inquires sarcastically, "With your musket and your courage on display?" In another scene, privation plagues the home front, and Ada wants Inman to stop fighting, leave the army, and return to her. "Come back to me is my request," reads her letter to him. He promptly deserts, affirming women's power to undermine the Confederate war effort. Later in the film, the rough yeoman prototype Ruby Thewes learns that her father, himself a Confederate deserter, has been shot. She pronounces the war "bullshit."

Men made the weather, she proclaims in her usual salty manner, and now they stand in the rain and say, "Shit, it's raining!" These and many other moments in *Cold Mountain* leave no doubt that Melanie Wilkes and her ilk would find few compatriots among their North Carolina sisters on Cold Mountain.

Few appealing characters in *Cold Mountain* exhibit any pro-Confederate sentiment. The Home Guard, commanded by a simplistically evil officer named Teague, represents the most obvious expression of the Confederate state. Early in the war, Teague announces that the Home Guard will watch over Cold Mountain while the area's men are away fighting with Confederate armies. He later says deserters will be executed and anyone who helps them deemed a traitor to the Confederacy. Teague's men pillage and kill at their whim, presenting an inaccurate portrait of the Home Guard that conflates bushwhackers, deserters, guerrillas, and other irregular units. In one graphic scene, the Home Guard murders a yeoman farmer in cold blood, tortures his wife, and kills two sons who are trying to avoid Confederate service. A dispirited Inman refers to Confederate soldiers as fools "sent off to fight with a flag and a lie," leaving viewers to conclude that the Confederacy duped the poor fellows into donning gray uniforms. A military surgeon's comments support this idea. Looking out at slaves working in a field, he speaks scornfully about the cause for which wounded men in his hospital are fighting. The fools are dying for rich slaveholders, he says, in a classic example of the "rich man's war, poor man's fight" formulation. It seems that all the nice white folks in the Confederacy are deserters, soldiers suffering from false consciousness, or disgruntled women against the war, while the Home Guard consists of pro-Confederate fiends who wrap themselves in patriotism and torment their neighbors.[29]

Cold Mountain does align with Lost Cause writers in largely removing slaves and slavery from the story. Unlike Frazier's novel, Minghella's film imagines western North Carolina as very white — almost as white as the *Andy Griffith Show*'s Mayberry, which was set in the same part of the world. Although fewer black people lived in mountainous North Carolina than in piedmont or tidewater areas, the absence of African Americans rings false. Slavery and black people serve principally to help leading white characters manifest enlightened attitudes. Ada finds herself in western North Carolina after leaving Charleston, South Carolina. The daughter of a slaveholding clergyman from the birthplace of secession, she nevertheless expresses happiness at escaping "from a world of slaves and corsets and cotton." Following her father's death, Ada frees the family's slaves.

Antislavery sentiment among women from South Carolina's slaveholding class was not unknown, as abolitionists Sarah and Angelina Grimké most famously demonstrated. Yet Ada would have belonged to a statistically insignificant minority. The film offers no explanation for her actions, which imply covert abolitionism. Inman also distances himself from proslavery Confederates. One night he stumbles upon a preacher carrying a black woman's limp body. The man had gotten her pregnant and, having drugged her, is on his way to drown the unfortunate soul. Inman saves the woman, ties the preacher to a post, and continues his journey back to Cold Mountain. Along the way he runs into a group of African Americans running toward freedom. "I've got no quarrel with you," he tells them, but they move on past. Soon the Home Guard arrives, dogs in tow, to chase Inman and the African Americans, who join one another as victims of predatory Confederate oppression.

Anyone watching *Cold Mountain* might wonder how the Confederacy lasted four years. What regime would not collapse quickly under the weight of women unhappy with the war, yeomen duped into fighting for slaveholders, and a Home Guard deployed to terrorize citizens? As with *Gods and Generals*, the problem lies in the film's emphases. *Cold Mountain* usefully portrays aspects of conflict on the home front seldom captured on film. Many men and women in the Confederacy opposed the war, and desertion plagued every southern army. Parts of mountainous North Carolina experienced lethal internal tensions, sometimes tied to heavy-handed actions by Confederate conscription officers in the state. Guerrillas, bushwhackers, and local troops often preyed on civilians. But the large majority of white southern women — especially slaveholding women like Ada Monroe — supported the Confederate nation until very late in the conflict. An equally large proportion of Confederate soldiers, most of them nonslaveholders like Inman, remained in the ranks. Nothing like Minghella's Home Guard existed, and Ada's stance regarding slavery can be dismissed as profoundly anachronistic. Minghella's anti–Lost Cause version of the Confederacy, though more appealing to most modern audiences than *Gods and Generals*, continues a long Hollywood tradition of ignoring historical facts in favor of good storytelling.[30]

The Lost Cause tradition may have enjoyed its last hurrah in *Gods and Generals*. In a cultural landscape profoundly shaped by the civil rights movement, the Confederate slaveholding republic has lost much of its once powerful romantic appeal. Residual influence likely will rest with television, where *Gone with the Wind* and other films with Lost Cause themes are always available, and in the availability of older films in other formats. The degree to which future Hollywood productions will vanquish the Lost Cause from *popular* understanding of the Civil War remains to be seen.

NOTES

1. For a fuller discussion of Lost Cause symbols in the 1980s and 1990s, see the introduction and chapter 1 of Gary W. Gallagher, *Causes Won, Lost, and Forgotten: How Hollywood Shapes What We Know about the Civil War* (Chapel Hill: University of North Carolina Press, 2008). For the grosses of *The Birth of a Nation* and *Gone with the Wind*, see Bruce Chadwick, *The Reel Civil War: Mythmaking in American Film* (New York: Knopf, 2001), 132, 187.

2. On the Lost Cause, see Gaines M. Foster, *Ghosts of the Confederacy: Defeat, the Lost Cause, and the Emergence of the New South, 1865–1913* (New York: Oxford University Press, 1987); Gary W. Gallagher and Alan T. Nolan, eds., *The Myth of the Lost Cause and Civil War History* (Bloomington: Indiana University Press, 2000); and Alice Fahs and Joan Waugh, eds., *The Memory of the Civil War in American Culture* (Chapel Hill: University of North Carolina Press, 2004).

3. On Dixon and Griffith, see John Hope Franklin, "Silent Cinema as Historical Mythmaker," in *Hollywood's America: United States History Through Its Films*, ed. Steven Mintz and Randy Roberts (St. James, N.Y.: Brandywine, 1993), 42–47.

4. Joan L. Silverman, "Birth of a Nation," in Charles Reagan Wilson and William Ferris, eds., *Encyclopedia of Southern Culture* (Chapel Hill: University of North Carolina Press, 1989), 947; Francis Hackett, "Brotherly Love," *New Republic* 1 (March 20, 1915), 185; Chadwick, *Reel Civil War*, 131–32; Franklin, "Silent Cinema," 48. Franklin's essay offers a good overview of the negative reaction to the film.

5. Selznick originally had planned for 2,500 extras as wounded soldiers in the scene at the railroad station, changing to 1,600 humans and 1,200 dummies because of budgetary constraints. The Screen Extra's Guild insisted that all the "wounded" be real bodies. Selznick agreed, but the guild could supply no more than 1,500 people. See Bob Thomas, *The Story of Gone with the Wind* (New York: National Publishers, 1967), [23].

6. For an interesting discussion of Selznick's decisions relating to African American characters and race in *Gone with the Wind*, see Leonard J. Leff, "Gone with the Wind and Hollywood's Racial Politics," *Atlantic Monthly* 284 (December 1999): 106–14.

7. The main characters in *Gettysburg* are Robert E. Lee (Martin Sheen), James Longstreet (Tom Berenger), George E. Pickett (Stephen Lang), Lewis A. Armistead (Richard Jordan), A. J. L. Fremantle (James Lancaster), James L. Kemper (Royce D. Applegate), Joshua L. Chamberlain (Jeff Daniels), Buster Kilrain (Kevin Conway), and Tom Chamberlain (C. Thomas Howell). New York publisher David McKay published *The Killer Angels* in 1974. For a discussion of the historical accuracy of Shaara's novel, see D. Scott Hartwig, *A Killer Angels Companion* (Gettysburg, Pa.: Thomas, 1996). For a thoughtful essay on the film, see William Blair, "The Brother's War: Gettysburg the Movie and American Memory," in *Making and Remaking Pennsylvania's Civil War*, ed. William Blair and William Pencak (University Park: Pennsylvania State University Press, 2001), 245–60.

8. On Gettysburg as an overblown turning point, see Gary W. Gallagher, "Gettysburg:

A 2003 Perspective," in *Gettysburg Commemorative Issue*, a joint special issue from the editors of *Civil War Times Illustrated*, *Civil War Times*, and *Military History* (Summer 2003): 80–90.

9. The re-enactors playing Confederate soldiers broke into unscripted applause and shouting when Martin Sheen, as Lee, rode by during shooting. Ron Maxwell decided to keep the scene in the film. For a historical example of this phenomenon, see Edward Porter Alexander, *Fighting for the Confederacy: The Personal Recollections of General Edward Porter Alexander*, ed. Gary W. Gallagher (Chapel Hill: University of North Carolina Press, 1989), 345–46. Lee's best artillerist, Alexander likened the outpouring of emotion to "a military sacrament."

10. James Longstreet's reputation underwent a remarkable transformation in the late 1980s and 1990s, due in large measure to the flattering portrayals in Shaara's *The Killer Angels* and Maxwell's *Gettysburg*. In July 1998, admirers unveiled a statue of "Old Pete" on the battlefield at Gettysburg.

11. *The Killer Angels* does not include a scene with Tom Chamberlain interrogating captured Confederates. The younger Chamberlain merely recounts the conversation, and the allusion to "rats," to his brother Joshua.

12. Longstreet's *From Manassas to Appomattox: Memoirs of the Civil War in America* (Philadelphia: Lippincott, 1896) makes no mention of freeing slaves. Longstreet's most recent biographer notes that when Lee asked his lieutenant's opinion about enrolling slaves as soldiers in the last winter of the war, Longstreet "opposed the idea because it would mean the 'necessity' of abolishing slavery in the future without 'materially aiding us in the present'" (Jeffry D. Wert, *General James Longstreet: The Confederacy's Most Controversial Soldier, A Biography* [New York: Simon and Schuster, 1993], 397).

13. On Lee as a nationalist, see Gary W. Gallagher, *Lee and His Army in Confederate History* (Chapel Hill: University of North Carolina Press, 2001), 162–75.

14. The main characters in *Sommersby* are John "Jack" Sommersby (Richard Gere), Laurel Sommersby (Jodie Foster), Judge Barry Conrad Isaacs (James Earl Jones), Joseph (Frankie Faison), and Orin Meecham (Bill Pullman).

15. Journalist John T. Trowbridge's travels through Tennessee immediately after the war revealed considerable white antipathy toward freed slaves — suggesting the degree to which Sommersby's ideas about race would have stood out among his white peers. From near Memphis, Trowbridge described the reaction among "Southern ladies and gentlemen" on a train who looked out of their car to see homeless black people camped near the tracks. "That's freedom!" they said scornfully. "That's what the Yankees have done for 'em!" "They'll all be dead before spring. Niggers can't take care of themselves. How much better off they were when they were slaves!" (John T. Trowbridge, *The Desolate South, 1865–1866*, ed. Gordon Carroll [New York: Duell, Sloan and Pierce, 1956], 176.)

16. The main characters in *Ride with the Devil* are Jacob "Jake" Roedel (Tobey Maguire), Jack Bull Chiles (Skeet Ulrich), George Clyde (Simon Baker), Daniel Holt (Jeffrey Wright), Sue Lee Shelley (Jewel Kilcher), and Pitt Mackeson (Jonathan Rhys Meyers).

17. *Ride with the Devil* does not exaggerate the brutality of Missouri's war. See Michael Fellman, *Inside War: The Guerrilla Conflict in Missouri during the Civil War* (New York: Oxford University Press, 1989), and Albert Castel and Thomas Goodrich, *Bloody Bill Anderson: The Short, Savage Life of a Civil War Guerrilla* (Mechanicsburg, Pa.: Stackpole, 1998).

18. The main characters in *Gods and Generals* are Robert E. Lee (Robert Duvall), Thomas J. "Stonewall" Jackson (Stephen Lang), Joshua Lawrence Chamberlain (Jeff Daniels), Buster Kilrain (Kevin Conway), Thomas Chamberlain (C. Thomas Howell), Jim Lewis (Frankie Faison), Anna Morrison Jackson (Kali Rocha), Jane Beale (Mia Dillon), Martha Beale (Donzaleigh Abernathy), and Fanny Chamberlain (Mira Sorvino).

19. *New York Times*, March 9, 2003, The Word, p. 14; *Washington Post*, February 21, 2003, C1, C4; *Journal of American History* 90 (December 2003): 1123 (review by Steven E. Woodworth).

20. John E. Stanchak, "Gods and Generals," *Civil War Times* 41 (December 2002): 37; Dennis E. Frye, "The Making of 'Gods and Generals,'" *North & South* 5 (October 2002): 24; Bill Kauffman, "The Civil War Returns," *American Enterprise* 14 (March 2003): 25. See also Kathryn Jorgensen, "'Gods & Generals' Opens Nationally; Movie Critics Boo," *Civil War News* 28 (April 2003): 1, 30.

21. In Shaara's book (New York: Ballantine, 1996), Union officers Winfield Scott Hancock and Joshua Lawrence Chamberlain have much larger parts and Jackson a much smaller one. In terms of northern characters, Francis Preston Blair Sr., long a figure on the Washington political scene, appears early in the film to offer Lee command of U.S. forces mustering outside Washington.

22. Jane Howison Beale's journal has been published as *The Journal of Jane Howison Beale of Fredericksburg, Virginia, 1850–1862* ([Fredericksburg, Va.]: Historic Fredericksburg Foundation, 1979). In it, Beale expresses considerable concern about slaves who have run away to Union forces. Her entries concerning the battle of Fredericksburg mention Martha just once—on December 11, 1862: "We were aroused before day by Gen. Lee's 'Signal guns,' but not knowing their special significance, we did not hurry ourselves, until 'Martha' our chamber maid came in and said in a rather mournful tone, 'Miss Jane the Yankees are coming, they have got two pontoons nearly across the river'" (69).

23. In March 1868, Lee remarked to a former Confederate staff officer that he told Jefferson Davis "often and early in the war that the slaves should be emancipated, that it was the only way to remove a weakness at home and to get sympathy abroad, and to divide our enemies, but Davis would not hear of it." No wartime documents corroborate this statement. See William Allan, "Memoranda of Conversations with General Robert E. Lee," in Gary W. Gallagher, ed., *Lee the Soldier* (Lincoln: University of Nebraska Press, 1996), 12. Very late in the war, Lee did support placing slaves in the Confederate army and granting freedom to those who served honorably. There is no evidence that he advanced such an idea during the period covered in *Gods and Generals*.

24. Stanchak, "Gods and Generals," 37. A recent book that seems to take the film's handling of Jackson and Jim Lewis as a point of departure is Richard G. Williams Jr., *Stonewall Jackson: The Black Man's Friend* (Nashville, Tenn.: Cumberland House, 2006), for which James I. Robertson Jr. wrote an appreciative introduction that describes Jackson as "a spiritual teacher for scores of slaves and freedmen as well as the best friend many of them ever had" (12). Robertson's *Stonewall Jackson: The Man, the Soldier, the Legend* (New York: Macmillan, 1997), 191–92, summarizes the general's views about slavery in less enthusiastic terms. The historical record offers little to support Williams's flattering portrait.

25. James I. Robertson Jr., *Gods and Generals: The Paintings of Mort Künstler* (n.p.: The Greenwich Workshop Press, 2002), 13.

26. The main characters in *Cold Mountain* are Inman (Jude Law), Ada Monroe (Nicole Kidman), Ruby Thewes (Renée Zellweger), Teague (Ray Winstone), Reverend Monroe (Donald Sutherland), Reverend Vessey (Philip Seymour Hoffman), Sally Swanger (Kathy Baker), and Sara (Natalie Portman).

27. *USA Today*, December 24, 2003, 1D; *Washington Post*, December 25, 2003, C1; *Journal of American History* 91 (December 2004): 1128–29 (review by John C. Inscoe); *New York Times*, December 21, 2003, Section 2, p. 28. For a discussion of the film by historians Edward L. Ayers, Stephen Cushman, and Gary W. Gallagher, see Bob Thompson, "Civil War, Take 2," in *Washington Post*, December 24, 2003, C1, C8. For a discussion of the historical accuracy of Frazier's novel, see Paul Ashdown, *A Cold Mountain Companion* (Gettysburg, Pa.: Thomas, 2004).

28. *Los Angeles Times*, December 28, 2003, p. E39. For an assessment of the film aimed at Civil War enthusiasts, see John E. Stanchak, "Cold Mountain," *Civil War Times Illustrated* 42 (February 2004): 32–39.

29. David Williams, *A People's History of the Civil War: Struggles for the Meaning of Freedom* (New York: The New Press, 2005), builds on earlier scholarship highlighting disaffection in the Confederacy to craft a picture similar to that presented in *Cold Mountain*. A much different interpretation emerges in a number of recent studies that describe considerable tenacity and sense of purpose on the Confederate home front. For examples, see William Blair, *Virginia's Private War: Feeding Body and Soul in the Confederacy* (New York: Oxford University Press, 1998); Gary W. Gallagher, *The Confederate War* (Cambridge, Mass.: Harvard University Press, 1997); Anne Sarah Rubin, *A Shattered Nation: The Rise and Fall of the Confederacy, 1861–1868* (Chapel Hill: University of North Carolina Press, 2005); and Mark V. Wetherington, *Plain Folk's Fight: The Civil War and Reconstruction in Piney Woods Georgia* (Chapel Hill: University of North Carolina Press, 2005).

30. Martin Crawford, *Ashe County's Civil War: Community and Society in the Appalachian South* (Charlottesville: University Press of Virginia, 2001), presents a complicated picture of loyalty and disaffection in one North Carolina county. For firsthand testimony from across the state, see W. Buck Yearns and John G. Barrett, eds., *North Carolina Civil War Documentary* (Chapel Hill: University of North Carolina Press, 1980). Phillip Shaw Paludan, *Victims: A True Story of the Civil War* (Knoxville: University of Tennessee Press, 1981), explores the murder of thirteen Unionist prisoners in western North Carolina.

Battle over the Bodies

Burying and Reburying the Civil War Dead, 1865–1871

⊰ DREW GILPIN FAUST ⊱

Neither conflict nor violence came to an end with the surrender of Confederate armies in the spring of 1865. Reconciliation would require decades, as North and South struggled over the meaning of the war and the character of the newly triumphant American nation. And intersectional harmony would at last come about, as David Blight has so powerfully illustrated in *Race and Reunion*, through the creation of a national ideology of shared loss and sacrifice that all but erased the place of slavery and emancipation in the memory of the war's origins and purposes. The Civil War dead — and the bravery and suffering common to the fallen of both North and South — became the foundation for renewed national unity. In the war's immediate aftermath, however, the dead played a quite different role, serving as a divisive, rather than a unifying force, pitting former Confederates against Yankees, black southerners against white southerners, in a battle over the disposition and treatment of the 620,000 men who had lost their lives in the conflict.[1]

In April 1865, the work of killing was officially complete, but the claims of the dead persisted. Many soldiers lay unburied, their bones littering battlefields across the South; still more had been hastily interred where they fell, far from family and home; hundreds of thousands remained unidentified, their losses unaccounted for. The end of combat offered an opportunity to attend to the dead in ways war had made impossible. Information could now flow freely across North and South; military officials would have time to devote to compiling and scrutinizing casualty records; bodies scattered across the defeated Confederacy could be located and identified; the fallen could be honored without encroaching on the immediate needs of the living.

For the Union military, war's end permitted systematic assessment of losses that the unrelenting pressures of battle had prohibited. In July 1865,

In the spring of 1862, a northern photographer made this study of rough wooden markers over graves of soldiers killed eight months earlier in the First Battle of Bull Run. Untold thousands of Union and Confederate dead lay in graves lacking even this type of temporary identification. Francis Trevelyan Miller, ed., *The Photographic History of the Civil War*, 10 vols. (New York: Review of Reviews, 1911), 9:278.

Quartermaster General Montgomery Meigs ordered every Union commander to submit a report of "all interments registered during the war." Wartime records had noted only 101,736 registered burials, fewer than a third of the estimated total of Union fatalities. It was clear that hundreds of thousands of northern soldiers lay in undocumented locations, their deaths unknown to their families as well as to military record keeping.[2]

Official policy toward the dead would evolve slowly over the next several years, but immediate action seemed imperative, as a matter of both decency and expediency. The longer bodies were left without proper burial, the more vulnerable they became to depredation, either by ex-Confederates or by rooting animals, and the less likely they were to be identifiable. Military commanders improvised in face of need and opportunity. In June 1865, Assistant Quartermaster James Moore was ordered to the Wilderness and Spotsylvania "for the purpose of superintending the interments of the remains of Union soldiers yet unburied and marking their burial-places for

African American burial crews disinterring Union dead on the Cold Harbor
battlefield shortly after the war. Such work was carried out at numerous
sites across the former Confederacy. Library of Congress.

future identification." Moore found hundreds of unmarked graves, as well
as skeletons that had been left for more than two years without the dignity
of burial. On these two fields, he estimated he oversaw the interment of
1,500 men, although the scattering of so many bones made an exact count
impossible. Soldiers of the U.S. Colored Troops, not yet mustered out of
service, did the often repellent work.[3] As soon as Moore had completed this
assignment, he was sent to the site of the notorious Confederate prison at
Andersonville, Georgia, where so many Union soldiers had perished. His
expedition documented 13,363 bodies and succeeded in identifying 12,912.
All were reinterred in marked graves, and on August 17, their resting place
was dedicated as the Andersonville National Cemetery.[4]

In the Western Theater, similar efforts were under way. On June 23,
1865, Maj. Gen. George H. Thomas, commander of the Department of the
Cumberland, had ordered Chaplain William Earnshaw to identify and
rebury Union soldiers in the vicinity of Murfreesboro, Tennessee, in the
Stones River National Cemetery, established in 1864 to commemorate the
bloody battle that had taken place there late in 1862. Earnshaw began

searches of the surrounding area, investigating old sites of camps and garrisons within a radius of nearly a hundred miles.

In the summer of 1865, however, the ultimate intentions of the federal government toward the war dead were not yet clear. Only slowly in the years following southern surrender did a general sense of obligation toward the dead yield firm policy. The orders of individual military commanders ultimately combined with legislative authorization and funding to create an enormous and comprehensive postwar reburial program intended to locate every Union soldier across the South and inter all within a new system of national cemeteries. But this was not the goal at the outset. Widespread and continuing public discussion about the dead gradually articulated a set of principles that influenced military and legislative action. The experience of federal officials, like James Moore, assigned to begin the interment and identification of the slain shaped attitudes as well, as the actual conditions of wartime graves and burials became known. Transcendent ideals of citizenship, sacrifice, and national obligation played an important part in the emergence of the national cemetery system. But ever-growing concerns about southern mistreatment of gravesites and bodies became a powerful force in the establishment of what was arguably the most elaborate federal program undertaken in nearly a century of American nationhood.

In October 1865, sobered by the difficulties he had already encountered in the attempt to compile reliable lists of the dead, Quartermaster General Montgomery Meigs issued another general order, calling upon officers to provide a survey of cemeteries containing Union soldiers. He requested details about the location and condition of graveyards, the state of relevant records, and officers' recommendations for the protection and preservation of remains. After interruptions necessitated by summer heat, Moore in the East and Earnshaw in the West resumed their efforts under these new guidelines, and on December 26, Edmund B. Whitman was relieved of his regular duties as a quartermaster and assigned responsibility "to locate the scattered graves of Union soldiers" across a wide area of Kentucky, Tennessee, Georgia, Mississippi, and Alabama. The extensive records Whitman left describing his efforts over the next half decade provide unparalleled insight into both the condition of the Union dead and the evolution of federal policy.[5]

As he contemplated his assignment, Whitman concluded that "*a knowledge and a record of every grave*" must be "*in the possession of some living person.*" Whitman composed a circular titled "Important Information Wanted," addressed to "Surgeons, Chaplains, Agents of Sanitary and

Christian Commissions, Quartermasters, Officers or Soldiers," and forwarded it to 300 newspapers and periodicals for publication.[6] The request provoked an outpouring of responses. Relatives begged Whitman to find the remains of lost kin; other correspondents furnished "drawings and descriptions" indicating the exact spot where a friend or comrade had been buried. Often, Whitman reported, these proved "so minute and accurate in the details, that any person could proceed with unerring certainty to the very grave."[7] Chaplains wrote to Whitman with complete lists of regimental dead and their places of burial; one clergyman who had returned home to New Bedford, Massachusetts, provided documentation for 200 graves in Tullahoma, Tennessee. Many soldiers seemed to have "whiled away boredom copying names from graves," lists that they eagerly forwarded in response to Whitman's request. Surgeons sent plans of hospital burial grounds with numbered graves and rolls of names. Officers who had been in charge of burial parties on the field had sometimes prepared plots of interments. "In the case of the 46th Ohio Regiment," Whitman reported, "such a paper, stained and soiled at the time of burial," would lead "to the identification after the lapse of more than 4 years of the entire group of dead from that regiment on the Shiloh battlefield."[8]

On March 1, 1866, Whitman left Nashville on his mission, heading first to the site of the 1862 battle of Fort Donelson. The "entire country over which the war has extended its ravages," he soon recognized, "composes one vast charnel house of the dead."[9] Whitman proceeded with a sense of growing urgency, recognizing that information and even the bodies themselves were highly vulnerable to both human and natural forces. He and other federal officers had begun to hear of numbers of distressing incidents of vandalism of Union graves and bodies. Accounts reached Whitman of corpses thrown naked and facedown into graves, of a body left lying to rot with a pitchfork still impaled in its back, of "constant depredation of headboards" in battlefield burial grounds. When he pursued a father's request that his son be moved from where he had fallen on the field in Georgia to the national cemetery in Chattanooga, Whitman learned that the body had already been claimed by local men "for the purposes of studying anatomy." Only two small arm bones, one hand bone, and his clothing remained in Oliver Barger's ransacked grave. Whitman received numerous reports of violence perpetrated against those who dared care for Union bodies or graves. In Kentucky, a man had even been killed for permitting two Yankees to be buried in his yard. A "constant depredation of Headboards and other trespasses and defilements, are constantly occurring,"

Whitman's superior officer in Nashville reported to the quartermaster general in Washington.[10]

In February 1866, Maj. Gen. George Thomas issued an order forbidding desecration of Union graves and directing specifically that they must not be mutilated or obliterated in the course of the spring plowing season, about to begin for the first time since the end of the war. By April, concerns about vandalism had reached Washington, and Congress passed a joint resolution requiring the secretary of war "to take immediate measures to preserve from desecration the graves of the soldiers of the United States who fell in battle or died of disease . . . and secure suitable burial places in which they may be properly interred." Now the legislative branch joined the military in explicit engagement in the disposition of the Union dead.[11]

Whitman's superiors delivered elaborate orders about his responsibilities and their goals: he was to locate graves, mark and protect isolated burial spots, and "form some plans" about graves that should be moved and about sites to which they might be relocated. Whitman's instructions insisted that bodies that had been decently interred should be left where they lay except when "a savage and vindictive spirit on the part of the disloyal inhabitants" suggested "a disposition to molest the remains." Increasingly, Whitman was coming to regard such vengefulness as less the exception than the rule.[12]

In the year since Appomattox, the defeated white South had moved from stunned disbelief to a posture of growing defiance. Encouraged by President Andrew Johnson's sympathy, former Confederates tested the limits of northern will, challenging Yankee claims to the fruits of victory. In the summer of 1865, southern legislatures passed restrictive and discriminatory Black Codes, designed to reestablish slavery in all but name; in the fall, the recently rebellious states elected former Confederate military officers and politicians to represent them in Washington; throughout the South, white southerners perpetrated and tolerated relentless violence against freedpeople. The hundreds of thousands of Union bodies in their midst proved an irresistible target for southern rage and represented as well an opportunity to express the refusal to accept Confederate defeat. It had proved impossible to overcome a live Union army, but bitter Confederates could still wage war against a dead one.[13]

A particularly virulent outbreak of white violence in fact served as a direct cause of intensified congressional interest in Union graves. During the first four days of May 1866, Memphis erupted in what were generally designated as riots, although the death toll of forty-six blacks and two whites suggests that those who wrote of a "massacre" were more accurate. Ninety-one houses, all but one occupied by African Americans, four churches, and twelve schools were destroyed. Fear became so widespread among African Americans in the area that Whitman reported he was for some time unable to get black laborers to continue to work for him. Congress promptly dispatched a committee of three members of the House of Representatives to investigate causes of the disturbance. Ultimately, the legislators made recommendations about controlling white defiance that played a significant role in the movement toward military Reconstruction. But the assistant quartermaster of the Division of the Tennessee, George Marshall, seized the opportunity provided by the congressmen's presence in Memphis to impress upon them the importance of the effort to bury the Union dead and the danger in which many soldiers' bodies lay. A delegation including Chaplain William Earnshaw, who had been overseeing reinterments at Stones River, convinced the congressmen that a comprehensive reburial program was imperative to ensure the safety of Union graves. The committee chair, Elihu Washburne of Illinois, was particularly moved by the account of Union dead scattered across the South, and Whitman believed that this meeting led directly to the National Cemeteries Act that passed, along with a fifteenfold increase in appropriation, in the next Congress. But even before the bill became law, it was clear that after the discussion in Memphis, the reinterment effort would assume a new and enhanced scope and importance.[14]

As spring unfolded, Whitman proceeded through the battlefields of Tennessee — Fort Donelson, Fort Henry, and then Shiloh. There, at the site of the battle that had first intimated the scale of slaughter to come, he encountered human bones scattered in "large quantities," and he learned from nearby inhabitants that their hogs, customarily left free to forage, were no longer fit to be eaten "on account of their living off the dead." Sweeping the field "deployed in the manner of a skirmish line," Whitman and his men sought to cover every foot of terrain involved in the battle. A list of 315 gravesites that had been compiled by a Sanitary Commission agent just after the battle proved of critical assistance, and Whitman's party recorded and marked by compass points 178 different areas containing graves, including twenty-one burial trenches that held, he estimated, 250 bodies. Whitman was deeply moved by finding many soldiers in regimental groups, obviously carefully interred at the end of the battle by their comrades. These would be kept together when they were later removed to the National Cemetery. In all, Whitman discovered 1,874 Union dead, of which 620 were identified by headboards or other inscriptions. About 200, he estimated, had been removed by relatives or friends. Keeping in mind the idea of siting national cemeteries at points of great historical interest, Whitman selected a potential spot on the Shiloh field.[15]

Near Memphis, Whitman encountered a road built over Union graves that had been all but destroyed by teams and carts, and he wrote sadly of 810 neglected Union graves in a cemetery three miles from the city. Nine hundred Rebel graves in the same burial ground were carefully tended, with identities listed in a sexton's book. The "Association of Southern Mothers," he learned, had assumed responsibility for these Confederate dead, while their victorious Union counterparts lay dishonored beside them.[16]

Locating the many graves scattered beyond actual battlefields — casualties from skirmishes, or wounded men who died on the march, or men who succumbed to disease — required Whitman to seek information from local citizens who might have seen or heard of buried soldiers — or even assisted in their interments. "As a rule," he later remembered, "no residence or person was to be passed without the inquiry. 'Do you know, or have you heard of any graves of Union soldiers in this neighborhood?'" When he arrived in Oxford, Mississippi, Whitman called upon the town postmaster, a federal employee, after all, who might be expected to be both knowledgeable and helpful to a Union official. Whitman received not assistance but a warning. The postmaster declared that he would not dare tell a Yankee soldier about Union graves, even if he knew of them. Since the postmaster had taken the loyalty oath to qualify for his position at the end of the war, all his friends, cultivated during nineteen years of residence in the town, had abandoned him. He had even been asked to cease attending his church. "I am informed," Whitman wrote his commanding officer, "that a disposition has been shown in this vicinity to obliterate and destroy all traces of the graves union soldiers find scattered in the country."[17]

Farther south, the Union dead seemed in even more distressing circumstances. Whitman discovered "immense numbers" of bodies in the area between Vicksburg and Natchez — perhaps, he thought, as many as 40,000. These corpses were in every imaginable place and condition — buried on river embankments and then wholly or partially washed away (there were even reports of coffins floating like little boats down the Mississippi toward the sea), abandoned in "ravines and jungles and dense cane brakes" and never buried at all. A farmer named Linn who wanted to extend his cotton fields had ploughed up about thirty Union skeletons and then delivered the bones "*in bulk*" to the Vicksburg city cemetery. Not far away, a Union graveyard had been leveled entirely to make way for a race course.[18]

As Whitman pursued his explorations, 300 black soldiers at the Stones River National Cemetery continued to collect and rebury Union bodies from the wide surrounding area at the rate of between fifty and a hundred a day. Stones River represented a pioneering example of the comprehensive reburial effort that by the summer of 1866 had come to be seen as necessary across the South. It also represented the critical role African Americans had come to play in honoring the Union dead. Almost invariably, units of U.S. Colored Troops were assigned the disagreeable work of burial and reburial, but individual black civilians also proved critical to Whitman's effort to locate corpses and graves.[19]

"Justice to the race of freedmen," Whitman reported to headquarters, demands "a tribute of grateful mention." Rebuffed in his search for information by whites like the Mississippi postmaster, Whitman learned to turn to black southerners for help as he traversed the South in the spring and fall of 1866. "Most all the information gained" at one Georgia location, he reported to his journal, "was from negroes, who, as I was told . . . *pay more attention to such matters than the white people*." There was a good deal more at issue here than just attentiveness, Whitman soon recognized. Black southerners cared for the Union dead as a gesture of political assertiveness as well as a demonstration of gratitude and respect.[20]

During the war, African Americans had risked their lives burying Union soldiers and trying to preserve both their names and their graves. About two miles from Savannah, in a corner of "the Negro Cemetery," lay seventy-seven "graves of colored soldiers" in four neat rows. All but three were identified, all in "very good condition," and all marked with "good painted headboards." This was the last resting place of the dead of a unit of U.S. Colored Troops, carefully buried and tended by the freedpeople of the area. Whitman encountered other sites where former slaves had interred Yankees and still watched over their graves. Behind an African Colored church near Bowling Green, Kentucky, for example, 1,134 well-tended graves sheltered both black and white Union soldiers. A black carpenter nearby provided the most useful information about the area because he had made coffins and helped to bury many of the Union dead himself.[21]

Whitman benefited from assistance and information provided by freedmen throughout his travels. Moses Coleman, "an intelligent negro," sought Whitman out to tell him about the graves of nine Union soldiers who had been shot by Confederate cavalry after being taken prisoners, "one of whom," Whitman reported, "he saw shot after being compelled to climb a tree." A freedman eagerly offered the names and locations of two soldiers he had buried more than a year before; another former slave reported his employer's desecration of soldiers' graves and offered to identify thirty on his plantation that still remained undefiled. Black southerners showed little hesitation in choosing sides in this bitter warfare over the disposition of the dead.[22]

At the end of June, Whitman proposed sites for national cemeteries at Fort Donelson, Pittsburg Landing, Corinth, Memphis, and Vicksburg, and presented his views about the future to the chief quartermaster of the Military Division of the Tennessee. The experiences of the preceding months, he reported, had produced a "daily deepening in my own mind" of the importance of this federal obligation to the dead, as he had witnessed the "total neglect" or "wanton desecration" of Union graves by a southern population whose "hatred of the dead" seemed to exceed their earlier "abhorrence of the living."[23]

In early September, Whitman continued his explorations, moving through Kentucky from the Tennessee line to the Ohio River, embarking again in late October to Chattanooga and Chickamauga, then along the line of Sherman's March, and back through Macon and Andersonville by the close of the year. By the end of his journey, Whitman estimated he had traveled 30,000 miles in his search for the dead. The increasing local violence resulting from growing national conflict over Reconstruction made Union bodies and graves, not to mention his own mission, ever more vulnerable. "The country in that section," Whitman wrote from Lexington, Kentucky, in late September 1866, "is in a very unsettled state and the lives of Union men are unsafe." Collectively, his communications to headquarters powerfully reinforced "the necessity of . . . universal disinterment and collection of the scattered remains into permanent National Cemeteries."[24]

In early 1867, Whitman's views were at last enshrined in law, as well as War Department policy. With "An Act to Establish and Protect National Cemeteries," passed by Congress in February 1867, and the creation of seventeen additional cemeteries in the course of that year, the federal government legally signaled its acceptance of responsibility for those who had died in its service. The locating and recording of graves Whitman had undertaken in his 1866 expeditions would be transformed into a comprehensive program of reburial, combined with acquisition of land for a system of government cemeteries adequate to hold hundreds of thousands of soldiers' remains.[25]

Across the Military Division of the Tennessee, Whitman reaped what he described as a "Harvest of Death," reporting that by 1869 he had gathered 114,560 soldiers into twenty national cemeteries within his assigned territory. Each body was placed in a separate coffin, its original burial site recorded, its final destination documented by cemetery section and grave number. Reinterments cost an average of $9.75 a body, with two to three dollars of this for the coffin.[26] As Whitman supervised the removal of tens of thousands of bodies to national cemeteries in the Division of the Tennessee, so the work begun in 1865 by Moore and Earnshaw continued in other parts of the South. Charged with responsibility for burials in Virginia, Maryland, and Washington, D.C., Moore collected more than 50,000 bodies into national cemeteries. When the reinterment program was completed in 1871, 303,536 Union soldiers had been buried in seventy-four national cemeteries, and the War Department had expended $4,000,306.26 on the effort to gather the dead. Quartermaster General Meigs reported that 54 percent of the men had been identified as a result of careful attention to bodies and their original graves, as well as extensive research in military hospital records, muster rolls, casualty reports, and even documentation gathered by the Sanitary Commission about deaths and burials. Some 30,000 of these dead were black soldiers, buried in areas designated "colored" on the drawings that mapped the new national cemeteries and enumerated in columns marked "black" on the forms officially reporting the progress of interments. Separated into units of U.S. Colored Troops in life, these soldiers were similarly segregated in death, and only about a third of them were identified. The notions of equality of citizenship that animated the reburial program clearly had their limits, despite the critical role African Americans had played in the identification and interment of the war's dead.[27]

The reburial program represented an extraordinary departure for the federal government, an indication of the very different sort of nation that had emerged as a result of Civil War. The program's extensiveness, its cost, its location in national rather than state government, and its connection with the most personal dimensions of individual's lives all would have been unimaginable before the war created its legions of the dead, a constituency of the slain and their mourners, who would change the very definition of the nation and its obligations.[28]

But this transformative undertaking included only Union soldiers. These were the staunch defenders the nation sought to honor; these were the bodies imperiled by vengeful former Confederates; these were the men whose survivors bombarded the War Department with petitions for information about deaths and burials. But the contrast with the absence of official concern for the Confederate dead was stark.[29] This differential treatment of the dead had powerful, and seemingly unanticipated, effects. Southern civilians, largely women, mobilized private means to accomplish what federal resources would not. Their efforts to claim and honor the Confederate dead — and the organizations they spawned — became a means of keeping sectionalist identity and energy not just alive, but strong.

The April 1866 joint congressional resolution proposing the national cemetery system had provoked an outraged response from white Virginians. Northerners were wrong, the *Richmond Examiner* proclaimed, to think that the Confederate was "the less a hero because he failed." Calling upon Richmond's churchwomen to assume responsibility for Virginia's fallen, the paper underscored the irony of defining southerners as outside a nation with which they had been forcibly reunited. If the Confederate soldier "does not fall into the category of the 'Nation's Dead' he is *ours* — and shame be to us if we do not care for his ashes."[30]

On May 3, 1866, a group of Richmond women responded to the *Examiner*'s call, gathering to found the Hollywood Memorial Association of the Ladies of Richmond, and recognizing both the obligation and the challenge before them. As Mrs. William McFarland, newly installed association president, acknowledged, the former Confederate capital was "begirt with an army of Confederate dead." Thousands of men lay in neglected graves in Hollywood Cemetery or in Oakwood, its counterpart in the eastern edge of the city, conveniently close to the site where Chimborazo, the South's largest military hospital, had stood. Tens of thousands more lay scattered on the many battlefields that surrounded the city. Mrs. McFarland believed that these soldiers belonged not just to Richmond, but to the South, and it was to the Women of the South that she directed her appeal.[31]

The association began repair of the 11,000 soldiers' graves dug at Hollywood during the war. Nearly all needed remounding and returfing, and few had adequate markers. The ladies worried too about the bodies scattered through the countryside, which they believed should be gathered, like the Union dead, into hallowed and protected ground. With the help of farmers from battle sites on the city's outskirts, the association arranged for the transfer of hundreds of bodies to new graves in the Richmond cemetery during the summer and fall of 1866.

The northern reburial movement was an official, even a professional effort, removed by both geography and bureaucracy from the lives of most northern citizens; it was the work — and expense — of the Quartermaster

Corps, the U.S. Army and the federal government. In the South, care for the Confederate dead was of necessity the work of the people—at least the white people; it became a grassroots undertaking that mobilized the white South in ways that extended well beyond the immediate purposes of bereavement and commemoration.

Winchester, in the northernmost part of Virginia, had been another site of almost unrelieved military activity, including three major battles of Winchester, one each in 1862, 1863, and 1864; the town was said to have changed hands more than seventy times in the course of the war. The dead surrounded Winchester as they did Richmond, and women organized similarly to honor them. Fanny Downing, who assumed the presidency of the Ladies Association for the Fitting Up of Stonewall Jackson Cemetery issued an "Address to the Women of the South" that echoed Richmond's Nancy McFarland. "Let us remember," her broadside cried, "that we belong to that sex which was last at the cross, first at the grave. . . . Let us go now, hand in hand, to the graves of our country's sons, and as we go let our energies be aroused and our hearts be thrilled by this thought: *It is the least thing we can do for our soldiers.*"[32]

Downing invoked the long tradition of female responsibility for mourning, but her invocation of allegiance to a country that had supposedly surrendered its existence suggested a second motivation for women's leadership of the southern reburial effort. To respectfully bury one's neighbors and kin was a personal and private act; to honor those who had risen up in rebellion against the national government was public and political. Yet women were regarded in mid-nineteenth-century America as apolitical in their very essence; their aggressions and transgressions could be—and largely had been—ignored during the war. Even amidst the escalating conflicts of Reconstruction, their gender would provide them wide leeway as they enacted a role they had played since they took Jesus from the cross. Mrs. Charles J. Williams, secretary of the Georgia Ladies Memorial Association, clearly understood the nature of this gendered claim. "Legislative enactment may not be made to do honor to [Confederate] memories," as it had to those of the Union dead, "but the veriest radical that ever traced his genealogy back to the deck of the Mayflower, could not refuse us the simple privilege of paying honor to those who died defending the life, honor and happiness of the Southern women." But the "simple privilege" of memorializing the Confederate dead—like so many women's actions during the war itself—was in fact highly political. Ensuring the immortality of the fallen and of their memory became a means to perpetuate southern resistance to northern domination and to the reconstruction of southern society.[33]

On October 25, 1866, a crowd 5,000 strong gathered to dedicate Winchester's Stonewall Cemetery, graveyard for 2,494 Confederate soldiers who had been gathered from a radius of fifteen miles around. Gen. Turner Ashby, a dashing cavalry commander and local hero who had been killed in 1862, served as the ranking officer among the dead, as well as a focus of the day's ceremonies. His old mammy was recruited to lay a wreath on his grave in a pointed celebration of the world for which the Confederacy had fought. The American flag flying in the adjoining National Cemetery, where 5,000 Union soldiers had already been interred, provoked a "good deal of rancor" from the crowd, and the members of the U.S. Burial Corps, at work caring for the federal dead, were jeered and insulted. Twenty-five hundred Confederates on one side; 5,000 Yankees on the other: perhaps this was the 4th Battle of Winchester, the one in which all the soldiers were already dead.[34]

Women founded memorial associations almost everywhere there were concentrations of Confederate bodies. In Nashville, Vicksburg, Chattanooga, Atlanta, Marietta, Appomattox, Petersburg, Spotsylvania, and Fredericksburg, women gathered the southern slain in a movement that was at once profoundly personal and inevitably political. Some historians have argued that memorial activities in the immediate postwar South did not possess the explicitly partisan intentions of later commemorations, those that occurred after the founding of the United Confederate Veterans and the Daughters of the Confederacy in the last decade of the century. Tied to the politics of Jim Crow, disfranchisement, and state rights, Confederate memory became in that era a political force that effectively undermined the emancipationist, nationalist, and egalitarian meaning of the war. But the activities of the Ladies Memorial Associations, undertaken in considerable degree as a direct response to the exclusion of Confederates from national cemeteries, were explicitly sectional, intended to proclaim continuing devotion to the Confederacy, as well as to individual husbands, fathers, brothers, and sons. The Reverend John L. Girardeau, an eminent Presbyterian and theologian, was the featured orator at the 1871 ceremony marking the reinterment of the Gettysburg dead at Charleston's Magnolia Cemetery. He made the political nature of the gathering clear when he insisted, "we are not here simply as mourners for the dead." The event addressed "living issues," he explained, which involved "the principles which led to our great struggle," principles, in his words, like state rights and opposition to "Radicalism" and to racial "amalgamation." The living, he noted, confronted a compelling and unavoidable question: "Did these men die in vain?" Honor to the dead required the continuing defense of Confederate ideals, which had been "defeated, not necessarily lost." Only vindication of the original purposes of the conflict could ensure the meaning of so many men's sacrifice. The Confederacy would not live on as a nation, but its dead would in some sense become its corporeal and corporate representation, not only a symbol of what once was, but a summons to what must be.

Neither northern nor southern participants in the commemoration and reburial movement were — in Girardeau's words — "simply . . . mourners." Instead, they became in a very real sense the instruments of the power and civic immortality of the dead. Gathering scattered bodies into mass cemeteries with graves marshaled in ranks like soldiers on the field of battle made the dead a living reality, a force in their very visibility. These Civil War cemeteries — both North and South — were unlike the graveyards Americans knew before the war. These were not clusters of family tombstones in churchyards, nor garden cemeteries symbolizing the union of man and nature. Civil War cemeteries contained row after row of humble, identical markers, hundreds of thousands of men, known and unknown, who represented the unfathomable cost of the war, men whose very numbers demanded attention and meaning. The reburial movement created a constituency of the slain, insistent in both its existence and its silence — rows and rows of men whose very absence from American life made them a presence that could not be ignored.

NOTES

1. David Blight, *Race and Reunion: The Civil War in American Memory* (Cambridge, Mass.: Harvard University Press, 2001).

2. On general orders, see Brevet Brigadier General J. J. Dana to Brevet Major General J. L. Donaldson, March 19, 1866, in E. B. Whitman, Letters Received, RG 92 A-1 397A, National Archives and Records Service, Washington (repository hereafter cited as NA); and E. B. Whitman "Cemeterial Movement" in Whitman, Final Report, 1869, RG 92 E646, NA; "Civil War Era National Cemeteries," 8, ⟨http://www.va.gov/facmgt/civilwar .htm⟩ (accessed on April 21, 2000). See also U.S. War Department, Quartermaster General's Office, *Compilation of Laws, Orders, Opinions, Instructions, etc. in Regard to National Military Cemeteries* (Washington: Government Printing Office, 1878); and *Roll of Honor: Names of Soldiers Who Died in Defence of the American Union*, 27 nos. (Washington: Government Printing Office, 1865–71).

3. Special Order No. 132 in Report of Captain J. M. Moore, Report of the Quarter-

master General, November 8, 1865, in Report of the Secretary of War, *Executive Documents Printed by Order of the House of Representatives During the First Session of the Thirty-Ninth Congress, 1865–66* (Washington: Government Printing Office, 1866) 3:264–66; James M. Moore to Quartermaster General Montgomery C. Meigs, July 3, 1865, M619 208Q 1865, Roll 401, NA. See also Requests Received by Col. James Moore, 1863–66, RG92 E581, NA; Requests for Information Relating to Missing Soldiers, 1863–67, RG 92 E582, NA; and Letters Received by Tommy Baker, Clerk of Office of Burial Records, 1862–67, RG 92 E580, NA.

4. Clara Barton, Journal, July 8, 12, August 5–6, 17, 1865, Clara Barton Papers, Library of Congress; Clara Barton to Edmund Stanton, n.d., ibid.; see Requests for Information, RG 92 E582, NA; Elizabeth Brown Pryor, *Clara Barton: Professional Angel* (Philadelphia: University of Pennsylvania Press, 1987), 138–42; Monro MacCloskey, *Hallowed Ground: Our National Cemeteries* (New York: Richards Rosen Press, 1968), 32; and Report of Captain J. M. Moore, Report of the Quartermaster General, November 8, 1865, in Report of the Secretary of War, *Executive Documents Printed by Order of the House of Representatives During the First Session of the Thirty-Ninth Congress* (Washington: Government Printing Office, 1866), 3:264–66. See also John R. Neff, *Honoring the Civil War Dead: Commemoration and the Problem of Reconciliation* (Lawrence: University Press of Kansas, 2005), and Edward Steere, "Genesis of American Graves Registration, 1861–1870," *Military Affairs* 12 (Fall 1948): 149–61. See Edmund Whitman Papers, 1830–76, Schoff Civil War Collection, William L. Clements Library, University of Michigan, Ann Arbor; and Class of 1838 Class Book and "1838: Whitman, Edmund Burke," Alumni Biographical File, Harvard University Archives, Cambridge, Mass.

5. Meigs, quoted in Whitman, "Remarks on National Cemeteries," *The Army Reunion* (Chicago: S. C. Griggs and Co., 1869), 227.

6. E. B. Whitman to Thomas Swords, February 13, 1867, and Whitman, Final Report; "Circular," January 24, 1866, in E. B. Whitman, Letterpress Book, vol. 1, RG 92 E-A1-397A, NA.

7. Whitman, Final Report; A. T. Blackmun to Whitman, 1865, John H. Castle to Whitman, January 24, 1866, Letters Received, RG 92 E-A1-397A, NA.

8. E. B. Whitman, Report, May 5, 1866, Cemeterial Reports and Lists, RG 92 E-A1-397A, NA; Whitman, Final Report.

9. E. B. Whitman to J. L. Donaldson, June 26, 1866, E. B. Whitman, Letterpress Book, vol. 1, RG 92 E-A1-397A, NA; E. B. Whitman, Daily Journal, vol. 2, RG 92 E-A1-397A, NA; Whitman, "Remarks on National Cemeteries," 229.

10. Lieutenant Thomas Albee to Thomas Van Horne, November 28, 1865, E. B. Whitman, Letters Received, RG 92 E-A1-397A, NA; Brevet Major General J. L. Donaldson to Quartermaster General Montgomery Meigs, December 9, 1865, ibid.; Barger to E. B. Whitman, February 24, 1866, ibid.; Journal of a Trip Through Parts of Kentucky, Tennessee, and Georgia Made to Locate the Scattered Graves of Union Soldiers, [1866], vol. 1, p. 93, RG 92 E685, NA.

11. Whitman, Final Report, Appendix; Whitman, "Cemeterial Movement," in ibid.; clipping, April 4, 1866, Letters and Reports Received Relating to Cemeteries, RG 92 E569, NA.

12. Brevet Major General J. L. Donaldson to Col. M. D. Wickersham, April 17, 1866, Letters Received, RG 92 E-A1-397A, NA; Brevet Brigadier General J. J. Dana, Remarks

of the Quartermaster General, May 26, 1866, Cemetery Reports and Lists, RG 92 E-A1-397A, NA.

13. See Dan T. Carter, *When the War Was Over: The Failure of Self-Reconstruction in the South, 1865–1867* (Baton Rouge: Louisiana State University Press, 1985); George C. Rable, *But There Was No Peace: The Role of Violence in the Politics of Reconstruction* (Athens: University of Georgia Press, 1984); and Eric Foner, *Reconstruction: An Unfinished Revolution, 1863–1877* (New York: Harper and Row, 1988).

14. Whitman, Final Report; United States Congress, House of Representatives, Select Committee on the Memphis Riots, *Memphis Riots and Massacres, 1866* (1866; reprint, Miami, Fla.: Mnemosyne, 1969).

15. E. B. Whitman to Brevet Major General J. L Donaldson, March 26, April 18, 1866, E. B. Whitman, Letterpress Book, vol. 1, RG 92 E-A1-397A, NA; E. B. Whitman, Cemeterial Reports and Lists, June 27, 1866, RG 92 E-A1-397A, NA; Journal of a Trip.

16. E. B. Whitman to Major General J. L. Donaldson, April 29, 1866, E. B. Whitman, Letterpress Book, vol. 1, RG 92 E-A1-397A, NA.

17. Whitman, "Remarks on National Cemeteries," 229; E. B. Whitman to Major General J. L. Donaldson, April 30, 1866, E. B. Whitman, Letterpress Book, vol. 1, RG 92 E-A1-397A, NA.

18. E. B. Whitman to Major General J. L. Donaldson, May 24, 1866, and E. B. Whitman to Brigadier General H. M. Whittlesey, May 15, 1866, E. B. Whitman, Letterpress Book, vol. 1, RG 92 E-A1-397A, NA.

19. Brevet Brigadier General J. J Dana, Remarks of the Quartermaster General, May 26, 1866, Cemeterial Reports and Lists, RG 92 E-A1-397A, NA.

20. E. B. Whitman to Brevet Major General J. L. Donaldson, June 26, 1866, E. B. Whitman, Letterpress Book, vol. 1, RG 92 E-A1-397A, NA; Journal of a Trip, 2:26.

21. Journal of a Trip, 1:218, 240; 2:26.

22. Ibid., 2:26.

23. E. B. Whitman to Brevet Major General J. L. Donaldson, June 19, 26, 1866, E. B. Whitman, Letterpress Book, vol. 1, RG 92 E-A1-397A, NA.

24. Ibid., September 23, 1866; Whitman, Final Report.

25. *Congressional Globe*, 39th Cong., 1st sess., February 18, 1867, p. 1374.

26. Whitman, Final Report; Meigs statement of December 22, 1868, quoted in *Congressional Globe*, 42nd Cong., 2nd sess., May 8, 1872, p. 3220.

27. Report of the Quartermaster General, Report of the Secretary of War, *Executive Documents Printed by Order of the House of Representatives During the Second Session of the Forty-Second Congress* (Washington: Government Printing Office, 1872), 2:135–36; Report of the Quartermaster General, Report of the Secretary of War, *Executive Documents Printed by Order of the House of Representatives During the Third Session of the Forty-First Congress* (Washington: Government Printing Office, 1871), 2:210; Therese T. Sammartino, "Civil War Era National Cemeteries," 16, ⟨http://www.va.gov/facmgt/civil war.htm⟩; total cost from Charles W. Snell and Sharon A. Brown, *Antietam National Battlefield and National Cemetery, Sharpsburg, Maryland: An Administrative History* (Washington: U.S. Department of the Interior, National Park Service, 1986), 29; Leslie Perry "The Confederate Dead," clipping from *New York Sun*, [1898], in RG 92 585, NA. See bound volume of plats of national cemeteries, E. B. Whitman, Final Report, RG 92 E646, NA. See also letter from Sara Amy Leach, Senior Historian, National Cemetery Ad-

ministration, Department of Veterans Affairs to Drew Gilpin Faust, October 5, 2004, for details of African American burials. She notes that segregated burials seem to have been undertaken by custom rather than explicit regulation and were not evident in cemeteries for soldiers' homes, where burials were chronological. For forms see "Weekly Report of the Number of Interments," July 28, 1866, Letters and Reports Received Relating to Cemeteries, RG 92 E569, NA.

28. Whitman, "Remarks on National Cemeteries," 225.

29. "Burial of the Rebel Dead," *New York Times*, January 30, 1868, p. 4; Russell F. Weigley, *Quartermaster General of the Union Army: A Biography of M. C. Meigs* (New York: Columbia University Press, 1959), 308–10.

30. *Examiner* quoted in Mary H. Mitchell, *Hollywood Cemetery: The History of a Southern Shrine* (Richmond: Virginia State Library, 1985), 64.

31. "To the Women of the South," in *Daily Richmond Enquirer*, May 31, 1866, clipping in Hollywood Memorial Association Papers, Museum of the Confederacy, Richmond.

32. Downing cited in Anne Sarah Rubin, *A Shattered Nation: The Rise and Fall of the Confederacy, 1861–1868* (Chapel Hill: University of North Carolina Press, 2005), 234.

33. Ibid., 235; Neff, *Honoring the Civil War Dead*, 146–48. On women and politics in the Civil War, see Drew Gilpin Faust, *Mothers of Invention: Women of the Slaveholding South in the American Civil War* (Chapel Hill: University of North Carolina Press, 1996).

34. "Virginia—Dedication of the Stonewall Cemetery—Feeling of the Southern People—Miscellaneous Incidents," *New York Times*, October 29, 1866, 8. On Ashby, see Confederated Southern Memorial Association, *History of the Confederated Memorial Associations of the South* (New Orleans: The Graham Press, 1904), 149. For a discussion of several Ladies Memorial Associations in Virginia, including the ones in Richmond and Winchester, see Caroline E. Janney, *Burying the Dead but Not the Past: Ladies' Memorial Associations and the Lost Cause* (Chapel Hill: University of North Carolina Press, 2008).

Not a Veteran in the Poorhouse

Civil War Pensions and Soldiers' Homes

⊰ JAMES MARTEN ⊱

The Vietnam War sparked conflicts between veterans and nonveterans, inside the veteran community, and within individual veterans that still resonate with many Americans. These tensions have been staples of literature, popular culture, and news reporting for thirty years. *Coming Home* (1978), *First Blood* (1982), and *In Country* (1989) are just a few of the movies featuring troubled veterans. Dozens of memoirs and novels explore the points of view and experiences of the men who served in Vietnam. Tim O'Brien, a veteran and award-winning author, infuses all of his stories and novels with an awareness of the costs of war. *In the Lake of the Woods* (1994), for example, traces the sudden decline of a promising politician who, it is discovered, participated in a My Lai–style massacre while serving in Vietnam. The scars from Vietnam still surface from time to time; indeed, one theme of the 2004 presidential election between George W. Bush and John Kerry revolved around competing memories of the war.[1]

Not surprisingly, the public awareness of the internal and external conflicts and challenges facing returning veterans carried over into reporting on men and women returning from serving in Iraq. In addition to generic but sincere accounts of homecomings for Reserve and National Guard units, reporters tended to focus on the difficulties of their transition back to their pre-Iraq lives and on the plight of disabled vets.[2]

The lives and perceptions of Vietnam and Iraq war veterans clearly reside in "contested" terrain, a conceptual and historiographical land where the meanings of historical events are constantly shifting. Historians of the Civil War also can often be found exploring this uncharted ground, as they examine the ways in which gender and race, for instance, affected perceptions and realities, or when they struggle with inaccurate but still popular impressions of Reconstruction, or when they deal with the issue of "memory."[3]

Despite the contested nature of so much Civil War historiography, the notion has rarely been applied to Civil War veterans.[4] After all, we have cozy images of the old soldiers fading into comfortable archetypes of reconciliation between North and South, reminders, on certain days of the year, in their musty uniforms and white goatees, of the fight to save the Union. We have the graceful words of Oliver Wendell Holmes Jr. to remind us. In 1884 he told the men of the Grand Army of the Republic's John Sedgwick Post No. 4 in Keene, New Hampshire, that, "Through our great good fortune, in our youth our hearts were touched with fire. It was given to us to learn at the outset that life is a profound and passionate thing. While we are permitted to scorn nothing but indifference, and do not pretend to undervalue the worldly rewards of ambition, we have seen with our own eyes . . . the snowy heights of honor, and it is for us to bear the report to those who come after us."

Holmes firmly reminded his listeners that veterans were noble symbols and a separate breed: "The generation that carried on the war has been set apart by its experience." He spent much of the speech listing experiences that a man who did not fight in the war could never know, including his own combat injuries. "Accidents may call up the events of the war," he explained. "You see a battery of guns go by at a trot, and for a moment you are back at White Oak Swamp, or Antietam, or on the Jerusalem Road. You hear a few shots fired in the distance, and for an instant your heart stops as you say to yourself, The skirmishers are at it, and listen for the long roll of fire from the main line." Old comrades meet and reminisce—not about their families or careers, as most men would do, but about such terrible and manly moments as "when you were nearly surrounded by the enemy, and again there comes up to you that swift and cunning thinking on which once hung life or freedom—Shall I stand the best chance if I try the pistol or the sabre on that man who means to stop me?" In another passage, Holmes cataloged the members of his generation of Boston aristocrats who did not survive the war; they had names like Cabot, Putnam, Lowell, Revere, and Abbott. He recalled a scene from the Seven Days, the last time he saw James J. Lowell alive: "When I looked down the line at . . . the officers . . . at the head of their companies. The advance was beginning. We caught each other's eye and saluted. When next I looked, he was gone."[5]

Of course this "old soldier"—he was all of forty-three—was talking to other old soldiers. But the civilians in the audience would have realized that Holmes was setting out differences between those who had fought in the war and those who had not. There were certain experiences that could not be shared; there were certain nightmares that could not be explained; there had been sacrifices and losses that civilians could barely imagine.

It was the chasm between those who fought in the war and those who did not—and what that fight should mean twenty years after the war—that provided one of the two most important conflicts among northern veterans: the debate over the Federal pension system for disabled Union veterans. Despite general agreement among most Americans that the United States owed soldiers some form of pension, the size and scope of that pension proved to be controversial. In an era when few Americans received pensions of any kind and when most voters favored a limited role for the federal government, both proponents and opponents of pensions had to choose their words carefully as they debated the responsibilities of the republic to the men who had fought for it and the motivations of the men receiving them.[6]

At stake were a number of key American values: what did a democratic nation owe the men who *volunteered* to risk their lives for their country? What should be expected of the veterans as symbols of Union, honor, and sacrifice? How much sacrifice should be expected of those volunteers, and for how long? How did the normal American assumptions about self-reliance and charity apply to men whose lives had been ruined by war? That any of these questions would arise in 1865 about Civil War veterans would have been surprising to most Americans, who rarely doubted the worthiness of the men who had fought for the Union. Most programs to care for veterans, widows, and orphans took their inspiration from a passage in the famous final paragraph of Abraham Lincoln's second inaugural address: "With malice toward none, with charity for all, with firmness in the right as God gives us to see the right, let us strive on to finish the work we are in, to bind up the nation's wounds, to care for him who shall have borne the battle and for his widow and his orphan, to do all which may achieve and cherish a just and lasting peace among ourselves and with all nations."[7]

Lincoln's suggestion that the nation care for the northern victims of war became, for many, an irrevocable vow following his assassination and the victorious close of the war. Who could argue with the necessity and justice of building soldiers' homes, extending pensions to disabled volunteers, and providing a measure of support for wives and children of men who had died in the war? For a time, the generosity of the nation went unquestioned, but that changed by the 1880s and 1890s. The annual cost of pensions rose from $29 million in 1872 to $106 million by 1890, largely due to the 1879 "Arrears Act," which dated pensions from the date of death or disability rather than the date the pension was awarded, and the "Disability Act," which established that a veteran need not have incurred a disability while in the service in order to receive a pension.[8]

The pension debate that raged in Congress during those decades took often predictable turns: Republicans supported expanding and increasing pensions, while Democrats opposed further drains on the Treasury. There was an inevitable sectional element to the debate, as well as straightforward concern about the escalating costs. But there was also debate about whether or not the pensions program was being administered effectively, about the widespread — or at least the appearance of widespread — fraud, and about the worthiness of some of the veterans receiving pensions.

The other conflict arose from the ways that veterans saw themselves and how they believed others saw them. Assessing veterans' attitudes in this regard is tricky, of course, but a number of Gilded Age institutions provide a lens through which they can be glimpsed: the state and federal soldiers' homes built to care for the disabled and, eventually, the elderly veteran volunteers of the Civil War. The National Asylum for Disabled Volunteer Soldiers was established by Congress in the spring of 1865 (later called the National Home for Disabled Volunteer Soldiers [NHDVS], it was the direct predecessor of the Veterans Administration). By 1867, the first three homes had opened in Maine, Ohio, and Wisconsin. Over the next two decades, eight more national homes would be established, and most northern states would create their own homes for veterans. The decision to open these homes was not controversial, and Americans generally approved of the expense to support worthy veterans unable to care for themselves. One historian has estimated that just fewer 100,000 men spent time in a soldiers' home.[9]

One reason for the homes' popularity was their integration into the host communities. They became tourist attractions and parks for neighboring towns and cities. In Milwaukee, the NHDVS welcomed 60,000 visitors a year and hosted an annual Fourth of July celebration and fireworks display. In Milwaukee, and elsewhere, the home's quiet and apparent sobriety stood in stark contrast to the rowdy beer halls and amusement parks of Milwaukee. "Here are tolerated none of the riotous worshippers at the sickening shrine of Bacchus," according to the *Milwaukee Sentinel*. "Here the lovers of order and innocent amusements can while away a leisure hour, with no apprehension of disturbance from the interference or the clamorous babblings of the vulgar and dissipated."[10]

In keeping with this calm image, Americans liked to think of the men living in these homes as dignified graybeards. But these pleasantly benign notions of old soldiers ignored the circumstances in which the soldiers lived and obscured the very real conflict in the ways that the soldiers themselves accepted their dependence. The first soldiers to enter the homes were truly disabled; the rules, which were never strictly enforced, were relaxed in the 1880s to admit men whose only disability was old age. Many inmates entered in their forties or fifties, and endured many years of living in barracks, eating institutional food, spending empty hours wandering the grounds, reading, or doing odd jobs. Surrounded by other old soldiers, they were, in fact, alone in the world, unneeded and largely forgotten. Although promoted as a key way for the nation to repay its debt to the soldiers, Civil War soldiers' homes demanded that inmates give up freedom and privacy for Spartan comfort and modest security. No wonder interior conflicts about their self-worth plagued some of the men, perhaps especially those who sensed that their families were embarrassed.

ALTHOUGH MEMORIAL DAY speeches generally stuck to traditional odes to the Union cause and to the valor of Union soldiers, two such speeches, delivered only a few years apart, offered competing interpretations of the pension program. The first laid out the typical arguments for expanding the roll of pensioners; the second presented the case against the blithe awarding of pensions to virtually all old soldiers. That each speech was delivered by a veteran suggests that the public debate raging over the pension system was also taking place within the ranks of veterans themselves.

"Old age, decrepitude and disease are reaping an abundant crop" among Union veterans, declared Charles W. Johnson, chief clerk of the U.S. Senate, on Memorial Day in 1887. Johnson was speaking in Minneapolis on "the veteran of 1861–6 and the citizen of 1887." Like a kind of ghost of Memorial Days past, he offered images of martial glory during the fight for the Union nearly a quarter century before; like the ghost of Memorial Days present, he asked his audience, "Look at these soldiers! Look at their gray hairs, their furrowed cheeks, their bent forms, their tottering limbs and trembling hands. They cannot carry rifle, knapsack, ammunition and rations, and march over rough roads, ford streams, stand on picket in pelting rains, endure exposure and fatigue. Their eyesight is dim. They cannot aim. They are not fit for service. They are not soldiers. They cannot undertake new enterprises in civil life. They cannot learn new ways." Johnson suggested that their decrepitude encouraged Americans to ignore them, even to hold them in contempt.[11]

And when they returned from that victory, Johnson suggested, "they took up the burdens of civil life cheerfully, ardently,—they went west, north and south; they entered public lands, they felled forests, broke the virgin soil of wood and prairie . . . ; they built cities and railroads; they opened mines, manned the looms." In Washington, many performed honorable service in government jobs. In short, the veterans had saved the Union on the battlefield and then helped that Union grow more powerful in their peaceful pursuits after the war. Now, with wounds and sickness and old age catching up to them, they needed to collect on the moral debt owed them by their fellow citizens, from the man "who did not enlist; who perhaps sustained the war in an honorable way while it was going on; or [from] that other citizen who was too prudent, too prosperous or too young to enlist, or the foreign born citizen who has come to America since the war."[12]

Acknowledging the raging debate over pensions, Johnson connected the public's reluctance to accept its responsibilities to veterans to the growth of materialism: the love of money and the admiration for men whose only accomplishment was making money. The glittering celebrity of the capitalists and the dynamic consumerism encouraged by the growing economy had distracted the public from its former admiration for the veterans. Rather than honoring veterans, "in our day the men who grow suddenly rich in speculation, in chicanery and vulgar cunning, whose flashing equipages go rolling by, are shown the highest seats and sway the world." But living up to the promises made, or at least implied, to the veterans when they went off to war, honoring those men for their sacrifices in the modest ways made available by the government, would serve as counterpoints to the "corroding influence" of the undue worship of material wealth. In a sense, the old soldiers were conducting one last campaign for the soul of America. "The presence of the Veteran of the Union is a constant reproach against the tendency of our times," thundered Johnson, and "awakes an impulse toward a better and higher citizenship."[13]

These men could be materially honored and the nation could pay its moral debt to them by retaining the preference given to veterans for federal jobs — now threatened by civil service examinations and patronage handed out by the resurgent Democratic Party — and by granting a pension to every elderly or disabled veteran, even if his disability was not caused by military service. "These Veterans have done and are doing every duty" asked of them, concluded Johnson, and now "it is the duty of the citizen to see that there is not a Veteran in want; not a Veteran in the poorhouse."[14]

The image of veterans spending their last years in almshouses, county poor farms, or other charitable institutions that elicited long-held notions of fear and contempt was a powerful emotional and political tool. It had helped spur the building of state soldiers' homes in the 1870s and 1880s, and the Grand Army of the Republic constantly stressed its devotion to keeping veterans out of county institutions through GAR "relief funds." The rhetoric soared in 1887, the year in which Johnson gave his speech, when President Grover Cleveland vetoed the most generous pension bill to date and angered veterans by advocating the return of captured Confederate battle flags. Pensions became a huge issue in the election of 1888, when Benjamin Harrison, backed by the GAR, defeated Cleveland.[15]

Although few Americans believed that aging veterans should be allowed to die in such degrading conditions, many insisted not all veterans needed help from the government. The premise that the nation had a duty to its old soldiers was turned upside down by another veteran speaking on a Memorial Day a few years earlier. On the same day in 1884 that Holmes uttered his famous words in New Hampshire, Theodore C. Bacon held forth in Canandaigua, New York, on "the veteran soldier's duty to his country." Bacon had served in the 17th Connecticut Cavalry and as a staff officer for Brig. Gen. John Buford. He began his talk to the Albert M. Murray Post of the GAR by saying that he had little to add to the traditional "wisdom" and "eloquence" that had become commonplace in Memorial Day speeches. He could hardly "add a new resplendence to the halo of eulogy with which, from year to year, we have been wont to crown the memories of those who have died for us."[16]

Bacon chose to turn the tables on the veterans in his audience; rather than telling the nation what it should do for its old soldiers, he suggested to the veterans what they owed their country. Rather than suggesting that the American people would be judged based on how they treated veterans, he argued that veterans had the higher standards to live up to simply because they were veterans.

After delivering an admiring and somewhat exaggerated account of the way in which Oliver Cromwell and the veteran of his New Model Army blended peacefully and prosperously back into society after the English Civil War, Bacon declared that "the first duty of the veteran soldier to his country, in this nineteenth century as in the seventeenth, in America as in England" is "that he shall be in time of peace its best and most active citizen." He should, of course, obey the law, but he should also help restore the nation's prosperity, repair the damage wrought by war, and "be . . . most diligent of all in restoring that frightful waste." Bacon urged veterans to make themselves available to state militias, which, since the war, had deteriorated disgracefully. In a comment that revealed as much about his own attitudes toward the poor as it did about the pension issue, Bacon complained that the militias had declined so much that they would be unable to put down the riots that were sure to come in the cities teeming with immigrants and dissatisfied poor folks who were a demagogue away from becoming "armed and raging multitudes." Finally, because their military training and their sacrifice had made them "in some sense a superior caste," they must "not forget the duties that belong to superiority." They should display their uniforms, flags, weapons, and medals proudly, but only at times and in places that honored those symbols of their service. "If you have fallen into vicious or criminal ways, shelter yourself from the cold with anything rather than that old blue coat," he ordered, when "you descend into dens of vice or jail." It was appropriate to display their framed officer's commission in their shop or office but not "in your tippling house or your gambling hell."[17]

In short, old soldiers must live up to their responsibilities as heroes and recall the honor they acquired by serving their country. And they must remember the patriotism that led them to war. Bacon distinguished between soldiers who had volunteered and those who came into the army late in the war, when bounties inspired unworthy men to don the blue and substitutes entered the army only for monetary gain. "There were still noble men — patriotic men, unselfish men — breasting the storm of bullets, with higher motives than the bounty, the so-many-dollars-a-month-and-found, or the future claim upon the public treasury, impelling them." But they had become more and more rare as the war dragged on. The connection of material gain to military service at the expense of pure patriotism had "demoralized our armies, lost our battles, depraved the public sentiment, and burdened nations, states, counties and towns with prodigious accumulations of indebtedness."[18]

The "evil influence" of such mercenary self-interest "is even now persistent and efficient" in the calls by politicians, claims agents, and greedy old soldiers for the so-called service pension, "the most stupendous schemes of retroactive payments that the world had ever dreamed of . . . projects of spoliation in the presence of which all prior measures seem insignificant." "True soldiers" would never associate themselves with this large-scale public larceny. Yet the aggressive promotion of such programs by a few GAR newspapers, opportunistic politicians, and profit-seeking agents had earned for all veterans reputations "as mercenaries, haggling for their pay; or as mendicants, begging for alms." Old soldiers owed it to the nation to "give the lie" to such stereotypes, to reject the burden placed on poor taxpayers by the "pretended demand of veteran soldiers."[19]

Not surprisingly, Bacon's urgings inspired few veterans to forsake the

Materialism

payments they believed they had earned, and the pension issue was never fully resolved. Although the pension rolls kept expanding and the amount spent on pensions kept increasing, the GAR and other veterans' groups failed to achieve what had become their pet scheme by the 1890s: a "service" pension for all men who had served in the Union army, regardless of their physical or economic condition. Values-laden rhetoric about soldiers' worth and a nation's duty to its veterans would continue to provide a hard-edged counterpoint to the sentimentalized celebration of their heroism and sacrifice.

DESPITE CRITIQUES FROM Bacon and others, sentimentality flourished in discussions of soldiers' homes. Louisa May Alcott wrote the story "My Red Cap" in support of the 1881 Soldiers' Home Bazaar in Boston. In the spirit of the Sanitary Fairs held during the Civil War, the bazaar published a journal throughout the ten-day run of the fair. In addition to news about exhibits and information about the Massachusetts Soldiers' Home in Chelsea (the home was already open; proceedings from the bazaar would establish an endowment for operating expenses), Alcott told the story of a fictional veteran named Joe Collins, a steady, modest yeoman whose patriotism called him away to war. The narrator meets him early in the war as she distributes apples to departing soldiers; she comes across him after he returns home minus an arm. He loses his fiancée to a man who did not fight in the war, and his crippling wound prevents him from pursuing a career. He works as a messenger—hence the red cap of the title—supported in part by the work the narrator throws his way. When he stops coming, she goes in search of him and finally finds him living in a single mother's home, taking care of her children for room and board while she scratches out a living doing laundry. He owns only the clothes on his back (he sleeps with only his old army coat for a blanket) but refuses to be sent to a poorhouse. When the narrator finds him, he is his old, polite, modest self. "There ain't much left of me but bones and pain," he admits, but "I'm powerful glad to see you all the same." He gladly accepts an invitation to go into the new soldiers' home. Once ensconced in that happy place, his health improves and, as the narrator writes, "A happier man or a more grateful one it would be hard to find." She goes on: "If a visitor wants an enthusiastic guide about the place, Joe is the one to take, for all is comfort, sunshine, and goodwill to him; and he unconsciously shows how great the need of this refuge is, as he hobbles about on his lame feet, pointing out its beauties, conveniences, and delights with his one arm."[20]

This kind of happy ending did, of course, occur. But the reality for many veterans consigned to soldiers' homes was, inevitably, less inspiring, as each old soldier dealt with his own demons and fought to maintain a sense of worth and personal dignity. Interestingly, although very few accounts by inmates of the federal or state homes have survived, the handful that are available provide ample evidence of the doubt and anger that characterized many of the institutionalized veterans of the Civil War.

The source revealing the most positive attitude demonstrated by an inmate of a home are the letters written by Temple Dunn, who entered the NHDVS in 1904. Dunn had mustered out of the 49th Indiana as an eighteen-year-old corporal; following the war he became a respected educator and a failed businessman. After a decade of hard luck during the depression that followed the Panic of 1893, the sixty-year-old finally checked himself into the Central Branch in Dayton, Ohio.

Dunn's letters reveal a man who knew that his admission to the home carried connotations unbecoming to a Gilded Age male, and he fought to maintain his honor and confidence. His correspondence is interesting not because he was particularly unhappy at the home—in fact, he seemed to make a conscious effort to *be* happy—but because they show that his only child, a daughter named Bettie, was deeply disturbed by the idea of her father accepting the nation's gratitude in this way. She was not the only American to see shame in wearing the plain blue uniforms of the NHDVS. Newspapers and GAR magazines published frequent articles and editorials assuring Americans that home-bound veterans were not paupers but warriors receiving their just rewards. But the rather defensive tone of the articles indicated that just the opposite assumption was common currency among Gilded Age Americans.[21]

Dunn's surviving letters from his time at the home, which cover just under three years, are chatty missives to his daughter, Bettie. Their relationship is clearly close and loving. But Bettie did not want her father living in a soldiers' home. Dunn made the decision on his own and felt it necessary to assure her there was no shame in accepting support from a grateful nation. That he felt the need to do so suggests his awareness that the attitudes of the public toward old soldiers were more ambiguous than most public rhetoric would suggest.

A deeply religious man, Dunn began his first letter with a biblical reference: "Let not your heart be troubled." He apparently hoped that his evocation of John 14:1 would make the news easier for Bettie to take. "It has been coming a long time," he wrote. "I have not been able to command courage enough to speak to you about it." He assured her that he had thought and prayed and wept about the decision but was satisfied it was the best thing to do. "All my regrets are for you, and all the tears it has cost me have been for you. . . . I beg of you not to make it harder for me to bear by bemoaning more than you must my situation." Dunn hated the thought of being a burden to anyone, especially Bettie, and he desperately wanted to avoid cashing in a life insurance policy that would be his only material legacy to his only living child. He assured her that he would be well fed, well clothed, and well housed, and that there would be "a great many arrangements to contribute to my religious, social, and intellectual life." Moreover, he believed the country owed him the security and limited comfort that the home could provide. "I deserve, and richly deserve, everything that can be done for me here. The debt can never be overpaid." He took pains to suggest that his job search would continue and that he might only stay at the home over the winter. "I am sure I may trust you to put only the most generous construction upon my actions."[22]

But his sunny outlook could not erase an uncomfortable sense that he had, by going to the home, entered a status that would raise eyebrows among neighbors and inspire guilt in family members. Dunn inadvertently revealed much about common middle-class attitudes about the home that ran counter to public admiration for veterans and patriotic rhetoric about the homes' function in rewarding worthy saviors of the Union. In a telling passage from his first letter, he declared, "I shall direct this to you in a Home envelope, making no effort at concealment. Let us be right out with it. My pride has fully succumbed, and I trust yours will yield without too much pain to you." Later in the same letter he asked Bettie to "not try for a moment to conceal my whereabouts. Just say I cannot bear to be a burden to others who have their own burdens to bear."[23]

Although Bettie's letters to Dunn have not survived, it is clear that her father's assurances and proud descriptions of the home grounds failed to move her, at least at first. Dunn's response to the first two letters she sent him after entering the home offers a pretty good idea of what Bettie had said:

> Your sorrow-burdened letter — and the preceding one — are here this morning. You make a powerful appeal, but you are wrong. My course is the soul of honor. I am not making a disgraceful surrender. I am not physically able to prosecute a determined fight, and am doing the only thing that is open to me as I see it. I am as anxious not to become a burden upon you as upon others — though I know — O, how well I know it — you would bear it as no one else in the wide world would. . . . Step by step I have fought it out with myself, for a long

time; and I do not think of changing my purpose. . . . [A]s I see my situation, I have done the right thing.

In an extremely telling passage, Dunn wrote that, "out of respect to your mistaken notion," he would mail this letter in a plain envelope (indeed, this and virtually all subsequent letters are written on plain paper rather than NHDVS stationary). "I am sorry I may not just use the Home envelope. It will very soon be known, and it would be better not to attempt any concealment." He closed, "*Sorry* to give any answer which is the opposite of what you ask for."[24]

Despite what must have been an emotionally wrenching beginning, Dunn's acceptance of his position grew over time. Small comments and bits of news in the regular letters he sent to Bettie indicate his satisfaction. He supervised a crew of three men in some sort of "pleasant" but unnamed work; kept his promise to send small amounts of money to her out of his quarterly pension payment (much of it went to refurbishing her house); decorated a letter written on Flag Day in 1905 with a hand-drawn American flag; described from time to time the great food served at the home; reported his progress in reading the Bible from beginning to end; suggested ways for her to view a partial eclipse of the sun; and began brushing up his Latin.

In Dunn one sees a veteran accepting his nation's charity but not giving up his self-respect. That he remained a clear-thinking, engaged parent, unbowed by what apparently seemed to him to be a temporary situation, is obvious from the fatherly advice that appears in his letters to Bettie. At one point, Bettie experienced an emotional religious conversion and apparently — and inexplicably, given Dunn's open piety — feared her father's disapproval. Dunn assured Bettie that it did not bother him at all: "I bid you God-speed in your nearness to Him, I shall be very near you at your nearest — with His blessing." In a marginal note indicating a sense of humor largely invisible in his other letters, he offered a biblical tongue-twister: "Can you say and smile while you say it over and over 'Simply to thy cross I cling?'" Bettie's sometimes troubled religious experiences appeared in a number of letters.[25]

In the absence of a mother, Bettie relied on her father for advice when, in the summer of 1905, she entered a relationship with a man named Tom. Dunn was delighted at the prospect of her marriage, but he gave her reasonable — if somewhat old-fashioned — advice about how to act in public (being "silly over each other" would simply draw attention to themselves; once she has committed herself to Tom, she should pay less attention to other men) and modern-sounding advice not to stop stating her opinions, even if they conflicted with her husband's. Bettie had apparently wondered if she was settling for a man less brilliant than she had hoped to marry; the good father replied, "If you *respect* Tom (as you must, if seems to me, for I do *thoroughly*) and love him, that beats all the merely *brilliant* things in the world. Merely brilliant marriages are dangerous." He acknowledged in another letter that she was past the age of "tenderest sentiment"—she was twenty-eight at the time—and felt rather sad that she had missed the excitement of young love. Nevertheless, by the summer of 1906 Bettie was engaged and Dunn was preparing the wedding invitations.

Perhaps because she appreciated the fact that the home had not deprived her of a father, Bettie did eventually come around to her father's point of view regarding the home, and she even visited him on at least one occasion. After her departure, Dunn wrote, many of the veterans "came to me with warm handshakes and warmer congratulations over my having you. I was very proud of the way they sized you up." He was also proud of the kindness and maturity she showed in speaking to "my friends." Your "manner was *superb*! *God bless you*!!"[26]

In the last surviving letter to Bettie he described a new job at the home—difficult, but rewarding—and expressed his determination that, when he finally did come to live with Bettie and Tom, he would not be a burden but actually a help around the house. Interestingly, for the first time in nearly three years, he wrote the letter on NHDVS stationary. Dunn apparently left the home shortly afterward, although no record of his later life exists.[27]

On the surface, Dunn's cheerful resignation and his determination to make the best out of an imperfect situation reveal him as a stereotypical inmate of a soldiers' home. But his response actually reflects the attitudes Americans assumed in their veterans. Dunn was clearly aware that a significant portion of the population believed that there was something lacking in the character of the men living off of government largesse. Of course, entering a soldiers' home also suggested that one's family was unable to assume his care, which put the family in a bad light. In any event, becoming an inmate at a soldiers' home could inspire conflict within families—as well as within the men themselves.

The latter was especially the case with Henry Clinton Parkhurst, who wrote in August 1910, while he was an inmate at the soldiers' home in Napa, California, that "some men enter soldier-homes from necessity or for temporary convenience. Others find in a soldier-home a luxurious hotel—a glorious place where they can eat, sleep, play cards, blather by the hour, and wear out clothes, without having to work." Parkhurst was a newspaperman and writer as well as an alcoholic; he claimed to have helped found the veterans' home in Napa.

His writings are filled with descriptions of conflict with other veterans and with himself. In the first line of an unpublished manuscript titled "The Soldier Home Troops," he indicates his general distaste for soldiers' homes: "Who enters here leaves pride and self-respect behind." Parkhurst had been in and out of homes all over the country throughout his middle and early old age, and he hated them thoroughly. Although he claimed that he had voluntarily checked into homes to write—he completed at least one book manuscript—his absolute contempt for other inmates suggests a degree of self-loathing that no self-respecting amateur psychologist could miss.[28]

Parkhurst had seen hard service during the war as a member of the 16th Iowa Infantry. He entered the army as an eighteen-year-old in 1862 and reenlisted in 1864. He fought at Iuka and Corinth and was captured at Atlanta, after which he spent six months at the Andersonville and Florence prison camps. During his peripatetic career as a journalist in Iowa, New York, and California, he sometimes found it financially and personally convenient to enter state or national veterans homes for limited periods of time.

At the beginning of a dozen tightly transcribed pages Parkhurst wrote, "It is not worth while complaining about soldiers' homes or scribbling much about them. They are all alike—rotten with graft—and a man of intelligence who is forced to live in one of them is to be pitied." He complained about the negligence and poor management of the officials, the bad habits and foreign origins of the inmates, and the "fact" that most men living in the homes by the 1890s and early 1900s were not actually veterans, but short-timers, militiamen, or out-and-out frauds. He referred to them as "cattle" and "human hogs"; out of any one hundred inmates, "not more than four or five would be worth talking to [for] five minutes. They are the utter scum of civil and military life—the ignorant refuse of jails, alms-houses, insane asylums and penitentiaries." And these were the men—hardly the stereotypes of old soldiers presented in sentimental stories and articles—with whom he was forced to live.[29]

Parkhurst's contempt stemmed from his own difficult service and from his conservative belief, apparent in his writings, that real men should be able to stand on their own two feet. "No man should be maintained for life at public expense, and be allowed a pension besides," he wrote, "unless he could prove he had served six months at the front, in actual warfare." Even disabled men who could not prove such service should be sent to the poorhouse, along with the "riff-raff" of the regular army and navy. "To establish expensive places and call them 'soldier homes,' and then make them dumping grounds for the filth and scum of society—for professional paupers, army deserters, insane persons, tramps, jail-birds, men fresh from penitentiaries, men who have no shred or sign of military papers, or who have found or bought the papers of dead soldiers—to do this is a sham and hypocrisy and an imposition on tax-payers."

Parkhurst's catalog of criminals and miscreants was impressive. He claimed that at least 5,000 men were living in soldiers' homes under the assumed names of dead soldiers. His evidence was anecdotal but powerful: a hard-working mechanic who had retired to the national home in Hampton after happening across discharge papers in the drawer of a bureau he had purchased at an auction; an acquaintance who, upon surveying the roll of members of the national home near Los Angeles, found his own name! Parkhurst himself had come under the authority of sergeants (homes were organized into companies, with captains, sergeants, etc.) with highly suspect records: one, a career criminal and member of a home guard company in Nevada, had lived for thirty years in the home; another had been a gambler and pimp, a brawler and saloon keeper, a forger and an inmate of San Quentin (after shooting a man in a fight); a third had, during the war, been put in charge of a captured vessel filled with cotton and immediately deserted to the Rebels.

A second document, written about two weeks after "The Soldier Home Troops," continued his screed against soldiers' homes. "The Bug House," his term for the home, began with the story of a knife attack by a "vicious inmate" on an inoffensive barber. Parkhurst broke up the fight by battering the attacker with a board. He predicted that the latter would not be punished. It was the second knife fight in the home in two weeks. Punishments were rare; "no criminal is ever turned over to the civil authorities, lest public criticism should be excited." Parkhurst claimed that murders at the national homes were "not infrequent" but that the perpetrators were regularly pronounced insane and shipped off to the asylum for insane soldiers in Washington. After they were "cured"—usually in about a year— they were sent to another home, "to probably kill another man there." Parkhurst admitted that "there are many good fellows, and many good soldiers in every soldier-home." However, he estimated that "two-thirds of the inmates are low, dirty, lazy, ignorant, drunken, obscene European paupers and 'dead beats' whom it is a burlesque to call 'old soldiers.' . . . They are simply human scum, and when the last one of them is dead, it will be a blessing to the country."[30]

Not quite three years later, Parkhurst was living at the Iowa Soldiers' Home in Marshalltown. He was about sixty-nine years old, but his age and the change of scenery had not moderated his contempt. Reflecting a quaint notion about germ theory, he reported that he resisted using common drinking cups, kept his towel separate from the other veterans, and always scrubbed out the tub before bathing for fear of contracting cancer or syphilis, the latter of which apparently raged at epidemic levels. His litany of accusations continued; one of the "captains" of a veterans' company — whose name he wrote but then crossed out — "is a favorite at Headquarters, not withstanding the fact that he was convicted of the degraded crime of sodomy." The sentencing judge had given him the choice of going to the penitentiary or to the soldiers' home — "an insult to every soldier of the Union army." Another "filthy vagabond" suffering from venereal disease who was, nevertheless, a pet of the home governor carried on conversations "so obscene and disgusting that it would not be allowed in an ordinary house of ill fame."

Parkhurst could not believe that these men had ever been soldiers — at least not good soldiers. They were "so ignorant of military drill that they can't 'keep step,' and any brief march throws them into confusion." They mishandled their guns and could barely get off the volleys required at official funerals. Many spent their time tracking private pension bills in the *Congressional Record*; others plotted scams of the government that included crutches, fake illnesses, and forged documents. A number of men who claimed complete disability carried on businesses outside the home grounds. A telling anecdote, at least to Parkhurst, was the fact that, rather than talking about generals and battles, as "real" old soldiers would do, the old men engaged in "incessant filthy talk about women; and angry blathering about pension bills."

In a rare moment of self-reflection, Parkhurst conceded that, at a certain level, he was also a "fakir like these other dead beats"; he was not physically disabled and chose to live in the homes from time to time to save money while working on articles and books. But he refused to feel guilty: "As long as government money hangs on limbs of trees, I feel justified in helping myself to some of it." Unlike most of his fellow inmates, believed Parkhurst, "I did the country real service in dangerous times." He ended "The Soldier Home Troops" with the prediction that the soldiers' homes would "continue to be patriotic dens of graft, havens for crafty and undeserving paupers, and a hotel for the drunken filth and scum of the land." He concluded that "the best way for a real soldier to rest their ills is to keep out of them. That is what I intend to do."[31]

Unlike Parkhurst, Charles Morehouse could not avoid entering a soldiers' home. Although his financial situation is unclear, Morehouse's declining health forced him into the Minnesota State Soldiers' Home. He spent most of 1912 — the last year of his life — in the home in St. Paul. Apparently dying of a bladder ailment, for which he received excruciating treatments every few weeks, he also suffered from extreme loneliness and exhibited an absolute distaste for all elements of life at the home. The New York native and veteran of three years' service in two different Ohio regiments stayed in a Minneapolis boardinghouse for several weeks after submitting his application to the home in early February; about the day he arrived at the home, he wrote in his diary, "God only knows the sad and sorry memory of the following days and nights. Oh the pain and the hunger for the touch of a home hand and the sound of a home voice." If Temple Dunn's conflict was with outsiders' perceptions of home inmates, and if Henry Parkhurst's bitterness stemmed from the degraded company he was forced to keep in the several homes in which he lived, Morehouse's conflict was virtually entirely internal: the home was not a home and he mourned for the life he could no longer have.[32]

Morehouse's pain and feeling of isolation fairly leap from the pages of his little diary. He occasionally gave himself completely over to despair, wondering if he would ever see a friendly face again. When family and friends came to visit, which they did every two or three weeks, he generally met them in downtown St. Paul or Minneapolis, where they would have lunch at a hotel and do a little shopping. Although they did, from time to time, come to the home, Morehouse would usually take them to a nearby park; he apparently did not want them to see him in his dreary new place of residence. Even when family visited, as his son, daughter, and one or two other women did during his second week in the home, he remained unhappy. Their departure left him "sad because it all seemed so *different* from *what* I *expected*—almost as [though] they do not care for me and my broken heart."[33]

Morehouse refused to allow himself to settle into his new life. He referred by name to fellow veterans on only two or three occasions; he constantly tried to escape the confines of the home grounds; he hated the surgeon, only barely tolerated the chaplain, and found the quartermaster "not congenial." He described the home in terms of what it was not: his own home. He took a little bit of masochistic pleasure in describing the pitiful meals of weak soup and poor meat and regularly referred to the "vile suppers" served to the old men. He was grateful when a friend sent him a potted hyacinth; although it reminded him of Easter, he thought it "out of place" in his "barn like room."[34]

Morehouse rarely mentioned other soldiers except to complain about their drunkenness and incessant playing of the "music box." Early in the spring he ventured to the "Falls"—the Minnesota Soldiers' Home was perched on a bluff over the Mississippi near Minnehaha Falls. He complained that the "usual amount of booze was consumed which just makes me sick." Morehouse hated it when the other veterans tried to be friendly, when "Old Andy" and "Bill" "jogged up" one evening, for example; "they with others made the night hideous." He complained on another occasion that the "gang are keeping up the jamboree" and, on an especially boring day, wrote that "the gang are tapering off on their orgies a trifle." It was even worse when the weather warmed up; a nice Sunday afternoon in June was ruined when "in the park there was a perfect mob which set me wild."[35]

By mid-April, Morehouse's entries were dominated by day-by-day reports of the "exquisite" pain caused by his worsening bladder ailment and the excruciating and invasive treatments—called the "washing out process"—conducted every week or two by the home surgeon or by his slightly gentler doctor-friend in St. Paul (who also had the advantage of having a pretty receptionist with whom Morehouse liked to chat). The pain kept him awake virtually every night, but the treatments were so frightful that he frequently reported not having the nerve to go to them.[36]

Months before he reached the final medical crisis that took his life, Morehouse wrote, "All of this isn't life—it is just agony." Three days after recording that sentiment, he complained of being "too despondent to go out" of the barracks. He was obviously accustomed to calling on his religious beliefs at such times, and he reported, "I try hard to get the Christ Spirit into my mind and actions every day—but there is but little encouragement in this place. God help us all." Two weeks later he recorded a long, cold weekend spent indoors, where he "roosted on the ragged edge of despair and pain." His nearly daily entries dwindled throughout the last half of 1912, from roughly once a week to even less, skipping from midsummer to late October. Morehouse's last dated entry recorded a light snow on November 23; he died less than two months later.[37]

OLIVER WENDELL HOLMES JR. had started out in his 1884 speech to find common ground with the civilians in his audience. "To the indifferent inquirer who asks why Memorial Day is still kept up," he said, "we may answer, it celebrates and solemnly reaffirms from year to year a national act of enthusiasm and faith. It embodies in the most impressive form our belief that to act with enthusiasm and faith is the condition of acting greatly. To fight out a war, you must believe something and want something with all your might. So must you do to carry anything else to an end worth reaching." He was neither the first nor the last to suggest war as a metaphor for struggle and determination and achievement, and it truly was a way to unite those men whose hearts had been touched by fire and those civilians who, at best, had merely warmed their hands by that same fire.[38]

But soldiers and civilians did not necessarily think about this very real war in the same way; nor did they necessarily agree on the ways in which a nation should show its gratitude to those battle-singed veterans. The band of brothers who had shared the hardships and glories described by Holmes were separated from nonveterans by their experiences and had very different notions of how they could be repaid for their sacrifices. And only a fraction of those veterans ended up in soldiers' homes, where some of them sank into depression like Charles Morehouse, who complained of the "unreal life as this is" and asked, "Where, oh where are the sweet sincerities of the olden days?" These public and private conflicts over the granting of pensions and over the nature of life at soldiers' homes show that the conflicts within the conflict kept burning long after the fire of the Civil War had burned out.[39]

NOTES

1. Larry J. Sabato, ed., *Divided States of America: The Slash and Burn Politics of the 2004 Presidential Election* (New York: Pearson/Longman, 2006), is a useful anthology on the issues and campaign strategies of the 2004 election. The most important attack on Kerry's war record is John E. O'Neill and Jerome R. Corsi, *Unfit for Command: Swift Boat Veterans Speak Out Against John Kerry* (Washington: Regnery, 2004).

2. Typical of the articles on Iraq were two that appeared under a Cox News Service dateline: "PTSD rates in current wars may top Vietnam" and "Drugs part of life in combat," *Milwaukee Journal Sentinel*, November 27, 2006.

3. Civil War–era historians plowing contested ground have devoted a great deal of attention to memory. See, for example, David W. Blight, *Race and Reunion: The Civil War in American Memory* (Cambridge, Mass.: Harvard University Press, 2001), and Alice Fahs and Joan Waugh, eds., *The Memory of the Civil War in American Culture* (Chapel Hill: University of North Carolina Press, 2004). Other representative works on Civil War memory examine the battle of Gettysburg's continuing legacy: Carol Reardon, *Pickett's Charge in History and Memory* (Chapel Hill: University of North Carolina Press, 1997), and Jim

Weeks, *Gettysburg: Memory, Market, and an American Shrine* (Princeton, N.J.: Princeton University Press, 2003).

4. The major exception is Eric T. Dean Jr., *Shook over Hell: Post-Traumatic Stress, Vietnam, and the Civil War* (Cambridge, Mass.: Harvard University Press, 1997). Larry M. Logue's brisk *To Appomattox and Beyond: The Civil War Soldier in War and Peace* (Chicago: Ivan R. Dee, 1996), introduces a number of sources of conflict over veterans' affairs, while Stuart McConnell's *Glorious Contentment: The Grand Army of the Republic, 1865–1900* (Chapel Hill: University of North Carolina Press, 1992), explores the dynamics of competing attitudes within an organization whose members are generally, and mistakenly, considered to have thought exactly alike on most issues. Stewart O'Nan offers a fictional account of a Civil War veteran with symptoms of post-traumatic stress syndrome in *A Prayer for the Dying* (New York: Henry Holt, 1999).

5. Mark DeWolfe Howe, comp., *The Occasional Speeches of Justice Oliver Wendell Holmes* (Cambridge, Mass.: Harvard University Press, 1962), 15, 8, 9.

6. Useful accounts of the pension programs and the issues they raised are Theda Skocpol, *Protecting Soldiers and Mothers: The Political Origins of Social Policy in the United States* (Cambridge, Mass.: Harvard University Press, 1992), and Megan J. McClintock, "Civil War Pensions and the Reconstruction of Union Families," *Journal of American History* 83 (September 1996): 456–80. The classic political and institutional history of the pension system is John William Oliver, *History of the Civil War Military Pensions, 1861–1865* (Madison: University of Wisconsin Press, 1917).

7. Abraham Lincoln, *The Collected Works of Abraham Lincoln*, ed. Roy P. Basler, 9 vols. (New Brunswick, N.J.: Rutgers University Press, 1953–55), 8:333.

8. Claudia Linares, "The Civil War Pension Law," Working Paper 2001-6, Center for Population Economics, University of Chicago, 2001.

9. Larry M. Logue, "Union Veterans and Their Government: The Effects of Public Policies on Private Lives," *Journal of Interdisciplinary History* 22 (Winter 1992): 423. The best account of the founding and administration of the homes is Patrick J. Kelly, *Creating a National Home: Building the Veterans' Welfare State, 1860–1900* (Cambridge, Mass.: Harvard University Press, 1997). See also Judith Gladys Cetina, "A History of Veterans' Homes in the United States, 1811–1930" (Ph.D. dissertation, Case Western Reserve University, 1977). Although they are beyond the purview of this essay, Confederate states also established homes for elderly Confederate veterans. See R. B. Rosenberg, *Living Monuments: Confederate Soldiers' Homes in the New South* (Chapel Hill: University of North Carolina Press, 1993).

10. *Milwaukee Sentinel*, July 17, 1871. For more on the relationship between the Milwaukee branch of the NHDVS and the city, see "'A Place of Great Beauty, Improved by Man': The Soldiers' Home and Victorian Milwaukee," *Milwaukee History* 22 (Spring 1999): 2–15.

11. Charles W. Johnson, *The Veteran of 1861–5 and the Citizen of 1887* (Minneapolis: Harrison & Smith, 1887), 5, 6.

12. Ibid., 7–8.

13. Ibid., 12–13.

14. Ibid., 18–19.

15. Kelly, *Creating a National Home*, 93–98; McConnell, *Glorious Contentment*, 124–41; Logue, *To Appomattox and Beyond*, 97–99.

16. Theodore Bacon, *The Veteran Soldier's Duty to His Country* (Rochester: *Rochester Union and Advertiser*, 1884), 3. For the debate within the GAR over pensions, see McConnell, *Glorious Contentment*, 152–56.

17. Bacon, *Veteran Soldier's Duty to his Country*, 6–10.

18. Ibid., 11–12.

19. Ibid., 12–13.

20. Louisa May Alcott, "The Red Cap," *The Sword and the Pen*, December 10, 1881, 3, 4.

21. For American attitudes about residents of poorhouses during this period, see Michael B. Katz, *In the Shadow of the Poorhouse: A Social History of Welfare in America*, rev. ed. (New York: Basic Books, 1996), 88–102.

22. Temple H. Dunn to "My Dear Bettie," September 14, 1904, folder 1, Temple H. Dunn Papers, Manuscript Section, Indiana State Library, Indianapolis.

23. Ibid.

24. Ibid.

25. Ibid., May 21, 1905.

26. Ibid., August 19, September 3, December 2, 1905, July 7, 1906.

27. Ibid., June 27, 1907.

28. Henry Clinton Parkhurst, "The Soldier Home Troops," n.p., unpublished manuscript, box 5, Scrapbook, Henry Clinton Parkhurst Collection, State Historical Society of Iowa, Iowa City (repository hereafter cited as SHSI).

29. Although Parkhurst clearly exaggerated the vices enjoyed by his fellow inmates, alcoholism and the attending medical and disciplinary problems flourished at many soldiers' homes. See, for example, Kelly, *Creating a National Home*, 141–49, and James Marten, "Nomads in Blue: Disabled Veterans and Alcohol at the National Home," in David A. Gerber, ed., *Disabled Veterans in History* (Ann Arbor: University of Michigan Press, 2000).

30. Parkhurst, "The Bug House," n.p., unpublished manuscript, Parkhurst Collection, SHSI.

31. Parkhurst, "Iowa Soldiers' Home," unpublished manuscript, and Parkhurst, "The Soldier Home Troops," both in Parkhurst Collection, SHSI.

32. Charles Morehouse Diary, March 13, 1912, Minnesota Historical Society, St. Paul.

33. Ibid., April 3, 1912.

34. Ibid., March 28, 29, 1912.

35. Ibid., March 5, April 8, 12, 13, June 9, 1912.

36. Ibid., April 9, 1912.

37. Ibid., April 11, 14, 25–27, November 23, 1912.

38. Howe, comp., *Occasional Speeches of Justice Oliver Wendell Holmes*, 6.

39. Morehouse Diary, June 8, 1912, Minnesota Historical Society, St. Paul.

William T. Sherman in Postwar Georgia's Collective Memory, 1864–1914

⊰ CAROL REARDON ⊱

In February 1891, shortly after the death of William Tecumseh Sherman, a Georgia journalist posited an intriguing question: "How shall we judge a man who was one day all fire, and the next day all ice: forgiving one moment, and relentless the next, a patriot today and a partisan tomorrow?"[1] This query suggests that, after the passage of nearly thirty years, Georgians' collective memory of the famed Union general could provoke surprisingly reflective consideration. Indeed, by the time of the Civil War's golden anniversary, Sherman's place in Georgia's past did not rest solely on bitter recollections of the military events of 1864. Through the years, the political and social crises of Reconstruction, the blossoming of both the Lost Cause and the New South mentalities, and the rise of Jim Crow had spawned a surprising diversity in the ways in which Georgians remembered him.

From the time the Union army launched its offensive from Chattanooga in May 1864 until it marched into South Carolina in January 1865, many Georgians experienced sociologist Arthur G. Neal's three "ingredients" of trauma: "some form of bafflement, some level of suffering, and perceptions of evil in human affairs."[2] Thousands in the direct path of the Union army experienced the near-total collapse of the familiar rhythms of their daily lives, confronting confusion, insecurity, and loss first as individuals and families and then as citizens of a larger political entity. To make sense of the chaos breaking around them, Georgians demanded to know what happened and, even more importantly, why it had happened.

During the 1864 campaign, few Georgians truly comprehended what had happened to their state. Newspapers and the telegraph system brought only incomplete and contradictory assessments of fast-breaking events that might provide context for an individual's or family's own experiences — or contradict them entirely. In a single issue of a Georgia newspaper during Sherman's March to the Sea, for instance, readers could find detailed, block-by-block lists of destroyed buildings in Atlanta and, a few columns away, find confident boasts that loyal citizens most certainly would take up arms to defeat Sherman before he could ever wreak any such havoc. Reports of outrages against women and children attributed to Sherman's "bummers" appeared in the same issue as stories of unexpected benevolence extended by the northern invaders. Georgians read of faithful slaves saving their masters' lives and property and of other slaves willingly pointing out to Yankee soldiers the caches of food and valuables their masters had hidden.[3] In short, wartime Georgians could construct no single vision of what had happened to their state beyond a general understanding that, in scale and scope, it eclipsed all of the war's other horrors.

Even in the absence of a shared experience, all Georgians—including those far from Sherman's path—demanded to know who bore the responsibility for their prostration. The ways in which they affixed the blame for their plight validates Jacqueline Campbell Glass's observation that Sherman's march through the Carolinas in early 1865 possessed both physical and psychological dimensions. In Georgia, the psychological effects would reveal themselves—sometimes in surprising ways—during and for decades after the war and shape how Georgians remembered the grim-visaged Ohioan.[4]

Even during the war, thousands of Georgians viewed Sherman's army as only one agent of their state's devastation. Since 1861, Union naval and ground forces raided coastal Georgia. The Confederate Army of Tennessee had wintered in North Georgia in 1863–64, stripping bare the meager larders of their fellow southerners. Union cavalry raids—from Maj. Gen. George Stoneman's foray in July 1864, to Brig. Gen. H. Judson Kilpatrick's operations in November and December of that year, to Maj. Gen. James H. Wilson's April 1865 strike—slashed through portions of western and west central Georgia where Sherman's army never visited. Soldiers in Union blue never entered large parts of south Georgia, but frequent rumors of impending invasion created tensions of their own. And Georgians did not affix all blame for their recent misfortune on the armies. The state's fractious political and social system and its contentious relationship with the Richmond government supplied a long list of others who contributed to Georgia's recent fate.

As a Georgia journalist had opined a few months before the start of Sherman's offensive, "We are fighting each other harder than we ever fought the enemy."[5] In the aftermath of the passage of the armies, some saw the destruction as God's judgment on their cause or the weakness of their commitment to support it. Still others vented their rage against the collaborationist activities of the state's Unionist minority, strongest in the northern counties of "Cherokee Georgia" but embarrassingly evident elsewhere as well. Georgia governor Joseph E. Brown, already under public assault for his weak response to 1863's hard drought and perceived inequities in the impressment system, drew heated criticism for his ineffectual efforts to organize a defense. Brown expected Jefferson Davis to send Confederate troops from other theaters to defend Georgia's essential industrial and agricultural base, but the governor's strident state rights advocacy placed him at odds with Richmond on Confederate manpower policy and other key issues. While no reinforcements came, Davis insulted many Georgians when he traveled south in September 1864 to exhort residents to rally to arms, proclaiming that, "If there is one who will stay away at this hour, he is unworthy of the name of a Georgian."[6] Georgians in unaffected areas blamed those who had suffered the most, complaining that the Yankees ate well "owing altogether to the unwillingness of the people along the route to destroy what provisions they could not carry away and drive off their stock."[7] Affairs in North Georgia grew so grim by early 1865 that an Athenian admitted that "I am more than mortified to say so, but the people generally were infinitely better off when the Yankees occupied the country," and joined those Georgians who turned against Brown for failing to restore order to the region.[8]

In the dark days immediately after the Confederacy's demise, then, Georgians did not hold Sherman alone accountable for the fate of their state. A journalist standing amid the burned remains of a Georgia train depot noticed a rugged and ragged soldier clothed in fragments of a tattered gray uniform. With deep sadness washing over his face, the weary veteran surveyed the destruction, recalled the memory of Union artillery shelling the station — then a makeshift hospital filled with wounded and served by a civilian medical staff that included female nurses — and quietly asked, "How can we forget or forgive, with all those ruins staring us in the face?"[9] In asking an important question that touched on all three of Neal's "ingredients" but in positing no easy answer, that soldier had encapsulated the anguish facing many Georgians at war's end. While Sherman's offensive physically devastated only specific regions in Georgia, it helped to unravel the entire state's already fragile political and social fabric, leaving it little strength and no common vision to face the trials yet to come.

Individually, Georgians applied themselves energetically to the arduous task of repairing the war's physical damage. After all, "to a dauntless people no disaster is irreparable," wrote one postwar chronicler.[10] To those upon whom Sherman's army visited destruction, he remained the personification of evil. A visiting journalist chatting with a hard-pressed family in late 1865 reported, "[H]ow they did execrate Sherman!" for all their troubles, big and small, including the loss of the cows that provided milk to cut the bitterness of their rye-coffee.[11] When another traveler asked Georgians about the war's major figures, they condemned Jefferson Davis as "a fourth-rate man" but deemed Sherman to be "a child of hell."[12] A Georgian in 1866 compared Sherman unfavorably with Abu Beker, "a wild, untutored Arab of the sixth century," who, while spreading Islam into Syria, had ordered: "Destroy not the palm tree, nor fruit trees of any kind, waste not the corn fields with fire; nor kill any cattle excepting for food." The writer marveled at the contrast between "the Mahomedan" and "Sherman the Christian," who said "burn and destroy; lay waste the corn field with fire; kill the cattle, [and] forage upon the smoke houses as you pass along."[13] Still, in time, the physical scars would heal.

The same could not be said for the psychological blows inflicted during the political Reconstruction that followed close on the heels of military defeat. Well into the twentieth century, Georgians came to describe Reconstruction—and not the Civil War—as the state's lowest point. Indeed, it represented the gathering of "clouds blacker than war" or a "second invasion of the South" that proved to be "far more disastrous than the first."[14] The Radical Republicans, who restructured the state government in ways that upset long-standing social and political norms, provided Georgians with a whole new set of despicable villains. Sherman may have served as a major agent of destruction in 1864, but he did not necessarily rank high among the state's most hated tormentors after the war ended.

Indeed, during the early phase of Reconstruction, the general's place in Georgia's civic discourse depended entirely upon context. In the years immediately after the war, Sherman won some Georgians' praise for offering generous surrender terms to Gen. Joseph E. Johnston in April 1865. Georgia editors lauded both his opposition to the Radicals' initial demand for a military occupation of the defeated Confederacy and his "adhesion without reserve" to Andrew Johnson's plan to restore the southern states into the federal Union.[15] When most Georgians utterly refused to support the first presidential run of Ulysses S. Grant, whom they viewed as a tool of the Radical Republicans, a Macon editor suggested—without evident sarcasm or hyperbole—a ticket behind which Georgians could rally: "Military power must be met at the polls with military power and influence. As many just grounds of complaint as we have against Lt. Gen. William T. Sherman, we are willing to over look all the past and make him, with our own pure and immortal Lee, the great standard bearer of the Constitution in the Presidential battle of 1868."[16] Indeed, for years to come, some Georgia political writers preserved a positive image of Sherman for his opposition to harsh treatment of the defeated South, noting that, when compared to certain Radical Republicans, he was "an angel of light."[17]

Not all Georgians could accept that glowing portrayal. For them, memories of a destructive Sherman provided the perfect standard to guide discussion of postwar political affairs. In the late 1860s, former governor Brown became the target of especially heated invective from his in-state political foes and even former wartime allies for counseling cooperation with the Radicals. Benjamin H. Hill, one of Georgia's Confederate senators and an ardent supporter of Jefferson Davis, reluctantly attended a Republican banquet in Savannah, where he endured salutes to the architects of Union military victory. He suggested to a New York reporter that the organizers had erred greatly in omitting to "thank Joe Brown and those who acted with him" for doing "more to embarrass and weaken the Confederacy than the armies of either Grant or Sherman."[18] The practice of Georgians blaming fellow Georgians for the sorry condition of their state during the Civil War continued into Reconstruction and beyond.

Also revealing about Sherman's place in Georgians' postwar collective memory are those elements of their day-to-day civic lives where the general claimed no place at all. In public events as diverse as commemorations to honor the war dead or promotional efforts to lure economic investment, Georgians tended to remonstrate against the current threat of Radical rule rather than the horrors of the past that Sherman represented. "[L]et us look away from the gloom of political bondage, and fix our vision upon a coming day of triumph, when principles, born of truth and baptized in the blood of our brothers, shall out live the persecutions of merciless enemy and the treachery of unhallowed ambition," intoned one orator at a Confederate Memorial Day ceremony in Putnam County in 1868.[19] Only the day most frequently chosen for these ceremonies—established officially in 1874 as April 26—traced a link to Sherman; it marked the day he received Gen. Joseph E. Johnston's surrender in North Carolina.

Sherman's ambiguous and multifaceted image in Georgia's immediate postwar collective memory began to change, however, as the worst of Reconstruction passed. By the mid-1870s, when southern efforts to preserve for posterity a "true history" of the Confederate war began to blossom, Georgians joined in the fight. Indeed, they had specific reason to embrace this cause. In the immediate postwar years, northern publishers printed a number of books about Sherman's decisive 1864 campaign that uniformly condemned pro-Confederate Georgians, praised the state's Unionists, lauded the end of slavery, and seldom criticized Union soldiers for destroying private property or maltreating noncombatants. George Ward Nichols, who served on Sherman's staff, repeatedly gloried in the emancipation of Georgia's slaves, considering "the faith, earnestness, and heroism of the black man" to be "one of the grandest developments of this war." He showed no remorse for the energy exerted by Sherman's soldiers to find hidden treasures, noting, "It was all fair spoil of war, and the search made one of the excitements of the march."[20] Ohioan George W. Pepper featured frequent vignettes about Georgia Unionists who provided support to Sherman's men, but, unlike Nichols, he blended stories of elated slaves who welcomed the arrival of northern soldiers with chilling tales of mobs of unrestrained blacks in Atlanta and elsewhere committing "every possible species of outrage."[21] Popular travel narratives by Sidney Andrews, Whitelaw Reid, John Dennett, John T. Trowbridge, John H. Kennaway, and others reinforced an image of a countryside justifiably laid to waste, a people demoralized and divided against itself, a political and social structure in upheaval, and a future full of uncertainty and doubt, all inflicted under the rallying cry of "Bully for old Billy, we follow him!"[22] These popular works invariably exposed to all—Georgians and outsiders alike—the Empire State's deepest wartime anguish.

During the early days of Reconstruction, few Georgian authors found a way to reach a national audience to challenge the veracity of these northern narratives. Alternative interpretations that condemned Union soldiers' brutality and destructiveness usually found space only in Georgia newspapers or other venues of limited circulation. A typical comparison contrasted the inhumanity of Sherman's men in Georgia in 1864 with the moral rectitude of southern soldiers who followed Robert E. Lee into Pennsylvania in 1863. After noting that "hardly a rail was burned" in the Keystone State, a Georgia journalist explained that, to find Sherman's path, "You'll need no guide, for lone chimneys stand, like spectral sentinels, guarding the wreck and the ruin, the devastated fields and the desecrated altars that line the reckless soldier's route."[23]

Georgians' interest in the southern effort to publish "correct" histories of the war blossomed to full bloom in 1875, when Sherman published his controversial memoirs. When considering his Georgia campaign, the general asserted that "little or no damage was done to private property." Moreover, he recalled no reports of murder or rape of civilians and accused Wheeler's Confederate cavalry—not his own men—of destroying crops in the field. He admitted that the "bummers" committed "many acts of pillage, robbery, and violence" in interpreting his instructions to "forage liberally on the country," but he also stressed that his official orders included a specific prohibition against soldiers entering civilian homes. Most of all, after claiming to have inflicted at least $100 million in damage, he showed no remorse for any of his decisions.[24] To the surprise of no one, southern reviewers described the memoir as "stimulating fertilizer" and accused Sherman of overstepping "all bounds of delicacy and propriety (not to say common decency)."[25]

Seething Georgians could not permit Sherman's narrative to go unchallenged. In the vanguard of the literary counterattack, Charles Colcock Jones Jr. — Lt. Gen. William J. Hardee's former chief of artillery during the siege of Savannah in 1864 — publicly pledged himself to preserving Georgia's "true" Confederate military history. Determined to rebut northern histories "written chiefly by those who made light of [Georgia's] afflictions, laughed at her calamities, gloated over her losses, and lauded her spoilers," he ultimately crafted Georgia's first generally accepted collective memory of Sherman. Until his death in 1893, Jones produced a steady stream of books and pamphlets, submitted items to *The Southern Historical Society Papers*, and delivered many public addresses, all designed to produce a "true history" of Civil War Georgia that, among other things, recast Sherman as a clearly defined — and entirely unsympathetic — central figure. For his efforts, a fellow Georgian labeled Jones "the greatest American historian after George Bancroft."[26]

Jones challenged several specific elements of the narrative constructed by postwar northern writers. As historian Michael Kammen has argued, the creation of social memory must also consider social amnesia, so it is not surprising that Jones began by deleting some disquieting memories of Georgia's wartime experience.[27] First, he reduced the complexities of Sherman's May-to-December campaign from Chattanooga to Savannah to focus on the burning of Atlanta and the March to the Sea in November and December. This approach permitted him to erase the memory of the strong Unionist presence in North Georgia that northern writers had showcased. Second, he diminished the military importance of Sherman's "predatory" march, since, after all, it was "inaugurated with a full knowledge of [Georgia's] weakness, conceived largely in a spirit of wanton destruction, conduced in many respects in manifest violation of the rules of civilized warfare, and composed in the face of feeble resistance." Third, playing down the significance of the march permitted him to attack Sherman's military character and capacity, deeming it "positively erroneous" to denote the campaign a "triumph of consummate military skill and valor" and depicting the general as a "man devoid of all feelings of propriety." Fourth, he celebrated the resistance of Georgia's civilians, especially the women who endured so much "when death and desolation stalked like all devouring demons through our war-convulsed land." Fifth, he damned Sherman and his men for the way in which they treated Georgia's slaves. Once a slave owner himself, Jones noted that nearly 100,000 blacks "were seduced for their allegiance," left their plantations, and then, too often, were abandoned by Sherman's men to die. Finally, he saluted Georgia's soldiers as "lovers of liberty, combatants for constitutional rights, and as exemplars of heroic virtue, benefactors of their race" — but he saved such accolades only for those who served in the Home Guard and in the Army of Northern Virginia, and not those under Johnston and Hood who abandoned Georgia at its time of direst need. He rescued from obscurity a skirmish at Honey Hill in South Carolina, to show that Georgia state troops rallied to the defense of the Palmetto State — whose troops did not reciprocate — while Sherman devastated their own homes.[28]

Georgia journalists, authors, and historians drew heavily on Jones's various themes from the 1870s through the 1890s. Residents of Georgia cities left relatively unscathed in 1864 explained their salvation as evidence of Sherman's ineptitude. After outlining the military significance of Augusta's arsenal and other facilities, a former Confederate officer finally concluded that Sherman spared that city due to either "gross incapacity, or a desire to prolong the strife and inflict injuries upon private citizens rather than upon the resources of a hostile government."[29] Savannah residents concurred that no great military significance attached to Sherman's capture of their city. In fact, the general actually "lost an easy and brilliant opportunity of capturing Hardee's entire command of about 10,000 men with that city."[30] Georgians seemed to agree that Sherman's March to the Sea caused much damage, but that alone did not make it "an achievement worthy to live for all time in 'song and story.'" They deemed it "a very commonplace affair."[31]

By the late 1870s, Sherman's place in Georgia's past had begun what appeared to be a steady spiral down toward demonization. Press coverage of his arrival in Georgia in January 1879 and again in November 1881 — the only two times he visited Atlanta after his men torched it in 1864 — demonstrated just how quickly popular sentiment had begun to harden. During his 1879 visit, Atlantans greeted him with restrained courtesy. The press covered his tour of the city's new business district and his review of the U.S. Army troops at Fort McPherson without notable rancor and reported nothing about an unsettling exchange between Sherman and a group of 200 Georgians near Cartersville.[32]

His reception changed dramatically, however, when he returned for the International Cotton Exposition in November 1881. This time, Sherman arrived shortly after the publication of Jefferson Davis's own memoirs. The former president — in language similar to that used by Jones — had saved some of his harshest invective for the March to the Sea. "The arson of the dwelling-houses of noncombatants and the robbery of their property, extending even to the trinkets worn by women, made the devastation as relentless as savage instincts could suggest."[33] While Davis promoted his book, an Indianapolis editor asked him his opinion of Sherman. "The truth is," Davis commented, the general "is a vain man, who has been ruined by success and flattery, and is possessed of a chronic hallucination that he is a great general. He is really a man of very mediocre talents," he concluded, hinting that if Sherman had faced Stonewall Jackson instead of Johnston — whom Davis despised — "a different tale would have been told."[34]

Comments such as these helped to heal the breach between Davis and Georgians who believed he had abandoned them to their fate. Thus, when it was rumored that exposition organizers planned to rename a salute to Mexican War veterans as "Sherman Day," editors across Georgia now howled in protest, decrying any effort to "receive and welcome with open arms the despoiler of Atlanta" and "the man who wantonly insulted our mothers, wives and sisters."[35] They noted with disgust that the date of the proposed "Sherman Day" coincided with the anniversary of the start of the March to the Sea.[36] Even though Sherman stayed out of the limelight, only speaking briefly to avow, "I am as friendly to Georgia as I am to my own native state of Ohio," he won few plaudits on his last visit to the Empire State.[37]

Davis's harsh comments also became the opening salvo of an intermittent literary war between the former president and Sherman that gave Georgians even more reasons to embrace their former president and to recast the general even more firmly in the villain's role.[38] In 1885, famed South Carolina poet Paul Y. Hayne, now residing in Augusta, crafted an ode titled "Davis and Sherman" to slam "Tecumseh's brazen trumpet blare / Thro' tortuous labyrinths of false acclaim," while saluting the former Confederate leader, who "from desolate heights of his sublime despair, / Hurls swiftly back the base imputed shame!" The poet assured Davis, "Such poor creatures as Sherman on the *one* hand, or the renegades of what I believe is called '*The New South*' on the other, can never disturb your tranquility."[39]

As Hayne's comment suggests, the 1880s saw the emergence of another war for Georgia's soul, a struggle between two groups of southerners, each desiring to use its section's recent past to support its own vision for its future. The partisans of the Lost Cause fed on the memory of wartime sacrifice and devastation; rejected slavery — which they deemed a benevolent institution — as a basic cause of the conflict; argued that constitutional principles underpinned secession; believed that defeat resulted from the North's overwhelming numbers and resources rather than southern social or political weaknesses; and considered all Confederate soldiers — not merely those who fell in battle — worthy of honor and respect. Georgia's Lost Cause adherents accepted Jones's views on Sherman, despising him for his unconscionable war upon civilians and the destruction of their way of life, including emancipation. Another view embraced the vision of the New South. Its advocates honored the courage of all Confederate soldiers, but they also believed that economic progress in a free labor economy and national reconciliation best served the South's future. Their frequent cooperation with northerners in various business ventures often required New South Georgians to reduce the potential for a flare-up of sectional hostilities by crafting a quite different narrative of the state's recent past, one that conflicted sharply with Jones's work by muting or even ignoring Sherman's inflammatory role in it.

Georgia's New South and Lost Cause sentiments collided most directly in Atlanta. At war's end, Atlantans — whose many newcomers included significant numbers of northerners — eagerly embraced the challenge of rebuilding the city. By the 1880s, promoters invariably chose to look to the promise of the future rather than dwell on the devastation of the past. Atlanta, a city booster wrote, "is essentially a new place — modern, cosmopolitan, democratic — a fresh production, wholly practical, without antiquities or prejudices" that represents "all types, ideas, and nationalities, fused into one vital, resolute, outstretching concentration of power and growth." While noting the city's destruction — but never once mentioning Sherman by name — he touted instead its rebirth as "the gallant work of redemption." The city possessed Confederate monuments and cemeteries, yes, but it also boasted of a "spirit of fraternity" evidenced by its active Battle Monument Association of the Blue and Gray and its flourishing Grand Army of the Republic (GAR) post.[40]

But the Old South spirit still lived in Atlanta, too. In 1886, Governor John Brown Gordon invited Jefferson Davis to the city to unveil a monument honoring former Confederate senator Benjamin Hill, one of the president's strongest allies.[41] A Confederate veteran who observed the city's public reception for Davis, "the patriot who for them embodied the dear 'Lost Cause,'" considered it to be "beautiful beyond words to express."[42] Still, introducing the former president that day was influential city editor and booster Henry Woodfin Grady, who just a few months later delivered his famous "New South" speech in New York City, during which he acknowledged General Sherman's presence by noting that he was "considered an able man in our parts, though some people think he is a careless man about fire."[43] Depending on circumstance, as this event illustrated, New South and Lost Cause partisans could work in concert, but the former saw a growing need for an alternative collective memory of Georgia's war years that did not depict Sherman as a demonic despoiler.

For much of the 1880s, the John B. Gordon–Alfred H. Colquitt–Joseph E. Brown triumvirate—composed of two former Confederate generals and the now "redeemed" war governor—controlled Georgia's Democratic Party and, in true New South spirit, compiled a long record of support for industrialization and northern investment. By decade's end, however, the party began to splinter. Georgia Democrats espousing open support for the values of the traditional Old South had reemerged to challenge the triumvirate's New South platform. As Georgian John McIntosh Kell, a former Confederate naval officer, explained, "To me there has never been a 'New South.' The blood of heroic sires and gentle mothers in the view of the present generation have made her what she is—a remodeled country, built upon the grandeur of the past and holiest memories a people ever inherited!"[44]

In 1887, Charles C. Jones—who claimed that the words he most hated were "*The New South* and *Boom*"—invited Governor Gordon to Augusta for Confederate Memorial Day ceremonies, specifically asking him to address the glories of the Old South. Aware of the growing divide in his own party, the governor responded instead with a message intended to bridge that chasm, mixing Lost Cause rhetoric with the New South values he embraced. He praised "the southern plantation home" as the root of a noble civilization. Showing no remorse over slavery's demise, he also argued, "it was far, very far, from being an unmitigated evil." He then blended these traditional ideals with a key element of the New South's rhetoric of progress: a conditional commitment to the cause of national reunion, vowing to extend his hand to northerners who respected those who wore the gray and to shun those who blamed the war on slavery or condemned those who took up arms to defend it.[45]

Gordon's New South Democrats lost control of the state in the 1890s, but he and his allies quickly found a new pulpit from which to assert a degree of political power and to continue promulgating their views. The United Confederate Veterans (UCV), established in Nashville in 1889, chose Gordon as commander in chief. The trademark of his subsequent leadership—a commitment to national reunion when celebrated with mutual respect—remained consistent. Although he never convinced all UCV members to embrace his vision wholeheartedly, Gordon planned for Georgia to play a leading role in reconciliation.

An excellent opportunity to advance the dual causes of national reunion and economic progress presented itself almost immediately. As early as 1881, Union veteran Henry V. Boynton—who once challenged the veracity of Sherman's memoirs—pushed for a "Gettysburg of the West" where veterans of the Army of the Cumberland might erect monuments. He preferred the Chattanooga and Chickamauga battlefields for this purpose, and the UCV chapter in Chattanooga, recognizing potential economic benefits from tourism, threw its support behind him. The success of the project required Georgia to transfer title of the land comprising the Chickamauga battlefield from state hands to the federal government—no small gesture in the former Confederacy—but several former Confederate generals, including Gordon, Colquitt, and Joseph Wheeler, lent their support to the venture. The endeavor fit the needs of Georgia's New South partisans. First, the battle of Chickamauga in September 1863 represented the state's bloodiest battle. Second, the Confederate Army of Tennessee—almost forgotten in Jones's interpretation of Georgia military history—won a great victory there, so their forgotten soldiers would be remembered. Finally, Sherman did not fight at Chickamauga, eliminating the need to accord him any attention at all.[46]

The Chickamauga gambit demonstrated once again that New South Georgians dealt with the unwelcome memories Sherman's name evoked by finding ways to ignore him entirely. The practicality of this approach seemed justified, given the state's mixed, but generally unsympathetic, public reaction to General Sherman's death in February 1891. A few Georgians—but only a few—adopted a slightly conciliatory tone, as did the Populist who opined that, based on comments the general had made in Memphis during the war, the "farmer's sub-treasury scheme" may well "have found favor in his eye." More commonly, Georgia journalists had harshly condemned Sherman's conduct in 1864. "Sherman burned Atlanta to the ground. . . . He left Atlanta utterly disemboweled," one newspaperman wrote as the general lay on his deathbed. When word came of Sherman's death, Georgia editors asked readers to remember "the utter heartlessness of the man, . . . his mean and vindictive nature" and "the self-admitted barbarity of his character."[47]

With a pattern of remembering Sherman negatively well established, New South advocates strove to remove the general from Georgia's public war commemorations. At the dedication of the Chickamauga battlefield park in September 1895, former governor Gordon established the common ground for Blue and Gray by declaring that the war was not fought "between the friends of freedom on one side and its foes on the other, but between its friends on both sides." Gen. James Longstreet called for a "hearty restoration, and cordial cultivation of neighborly, brotherly relations" between veterans of both armies.[48] As an extension of the Chickamauga dedication, Atlanta's GAR and UCV posts arranged a "Blue and Gray Day" in the city, complete with pamphlets describing battle sites around Atlanta and providing directions to statues honoring Union general James B. McPherson and Confederate general William H. T. Walker, both killed in the fighting in late July 1864. The introduction to the brief battle narrative began with one line — "The war is over" — and never once mentioned Sherman.[49]

Georgians did not manufacture these sentiments simply for the Chickamauga dedication and the Atlanta tour. Prominent New South advocates, including former Confederate general Clement A. Evans, delivered the same message frequently on the lecture circuit, hoping to douse desires "to stir the ashes of evil passions" and end "spiteful malevolence."[50] Even the UCV national encampment in Atlanta in July 1898, which drew 30,000 Confederate veterans, spawned no Sherman-bashing. In an elaborate cyclorama painting depicting a panoramic view of the battle of Atlanta — produced to support the presidential ambitions of John A. Logan, one of Sherman's subordinates, and featuring him prominently — Sherman himself remained an appropriately small figure in the background. The *Atlanta Constitution* printed an extended review of the war in Georgia, reversing the emphasis in the Jones interpretation to stress Chickamauga and the conventional campaign from Chattanooga to Atlanta rather than the burning of Atlanta or the March to the Sea. Indeed, the editors took only one risk, printing a pro-Confederate parody of Henry Clay Work's despised Union marching song, "Marching Through Georgia."[51] In a similar vein, orators made no mention of Sherman during the dedication of Georgia's monuments on the Chickamauga battlefield in 1899.[52]

Still, despite its New South image, even Atlanta could become unpredictable when contemporary issues of race collided directly with memories of the past. Despite Sherman's own doubts about the future of the black race, for good or ill, both black and white Georgians viewed him as emancipator. Postwar northern narratives all included scenes of ecstatic slaves wildly welcoming their grizzled liberator; George Pepper had recounted the delight of an old man in Atlanta who "just wanted to see de man what made my old massa run."[53] Black Georgians never forgot Sherman. When his train stopped briefly in Macon after his 1879 visit to Atlanta, the local white editor reported that the general's brief visit "was quite the theme with the colored population." Many declared Sherman to be "'a bigger man than Grant,'" and those who shook his hand were "looked upon something like the moon, which, by association with his majesty, the sun, imbibes some of his brilliancy."[54] As Atlanta emerged at the turn of the century as an important center of African American education and culture, some black leaders traced the start of their upward climb specifically to their liberation by Sherman and his men. "The shells of General Sherman's guns were the strokes of the hammer of liberty," one black educator had written in 1894, admitting that they had "rejoiced when they saw the Confederate flag fall like Lucifer and trail in the dust."[55] Jim Crow Georgia's growing racial unrest easily found one of its roots in the actions of Sherman and his men.

In 1906, racial tensions came to a head in Georgia's heated gubernatorial contest between Hoke Smith and Clark Howell, each representing a different faction of the state's Democratic Party. Race underpinned the most inflammatory campaign issues, which centered on disfranchisement of black voters and the segregation of rail cars and other public facilities. Just a few years earlier, in decrying black Georgians' lack of economic progress and decreasing civil rights, W. E. B. DuBois had refused to embrace Sherman as the liberator of his race, dubbing the general's decision to relegate freedmen to hard labor in abandoned coastal rice fields in 1865 as "that dark human cloud that clung like remorse to the rear of those swift columns."[56] Still, in this restive time, any reference to the general who freed Georgia's slaves and inspired hopes — even frustrated hopes — of political and social equality, provoked white racial passions.[57]

In late April 1906, white anger boiled over. While news of the great San Francisco earthquake filled the headlines of newspapers across the nation, Georgia editors gave over their front pages to a local story: an announcement from Savannah's acting mayor that he "Would Hang Sherman While on His March."[58] The headline referred not to the deceased general, of course, but to his son, Father Thomas Sherman. The Jesuit priest had been invited to accompany a small detachment — two officers and fewer than eight enlisted men from the 12th U.S. Cavalry—on a terrain study of his father's campaign from Chattanooga to Atlanta. To blend in, Father Sherman wore his blue uniform tunic from his Spanish-American War service as an army chaplain.

White Georgians of all political persuasions immediately expressed outrage. The mere mention of Sherman's name triggered public expressions of hostility to a degree not seen in years. As one veteran opined, "Father Sherman ought to know that it is too soon to make such a march. . . . These people have taught their children to hate the name of Sherman, and they do hate it."[59] A Georgia congressman who had believed that the war's hard feelings had finally dissipated now discovered the sole exception—"the memory of Sherman's causeless vandalism."[60] To some Georgians, the combination of Father Sherman in the company of soldiers wearing the blue uniforms of the U.S. Army—described first as a "military escort" and then, much worse, as a "body guard"—resembled a second invasion and, perhaps, even a second occupation. Even a senior GAR leader in Atlanta protested that providing a military escort was "outrageous."[61] President Theodore Roosevelt quickly issued a recall order, leading to gleeful Georgia headlines boasting, "Father Sherman in Full Retreat."[62] A disappointed Father Sherman later complained that "body guard" was a phrase "invented by some Georgian who had the wrong idea of my purpose."[63]

Only a few New South voices—and none in racially tense Atlanta—openly welcomed Father Sherman. In Dalton, local dignitaries including the sheriff and a clerk of the Georgia Superior Court enjoyed a cordial visit at his campsite.[64] In similar fashion, the town fathers at Cartersville welcomed Father Sherman with a reception that drew "nearly a score" of prominent local citizens. When the priest broke off his tour, the Cartersville editor expressed open regret. Other dignitaries had visited the North Georgia battlefields with such escorts, so he wanted his fellow southerners to "do what we can to foster a friendly feeling between north and south as General Sherman did back in '65."[65]

The furor of early May 1906 dissipated almost as quickly as it started. Although Georgians did not link Father Sherman's trip to the state's racially charged political atmosphere just then, such a connection slowly emerged after September 1906, when Atlanta experienced a violent race riot. In its aftermath, even a northern editor asked, "How does it happen that the blacks who took care of the helpless women and children during the war cannot now be trusted to live in the same town?" E. H. Hinton of Atlanta tied racial hostilities directly to emancipation, noting that forty years of freedom had "transformed the negro from a docile, kindly, confiding, good-natured, dependent servant into a jealous, envious, distrustful, resentful, and independent citizen" and demanded that the North "undo the wrong they have done."[66] After marveling at Father Sherman's willingness to "subject his father's memory to the denunciations sure to follow the recountings of his barbarous acts," a southerner expressed admiration for Georgia's "loyal slaves" during the war, who, unlike the Atlanta rioters, had shown no "restlessness" and committed no "outrages on women."[67] Articles on "the tender relations existing between the two races under the old regime"—already a staple in *Confederate Veteran* and other Georgia publications—flourished anew after Father Sherman's brief visit.[68]

Atlanta's reaction to the clergyman's visit proved to be a temporary aberration from its New South mentality. In the immediate aftermath of Father Sherman's ride, U.S. Army officers from Fort Leavenworth had curtailed their own tour of the North Georgia battlefields—an action the UCV applauded. But another group in 1907 went all the way to Atlanta unmolested after inviting local editors and curious citizens into their evening camps, where a southern-born officer invariably explained that they came only as students "To Study the Masterly Retreat of Gen. Joseph E. Johnston from Dalton to Atlanta."[69] In 1909, in a quest to bolster economic opportunities, city leaders in Atlanta and Chattanooga explored the possibility of building a modern new road to link the two cities. Publicity bluntly—and inaccurately—stated: "This road follows the route taken by Sherman in his famous march to the sea."[70] Still, no outrage followed. Nor did protests rise when Atlanta's Confederate Memorial Day parade that same year included a detachment of the U.S. Army's 17th Infantry regiment.[71] In 1913, when the GAR held its annual encampment in Chattanooga, a full-page illustrated spread in the *Atlanta Constitution* under the headline "Sherman's Army Once More to Invade Atlanta and Visit Its Battlefields" generated no outpouring of hostility. Indeed, when the Union men arrived in Atlanta, a substantial number of the city's leading Confederate veterans—including several who publicly condemned Father Sherman's excursion seven years earlier—organized a lively reception and tours for them.[72]

Amidst this vibrant New South version of Georgia's past that slighted or ignored Sherman's role in it, the undiluted Lost Cause sentiment first promulgated by C. C. Jones continued to thrive, especially south and east of Atlanta. The Georgia Division of the United Daughters of the Confederacy (UDC) now emerged as the chief steward of Old South values. From inception in 1895, its members accepted several missions: to organize women bound by ties of "loyalty to memories and principles" of the UCV, to be charitable toward Confederate veterans and their descendants, to erect monuments to Confederate heroes, and to propagate a "true" history of the Civil War that included the positive contributions of southern women.[73] Unlike New South partisans — or even many UCV leaders — they showed little interest in promoting national reconciliation. Indeed, they adopted as their own Jones's villainous image of Sherman and his tendency to ignore Georgia's wartime divisiveness. As Mrs. J. Jefferson Thomas of the Georgia UDC noted in 1896, "Sherman will be remembered as the General who destroyed Atlanta."[74] In time, however, they expanded their reach to include the entire Georgia campaign, not merely Sherman's burning of Atlanta and the March to the Sea.

The Georgia UDC tackled a wide range of projects, large and small. Early on, they reached beyond state lines to rally around thirteen-year-old Laura Galt of Louisville, Kentucky, who had refused to sing "Marching Through Georgia" in school. The Georgia UDC invited her to their state meeting and even suggested, unsuccessfully, that she replace the recently deceased Winnie Davis as "the Daughter of the Confederacy." They then launched a campaign to remove "Marching Through Georgia" from the nation's school songbooks. Citing instances when bands played the song at entirely inappropriate times, they feared that northerners and southerners alike might accept as true various references in the song that did not fit their preferred vision of Georgia's Confederate past, including allusions to slaves gleefully greeting Sherman's emancipators and persistent Unionism among some Georgia whites.[75]

The women of the Georgia UDC also oversaw the erection of at least seventy new Civil War monuments between 1895 and 1915, more than in any similar period since the war.[76] During Reconstruction, when Ladies Memorial Associations dedicated the first tributes to the southern dead and women, commemorative and dedicatory addresses seldom mentioned the general who brought war to their doorstep.[77] In the 1890s and into the early twentieth century, however, when the UDC hosted such events — still most often on Confederate Memorial Day on April 26 — open vilification of Sherman became a common theme. Sherman had left behind him "a desert of ashes" that left "homes devastated, hearts broken, hopes gone, [and] fathers, husbands, brothers, sons and lovers killed," Anna Carolina Benning reminded the members of the UDC chapter of Columbus in 1898.[78] Consistent with the UDC's commitment to promote the role of women in Confederate history, inscriptions on the new monuments now might include praise both for soldiers who fought on the battlefield and for female Georgians who resisted Sherman at home. A statue in Covington honored both local soldiers and "the noble women whose peerless patriotism and sublime lives of heroic and self-sacrificing service enhanced the holiness of that cause and prolonged the struggle for its supremacy." By 1910, Georgians even dedicated monuments specifically saluting the women of the Confederacy who, as the marker unveiled in Rome in 1910 attested, "made of war a season of heroism and of peace a time of healing" after Sherman's scourge.[79]

Robert E. Lee still owned Georgians' hearts, but, as one way to damn Sherman, Georgia women now extended long-delayed honors to the leaders and men of the Army of Tennessee that defended their state against the Yankees. A Lee's birthday celebration in Columbus in 1900 included, for the first time, a positive comparison between the Army of Northern Virginia's 1864–65 campaigns and the North Georgia operations of the men who served under that "master of defensive warfare," Joseph E. Johnston.[80] The UDC praised a Georgia couple who erected in 1902 a marker to Johnston's slain subordinate, Lt. Gen. Leonidas Polk, near his death site on Pine Mountain. In 1912, the UDC's Bryan M. Thomas chapter successfully raised $6,000 for a monument honoring Johnston himself — the only one of its kind — placed it near his Dalton headquarters, and touted his defensive campaign as "one of the most memorable in the Annals of War."[81]

In the most controversial of its efforts to erect monuments, the Georgia UDC took up the cause of Capt. Henry Wirz, commandant of the Andersonville prison camp and a heartily hated figure in the North. In 1905, Mrs. A. B. Hull of Athens criticized the camp's national cemetery filled with "magnificent monuments on every side, blazoning the most awful statements of brutality and proclaiming them as truths, and not one word to contradict them." Thus, they proposed a memorial not far from the stockade and cemetery where the offending northern monuments stood. Outraged Union veterans warned them not to do it. Even the UCV, which usually supported UDC programs, considered this proposal to be "like shaking the red flag" and "impolitic." The women persisted, however, and dedicated the marker on May 13, 1909, with the commandant's daughter unveiling the obelisk.[82] In rejecting Wirz's guilt, Georgians blamed Lincoln for letting Union prisoners die by refusing to exchange them for Confederate soldiers who might "insure the defeat of Sherman's well fed veterans," or they accused Sherman's men of burning the food that would have gone to feed the starving prisoners.[83]

One woman in particular made certain that Charles C. Jones's vision of Sherman became the standard interpretation of the Georgia UDC. Mildred Lewis Rutherford of Athens, a kinsman of Generals Thomas R. R. and Howell Cobb, filled the office of Georgia's UDC historian from 1895 until her death in 1928. A devout Lost Cause partisan, she believed passionately that Georgia had been the Confederacy's crown jewel. Embracing education as her most important weapon, she created scholarships for the children of Confederate veterans, supported the Lucy Cobb School for girls, sponsored historical essay contests, and organized Children of the Confederacy chapters.[84] She also endorsed the writing of a "true history" of Georgia's Confederate past that had to include a total demonization of Sherman and established a strict set of standards by which the UDC and UCV measured the acceptability of history and literature texts used in Georgia schools. She championed the preservation of the history of Georgia women during the war, both by supplying personal memories of those trying times — during Christmas 1864, "our Mammy told us Santa Claus could not cross Marse Sherman's lines" — and by encouraging Georgia's female authors to write about their own wartime struggles.[85] Rutherford's influence on the preservation of a Lost Cause interpretation of Georgia's Civil War history endured well into the twentieth century.

Still, she failed to claim a decisive victory. When the war's golden anniversary arrived, Sherman's place in Georgia's collective memory still bore two faces, one representing the New South and the other reflecting the Lost Cause. As the twentieth century progressed, context continued to dictate which interpretation might be used to best effect. In 1926, a New South piece in *National Geographic*, titled "Marching through Georgia Sixty Years Later," made no mention at all of Sherman or the events of 1864 as it touted the state's recent economic development.[86] By contrast, following the 1936 publication of Margaret Mitchell's *Gone with the Wind*, Georgians indulged in such a flurry of Lost Cause–inspired anti-Sherman rhetoric that literary critics blasted the book for perpetuating a "resplendent, satisfying, idiotic, and self-destructive" myth that "has been even more destructive than ever was the March."[87] By the eve of World War II, noted the author of a Georgia guide book, the "fire of sectional resentment no longer flames fiercely." But, he acknowledged, embers still glowed under the ash, adding, "Only the most modern young Georgians can discuss impersonally the reasons for the destructive march to the sea."[88]

In time, another spark rekindled those embers, restoring to prominence in Georgia's public memory the Lost Cause view of Sherman. Beginning in the 1950s, the emergence of the civil rights movement reawakened the resentment of many white Georgians against federal interference in state issues. In protest against the Supreme Court's decision in *Brown v. Board of Education* (1954) that paved the way for school integration, Georgia joined with several other southern states to add the Confederate battle standard to their flags. As federal troops provided security for integration of schools in neighboring states, Georgians wondered if they might again witness an invasion by the U.S. Army. Ku Klux Klan activity rose dramatically, with its public gatherings now freely using Confederate symbols in its efforts to promulgate its political agenda. Georgia's embrace of Lost Cause rhetoric and symbols persisted after passage of the Civil Rights Act and the Voting Rights Act of the 1960s. In a debate that peaked in the mid-1990s, Georgians argued about the continued inclusion of the Confederate battle flag on the state banner, splitting them into "reconstructionist" and "traditionalist" camps—also called the "fergit" and "fergit, hell" camps—that fit closely into the familiar patterns of the nineteenth century's Lost Cause and New South rhetoric.[89] New South victories came at high cost. One-term Democratic governor Roy Barnes lost his reelection bid in 2002, at least in part because he had supported the change in flag design, while his opponent, George E. "Sonny" Perdue III, openly supported the traditionalist's demand for a public referendum to decide between the new and old banners.[90]

The Vietnam conflict and its legacy likewise reinvigorated the Lost Cause perspective of Sherman and branded him with a twentieth-century label: war criminal. Those who relied upon this approached frequently cited an Emory Law School study that classified many—but not all—of Sherman's actions in Georgia as "war crimes."[91] The resurgence of various partisan groups dedicated to defending against attacks on southern culture and heritage built on these and similar arguments to condemn all those who would "whitewash" Sherman. Traditionalist Georgians expressed outrage at the publication of a spate of late-twentieth-century scholarly works— Mark Grimsley's *The Hard Hand of War*, most notably—that moderated Sherman's image as the destroyer of their state. "We have vilified him for more than 145 years," a native Atlantan wrote in 2004, wondering whether, now that northerners had "changed our character, our accent, our attitude and our traffic . . . [m]ust Yankees also change our history?" Another Georgian, rejecting scholars' assertions that many claims for Sherman's destructiveness could not be supported by recorded evidence, pretended to apologize for his family's long-standing hatred of the general, noting, "If they only had taken a little time of from rebuilding their torched homes, consoling their violated wives, mothers, and sisters and planting new crops for food, they could have 'documented' all of this to make it true."[92] When Governor Perdue and the Georgia Office of Travel and Tourism endorsed in 2004 a "Sherman Trail" to promote history tourism, Georgian Jeff Davis voiced strong opposition, lest "public acquiescence to political correctness" permit "a new revision of history designed to remove the stigma of one of America's most atrocious periods of terrorism."[93]

Contrasting dimensions of Sherman's image in Georgia's past survive today. Which facet reveals itself largely depends on the political or social context that inspires the calling forth of the general's memory. A popular North Georgia tourism website launches its marketing campaign with: "If the question was asked, 'Who was and still is the most hated and despised man in the history of Georgia,' the response would be William Tecumseh Sherman."[94] Such hyperbole is not historically accurate, however, and it obscures the famous Yankee's complicated and multifaceted place in Georgia's collective memory.

WILLIAM T. SHERMAN IN POSTWAR GEORGIA

NOTES

1. "A Man of Moods," *Atlanta Constitution*, February 18, 1891.

2. Arthur G. Neal, *National Trauma and Collective Memory*, 2nd ed. (Armonk, N.Y.: M. E. Sharpe, 2005), 6.

3. For a useful summary of Georgia and its tensions during 1864–65, see T. Conn Bryan, *Confederate Georgia* (Athens: University of Georgia Press, 1953), chap. 10.

4. Jacqueline Glass Campbell, *When Sherman Marched North from the Sea: Resistance on the Confederate Home Front* (Chapel Hill: University of North Carolina Press, 2003), 4.

5. *Milledgeville [Ga.] Confederate Union*, November 24, 1863, quoted in David Williams, *Johnny Reb's War: Battlefield and Homefront* (Abilene, Tex.: McWhiney Foundation Press, 2000), 82.

6. U.S. War Department, *The War of the Rebellion: A Compilation of the Official Records of the Union and Confederate Armies*, 127 vols., index, and atlas (Washington: Government Printing Office, 1880–1901), 52(2):588; *Macon Telegraph*, September 24, 1864; Jefferson Davis, *The Papers of Jefferson Davis*, ed. Lynda L. Crist et al., 12 vols. to date (Baton Rouge: Louisiana State University Press, 1971–), 11:61–63. Interestingly, Davis continued on to Montgomery and gave essentially the same speech. He delivered similar renditions in South Carolina as well.

7. *Columbus [Ga.] Ledger-Enquirer*, December 1, 1864.

8. *Atlanta Intelligencer*, January 22, 1865; reprinted in *Athens Southern Banner*, February 15, 1865.

9. John H. Kennaway, *On Sherman's Track; or, The South after the War* (London: Seeley, Jackson, and Halliday, 1867), 106, 118.

10. Lucian Lamar Knight, *A Standard History of Georgia and Georgians*, 6 vols. (Chicago: Lewis Publishing Company, 1917), 2:787.

11. Kennaway, *On Sherman's Track*, 118.

12. Sidney Andrews, *The South Since the War* (Boston: Ticknor and Fields, 1866), 232.

13. *Macon Daily Telegraph*, September 20, 1866.

14. Clark Howell, *History of Georgia*, 4 vols. (Chicago: S. H. Clarke Publishing Co., 1927): 1:587; United Daughters of the Confederacy, Georgia Division, *Reconstruction Period in Georgia, 1865–1875* (Statesboro, Ga.: Bulloch County UDC, 1916), 55.

15. *Macon Telegraph*, October 28, 1866. See also John F. Marszalek, *Sherman: A Soldier's Passion for Order* (New York: Free Press, 1993), 353–76.

16. "The Government of the United States—How to Change It," *Macon Weekly Telegraph*, July 5, 1868.

17. Knight, *Standard History of Georgia and Georgians*, 2:801.

18. "What Hon. B. H. Hill Told a New York Sun Correspondent," *Georgia Weekly Telegraph*, June 2, 1874.

19. Henry D. Capers, *An Address Delivered before the Ladies' Memorial Association of Putnam County, Georgia, April 28th, 1868* (Charleston: Walker, Evans & Cogswell, 1869), 5.

20. George Ward Nichols, *The Story of the Great March, from the Diary of a Staff Officer* (New York: Harper and Brothers, 1866), 101, 117.

21. George W. Pepper, *Personal Recollections of Sherman's Campaigns in Georgia and the Carolinas* (Zanesville, Ohio: Hughes Dunne, 1866), 79–80, 172, 229.

22. See, for instance, Kennaway, *On Sherman's Track*, 115. See also David W. Blight, *Race and Reunion: The Civil War in American Memory* (Cambridge, Mass.: Harvard University Press, 2001), 32–44.

23. "Message to the North," *Macon Weekly Telegraph*, September 11, 1868.

24. See William Tecumseh Sherman, *Memoirs of General William T. Sherman*, 2 vols. (New York: D. Appleton, 1875), 2:178–96; Blight, *Race and Reunion*, 161–65; and Marszalek, *Sherman*, 457–67.

25. Review of Boynton's *Sherman's Historical Raid* in *Southern Historical Society Papers*, ed. J. William Jones et al., 52 vols. (Richmond, Va.: Southern Historical Society, 1876–1959), 1:48, 424 (set hereafter cited as *SHSP*).

26. "Georgia Firsts," in *Miss Rutherford's Scrap Book*, 4 vols. (Athens: n.p., 1924), 2:18.

27. Michael Kammen, *Mystic Chords of Memory: The Transformation of Tradition in American Culture* (New York: Vintage, 1993 [1991]), 9.

28. See Charles Colcock Jones Jr., *The Siege of Savannah* (Albany, N.J.: Joel Munsell, 1874), 170–82; Charles C. Jones Jr., *Oration Pronounced by Col. Charles C. Jones, Jr. on the 31st October, 1878, upon the Occasion of the Unveiling and Dedication of the Confederate Monument, Erected by the Ladies Memorial Association of Augusta, in Broad Street in the City of Augusta* (Augusta, Ga.: Evening Sentinel Office, 1878), 1; Charles C. Jones Jr., *An Address Delivered before the Confederate Survivors Association, in Augusta, Georgia, at the Sixth Annual Meeting, on Memorial Day, April 26, 1884* (Augusta, Ga.: Chronicle Printing Establishment, 1884), 5–6. The themes developed in these two sources appear repeatedly in nearly all of Jones's writings. See also "The Battle of Honey Hill," *SHSP*, 13:355–67.

29. "A Curious Charge Against General Sherman," *Georgia Weekly Telegraph*, August 17, 1875.

30. A. R. Chisolm, "Some Corrections of Sherman's Memoirs," *SHSP*, 7:295.

31. E. L. Wells, "A Morning Call on General Kilpatrick," *SHSP*, 12:123.

32. "Reminiscences about General Sherman," *Confederate Veteran* 16 (July 1908): 352.

33. Jefferson Davis, *The Rise and Fall of the Confederate Government*, 2 vols. (New York: D. Appleton, 1881), 2:570.

34. "Jefferson Davis on Gen. Sherman," *Indianapolis Sentinel*, June 16, 1881, reprinted in *Georgia Weekly Telegraph*, June 24, 1881.

35. "'Sherman Day,'" *Augusta News*, November 17, 1881, reprinted in *Macon Weekly Telegraph*, November 18, 1881.

36. "The Destruction of Atlanta," *Atlanta Constitution*, November 18, 1881.

37. "At the Exposition," *Atlanta Constitution*, November 16, 1881; "Mexican Veterans," *Fort Wayne Daily Gazette*, November 16, 1881. See also, Marszalek, *Sherman*, 472.

38. See, for instance, Jefferson Davis to the Editor of the *St. Louis Republican*, November 6, 1884, in Dunbar Rowland, ed., *Jefferson Davis, Constitutionalist: His Life and Letters*, 10 vols. (Jackson: Mississippi Department of Archives and History, 1923), 9:474–75. See also Marszalek, *Sherman*, 472–75.

39. Paul Y. Hayne to Jefferson Davis, January 18, 1885, in Rowland, ed., *Jefferson Davis, Constitutionalist*, 9:335–36.

40. I. W. Avery, *Atlanta . . . The Advantages of Georgia, "The Empire State of the South"* (Atlanta: Constitution Publishing Company, 1885), 3–4, 24.

41. *Atlanta Constitution*, May 2, 1881; summary in Rowland, ed., *Jefferson Davis, Constitutionalist*, 9:441–43.

42. John McIntosh Kell, *Recollections of a Naval Life, Including the Cruises of the Confederate States Steamers "Sumter" and "Alabama"* (Washington: Neale, 1900), 295.

43. Edna Henry Lee Turpin, ed., *The New South and Other Addresses by Henry Woodfin Grady* (New York: Gordon Press, 1972), 31–32.

44. Kell, *Recollections of a Naval Life*, 5.

45. John B. Gordon, *The Old South. Addresses Delivered before the Confederate Survivors' Association in Augusta, Georgia, on the Occasion of Its Ninth Annual Reunion, on Memorial Day, April 26th 1887 by His Excellency, Governor John B. Gordon, and by Col. Charles C. Jones, Jr., LL.D.* (Augusta, Ga.: Chronicle Publishing Company, 1887), 7, 12. See also Gaines M. Foster, *Ghosts of the Confederacy: Defeat, the Lost Cause, and the Emergence of the New South* (New York: Oxford University Press, 1987), 83–85; and Blight, *Race and Reunion*, 41–42.

46. *Chattanooga and Chickamauga. Reprint of Gen. H. V. Boynton's Letter to the Cincinnati Commercial Gazette, August 1881*, 2nd rev. ed. (Washington: George R. Gray, Printer, 1891), 5, 54; National Park Service, *Chickamauga and Chattanooga National Military Park: An Administrative History*, chap. 1, pp. 1–7, ⟨http://www.cr.nps.gov/history/online_books/chch/adhi1.htm⟩ (accessed on August 9, 2006).

47. *Atlanta Constitution*, February 13, 17, 18, 20, 1891. See also Marszalek, *Sherman*, 479–99.

48. H. V. Boydton, comp., *Dedication of the Chickamauga and Chattanooga National Military Park, September 18–20, 1895* (Washington: Government Printing Office, 1896), 38–39, 41, 151–54.

49. Committee of the Atlanta Camp, United Confederate Veterans, *Battles of Atlanta. Short Sketch of the Battles Around, Siege, Evacuation and Destruction of Atlanta, Ga., in*

1864, with Map, Historic Places, Directory to Battle Lines, Prominent Characters Who Participated, etc. (Atlanta: n.p., 1895).

50. Clement A. Evans, "Our Confederate Memorial Day," *Confederate Veteran* 4 (July 1896): 222–23.

51. Georgia Board of Education, *Georgia: A Guide to Its Towns and Countryside* (Athens: University of Georgia Press, 1940), 181; *Atlanta Constitution*, July 20, 1898.

52. See the speeches in *Report of the Georgia State Memorial Board on Monuments and Markers Erected on Chickamauga Battlefield* (Atlanta: Franklin Printing, 1899), 35–58.

53. Pepper, *Personal Recollections of Sherman's Campaigns*, 171.

54. *Macon Weekly Telegraph*, February 4, 1879.

55. Edward Randolph Carter, *The Black Side: A Partial History of the Business, Religious, and Educational Sides of the Negro in Atlanta, Ga.* (Atlanta: n.p., 1894), 17.

56. W. E. B. DuBois, *The Souls of Black Folk* (1903; reprint, New York: Barnes and Noble, 2003), 20.

57. A concise summary of race issues in Jim Crow Georgia can be found in James C. Cobb, *Georgia Odyssey* (Athens: University of Georgia Press, 1997), 37–42.

58. *Atlanta Constitution*, May 1, 1906.

59. *Columbus Ledger*, May 3, 1906.

60. *New York Times*, May 2, 1906.

61. *Atlanta Constitution*, May 1, 1906.

62. Ibid., May 3, 4, 6, 1906.

63. *New York Times*, May 7, 1906. For the most complete coverage of this event, see E. Merton Coulter, "Father Sherman's 'March to the Sea,'" *Georgia Review* 10 (Winter 1956): 375–92.

64. *Dalton North Georgia Citizen*, May 3, 1906.

65. *Cartersville [Ga.] News*, May 3, 10, 1906.

66. E. H. Hinton, "The Negro and the South," *Confederate Veteran* 15 (August 1907): 367–68.

67. "Why General Sherman's Name Is Detested," *Confederate Veteran* 14 (July 1906): 295–98.

68. See, for instance, *Confederate Veteran* 14 (October 1906): 467, 547–48; 15 (March 1907): 127.

69. *Dalton North Georgia Citizen*, July 11, 1907; "Sherman's 'Achievements' in Georgia," *Confederate Veteran* 14 (July 1906): 300; Carol Reardon, *Soldiers and Scholars: The U.S. Army and the Uses of Military History, 1865–1920* (Manhattan: University Press of Kansas, 1990), 63.

70. *Atlanta Constitution*, June 10, 1909.

71. "How Atlanta Observed Memorial Day," *Confederate Veteran* 17 (July 1909): 341.

72. *Atlanta Constitution*, September 4, 1913.

73. Tommie Phillips LaCavera, comp., *The History of the Georgia Division of the United Daughters of the Confederacy, 1895–1995, Centennial Edition*, 2 vols. (Atlanta: United Daughters of the Confederacy, 1995), 1:59.

74. *Minutes of the Third Annual Meeting of the United Daughters of the Confederacy Held in Nashville, Tennessee, November 11, 1896* (Nashville: Foster & Webb, 1897), 5.

75. W. D. Pickett, "Why General Sherman's Name is Detested," *Confederate Veteran* 10 (July, August, September, October 1902): 292, 342–43, 419, 437; 11 (January, December

1903): 5–6, 532–34; 14 (September 1906): 398; 16 (October 1908): 503. See also Edwin Tribble, "Marching through Georgia," *Georgia Review* 21 (Winter 1967): 423–29.

76. At least sixty monuments were dedicated between 1906 and 1915 alone. Figures compiled from Georgia Division, United Daughters of the Confederacy, *Confederate Monuments and Markers in Georgia* (Fernandina Beach, Fla.: Wolfe Publishing Co., 2002).

77. Lizzie Rutherford Chapter, United Daughters of the Confederacy, *A History of the Origin of Memorial Day as Adopted by the Ladies' Memorial Association of Columbus, Georgia* (Columbus: Thomas Gilber, Printer, 1898), 18.

78. Ibid., 6.

79. Knight, *Standard History of Georgia and Georgians*, 2:104; Georgia Division, UDC, *Confederate Monuments and Markers in Georgia*, 113, 142, 268.

80. *Columbus [Ga.] Enquirer-Sun*, February 4, 1900; Henry R. Goetchius, *Robert Edward Lee: Gentleman, Scholar, Gallant Soldier, Great General, and True Christian* (Columbus, Ga.: n.p., 1900), 18, 21–27.

81. Georgia Division, UDC, *Confederate Monuments and Markers in Georgia*, 120, 187; *Confederate Veteran* 20 (May, December 1912): 203, 545; 21 (June 1913): 286–88.

82. For the details of this movement, see LaCavera, comp., *History of the Georgia Division*, 1:407–10; *Confederate Veteran* 14 (January, September, October, December 1906): 10–11, 394, 445–49, 558; 15 (January, February, March, April, May 1907): 17–19, 57, 107–13, 166, 201; 16 (January, May, June 1909): 9, 199–200, 263; and *Atlanta Constitution*, May 13, 1909.

83. *Confederate Veteran* 14 (January 1906): 11; "Sherman Helped Starve Union Prisoners," ibid., 512–13.

84. "Confederate Monuments and Cemeteries," *Confederate Veteran* 11 (January 1903): 17–18. See Rutherford's summary of commemorative activities in "Georgia Firsts," *Miss Rutherford's Scrap Book*, 2:17. See also Mrs. William H. [Rebecca Latimer] Felton, "Importance of the Education of the Poor Girls of the South," in *Minutes of the Fourth Annual Meeting of the United Daughters of the Confederacy Held in Baltimore, Maryland, November 12–12, 1897* (Nashville: Foster & Webb, 1898), 34–36.

85. Mildred Lewis Rutherford, "War Time Christmas in the Old South," *Miss Rutherford's Historical Notes* (Athens, Ga.: Self-published, 1926), 14:27.

86. Ralph A. Graves, "Marching through Georgia Sixty Years Later," *National Geographic* 50 (September 1926): 261–311.

87. See James W. Matthews, "The Civil War of 1936: *Gone with the Wind* and *Absalom! Absalom!*," *Georgia Review* 21 (Winter 1967): 462–69; Peveral H. Peake, "Why the South Hates Sherman," *American Mercury* 41 (August 1937): 441.

88. Georgia Board of Education, *Georgia*, 5–6.

89. For an extended discussion of these issues, see J. Michael Martinez, William D. Richardson, and Ron McNinch-Su, eds., *Confederate Symbols in the Contemporary South* (Gainesville: University Press of Florida, 2000), esp. chaps. 10 and 11.

90. *New York Times*, November 7, 2002.

91. See, for instance, Al Benson Jr., "Reparations? For Starters, How about Yankee War Crime Trials?" in *The Patriotist*, April 9, 2001, at ⟨http://www.patriotist.com/abarch/ab20010409.htm⟩ (accessed on July 6, 2007).

92. For reaction to Grimsley's book, see "The Long Shadow of Sherman's March," at ⟨http://people.cohums.ohio-state.edu/grimsley1/dialogue/long_shadow.htm⟩. See

also "Readers Respond to Efforts to Whitewash Sherman War Crimes," Georgia Heritage Coalition website, ⟨http://georgiaheritagecouncil.org/site2/news/reader-views-sherman051504.phtml⟩. Both sites accessed on July 6, 2007.

93. Jeff Davis, "Cleansing Sherman," Georgia Heritage Coalition website, ⟨http://georgiaheritagecouncil.org/site2/commentary/davis-cleansing-sherman.phtml⟩ (accessed on July 6, 2007).

94. "William Tecumseh Sherman, a North Georgia Notable," About North Georgia, ⟨http://ngeorgia.com/people/shermanwt.html⟩ (accessed on July 24, 2006).

The Nation's Greatest Hero Should Rest in the Nation's Greatest City

⊰ JOAN WAUGH ⊱

Before it was the General Grant National Memorial it was officially called Grant Monument. Visitors dubbed it "Grant's Tomb," and the nickname stuck. Commanding a hill 270 feet above the Hudson River on the north end of Manhattan's Riverside Park, the 160-foot gleaming granite and marble structure is one of the most impressive Civil War monuments ever built and the largest mausoleum in North America. Opened with great fanfare on the seventy-fifth anniversary of Grant's birthday on April 27, 1897, and funded entirely by popular subscription, the neoclassical building was designed to inspire awe. "His grave, his monument, his fame," predicted a contemporary, "will transcend all other attractions." Another predicted that people would forever learn "lessons of patriotism and fidelity from his monument."[1] Grant's Tomb quickly became a sacred pilgrimage spot for Union veterans and their families from all over the country. Many thousands gathered for regularly scheduled ceremonies honoring Grant's birthday, Memorial Day, and the Fourth of July. Prominent politicians and presidents selected the spot for speeches and important announcements. Foreign dignitaries visited frequently to pay their respects. Until 1916 it remained New York's most visited monument, drawing 500,000–600,000 people annually, outdistancing the Statue of Liberty, and maintaining extremely high levels of visitation until 1929.[2]

That year, aged survivors of the Grand Army of the Republic (GAR), the North's most powerful veteran organization, conducted their final ceremony at the tomb. The veterans, their families, and their immediate descendants declined in number after 1929, and the monument languished. Attendance dropped dramatically through the decades. Where the monument once stood alone, new additions to the area, including the towering Gothic Riverside Church, crowded it out, diminishing its presence. The lovely and remote rural park in which it was placed in the 1890s turned

Postcard of the Grant Monument, circa 1906. Author's collection.

into a dangerous crime-ridden neighborhood, called Morningside Heights, in the 1960s and 1970s. Additionally, the structure designed to summon feelings of reverence and contemplation seemed old-fashioned and ugly to modern sensibilities. One critic called it "clumsy and tasteless," while another described it as "pompous beyond even the requirements of a Mausoleum for a national hero."[3]

The Grant Monument Association, the private organization responsible for its upkeep, could not raise enough money to stop the building's deterioration. Nor did the situation change when the National Park Service took over the monument's care in 1958. By 1988, one scholar wrote that Grant's Tomb was the "least appreciated national monument in the country." Another observer was more graphic, calling it a "graffiti-scarred hangout for drug dealers and muggers."[4] The defaced monument offered little to the casual history buff. Unlike other important National Park sites, there was no visitor's center to interpret Grant's career, and no restrooms to accommodate tourist comfort. As interest in Civil War sites increased in the 1990s, due in part to Ken Burn's PBS documentary *The Civil War*, the monument's decay became a minor, and then a major scandal. Frank Scaturro, a Columbia University student volunteer at the tomb, went public with a scathing report charging neglect and abuse by the federal government that in turn generated media interest.[5] A 1994 *New York Times* editorial, titled "Dishonor for a Hero President," enumerated a sad list of woes that had befallen the tomb and called for the National Park Service to redress what had become a scandal attracting widespread attention.[6] Family descendants, led by Ulysses S. Grant Dietz, the great-great-grandson of

Grant, threatened to remove his body from New York City and re-inter his remains (along with those of his wife, Julia) in Illinois, when that state's legislature offered a burial place. In a Manhattan courtroom, the family charged that the tomb was "neglected and being abused by graffiti writers, skateboarders who use its stairs as a ramp, drug users and homeless people who urinate on the monument's wall." Responding to a chorus of protests, the Park Service embarked on a $1.8 million restoration project finished in time for the 100th anniversary commemoration of the monument's opening on April 27, 1997.[7]

Despite the improvements, Grant's Tomb remains a largely unvisited, chronically underfunded and ignored national monument. Where before thousands visited, now only hundreds do. Why is this so? The vagaries of New York's urban development combine with another plausible answer.[8] Grant did not evolve into the mythological figure envisioned by the monument's supporters. In 1897, Grant was equal in history and memory to Abraham Lincoln. He has not been regarded as so for many decades. One historian observed, "At the dawn of the twentieth century, Grant's Tomb stood as a central site of Civil War Commemoration, for national as well as New York audiences."[9] Lincoln transcended the Civil War, but Grant did not. Many if not most New Yorkers, as well as out-of-town tourists, are totally unaware of Grant's achievements. They do not know where Grant's Tomb is and do not care. In the 1990s, citizens expressed their opposition to using federal, state, or local funds for the tomb's improvement. "Are we so cowardly," a *New York Post* writer demanded, "that we can't stand up to a man who's been dead for a century? Are we going to let a corpse extort money from us?" The same author declared, "At a time when schools and parks are badly neglected, we shouldn't spend millions renovating a building that attracts so few visitors and has so little to do with the city's character."[10]

The story of the building of Grant's Tomb, not its decline, is my concern. Immediately after Grant's death, there was a concerted effort made by political, military, and cultural leaders ensuring the "Great Commander" was permanently entombed in an edifice worthy of his legacy. New York City emerged as the permanent burial site. Amid often bitter debates regarding the "New York Takeover," funds were raised, plans approved, an architect hired, and a monument erected. Public art emerges from a complex and contentious process involving businessmen, politicians, city and state government officials, artists, and the general public, organized into interest groups such as the Grand Army of the Republic. In examining this process with regard to Grant's Tomb, I draw attention to the relationship between memory and history expressed in monuments — especially those like Grant's, which are deliberately designed to foster a sense of national identity and unity (a topic that has attracted much attention among historians).[11]

Grant's Tomb, like most major "national" monuments, took a long time to be finished, evoked controversy at every stage of its development, and finally, at its completion, fell short of expectations. Despite such difficulties, there was never any doubt that Grant's monument would be built. Before 1865 Americans commemorated important events and persons in history, but the Civil War, understandably, brought a huge increase in memorials and dramatically reshaped America's "landscape of memory." The sheer scale of tragic death and heroic sacrifice inspired the honoring of both leaders and ordinary soldiers by erecting statues and other structures in many venues. Where before there were hundreds, now there were thousands of such memorials. Relatively few Civil War monuments were dedicated in the 1860s and 1870s. The rapid expansion began twenty to twenty-five years after Appomattox, coinciding with the building of Grant's Tomb and rising to a climax in the 1890s. Most were modest, inexpensive statues honoring the common soldier, although many grander monuments offered tribute to military and political heroes, and still others were elaborate commemorative arches straddling urban thoroughfares. Typically, monuments grand or humble were placed on battlefields or in cemeteries, small-town squares, and splendid urban plazas.[12]

Civil War monuments were paid for by public and private sources, and often featured some combination of both. The victorious North had the resources to build many more than the South, although that changed by the 1880s. In both sections veteran's groups, church or civic associations, and women's organizations held fund-raising events and donation drives to raise money for statues commemorating war-related activities. Unveilings featured patriotic ceremonies and speeches. Whether cut from granite or carved from marble, monuments were imbued with political and social meaning, revealing much about the war's legacy to the generation who lived through the era.[13]

The Grant Memorial easily fit and even surpassed the requirements for an important national monument. The man who led northern armies to victory and guided the country through Reconstruction as general and two-term president deserved the most impressive memorial the country could furnish. "The interest in General Grant's death has been very great," explained former president Rutherford B. Hayes. Hayes, who ended the war as a brevetted major general, made two speeches on the day of Grant's death at different GAR posts in Ohio. On both occasions, he urged veterans that a memorial be built that would "be worthy of the Republic, worthy of General Grant, and worthy of the righteous cause of which he was the most illustrious soldier." Hayes wrote a letter published by New York newspapers and carried nationwide in which he pleaded for a concerted effort by northern veterans in raising funds to erect a national monument at the site where Grant was going to be buried. "If the matter is promptly pushed by the Grand Army of the Republic while the public mind is intensely interested in all that concerns Gen. Grant," Hayes noted, "there is every reason for confidence that a national monument can be built."[14] Hayes's comments were echoed in numerous public forums where the issue of how to honor Grant's legacy was enjoined.

The results of one forum appeared in several *North American Review* "round table" discussions with selected public figures, cultural critics, painters, sculptors, and architects. The stated purpose was to answer the question: "Grant's Memorial: What Shall It Be?"[15] Although the combined background of the discussants revealed an elitist perspective, they also shared their generation's war experiences. Architect Henry Van Brunt served as a Union soldier, and Horatio Seymour was elected wartime Democratic governor of New York. Many, like sculptor Launt Thompson, had completed significant Civil War commemorative projects. They expressed a belief in Grant's importance to history as shown in this commonly expressed sentiment, "We should erect to his memory the grandest mausoleum or temple of modern times."[16] For all, Grant was a towering national icon whose achievement in preserving the Union deserved one of the greatest memorials in history. The published comments of these professional artists and prominent public figures illuminated the above common assumption that drove a similar but much broader public discussion on the monument's design.

The forum participants suggested that the tomb blend European neoclassicism with American-inspired themes and resources. The so-called Beaux-Arts movement of the late nineteenth century did not reject Old World forms but rather injected New World creativity and exuberance into monumental buildings and structures.[17] Indeed, roundtable critics suggested that Grant's Tomb should be comparable in majesty to the magnificent tombs of European military heroes such as Nelson, Napoleon, and Wellington. The painter W. H. Beard revealed the prevailing sentiments and hopes of himself and his colleagues when he said, "A loved and honored son of the nation has gone out from among us. There is no doubt but the nation at large will pour out from its abundance ample means to erect a structure adequate for the purpose . . . it should be simple, though full; pure, grand, unique." A cynic might dismiss Beard's words as an exercise in empty rhetoric. Monuments dedicated to great heroes typically evoke passionate declamations and fervent hopes especially before the reality of restricted budgets appear. Nevertheless, conversation about Grant's memorial continued unabated within and without the lofty halls of academe and sumptuous boardrooms, spilling over to newspapers, veterans' meetings, and in private correspondence. On August 12, 1885, a reporter captured the tone of the debates engaging a public eager to shape Grant's memorial, writing, "It is fitting, therefore, that it should be a modern and not a classic edifice, and that its emblems and friezes and tablatures should represent scenes from the life of the nineteenth century and on the physical plane of the American continent." Considerable newspaper space was given to the imminent monument, alongside the endless columns devoted to the story of Grant's death and funeral.[18]

. Before any memorial could take shape, Julia Grant and her family had to decide on a place of interment. Grant himself did not strongly favor one place over another. His only desire was that Julia be buried next to him. "There is one thing I would wish you and the family to insist upon," he told his oldest son, Frederick Dent Grant, "and that is that, wherever my tomb may be, a place should be reserved for your mother at my side." Grant wrote a note on June 23, 1885, to Fred mentioning three possible burial sites—Galena, St. Louis, and New York City, the last "because the people of that city befriended me in my need."[19] After Grant's death one month later, on July 23, immediate competition broke out among various places, but above all others New Yorkers were organized and aggressive in pressing their case. Just hours after Grant passed away, a telegram arrived from New York's Mayor William R. Grace offering land for Grant's burial in any city park the family designated. New York was first, but its offer was quickly followed with one from the Soldiers' Home in Washington, D.C., offering a prime interment site overlooking the capital city. Soon the family was inundated with applicants. As Fred remembered, "Upon the death of General Grant . . . many telegrams were immediately received, containing offers for various pieces of ground for his last resting-place."[20]

Fred asked Mayor Grace to send a representative to Mount McGregor to make a full report to the family. In a meeting held on July 24, the day after Grace's telegram arrived, the city official guaranteed that land in a public park would be set aside on which a "grand tomb" would be built.[21] Fred recalled that "it was decided that the offer made by New York was the most desirable one, as it included the guarantee . . . that his wife should be provided with a last resting-place by his side — there, this offer was accepted." Ending the suspense, official family spokesman Fred Grant announced to the public that his father would be buried in New York City. The Empire State newspapers expressed jubilance upon hearing the decision. The *New York Times*'s headline blared: "A Most Fitting Burial Place: The Nation's Greatest Hero Should Rest in the Nation's Greatest City."[22]

New York papers joyously reported a national consensus. Testimony from eight-six New Yorkers — including the mayor, politicians, government officials, businessmen, bankers, ex-generals, and lawyers — referred to Gotham as the nation's "real capital," while Washington was dismissed as the nation's "nominal capital."[23] New Yorkers stood on solid ground as the country's most populous and wealthy city. A prominent history of the city's architecture described its unique position, "Given that New York was not a state capital, its sense of itself as the representative American city was critical, giving rise to what might be called its metropolitan destiny: New York saw itself as a quasi-independent political and cultural entity that was both a microcosm of and a model for the nation as a whole."[24] New York's explosive growth was aided by an ever-expanding infrastructure that drove building and development downtown and into the hinterlands. The profits generated by wealthy and philanthropic-minded businessmen built important cultural institutions and beautiful architectural landmarks such as the Metropolitan Museum of Art (1880) and the American Natural History Museum (1877). The Statue of Liberty (1886) and the Brooklyn Bridge (1883) in different ways demonstrated the economic, political, and industrial preeminence of the city. Manhattan's Central Park was the stunning jewel in New York's crown, completed just after the Civil War. These massive projects of civic triumphalism demonstrated that New York, with a population of more than one million, was already a cosmopolitan, world-class city. It seemed only fitting to New Yorkers that General Grant, a national and international icon, would be buried and memorialized with a monument befitting the other landmarks.[25]

Although pleased, Mayor Grace knew that the family's decision would not be final until they formally approved a site and signed the contract. Moving seamlessly into the next phase, he recommended that the family consider "the prominent height in Riverside Park, on the banks of the Hudson."[26] The mayor believed Central Park was unsuitable because it had already become so familiar to New Yorkers that a tomb would seem intrusive, possibly even offensive.[27] After consulting with Julia, whose grief would keep her at Mount McGregor until after the funeral ceremonies, sons Fred and Jesse Grant left for the city. On July 27, officials arranged a tour offering several possible interment sites. The group, which included close family friend Gen. William T. Sherman, visited several places, mostly in Central Park and Riverside Park. As Grace anticipated, the former was deemed too noisy while the latter was greeted with approval by one and all. Returning to Mount McGregor and after consulting with his mother and family, Fred decided in favor of Riverside Park.[28] Approval for the scheme by the board of alderman was immediately forthcoming, as was its approval of Julia's resting place next to Ulysses. Riverside Park did seem an ideal location. Still incomplete in 1885, the area was beautiful and rural. Officially established in 1873, Riverside Park, like Central Park, was designed by Frederick Law Olmsted and Calvert Vaux. A local writer praised its serene beauty: "The view from this Mecca of the American traveler is one of the finest in the world—for thirty miles, on a clear day, up the Hudson toward West Point, and southward toward to the Battery, and across the Bay to the Narrows. The East River and Long Island Sound may be seen in the East, and the Palisades, Fort Lee, and the bold, steep leafy shores of New Jersey on the West."[29]

Others were less enamored with the choice. Upon hearing the news, Grant's minister Reverend John Newman blurted out, "Oh, it is such a lonely place there; and he was thoroughly a man of the people."[30] Some criticized the site as benefiting only the wealthy because at that time only carriages could get to Riverside Park (public transportation soon improved access). A disgruntled doubter noting the barren look of much of the park described it as "a neglected strip of unimproved land" and intimated that pressures by city officials to increase real estate values might have played a role in its selection. Undoubtedly profit motives did play a distant role; the area was designated as early as the 1860s as a prime target of real estate development for the wealthy. Olmsted and Vaux both expressed concerns (soon assuaged) that Grant's memorial did not belong in what was supposed to be a park for enjoyment and not solemn contemplation.[31]

Mayor Grace proposed an organization to facilitate the planned monument while public sentiment "was at its highest." He sent letters to a carefully selected list of prominent New Yorkers requesting their support for a Grant memorial. Over eighty gentlemen attended a meeting on July 28, 1885, and on that day the Grant Monument Association was officially established, united in the goal to build "a great national monument which shall appropriately testify to future ages" about "the grandest character of the century."[32] Among the founders were former Republican president Chester A. Arthur, Cornelius Vanderbilt II, and, serving as treasurer, powerful banker J. P. Morgan.[33]

The Grant Monument Association immediately announced a campaign to raise a million dollars. This was an unprecedented sum easily surpassing all previous memorials. Further details revealed that the entire cost of the monument would be borne by the private sector. In late July and early August of 1885 all signs seemed auspicious for a speedy outcome. There was even talk that the Grant Monument would be finished in five years. That prediction proved optimistic. The wealthy and prominent men occupying the top leadership roles did not have time to run an effective and efficient organization dedicated to fund-raising. Indeed, their failure to muster a quorum in many of the earliest, and most critical, executive committee meetings (between October of 1885 and February of 1886) seriously hampered the efficacy of fund-raising and drew much unfavorable notice in the press.[34]

The day-to-day administration was turned over to forty-one-year-old Richard Theodore Greener, who was appointed by Mayor Grace to the board of trustees. Elected to the salaried position of secretary, Greener worked in office space donated by the Mutual Life Insurance Company in midtown Manhattan. A fascinating figure, Greener was the first black graduate of Harvard College, and his distinguished resume included work as an educator, lawyer, professor, and diplomat.[35] As a high-profile leader in the African American community, Greener campaigned hard for the Republican Party in the early 1880s and professed admiration for President Grant, with whom he forged a personal acquaintance. Finding his salary inadequate for his large family's needs, he also served for several years as the city's chief examiner of the Municipal Service Board. Greener's most important task by far was to raise money *nationally* for the "Grant Fund." His highest accomplishment came in mobilizing the black community to support the monument, and small donations poured in from many states, as well as from the citizens of Monrovia, Liberia. One South Carolinian explained why so many blacks sent money: "We are grateful to and appreciate General Grant for the valuable service which he rendered . . . the erection of that great and glorious monument of freedom . . . of the American Negro."[36]

Greener and the Grant Fund enjoyed the unqualified support of the influential New York press. Whether Republican or Democratic, they happily served as the association's willing handmaidens in publicizing the Grant Fund. "An Appeal to the Country: The People Asked to Aid in the Erection of the Monument," ran an early headline. The reporter noted that the Monument Committee emerged from Mayor Grace's office to invite "the people of the United States to participate in the erection of a suitable memorial in honor of Gen. Grant."[37] The press printed every donor's name, and the majority of contributions were sent to newspapers such as the *New York Tribune*, the *New York Times*, and the *New York World* and forwarded on to the GMA's offices. Larger amounts from wealthy businessmen and corporations were lavishly praised in print. Western Union provided the first significant contribution of $5,000 and, in addition, offered their lines free of charge for citizens who wished to wire funds. A popular device proved to be the issuance of an elaborate "certificate" thanking the donor. Most people sent modest sums ranging from pennies to ten dollars. "Two Yankee Women" donated twenty cents, while "A German Who Gives up his Beer, 15c." Often a larger contribution was published near smaller ones, evoking a poignant contrast. Rutherford Stuyvesant's $250 was listed next to "Johnny's Mite's" ten cents and five cents from "A poor Soldier's Orphan." Donations came from veterans all over the country, including the states of Iowa, Louisiana, Pennsylvania, and Alabama.[38]

The most cursory analysis of the collections, however, revealed that, except for the African American populace, most of the subscriptions emanated from New York City, a troubling sign. The sad truth emerged that several weeks into the campaign only $50,000 had been raised, scandalously less than needed if the target of a million dollars was going to be reached in a timely manner. One newspaper stated the dilemma succinctly: "The New York Monument Committee have voted to raise one million dollars for a Grant Monument. They have raised about $50,000 which will probably be spent in sending begging letters to other parts of the country."[39] Knowledgeable supporters worried that a relatively brief window of opportunity existed for gathering funds expeditiously. In mid-August, Rutherford Hayes warned in a private letter that "the golden moment has already passed," adding, "further delay imperils all. . . . Experience [with monuments] shows that the funds, if raised by popular subscription, must be obtained at once."[40] The association's campaign faltered badly despite the stupendous outpouring of love and affection for General Grant. To the astonishment of many New Yorkers, the monument's placement in their city posed a serious public relations dilemma from the outset. Simply put, a majority of Americans rejected New York's self-proclaimed status as a national city. They did not open their wallets for a Grant memorial that few, at least for now, expected to visit. An Indiana newspaper declared, "We have not a cent for New York and would advise that not a dollar of help be sent to the millionaire city."[41] Jealously and resentment led to accusations that New York "seized" Grant's body for its own aggrandizement.

Sensing looming disaster, New York City–based journalists opened fire early with trenchant criticism. A *New York World* editorial lambasted the Grant Monument Committee for being entirely made up of New Yorkers. If it was the national monument it pretended to be, the *World* asked scornfully, than why not recruit men from all over the country? The paper concluded, "If Washington had been selected as the place of interment the Monument Committee would of course have been National in its composition. But it is to be hoped that the selection of New York as the burial place will not in any degree lessen the desire felt in other States to share in the erection of a fitting monument over Gen. Grant's grave. That ought to be a National Work."[42] Numerous out-of-state newspapers echoed these sentiments and recorded with pride that *their* citizens were ignoring New York's entreaties and building their own Grant monuments. Just a month into the GMA's fund-raising drive, Philadelphia had raised roughly the same amount of money toward a Grant monument. Likewise, Chicago's city fathers proudly announced that *their* Grant fund effort reached the princely sum of $45,000.[43]

Gotham editorials expressed the shock of many New Yorkers. Three examples provide the common tone. The *New York Post* responded in kind, charging that "the most astonishing of all [is] the manifestation of the curious jealousy excited by General Grant's desire that his body should lie among the people of New York."[44] Another editorial, appropriately titled "The National Monument," argued that "there is something particularly discordant in the querulous tones of petty jealousy and local spite." The third asserted, "It is fitting that the tomb of the greatest soldier and citizen of our later history should be in the commercial metropolis of the nations, where it will be visited and seen by the greatest number from all parts of our country as well as from foreign lands."[45]

A most worrisome aspect was the solid opposition from northern soldiers' organizations that overwhelmingly preferred Washington to New York City. An Ohio veteran remarked, "Our people are of the opinion that Washington is the proper location for a monument to so distinguished a character as the late General Grant and are willing to contribute to any other location believing that New York has no claims that are as prominent as other locations that have been mentioned."[46] The Grand Army of the Republic's commander in chief Samuel S. Burdette spoke for his constituency when he demanded Grant's burial in the true "national" city, Washington. He further rejected the association's request to merge resources and thus denied it a quick and lucrative fund-raising asset. Many pointed out the logic of Washington for Grant's mausoleum. Arlington National Cemetery, formally established in 1865, was the burial place of many Civil War soldiers, as was the slightly older Soldiers' Home Cemetery. The *Seattle Daily Post-Intelligencer* on July 26, 1885, urged that Grant's body "ought to be placed in state in New York, Philadelphia, and Washington, and then be buried there beside the soldiers who fought with him." In Washington, D.C., newspapers expressed disgust immediately after the decision was announced. They attacked New York's proposal as nothing more than a scam imposed by local politicians, conveniently ignoring or playing down the Grant family's stated preference.[47] In addition, prominent generals and politicians such as John A. Logan and Philip H. Sheridan pushed for their former commander to be interred in Washington. It seemed reasonable to veterans living outside of New York — city and state — that they would be just as likely, or more likely, to visit Grant's memorial in the national capital.

Two beloved figures among veterans, Rutherford Hayes and William Sherman, rallied to New York's defense. Hayes worked hard to arouse enthusiastic GAR efforts in support of New York, "where General Grant last resided and where more soldiers and citizens will see and enjoy it than would be the case [if it were placed] in any other locality."[48] Hayes sent a sharply worded letter to Burdette urging him to give up all opposition. The Grant family was not going to bend on this issue, insisted Hayes, who added that Burdette was being "misled by a temporary local delusion. General Grant's remains will forever rest on the banks of the Hudson."[49] Staunch monument supporter Sherman tried to win veterans over to his point of view in a speech to the 18th Annual Reunion of the Society of the Army of the Tennessee in Chicago. "Each city, town and even hamlet may have whatever monument they are willing to erect," Sherman assured veterans, "but it seems to me better that all should unite and build a strong, solid, simple monument . . . over his grave on the banks of the Hudson."[50]

The ultimate arbiter was Julia Grant. Seeking to put an end to the debate, Richard Greener and Mayor Grace asked her in late October 1885 to write a letter indicating strong support of New York. In a widely published reply, she pronounced Riverside Park in New York City the ideal spot for her husband's remains. Julia explained firmly that "Riverside was selected by myself and my family as the burial place of my husband, General Grant. First, because I believed that New York was his preference. Second, it is near the residence that I hope to occupy as long as I live, and where I will be able to visit his resting place often." Julia's letter dampened criticism. The *Kansas City [Mo.] Journal* pleaded for sanity on the issue. "It matters little where Grant may be buried, after all," it editorialized, "no matter where his tomb may be it will be visited, will become a hallowed spot . . . let the people unite in determining to help New-York to keep the trust she has assumed — the care of the tomb of Grant."[51]

The leadership of the Grant Monument Association used the support of Sherman and Hayes to smooth out relations between the association and the veterans. To some extent they succeeded. John Cameron, the adjutant general in Washington, issued a general order that suggested a donation of fifteen cents be raised from every member toward the national monument. The suggestion was only that, and was resisted by most veterans.[52] The majority of veterans preferred Washington, although time would soften their stance toward visiting the monument in New York. But they would not give enough money. Thus, the underlying problems of funding the monument nationally persisted. By Thanksgiving of 1885 the GMA announced it had reached the $100,000 mark. The figure would be impressive — but for the fact that $900,000 was needed to reach the target. Worse, 1886 saw donations slow to the barest trickle. The association faced a dilemma. They did not have enough money to begin construction, yet they needed a final design. Why should citizens give money to build a monument whose shape was a mystery? Gloom had settled over the whole project by the time veterans of U. S. Grant Post No. 327 held a ceremony at Grant's temporary tomb on Decoration Day in 1886. Reporters noted sarcastically that at least several hundreds of thousands of people had visited Grant's temporary tomb that day, but no concrete progress had been made toward a permanent resting place.[53]

Attempting to reinvigorate the process two years after Grant's death, the association held two competitions for the monument's design. The first, in 1887, ended in failure, but the second resulted in a winning design announced in September 1890.[54] It was awarded unanimously to the firm of thirty-six-year-old John Hemenway Duncan, a well-regarded New York City architect who designed the Washington Monument at Newburgh, New York. By the time he submitted his plan for Grant's Tomb he had already garnered several other major commissions, including the Soldiers and Sailors Memorial Arch (based on the Arc de Triomphe in Paris) at the entrance to Prospect Park in Brooklyn.[55] Duncan's Grant memorial was a neoclassical design inspired in part by one of the Seven Wonders of the World, the ancient tomb of King Mausolus in Asia Minor. Destroyed in the Middle Ages but excavated and reconstructed by nineteenth-century architects and scholars, Mausolus's tomb inspired the word "mausoleum" (a magnificent tomb). Borrowing as well from Greek, Roman, and French architecture, Duncan's imposing and impressive monument plan consisted of three levels, all to be constructed from light granite.[56]

The exterior featured a massive rectangular-shaped first level that soared to 100 feet. Placed on the "cube" was a dome supported by Ionic columns. In turn, the seventy-foot dome supported a "conical roof." Six huge Doric columns preceded the main entrance (one of three) located on the tomb's southern side. Duncan envisioned equestrian statues of Grant's four division commanders above the entrance portico. In addition, a bronze equestrian statue of Grant was planned for the mid-plaza area. Like many other recommended embellishments, the statues were later eliminated due to lack of funds, although the basic structure remained the same. The interior was equally elaborate, drawing inspiration from that of Napoleon's tomb in Paris. Once inside, visitors would enter a memorial hall large enough to hold roughly a thousand people. The upstairs gallery was lined with coffered barrel vaults and offered spectacular views of the Hudson River, the New Jersey coastline to the west, and the Long Island Sound to the east. Duncan later confirmed the obvious when he stated that his intention was "to produce an edifice which shall be unmistakably a Monumental Tomb, no matter from what point of view it may be seen."[57]

Across from the entrance and down a marble staircase was an open crypt where Ulysses and Julia would be entombed side by side in identical sarcophagi. Ample space was provided for displays of Civil War relics. Duncan's vision for the Grant Monument suited the association and the Grant family perfectly. They felt his design reflected a gravity that would most honor Grant. Richard Greener, one of Duncan's biggest supporters, remarked proudly, "I was one of the first to point out the simplicity, dignity, and fitness of [Duncan's design], as presenting the characteristics of the Conqueror of the Rebellion." Robert A. M. Stern presented a different view: "Duncan grasped the fundamental issue: to make a building that embodied not so much the character of Grant . . . but to create an American Valhalla, a shrine to American power." Montgomery Schuyler, an architectural critic, commented, "There is no question among those who saw the designs submitted for the Grant Monument, that the accepted design was by far the best of them, the only one, in fact, that could be seriously considered. The others were either unduly wild or unduly tame."[58] An added attractive feature of Duncan's design was that the construction could unfold in separate stages so fund-raising could continue throughout the process.

The crowds viewing the groundbreaking ceremonies on April 27, 1891, might be forgiven for breathing a collective sigh of relief that the tomb construction had finally begun. A select few, however, knew the association's coffers were so low that the entire sum collected since 1885 registered only $155,000. If more money were not raised, the construction would halt. As the desperate situation was publicized, criticism mounted once again among the press, the public, politicians, and veterans groups. "For seven years," fumed one ex-soldier, "the body of our old General-in-Chief had been allowed to remain in an open city park in a rude temporary shelter. This neglect had become a standing reproach and humiliating to every surviving Comrade."[59] The object of their combined wrath was the leadership of the Grant Memorial Association that demonstrated over the years it was inept and inert.

Simply put, the Grant Monument Association was not up to the task of finishing the memorial. Fund-raising continued to lag given the stiff national resistance to the monument's site in New York City. "Financially, Grant's tomb had become a local memorial honoring a national hero," wrote a scholar.[60] Yet the association's wealthy members eschewed aggressive measures, preferring to let the pennies and dollars trickle in. Passivity was not the only problem. Political infighting erupted in the fall and early winter of 1892 in disputes over employee salaries and high expenses, further diminishing capacity for effective direction. Two factions emerged to contest for the soul of the organization. One was led by the "old guard" and included Mayor Grace and Richard Greener. Another was led by former brigadier general, Grant aide, wealthy businessman, and prominent Republican trustee Horace Porter, who asserted that a significant shake-up was needed. This shake-up occurred between the groundbreaking ceremony described above and the more elaborate ceremony held the following year to lay the cornerstone of the monument. Porter assumed complete command of the association in spring of 1892.[61] Immediately installing his supporters, Porter cut the executive committee to six and streamlined the board of trustees, while simultaneously enlarging the organization's support circle by personally lobbying wealthy businessmen and prominent politicians to join the organization.[62] His appointment greatly improved relations with the GAR, and Porter pushed for the creation of an "autographic Honor Roll" of every GAR veteran placed in a special repository in the monument building.[63]

It is hard to imagine that the tomb could have been finished successfully without the charismatic leadership of Horace Porter. One historian dubbed him "the man most responsible for the Grant Monument."[64] Later, he added diplomatic experience to his résumé, earning appointment as the U.S. ambassador to France from 1897 to 1905. Tall and distinguished-looking with a bristly handlebar moustache, Porter was a talented orator, much in demand at memorial occasions and dedication ceremonies. In

A Grant Monument Association certificate for contribution with image
of Grant and signature of Horace Porter. National Park Service.

1897 he published what became a classic of Civil War literature, *Campaigning with Grant*, and also penned numerous articles about aspects of Grant's life, career, and character.[65] In short, Porter enjoyed access to, and commanded respect from, the highest levels of the American business, political, and military worlds. His unstinting loyalty to Grant affirmed the family's favorable impression of Porter's ability to make sure the monument was built. He received immediately the enthusiastic backing of Fred Grant, who previously worried that his father's monument would never be finished. "I feel assured," Fred wrote to Porter, "that this matter will reach a successful end soon now, with you in charge—all the world knows of your ability and energy, and I know of your devotion to my dear father."[66]

Fred Grant was correct in his assessment. Porter brought to his task passion, keen intelligence, and willingness to expend a prodigious amount of effort. In short, he was the right man at the right time to lead the Grant Monument Association. He articulated and implemented the winning strategy for finishing the memorial, abandoning the pretense that "the nation" was going to pay for the edifice. Porter instead turned the country's anti–New York sentiment into a potent fund-raising tool by appealing to the pride, generosity, and duty of all New Yorkers. In speech after speech he reminded various groups that the city made a sacred pledge to build a magnificent memorial to General Grant. "Let it be remembered," Porter said, "that our city authorities invited the family of General Grant to make the metropolis of the nation his permanent place of burial. . . . We have contracted a debt and like honest men we must pay it." He further warned that "in this crisis it is not the reputation of Gen. Grant which is on trial, it is the reputation of New York."[67] Anything less than meeting the original obligation, Porter concluded, would bring shame to the city and state.

Armed with this message—the tomb was still a national monument, but New Yorkers must bear the costs—Porter endeavored to make sure everyone who could contribute something did so.

Porter audaciously announced a target of $350,000 in sixty days. Then he laid the foundation to achieve that goal. Running the effort like a well-oiled military campaign, Porter appointed committees and subcommittees, identifying and targeting specific New York groups from plumbers and policemen to bankers and lawyers. All classes of people were targeted— donations of $5,000 from businessmen, contributions from humble and wealthy church congregations, smaller contributions from veterans, and pennies from working men all would be welcome. Thousands of schoolchildren participated in a citywide essay contest on Grant's contribution to American history, a brilliant publicity stunt that kept the cause fresh in people's minds. Porter especially liked having children participate in some way. "The greatest satisfaction I have in seeing the Grant Monument completed," he stated to a school official, "is that it will be an object lesson to the rising generation in loyalty, patriotism, and self-sacrifice."[68] Pushing forward, Porter ordered subscription books printed and placed in public places like train stations, hotels, and banks. Finally, he orchestrated a daily publicity barrage in the newspapers, constantly placing the plight of the memorial before the New York public. "It actually became a fad to raise money for the Grant Monument Fund," noted one account. The next big ceremony marking the progress of the tomb occurred on April 27, 1892, and Porter used the occasion to announce some good news.[69]

The May 7 cover of *Harper's Weekly* featured a solemn illustration by Thur de Thulstrup of President Benjamin Harrison laying the cornerstone of the Grant Monument. Standing beside him was Horace Porter, and in military attire, Gen. Grenville M. Dodge. Julia was seated in a place of honor, along with two of her sons and their families. Other distinguished guests included the vice president, the secretaries of war and the interior, and Generals Oliver O. Howard and John M. Schofield. Four thousand guests were seated in anticipation of the ceremonies, flanked by two thousand veterans. Beyond them an estimated fifty to seventy thousand people waited, enjoying the warmest of spring days at "the site of the monument [which] was the natural goal and culmination of one of the most delightful of suburban drives."[70]

The program was short and simple, and although the president's speech was more anticipated by the crowd, Porter's oration was enthusiastically received. The association's coffers had added roughly $200,000 to the $150,000 already collected, Porter proudly announced. He radiated confidence that the target would be met in thirty days, by the next Decoration Day, and exhorted the crowd to kept the money flowing. He reminded them of the progress accomplished—the foundation finished and the superstructure begun—and the progress anticipated. Porter asked the gathering to cherish the significance of the project they were all dedicated to finishing. It was in countless speeches such as this that Porter articulated a reverent vision for the Grant Monument. "The Monumental Sepulcher erected here will be the shrine at which American patriots will worship," he stated in typically florid prose, "Generations yet to come will pause to read the inscription on its portals, and the voices of a grateful people will ascend from this consecrated spot as incense rises from holy places, invoking blessings on the memory of him who had filled to the very full the largest measure of human greatness and covered the earth with his renown."[71] Soon after Porter finished, President Harrison awkwardly spread mortar over the bed of the cornerstone with a golden trowel, and to thunderous applause offered his own tribute to Grant.

In the weeks that followed, Porter intensified his relentless fundraising campaign and achieved spectacular results.[72] By Decoration Day 1892, all of the $350,000—the majority from New Yorkers—was collected and secured. Together with interest, the entire sum available for the construction of Grant's monument would total $600,000. Ninety thousand individuals had donated to the popular subscription drive. "Our citizens have contributed a fund larger than any ever received from voluntary contributions for any similar object in history," Porter proudly wrote.[73] It was a remarkable achievement, and Horace Porter deserved much of the credit.

Brimming with confidence and buoyed by a clear vision of what needed to be accomplished, Porter turned his formidable skills toward finishing the construction within a strict budget that had once been envisioned at one million dollars. Many features of Duncan's original design were eliminated and the structure itself slightly reduced in size. Outwardly, Porter was ever the enthusiastic leader, constantly assuring the people that the memorial would open on schedule. A master of public relations, he arranged for impressive ceremonies at the building site every April 27 and May 31—the anniversary of Grant's birthday and Decoration Day. In 1893, Porter learned that a naval review was going to take place in New York on Grant's birthday. He wrote the secretary of the navy to suggest that they use the occasion to fire a salute opposite the tomb. The navy was amenable, and the ceremonies had an added touch of pageantry.[74] Porter continued his speeches at venues in New York City and beyond, delivering elegant

Collection Box for donations to the Grant Monument.
National Park Service.

fund-raising tributes to the memory of his late commander. Between 1893 and 1897 he secured another $50,000, enabling the association to meet unexpected cost overruns.[75] Most of all, Porter was determined to bring the great promise of Grant's memorial to fruition. "The monument shall be flawless," he declared in a letter to the *New York World*.[76]

In the month before the opening, finishing touches were applied to the tomb and preparations made for the parade and the program. Under conditions of secrecy, Grant's body was removed from the temporary tomb and placed in the polished red granite sarcophagus a week and a half before the dedication. Thousands of people flocked into the area trying to catch a glimpse of the interior of the memorial. Anticipating huge crowds, Mayor Josiah Strong appointed a committee of 300 prominent citizens to the "Municipal Grant Monument Committee." Armed with $50,000 for expenses the committee was charged with the responsibility for the planning and execution of the ceremony. New York City officials declared a holiday, "Grant Day," and ordered schools, stores, and businesses closed. In contrast to the black-clad buildings of Grant's funeral, the city's streets were swathed in the bright national colors. "Stars and Stripes Everywhere," ran the headline in the *New York Herald*.[77]

Indeed the newspaper's own headquarters in Herald Square was just one of numerous buildings, stores, and private residences lavishly decorated for Grant Day. At least from early April, anticipation was running high as reported in the press. Day after day, newspapers across the country devoted major coverage to the finished tomb and made Grant's historical reputation the subject of a national discussion. Before an overflow crowd in Carnegie Hall, Professor Felix Adler delivered a talk to the Society for Ethical Culture titled "The Debt of the American People to Ulysses S. Grant." "Grant's Tomb the Mecca" and "Gathering to Pay Honor to the Dead Hero, Warrior," read banner headlines in the *San Francisco Chronicle*.[78] Many newspapers and journals offered special supplements with numerous pictures of the general and his family, lengthy biographies, discussions of his military campaigns and presidency, and, usually, headlines and articles featuring the theme of reconciliation—"The Gray Has Blended with the Blue," proclaimed the *Los Angeles Times*.[79]

A few days before the unveiling, the city's railroad stations and ferries disgorged legions of soldiers and ex-soldiers—from Regular Army, National Guard, and veteran's units—who marched through the festively decorated streets on their way to quarters. Marching along with them were ex-Confederate veterans from Maryland and Virginia, as well as a unit of 150 "Sons of Confederates," accompanied by the "Stonewall Brigade Band."[80] Along the way, all surely observed the parade-route bleachers being built—with seats going for 50 cents and boxes ranging from $1 to $50. Takers were fewer than might be expected—most of the one-million-plus spectators preferred to stand rather than pay. Perhaps they were thinking of saving money to buy souvenirs—badges, pieces of the tomb, pictures, little biographies of Grant—sold from stands lining the way up to the monument. One of the most popular souvenirs proved to be cheap copies of an official medal struck for the occasion. One side of the medal showed the newly built tomb, while the other depicted the familiar profiles of three presidents, Washington, Lincoln, and Grant. The motto below the profiles read: "Father, Savior, Defender."[81] As more and more visitors thronged into the city, hotel rooms were impossible to find at any price. Reporters jostled for the best interviews with distinguished guests. The day before the ceremony a special train arrived via Jersey City carrying President William McKinley and family in the first car and, in the second, Julia Grant and her daughter and three granddaughters, and Secretary of State John Sherman.

April 27 opened bitterly cold and windy with occasional bursts of rain. The weather did not deter the fifty thousand who began marching at 9:30 A.M. The solemn parade proceeded slowly from Madison Square, winding its way over to Riverside Drive. The front of the procession arrived at the tomb around 1:00 P.M. but the end not until 7:00 P.M., long after the ceremonies were over. At the tomb, huge grandstands seated a crowd of five thousand. Reserved seats in a special section held President McKinley, Vice President William Hobart, ex-president Grover Cleveland, the Grant family, cabinet members, members of the Supreme Court, thirteen governors, and twenty-eight representatives of the diplomatic corps. The invited military officials included some familiar names to the aging Civil War generation—William S. Rosecrans, Horatio G. Wright, Don Carlos Buell, Franz Sigel, Lew Wallace, Grenville M. Dodge, Oliver O. Howard, Daniel E. Sickles, James Longstreet, and Simon B. Buckner among them. Behind the crowd, the magnificent ships of the nation's Atlantic Fleet sailed up the glistening silver thread of the Hudson River. The ceremony at the tomb featured hymns, prayers by Bishop John P. Newman, a few remarks from President McKinley, and a longer oration given by General Porter. Afterward, most agreed that President McKinley's short but graceful tribute best captured the sentiment of the occasion:

> Let us not forget the glorious distinction with which the metropolis among the fair sisterhood of American Cities has honored his life and memory. With all that riches and sculpture can do to render an edifice worthy of a man, upon a site unsurpassed for magnificence, has this monument been reared by New York as a perpetual record of his illustrious deeds, in the certainty that as time passes around it, will assemble with gratitude and reverence and veneration men of all times, races, and nationalities. New York holds in its keeping the precious dust of the silent soldier, but his achievements—that he and his brave comrades wrought for mankind—are in the keeping of seventy millions of American Citizens, who will guard the sacred heritage forever and forever more.[82]

Grant's Tomb was complete. The monument was impressively austere, meant to inspire reverential reflection from endless generations of Americans. At least it started out that way. Union veterans and tourists came to the tomb to pay their respects to the general who won the war and secured

Joan Waugh

Crowd at the dedication of Grant's Tomb. National Park Service.

the peace, their war, their peace. In the early days, gentlemen were required to remove their hats, and a quiet, reverential atmosphere prevailed. In the first months, 560,000 men and women paid their respects. New Yorkers were vindicated. It seemed after all that New York City was the right place for Grant's national memorial. Not surprisingly, given the high expectations, reviews were mixed. The *New York Times*, which devoted a whole magazine supplement to the dedication, decreed the monument "too plain," yet, it added, "the tomb of Grant is upon the whole honorable alike to the community which possesses it and to the hero whom it commemorates."[83] In other words, it was more than a work of art and, as such, could not be judged solely on aesthetic qualities. Nearly thirteen years earlier, *Harper's Weekly* had called for Grant's memorial to embody a "massive simplicity," and somehow that phrase seemed just right for the tomb that commemorated "a modest man, a simple man, a man believing in the honest of his fellows, true to his friends, faithful to traditions, and of great personal honor."[84]

The spirit of the hugely successful memorial was captured by the novelist Henry James, who, after walking on the broad plaza leading up to the entrance, described Grant's Tomb as "a great democratic demonstration caught in the fact, unguarded, and unenclosed . . . as open as a hotel or a railway station to any coming and going." Another evaluation sprang from the pen of Lt. Gen. John M. Schofield, who reasoned why the tomb spoke to the common people: "It has been said that Grant, like Lincoln, was a typical American and for that reason was most believed and respected by the people. . . . Soldiers and the people saw in Grant . . . not one of themselves not a plain man of the people, nor yet a superior being whom they could not understand, but a personification of their highest ideal of a citizens, soldier or statesman, a man whose greatness they could see and understand as plainly as they could anything else under the sun." Most of all, Grant's Tomb represented a nation reunited — its creed, its ideals, its past, and its future. "It is to be our one great memorial of the struggle for union," declared an editor, "a monument not only to the foremost of our generals, but to the cause of 'liberty and union' and, in a sense, to all who fought and died for that sentiment."[85]

Despite controversies that had surrounded planning and construction of Grant's Tomb, the veterans, their families, and immediate descendants embraced the monument's celebration of national pride and patriotic values. Horace Porter's words and actions evoke this, as did many other declarations regarding the meaning of Grant's Tomb. Grant's was only the most impressive of the numerous Civil War art monuments constructed in the late nineteenth century. Together, these monuments called forth huge investments of money and of artistic effort but more importantly reflected the larger society's desire to immortalize the nobility and high ideals of the war. This desire to memorialize the deep appreciation so many people had toward those who sacrificed their lives explains the erection of statues and other structures in so many places to honor dead presidents, generals, and ordinary soldiers. National Park Service historian and tomb expert David M. Kahn summed up an era's position when he stated that the monument "in a very real sense symbolizes an entire generation's feeling not just about Grant, but about the Civil War and the role every foot soldier played in it."[86]

NOTES

1. Both quotations from *New York Times*, July 28, 1885.

2. The following are indispensable sources on Grant's monument: David M. Kahn, "The Grant Monument," *Journal of the Society of Architectural Historians* 41 (October 1982): 212–23; David M. Kahn, "General Grant National Memorial Historical Resource Study," unpublished manuscript (New York: National Park Service, 1980) (hereafter cited as Kahn, "Resource Study"); Neil Harris, "The Battle for Grant's Tomb," *American Heritage* 36 (August–September 1985): 70–79; G. Kurt Piehler, "The Changing Legacy of Grant's Tomb," unpublished paper, 1995, in author's possession; Eric A. Reinert, *"Grant's Tomb"* (New York: Eastern National, 1997); and Donald Martin Reynolds, *Monuments and Master-*

pieces: Histories and Views of Public Sculpture in New York City (1988; reprint, New York: Thames and Hudson, 1997), 214–23. A wealth of primary material related to the monument, including correspondence, financial records, and architectural competitions, is in the General Grant Monument Association Archives in Federal Hall National Memorial, New York City (collection hereafter cited as GMAA).

3. Reinert, *"Grant's Tomb,"* 22 (first quotation); *New York Times*, August 16, 1997 (second quotation).

4. Reynolds, *Monuments and Masterpieces*, 214 (first quotation); *New York Times*, April 10, 1994 (second quotation).

5. *New York Times*, December 19, 1993. Mr. Scaturro has subsequently graduated from law school and is currently working in Washington, D.C., where he remains active in the reestablished Grant Monument Association. The association's goal is to raise money for further improvements for the memorial, including a visitor's center (with restrooms) behind the tomb. The Grant Monument Association's website offers excellent information on the history of the tomb, as well as its current status, ⟨http://www.grantstomb.org/ind-gma.html⟩. See also the informative National Park Service site: ⟨http://www.nps.gov/gegr/⟩.

6. *New York Times*, January 2, 1994.

7. "For the Tomb of Civil War Hero, the New Battle is in Court," *New York Times*, April 27, 1994 (quotation). See also "Illinois Wants Grant's Tomb," *New York Times*, April 10, 1994; "No One in Grant's Tomb Unless It's Fixed, Family Warns," *New York Times*, October 16, 1994; "Peace Infuses Grant's Tomb," *New York Times*, April 23, 1999.

8. Plans for a grand ceremonial road leading up to Grant's Tomb that would lessen the "'great congestion' caused when marches ended" at the site were scuttled by opposition from competing real estate interests. (Quotation and story from *New York Times*, August 15, 1999.)

9. David Quigley, *Second Founding: New York City, Reconstruction, and the Making of American Democracy* (New York: Hill and Wang, 2004), 176.

10. Both quotations from *New York Times*, May 7, 1995.

11. Modern intellectuals, scholars of memory, and historians have studied the powerful emotions evoked in grand public art such as Grant's Tomb. A very small number of Civil War monuments and memorials became what Pierre Nora described as "sacred memory sites" (*lieux de memoire*). According to Nora, memory sites not only embody an integral part of a country's national heritage, but they also summon deep emotional feelings while at the same time educating people about a particular historical event. See Pierre Nora, *Realms of Memory: Rethinking the French Past*, vol. 1 (New York: Columbia University Press, 1996). Andre Malreaux famously said that "a culture will be judged by its statues" (Garry Wills, "The Meaning of Monuments," *Washington Post*, April 27, 1997). Marvin Trachtenberg wrote, "Monuments are a way . . . [to] . . . transmit communal emotions, a medium of continuity and interaction between generations, not only in space but across time, for to be a monument is to be permanent" (Trachtenberg, *The Statue of Liberty* [New York: Viking, 1976], 15).

12. Two excellent sources for war monuments are Thomas J. Brown, *The Public Art of Civil War Commemoration: A Brief History with Documents* (New York: Bedford/St. Martin's Press, 2004), and Kirk Savage, *Standing Soldier, Kneeling Slaves: Race, War and*

Monument in Nineteenth-Century America (Princeton, N.J.: Princeton University Press, 1997).

13. David J. Eicher, *Mystic Chords of Memory: Civil War Battlefields and Historic Sites Recaptured* (Baton Rouge: Louisiana State University Press, 1998); Kathryn Allamong Jacob, *Testament to Union: Civil War Monuments in Washington, D.C.* (Baltimore: Johns Hopkins University Press, 1998). John Bodnar and Michael Kammen published books on the relationship between memory and public art across three centuries of U.S. history, while Kurt Savage and Thomas Brown analyzed Civil War monuments exclusively. Their combined scholarship suggests that long after the excitement of the dedication ceremony fades away, national monuments were, and are, the favored places to stage patriotic events, parades, and speeches. Often monuments such as the Washington and Lincoln Memorials in Washington, D.C., became deeply embedded in popular consciousness through endlessly replicated images in postcards and paintings, as backdrops for television news reports, as settings for protests or music concerts, and in books, movies, and documentaries. See John Bodnar, *Remaking America: Public Memory, Commemoration, and Patriotism in the Twentieth Century* (Princeton: N.J.: Princeton University Press, 1992), and Michael Kammen, *Mystic Chords of Memory: The Transformation of Tradition in American Culture* (New York: Knopf, 1991).

14. Rutherford B. Hayes, *The Diary and Letters of Rutherford B. Hayes, Nineteenth President of the United States*, ed. Charles Richard Williams, 5 vols. (Columbus: Ohio State Archeological and Historical Society, 1922), 4:224 (first quotation); Hayes, "Aid for the Monument," *New York Times*, July 26, 1885 (second quotation).

15. Launt Thompson (New York sculptor), Calvert Vaux (architect who co-designed with Frederick Law Olmsted Central Park, Riverside Park, and Morningside Park), W. H. Beard (painter), Karl Gerhardt (sculptor of Grant's death mask), Henry Van Brunt (architect and author who served in the Civil War and whose firm executed the commission for Harvard's Memorial Hall), Olin L. Warner (sculptor), Wilson McDonald, Clarence Cook (painter and author), "Grant's Memorial What Shall It Be?" *North American Review* 141 (September 1885): 276–92. See also Horatio Seymour (former New York governor), John La Farge (artist and writer), Rufus Hatch (writer), Charles T. Congdon (Congregational minister), Dorman B. Eaton (lawyer and civil service reformer), "Notes and Comments," *North American Review* 141 (October 1885): 399–400; and C. M. Harvey, Mary A. Parker, Elizabeth A. Meriwether, Henry Forrester, F. B. Wixon, "Style and the Monument," from "No Name Essays," *North American Review* 141 (November 1885): 443–53.

16. *North American Review* 141 (September 1885): 281.

17. Architect Daniel H. Burnham brought the "Beaux-Arts" concept to its most brilliant fruition with Washington, D.C.'s Union Station and Library of Congress building. See Thomas S. Hines, *Burnham of Chicago: Architect and Planner* (New York: Oxford University Press, 1974).

18. Beard in *North American Review* 141 (September 1885): 279 (first quotation); *New York Tribune*, August 12, 1885 (second quotation).

19. Fred's letter appears in the *New York World*, September, 13, 1889. See also *New York Times*, July 24, September 7, 1885. Horace Porter's account in "The Tomb of General Grant," *Century Magazine* 53 (April 1897): 839–47, stressed New York as the favorite from the beginning. See also Kahn, "Resource Study," 10–12.

20. W. R. Grace to Julia Grant, July 23, 1885, Grant Family Archival Folder, GMAA; Fred's quotation from *New York World*, September 13, 1899. For details of the proposals, see Lt. General Hindeman to Col. Fred D. Grant July 23 or July 24, 1885, Grant Family Archival Folder, GMAA; *New York Times*, July 24, 1885; *New York Tribune*, July 26, 1885.

21. Frederick Dent Grant to William R. Grace, July 23, 1885, and F.D.G. to Horace Porter, March 24, 1892, Grant Family Archival Folder, GMAA.

22. *New York World*, September, 13, 1899 (Fred's quotation); *New York Times*, July 25, 1885 (headline).

23. *New York Times*, July 24, 1885.

24. Robert A. M. Stern, Thomas Mellins, and David Fishman, *New York 1880: Architecture and Urbanism in the Gilded Age* (New York: Monacelli Press, 1999), 16.

25. New York was not the only city to be remade by what architectural historians have called "The Architecture of National Power." The firm of McKim, Mead and White used neoclassical designs for the Boston Public Library, among many other buildings. See Leland M. Roth, *A Concise History of American Architecture* (New York: Harper and Row, 1979).

26. Mayor Grace's quotation in *New York Times*, July 26, 1885.

27. *New York Times*, July 28, 1885. On the Central Park controversy and opinions about where the general should be buried and what kind of monument should be built, see *New York Tribune*, July 25, 28, 29, 1885.

28. Confirmation of acceptance in letter to Col. Fred Grant from Charles Burnt, New York Department of Public Works, July 27, 1885, in Grant Family Archival Folder, GMAA; also reported in *New York Tribune*, July 29, 1885.

29. Martha J. Lamb, *The Guide for Strangers to General Grant's Tomb* (New York: J. J. Little, 1886).

30. As quoted in *New York Times*, July 29, 1885.

31. *New York World*, July 30, 1885 (criticism of public transportation); Kahn, "Resource Study," 19 (real estate boon). Discussions among architects, including Olmsted and Vaux, can be found in *New York Times*, August 8, 10, 11, 1885. The development of Riverside is discussed in Stern, Mellins, and Fishman, *New York 1880*, 741–44.

32. *New York Times*, July 24, 1885 ("at its highest" quotation); Kahn, "Grant Monument," 212–31 (second quotation p. 212).

33. The meetings of the Grant Monument Association are recorded in the Minute Books, 1885/1886, GMAA.

34. As quoted in Kahn, "Resource Study," 36.

35. Information on Greener and his role in the Grant Monument Association is from Ruth Ann Stewart and David M. Kahn, introduction to catalog, *Richard T. Greener, His Life and Work: An Exhibit and Tribute Sponsored by The National Park Service and The National Park Foundation* (New York: Schomburg Center for Research in Black Culture, New York Public Library, 1980), 1–15; Allison Blakely, "Richard T. Greener and the 'Talented Tenth's' Dilemma," *Journal of Negro History* 59 (October 1974): 305–21.

36. As quoted in Stewart and Kahn, *Greener, His Life and Work*, 11.

37. *New York Times*, July 31, August 1, 1885.

38. *New York Times*, September 11, October 28, 1885.

39. As quoted in Kahn, "Resource Study," 33.

40. Hayes to General S. S. Burdette, August 15, 1885, in Hayes, *Diary and Letters*, 4:232.

41. As quoted in Stewart and Kahn, *Greener, His Life and Work*, 12.

42. *New York World*, July 30, 1885.

43. *New York Tribune*, July 26, 1885 (the *Tribune* listed the discontented); *New York Times*, August 23, 1885 (Chicago statement).

44. As quoted in Kahn, "Resource Study," 19.

45. Quotations from *New York Herald*, July 25, 26, 1885.

46. *Army and Navy Register*, August 1, 1885, as quoted in Kahn, "Resource Study," 34.

47. "The Hero's Place of Burial: A Weak Washington Protest," *New York Times*, July 28, 1885. The article surveyed protests around the country.

48. Hayes, *Diary and Letters*, 4:224 (July 26, 1885). See also August 7, 1885, entry in ibid., 229.

49. Hayes to Burdette, August 15, 1885, in Hayes, *Diary and Letters*, 4:232 (for another letter to Burdette that emphasized more concerns, see ibid., 226); Hayes to James C. Reed, Secretary of the Monument Assn., May 25, 1892, in ibid., 5:84. Records show that by 1892 the GAR leadership was still being courted by the GMA. Two good examples are Horace Porter to Frederick Phisterer, Adj. General, Grand Army of the Republic, July 7, 1892, and Horace Porter to Major A. J. Weissert, Commander-in-Chief, GAR, March 6, 1892, in Grant Monument Association Letter Book, May 5, 1892–October 14, 1896 (item hereafter cited as Grant Monument Association Letter Book), container 1, Papers of Horace Porter, Manuscript Division, Library of Congress, Washington (repository hereafter cited as LC).

50. As quoted in *New York Times*, September 10, 1885.

51. Julia Grant to W. R. Grace, October 29, 1885, Grant Family Archival Folder, GMAA; Kansas City quotation reprinted in the *New York Times*, July 30, 1885. Julia Grant did not reside in New York City after 1894. She lived in Washington with her daughter and grandchildren, seldom venturing forth in public except to attend ceremonies honoring her husband, such as the dedication of the tomb in 1897. She died peacefully in 1902.

52. Horace Porter to Major Weissert, March 6, 1892, Grant Monument Association Letter Book, container 1, Papers of Horace Porter, LC.

53. GAR information in *New York Times*, September 16, 27, 1885; *New York Times*, October 28, 1885 (information on donations); Kahn, "Resource Study," 28–32.

54. Kahn, "Resource Study," 214–15; *New York Herald*, July 30, 1886.

55. *New York Herald*, September 13, 1890 (information on John Duncan); *New York Times*, October 20, 1929; Reinert, *"Grant's Tomb,"* 11; Kahn, "Grant Monument," 222–27.

56. Reynolds, *Monuments and Masterpieces*, 216. For discussion of the competition, see *New York Times*, April 25, 1897.

57. As quoted in Kahn, "Grant Monument," 227.

58. Stewart and Kahn, *Greener, His Life and Work*, 13 (Greener quotation); Robert A. M. Stern, Gregory Gilmartin, and John Montague Massengala, *1900: Metropolitan Architecture and Urbanism, 1890–1915* (New York: Rizzoli International Publishers, 1983); Kahn, "Resource Study," 143 (Schuyler quotation).

59. Quotation from "Grant's Tomb," folder 2, box 10, GMAA.

60. Piehler, "Changing Legacy of Grant's Tomb," 15.

61. The story is recounted in Maj. Gen. Grenville M. Dodge, *Personal Recollections of President Abraham Lincoln, General Ulysses S. Grant and General William T. Sherman* (Council Bluffs, Iowa: Monarch, 1914), 119.

62. Horace Porter to S. R. Van Duzer, May 10, 1892, Grant Monument Association Letter Book, container 1, Papers of Horace Porter, LC.

63. Joint fund-raising activities undertaken by the GAR and GMA are recorded in "G.A.R. Honor Role, 1892–1893," folder 2, box 10, GMAA. See also Horace Porter to General James Fry, May 12, 1892, Grant Monument Association Letter Book, container 1, Papers of Horace Porter, LC.

64. Reinert, "Grant's Tomb," 13; biographical sketch titled "Horace Porter," 16 pages, container 5, Papers of Horace Porter, LC.

65. Horace Porter, "Personal Traits of General Grant," *McClure's Magazine* 2 (May 1894): 507–14 (quotation p. 507).

66. Frederick Dent Grant to Horace Porter, March 24, 1892, Grant Family Archival Folder, GMAA. See also ibid., March 20, 1892.

67. *New York Times* Supplement, April 27, 1897, p. 4.

68. Horace Porter to E. H. Cook, May 14, 1892, Grant Monument Association Letter Book, container 1, Papers of Horace Porter, LC.

69. *New York Times*, April 26, 1897, p. 4 ("became a fad"); Porter, "Tomb of General Grant," 839–46.

70. *Harper's Weekly*, May 7, 1892, p. 439.

71. Quotation from "Address Delivered by General Horace Porter, Upon the Occasion of Breaking Ground for the Erection of the Monument to General Grant at River Side Park, N.Y., April 27th, 1891," pp. 14–15, container 4, Papers of Horace Porter, LC.

72. Horace Porter to Bradley Martin, May 5, 1892, Grant Monument Association Letter Book, container 1, Papers of Horace Porter, LC.

73. Horace Porter to Fred. Phisterer, July 7, 1892, Grant Monument Association Letter Book, container 1, Papers of Horace Porter, LC.

74. Horace Porter to Hon. Hilary A. Herbert, April 6, 1893, Grant Monument Association Letter Book, container 1, Papers of Horace Porter, LC.

75. Horace Porter to C. M. Beach, March 21, 1896, Grant Monument Association Letter Book, container 1, Papers of Horace Porter, LC. The sarcophagi ended up costing $10,000.

76. Horace Porter to Editor, *New York World*, April 16, 1895, Grant Monument Association Letter Book, container 1, Papers of Horace Porter, LC.

77. *New York Herald*, April 24, 25, 1897.

78. *New York Times*, April 27, 1897; *San Francisco Chronicle*, April 26, 1897.

79. *Los Angeles Times*, April 27, 28, 1897. See also the coverage in *Century Magazine* 53 (April 1897): 821–47, 937–50.

80. *New York Times*, April 28, 1897.

81. Medal in the Museum of the City of New York, Kahn, "Resource Study," 1.

82. "Official Programme of the Exercises at the Dedication of the Monument and Tomb of General Ulysses S. Grant Under the Direction of the Municipal Grant Monument Committee, Riverside, New York, April 27, 1897," pp. 1–4, container 4, Papers of Horace Porter, LC; Kahn, "Resource Study," 134–40. Extensive coverage was provided in *New York Times*, April 25–29, 1897.

83. *New York Times*, April 26, 1897, p. 6. One critic found the "upper portion to be out of scale with the massive square base" (Kahn, "Resource Study," 142–43).

84. *Harper's Weekly*, September 20, 1885; *New York Times*, July 24, 1885 (quotation by Longstreet).

85. Henry James, *The American Scene* (1907; reprint, London: Rupert Hart-Davis, 1968), 145 (quotation); Schofield letter printed in *San Francisco Chronicle*, April 26, 1897, as quoted in Kahn, "Resource Study," 142.

86. Kahn, "Resource Study," 3.

⊰ CONTRIBUTORS ⊱

WILLIAM BLAIR teaches at Penn State University and directs the George and Ann Richards Civil War Era Center. His publications include *Virginia's Private War: Feeding Body and Soul in the Confederacy, 1861–1865* and *Cities of the Dead: Contesting the Memory of the Civil War in the South, 1865–1914*.

STEPHEN CUSHMAN, a poet with a long-standing interest in the Civil War, teaches at the University of Virginia. He is the author of *Bloody Promenade: Reflections on a Civil War Battle*.

DREW GILPIN FAUST, the president of Harvard University, has published a number of books on southern and Civil War history. They include *The Creation of Confederate Nationalism*, *Mothers of Invention*, and *The Republic of Suffering: Death and the American Civil War*.

GARY W. GALLAGHER teaches at the University of Virginia. He has published, among other titles, *Causes Won, Lost, and Forgotten: How Hollywood and Popular Art Shape What We Know about the Civil War*, *Lee and His Army in Confederate History*, and *The Confederate War*.

J. MATTHEW GALLMAN's books include *America's Joan of Arc: The Life of Anna Elizabeth Dickinson*, *Mastering Wartime: A Social History of Philadelphia during the Civil War*, and *Receiving Erin's Children*. He teaches at the University of Florida.

JOSEPH T. GLATTHAAR has published several books on the Civil War, including *The March to the Sea and Beyond*, *Forged in Battle: The Civil War Alliance of Black Soldiers and White Officers*, and *General Lee's Army: From Victory to Collapse*. He teaches at the University of North Carolina.

HAROLD HOLZER is vice president for communications at New York City's Metropolitan Museum of Art. His many publications include *The Lincoln Image*, *The Union Image*, and *Lincoln Seen and Heard*.

JAMES MARTEN is the author of *Texas Divided: Loyalty and Dissent in the Lone Star State, 1856–1874* and *The Children's Civil War*. He teaches at Marquette University.

STEPHANIE MCCURRY teaches at the University of Pennsylvania and is the author of *Masters of Small Worlds: Yeoman Households, Gender Relations, and the Political Culture of the Antebellum South Carolina Low Country* and *Confederate Crucible: The Disfranchised and the Political Transformation of the Civil War South* (forthcoming).

JAMES M. MCPHERSON, who spent his teaching career at Princeton University, has published widely on the Civil War era. His books include *Battle Cry of Freedom*, *For Cause and Comrades*, and *Crossroads of Freedom: Antietam*.

CAROL REARDON teaches at Penn State University and has published several books on military and Civil War history, including *Pickett's Charge in History and Memory* and *Soldiers and Scholars: The U.S. Army and the Uses of Military History, 1865–1920*.

JOAN WAUGH is a specialist in Civil War history who teaches at the University of California, Los Angeles. Her books include *Unsentimental Reformer: The Life of Josephine Shaw Lowell*, *The Memory of the Civil War in American Culture*, and *U. S. Grant: American Hero, American Myth* (forthcoming).

Page numbers in italics indicate illustrations.